T0319814

Capital Movements and Corporate Dominance in Latin America

NEW DIRECTIONS IN POST-KEYNESIAN ECONOMICS

Series Editors: Louis-Philippe Rochon, *Laurentian University, Sudbury, Canada* and Sergio Rossi, *University of Fribourg, Switzerland*

Post-Keynesian economics is a school of thought inspired by the work of John Maynard Keynes, but also by Michal Kalecki, Joan Robinson, Nicholas Kaldor and other Cambridge economists, for whom money and effective demand are essential to explain economic activity. The aim of this series is to present original research work (single or co-authored volumes as well as edited books) that advances Post-Keynesian economics at both theoretical and policy-oriented levels.

Areas of research include, but are not limited to, monetary and financial economics, macro and microeconomics, international economics, development economics, economic policy, political economy, analyses of income distribution and financial crises, and the history of economic thought.

Titles in the series include:

Capital Movements and Corporate Dominance in Latin America

Reduced Growth and Increased Instability

Edited by

Noemi Levy-Orlik

Senior Professor, Economic Faculty, Universidad Nacional Autónoma de México, Mexico City, Mexico

Jorge Alonso Bustamante-Torres

Associate Professor, FES Acatlán, Universidad Nacional Autónoma de México, Mexico City, Mexico

Louis-Philippe Rochon

Full Professor, Laurentian University, Canada; Co-Editor of the Review of Political Economy, *Founding Editor Emeritus of the* Review of Keynesian Economics

NEW DIRECTIONS IN POST-KEYNESIAN ECONOMICS

Edward Elgar
PUBLISHING

Cheltenham, UK • Northampton, MA, USA

Cover image: Graffiti on the streets of Poznan, Poland. Photographed by Louis-Philippe Rochon, 2016.

Published by
Edward Elgar Publishing Limited
The Lypiatts
15 Lansdown Road
Cheltenham
Glos GL50 2JA
UK

Edward Elgar Publishing, Inc.
William Pratt House
9 Dewey Court
Northampton
Massachusetts 01060
USA

A catalogue record for this book
is available from the British Library

Library of Congress Control Number: 2021936631

This book is available electronically in the **Elgar**online
Economics subject collection
http://dx.doi.org/10.4337/9781800372146

ISBN 978 1 80037 213 9 (cased)
ISBN 978 1 80037 214 6 (eBook)

Printed and bound by CPI Group (UK) Ltd, Croydon, CR0 4YY

Contents

v

Contributors

Cecilia Allami is an Associate Professor in the Department of Political Economy, at the Universidad Nacional de General Sarmiento, Buenos Aires, Argentina.

Bruno Bonizzi is a Senior Lecture in Finance, Business School, University of Hertfordshire, Business School, UK.

Pablo Bortz is an Associate Professor, Universidad Nacional de San Martín/CONICET, Buenos Aires, Argentina.

Jorge Alonso Bustamante-Torres is an Associate Professor in the Socioeconomic Division, Faculty of Higher Studies Acatlán at Universidad Nacional Autónoma de México, State of Mexico, Mexico.

Nicole Cerpa Vielma is a doctoral student at the Business School, University of Leeds, UK.

Jennifer Churchill is a Senior Lecturer in Economics at UWE Bristol, UK.

Alan Cibils is the Chair Professor of the Political Economy Department, Universidad Nacional de General Sarmiento, Buenos Aires, Argentina.

Gonzalo Cómbita-Mora is an Associate Professor in the Department of Economics, Universidad de la Salle, Bogotá, and an Assistant Professor in the School of Economics, Universidad Nacional de Colombia, Bogotá.

Gary Dymski is a Senior Professor in the Business School, University of Leeds, Leeds, UK.

Ximena Echenique-Romero is an Associate Professor in the Economics Faculty, Universidad Nacional Autónoma de México, Mexico City, Mexico.

Nicole Favreau-Negront is a Research Assistant at the Economic Commission for Latin America and the Caribbean (ECLAC), Santiago, Chile.

Alejandro Garay-Huamán is a doctoral candidate at the University of Missouri, Kansas City, USA.

Annina Kaltenbrunner is an Associate Professor in Economics at Business School, University of Leeds, Leeds, UK.

Noemi Levy-Orlik is a Senior Professor, Economic Faculty, Universidad Nacional Autónoma de México, Mexico City, Mexico.

Álvaro Martín Moreno-Rivas is an Associate Professor in the School of Economics, Universidad Nacional de Colombia, Bogotá.

Samuel Ortiz-Velásquez is an Associate Professor in the Economics Faculty, Universidad Nacional Autónoma de México, Mexico City, Mexico.

Juan Pablo Painceira is a Senior Advisor of the Open Market Operations Department (Demab) at the Central Bank of Brazil (BCB), Brazil.

Esteban Pérez-Caldentey is the Coordinator of the Financing for Development Unit in the Economic Development Division at ECLAC, Santiago, Chile.

Louis-Philippe Rochon is a Full Professor of Economics at Laurentian University, Canada; Co-Editor of the *Review of Political Economy*, and is the Founder and Editor Emeritus of the Review of Keynesian Economics (2011–2018).

Gustavo Adrián Salazar is a Lecturer in the Escuela Politécnica Nacional, Universidad Central del Ecuador, Quito Ecuador.

Alexis Saludjian is an Associate Professor in the Instituto de Economia, Universidade Federal do Rio de Janeiro, Brazil.

Mimoza Shabani is a Senior Lecturer in Financial Economics at the University of East London, UK.

Hanna Szymborska is a Senior Lecturer at the Birmingham City Business School, Birmingham City University, Birmingham, UK.

Jan Toporowski is a Professor of Economics and Finance at the SOAS, London University, London, UK.

Marcelo Varela-Enríquez is a Senior Research Professor in the Instituto de Altos Estudios Nacionales, Universidad Central del Ecuador, Quito, Ecuador.

Acknowledgements

This book is a product of the research project IN3062120, "Capital mobility in the XXI century: A glance at markets and institutions in Latin America," supported by the DGAPA (Research Council) and the School of Economics at the Universidad Nacional Autónoma de México (UNAM), with the collaboration of the *Review of Political Economy*.

We would like to deeply thank the contributors for participating in this project, despite the problems caused by the current coronavirus pandemic, and we are grateful to Alan Sturmer, Katia Williford and Catherine Cumming, The Editors at Edward Elgar, for their guidance and assistance in the editing of this volume. This project was launched a mere few months before the start of the crisis, in January 2020. Despite the crisis, the authors were able to deliver their contributions on time. Equally important, and rather ironically, most of the chapters in this book dealt with social, economic, and political problems that the COVID-19 crisis has subsequently revealed. We hope this book contributes to a better economic, social, and political understanding that will enhance the well-being of all countries regardless of income level or development status.

We want to thank our PAPIIT project assistants, Jorge Luna and Guillermo Guerrero Chávez, who supported the research project and ordered the texts.

Noemi Levy-Orlik
Jorge Alonso Bustamante-Torres
Louis-Philippe Rochon

Introduction: the issues at stake

Noemi Levy-Orlik, Jorge Alonso Bustamante-Torres and Louis-Philippe Rochon

The dominant capitalist structures of the last third of the 20th century have been noteworthy for globalising and internationalising the social relationships of production, whose highest expression has been the cross-border movement of capital, which peaked in the 1990s (Levy-Orlik and Bustamante-Torres, Chapter 6 in this book). The political and economic agenda behind this model is dominated by Developed Countries (DCs), through a triad formed by their governments, banks and non-bank financial conglomerates, and non-financial conglomerates. Together, this triad maximises the gains of big capital through financial innovations supported by complex financial relations and global value chains (GVCs), which keep financial activities in the DCs and minimise production costs by sourcing production in Emerging and Developing Countries (EDeCs). The Global Financial Crisis (GFC) which exploded in 2008 weakened but did not break this economic and social order, with an uneven response in DCs and EDeCs (Painceira and Saludjian, Chapter 11 in this book), as the former embraced nationalist policies to curtail globalisation of their corporations while the latter doubled down on globalisation and internationalisation, further opening their economies and deepening their reliance on GVCs.

Financial deregulation and globalisation have deep roots in economic theory. The dominant theory legitimises capital mobility because it assumes that it homogenises productivity and expands the benefits of economic growth and prosperity. From this perspective, it has been observed, on the one hand, that capital movements are driven by surplus savings and shrinking profit margins in DCs, as their economies reach a stationary level of economic growth and development in processes of capital accumulation (Solow, 1963; Dowrick and Rogers, 2002), finding new opportunities to maximise profits in EDeCs. Thus, exporting capital from developed to less developed regions boosts its profitability because the latter have insufficient savings, and – given the scarcity of capital – profitability is high. In this context, unrestricted mobility of financial and productive capital seeks to homogenise levels of productivity on a global level, making it a mechanism which equalises economic growth between developing and developed regions. On the other hand, from the perspective of EDeCs, a lack of savings limits their economic growth, and in addition government intervention in the form of interest rate reductions and credit mobilisation towards priority productive sectors causes financial repression, which in turn reinforces economic stagnation (including investment spending) and productive heterogeneity (McKinnon, 1973). In this context, capital mobility is a driver of development for emerging economies, especially in the dynamic sectors of the productive process, and the hegemony transnational companies exercise in the most dynamic sectors (e.g. export industry) is justified on the grounds that it transfers technology with productive spillovers while boosting competitiveness, employment, and wages.

In this approach, the key to economic development is the diminishing marginal productivity of capital as the factor which determines return on investment and, given the equilibrium interest rate, establishes the volume of savings, and when savings and investment are equal capital returns are cancelled out. Therefore, free capital movement is essential to increasing savings in EDeCs, which fuels economic growth and development in those regions. This approach rejects the theories of underdevelopment based on structural inequalities.

The heterodox school of thought has opposite views. Finance triggers growth, including investment, and raises savings (as a result of higher income). In dominant oligopolistic structures (Kalecki, 1971; Steindl, 1952), finance is derived from companies' profits from previous periods (internal funds), and rentier capital – accumulated by the capitalist class – which doesn't return to the productive sector through capitalist spending in the same periods, creating business cycles.

In other words, financial capital produces economic cycles, with expansionary phases explained by financial inflation and high debt volumes, followed by contractive periods of slower economic growth, which in turn can cause economic stagnation. Thus, external capital flows do not necessarily have a positive impact on economic growth or expand finance, nor do they homogenise growth and productivity.

An overview of social relationships of production in the capitalist system in the last third of the 20th century shows that the predictions made by mainstream economic thought were not fulfilled, and on the contrary financial instability increased. Since the breakdown of the post-war financial system, complex financial relationships have gained in importance through cross-border capital movements (between developed and developing regions and within each region) with the novelty of EDeCs taking part in capital exports. In this context, medium-size multinational enterprises (MNEs) were created in emerging economies (see UNCTAD, n.d.), which, while extending their reach to all capitalist regions, did not increase competition, but rather accentuated structural imbalances within EDeCs and between developed and emerging regions.

The economic model that emerged from globalisation and internationalisation shifted manufacturing production to EDeCs (Lazonick and O'Sullivan, 2000) through GVCs (Aguiar de Medeiros and Trebat, 2018) and financial multinationals spread to all capitalist economies, without reducing inequalities. Latin America failed to become more competitive and the countries' external current account continued under structurally entrenched deficits, without achieving financial depth (in the stock and bond markets). This process had several repercussions.

First, productive costs shrank, especially those related to the workforce (Bellofiore et al., 2010), tax payments contracted, and clean technologies were delayed in EDeC production process, especially in Latin America. As a result, these economies' comparative advantages rested on low production costs and exploitation of natural resources, the control of which was transferred to international corporations, allowing them to extract maximum profit from developing economies.

Second, financial institutions were strengthened by the privatisation of social services (pensions, healthcare, education, etc.) that were commercialised in the form of insurance (medical, educational, pension funds, etc.) by institutional funds that channelled their financial flows to the leading international centres. This in turn spurred worldwide financial inflation, with massive financial gains, involving all economic agents (financial and non-financial corporations, government, and families). The singularity of this process is that the EDeCs were unable to develop or expand their own financial centres, bolstering international centres (Wall Street and the City in London), on the one hand, while reducing the scope of action for EDeCs. In this scenario, the goal of MNEs from EDeCs headquartered in developed countries is to gain access to more abundant, lower-cost liquidity from such financial centres.

Third, international financial flows were modified. On the one hand, their composition changed as foreign investment (portfolio and direct investment) took the lead, displacing international loans with the aid of financial innovation. On the other hand, the volume of capital movement increased sixfold, without increasing total savings in EDeCs – the substitution effect of foreign savings dominated over domestic savings – or financing. The most relevant effect of the internationalisation of financial systems is that EDeCs gained access to international capital through conversion of private instruments denominated in local currency into international units of account, creating a new form of international monetary asymmetry.[1] EDeCs, especially in Latin America and particularly in Mexico, succumbed to the illusion of unlimited access to international liquidity in exchange for almost complete opening of their financial systems, without deepening of their own financial markets. In fact, savings were separated from finance, the former being a product of production, restricted to domestic spaces, while the latter is provided by international agents (Borio and Disyatat, 2015). This process produced increased financial instability, because capital inflows depend on perceptions of EDeCs' economic performance among institutional investors and large international consortia. EDeCs were obliged to raise their interest rates and overvalue their currencies to attract foreign capital, which explains the excess liquidity that followed the 2008 GFC (due to FED quantitative easing) and the subsequent economic recession, starting in 2014 when the US attempted to normalise its monetary policy.

Fourth, the deregulation, globalisation, and internationalisation of productive processes imposed an export-based model, which debilitated domestic markets, due to the separation of supply and demand. Latin America took part in this productive process with severe disadvantages. Its appeal lay in its ability to supply raw materials and inexpensive labour. As a result, the productive process was not directed by a sector which produced investment goods (sector I in Marxist terms) and economies underwent a process of re-primarisation and labour organisation dominated by international contract manufacture or *maquila*.

The crises of the global and transnational production model were quick to appear, starting in EDeCs, linked to foreign capital movement and increased indebtedness, with strong contagious effects. The Mexican crisis (1994) topped the list of neoliberal crises sending powerful shockwaves throughout Latin America (Tequila Effect). DCs took longer to feel the effects of the globalised, financialised model, when the GFC struck the USA almost three decades later. Starting in 2007, financial movements in capital markets grew sluggish, triggering sharp financial deflation in October of the following year, followed by widespread MNE bankruptcies and the economic crash. The crisis also produced powerful shockwaves in Europe, due to the close financial ties between corporations on both sides of the Atlantic.

The DCs countered the 2008 GFC by implementing massive stimulus programs in 2009 (which they stopped in 2010), increased liquidity (quantitative easing) and diminished drastically the rate of interest, effectively halting bankruptcies and restarting economic activity, including financial trading. However, their economic recovery was slow and limited in scope (largely because the stimulus programs lasted only one year), with high unemployment because the terms of securitisation remained unchanged and the dominance of financial capital was maintained, with high levels of income concentration and poverty and growing volumes of debt to maintain consumption.

Once again, we find two answers for the crisis. Developed economies sought to restore "normalcy" by embracing nationalist policies, which have given way to a trade war between declining and emerging powers, hindering the recovery and continuity of the globalised export-based model and GVCs. Donald Trump came to power in the USA with the slogan "America First" and an unfulfilled promise to force transnationals to move their affiliates back to the US and reactivate employment, while the Brexit movement forced the UK to withdraw from the European Union (EU).

Considering the above arguments, the objective of this book is to discuss the dynamics of capital movements and the operations of corporations and, altogether, their effects on the productive and financial development of developing and emerging economies, particularly in Latin America. This book is divided into three sections and 14 chapters.

The first section deals with the Post-Crisis Capital Movement Trend and contains six chapters. Its purpose is to show that capital development has different effect in developed and developing and emerging economies countries. The first chapter, "*Financial geography and the 'social reality of finance': Aspatial or 'real space' analyses of financial crises?*" by Gary Dymski and Nicole Cerpa-Vielma, discusses globalisation from a heterodox perspective, not only considering time (following Post-Keynesians) but also space. The authors adopt an interdisciplinary framework between economy and geography and introduce the concept of "social reality of finance", illustrating their argument by exploring several economic models of financial crises in developing countries.

In the second chapter, written by Jan Toporowski, "*The transmission mechanism of financial crisis to developing countries: why the 'global financial crisis' wasn't global*", the author identifies three channels through which financial crises have been channelled to developing countries and emerging markets. The *financial* channel through illiquidity in the international monetary system that causes debt crises; the *monetary* channel, when exchange rates modify the value of external liabilities; and the *export* channel, when the value of exports falls below the value required to maintain production and service external debt. The developments of these channels, along with unconventional measures of monetary policy ensured that the 2008 financial crisis had only minimal effects in developing countries and emerging markets and concludes that capital controls are not an effective solution.

The next chapter, "*Foreign direct investment, inequality, and macroeconomic stability on the eve of the COVID-19 crisis*", by Hanna Szymborska, examines the relationship between foreign direct investment and income inequality. It focuses on the period following the Great Recession and seeks to understand the role of changing institutional setups in the global financial sector and the world economy after the 2007 crisis. The author analyses developed and developing countries, investigating trends in income inequality, balance of payments, and the outflows and inflows of FDI over time. The main findings are that the relationship between FDI and income inequality since 2008 is complex and the preliminary analysis of the available data does not reveal any systematic patterns between the different measures of income inequality and changes in FDI.

Jennifer Churchill, Bruno Bonizzi and Annina Kaltenbrunner, in Chapter 4, discuss "*Pension funds and domestic debt markets in emerging economies.*" These authors review the relationship between foreign and domestic pension funds in domestic financial markets of emerging economies, arguing that given their longer-time horizon, pension funds are expected to contribute positively to the development of large and deep domestic local currency bond markets, and hence ease fiscal and external constraints in these countries. However, this does not necessarily apply due to the hierarchic and structured international financial and monetary systems that are linked to external vulnerability and financial market instability.

In Chapter 5, Mimoza Shabani discusses *"The distribution of dividends of multinational banks operating in Latin America"*; here she analyses the distribution of dividends in multinational banks that operate in Argentina, Brazil, Chile, Colombia, Mexico and Peru, on the basis of bank level data, for the period 2013–2019. The findings suggest that Mexico and Peru have the highest foreign bank participation in their banking sector. However, foreign banks in Brazil, Chile and Mexico have made higher dividend payments to the shareholders of their parent banks. This also holds when looking at dividend payments in relation to their earnings. This suggests that a large share of earnings leaves the countries in which they operate in the form of dividend payments rather than being reinvested.

The last chapter of this section is *"The unique development of non-financial corporations in Latin America"* by Noemi Levy-Orlik and Jorge Alonso Bustamante-Torres, in which the authors discuss the impact of foreign flows on non-financial corporations, followed by a revision of FDI trends in term of volume and composition, looking at their impact on industrial development and its links with domestic financial markets. They also revise the development of Latin American non-financial corporations and argue that their overcapitalisation process differs from multinational corporations based in developed economies, for which they provide a detailed analysis of financial indicators of balance sheet and income statement from Chile, Brazil and Mexico.

The second section of this volume focuses on "Non-financial corporations and economic growth" and contains four chapters. The first is *"Capital flows, the role of non-financial corporations and their macroeconomic implications: an analysis of the case of Chile"*. Esteban Pérez-Caldentey and Nicole Favreau-Negront argue that the behaviour of the balance-of-payments, specifically the capital/financial account in Chile, is explained by financial and not real factors, reflecting the interactions of specific sectors. Particularly the rising importance of the international bond market is used by a minority of firms to issue debt in the international capital markets to counteract their falling profits. Thereby the international bond market is not a source of finance of real activity, turning into a space in which these firms can guarantee their financial survival.

In Chapter 8, entitled *"Foreign direct investment in the Mexican steel industry"*, Samuel Ortiz-Velásquez discusses foreign investment determinants in the Mexican steel industry, specifically three foreign subsidiaries: Tenaris-Tamsa, Gerdau-Corsa and Novametal-TIM corporations. The working hypothesis of this chapter is that investment is explained by microeconomic and institutional variables rather than macroeconomic determinants.

In the following chapter, Ximena Echenique-Romero discusses the *"Excess international liquidity and corporate financing in Mexico: reflections from USA monetary policy of quantitative easing"* in the light of three objectives. First, the relation of the USA quantitative easing policy and the structure of corporate refinancing in Mexico; second, the effects of the US international liquidity international interest rate differentials, the efficiency of international financial markets, and prices of financial assets; and finally, the connection of Mexican corporate financing and the stock market, highlighting that shares are the principal financing mechanism.

The last chapter of this section, written by Marcelo Varela-Enríquez and Gustavo Adrián Salazar discusses "*Foreign direct investment in Latin America: effects on growth and development, 1996–2017*". These authors examine the effectiveness of foreign direct investment on economic growth and development in Latin America between 1996 and 2017. They conclude that direct foreign investment contributes positively to economic growth measured by variations in GDP, while money flows captured from the balance of net income balance of payments and sent abroad negatively affect human development.

The final section of this book deals with "*Capital movement and economic patterns*" and contains four chapters. In Chapter 11, focusing on "*Latin American international integration and global value chains: what changed after the 2008 global financial crisis*", Juan Pablo Painceira and Alexis Saludjian discuss the development strategies of industrial countries (United States and the European Union) and developing economies (Latin America, particularly Brazil) after the GFC. According to the authors, the main international strategies of developed countries moved towards protectionism (USA and EU), while developing economies continued to support trade liberalism, reversing the strategies of international integration between countries of the centre and the periphery, affecting multinational companies' strategies, particularly China's role in the world economy and modifying finance issues.

In the following chapter, "*From 'downpour of investments' to debt crisis: the case of Argentina 2015–2019*", Cecilia Allami, Pablo Bortz and Alan Cibils argue that in Argentina, in the period of President Macri (2015 and 2019), a radically different macroeconomic policy plan was imposed. Against the expectations in this new period, deregulation and financial liberalisation neither creates a "*rain of investment*" nor equilibrated the structural external imbalances or achieved economic growth. Instead, a substantial increase in external portfolio investment took place, whose objective was short-term returns guaranteed by monetary policy and the Argentinian government was obliged to apply for rescue plans. which came along with the traditional stabilisation and adjustment packages.

In Chapter 13, Gonzalo Cómbita-Mora and Álvaro Martín Moreno-Rivas write on the issue of "*The hegemony of big corporations and internationalization of capital: a stagnation model with restricted democracy*". These authors state that the dynamics of Colombia's economy has favoured the consolidation of a productive structure that benefits large corporations. This chapter's hypothesis is that mining, energy sectors (dominated by multinational corporations) and national corporations in the agro-industrial sectors required the displacement of the Afro-descendant Indians and peasants from Colombian territories, aggravating the armed conflict and the combat against drug trafficking. To validate this argument, the authors construct a novel theoretical and empirical framework that considers economic analyses and political aspects that endanger the globalisation process.

In the final chapter, "*Extractive capitalism: transnational miners and Andean peasants in Peru*", Alejandro Garay-Huamán analyses the socio-economic impact of transnational extractive capital in the Andean communities of northern Peru, and the traditional socio-economic transformations within the limits of the development–underdevelopment duality. The relations between the capitalist and non-capitalist sectors are discussed in the light of dependency theory, production organisation and imperialism. On this basis, the author develops an alternative framework that accounts for the relation between transnational capital and the non-capitalist (peasant) sector connected through global chains of production, following the Marxist concept of class. Special emphasis is given to the production process, distribution, and the appropriation of surpluses, including extra-economic processes, required for the existence of these surpluses. All these concepts allow for an analysis of complex relationships between transnational corporations, the financial sector, the extractive sector workers, and peasants, within global production chains of gold, silver and copper.

NOTE

1. Kaltenbrunner and Painceira (2017) argue that financial globalisation introduced a new asymmetry between currencies of developed and developing countries, since it was a new mechanism of profit shifting for developed countries.

REFERENCES

Aguiar de Medeiros, C. and Trebat, N. (2018). Las finanzas, el comercio y la distribución del ingreso en las cadenas globales de valor: implicancias para las economías en desarrollo y América Latina. In Perez. Caldentey E. and Valdecantos S. (eds), *Estudios sobre financierización en América Latina, ABELES* (171–204). Chile: Cepal.

Bellofiore, R., Garibaldo, F. and Halevi, J. (2010). The global crisis and the crisis of European neomercantilism. *Socialist Register*, 47(1), 121–146.

Borio, C. and Disyatat, P. (2015). Capital flows and the current account. Taking financing (more) seriously. *BIS*, Working Paper 525, October.

Dowrick, S. and Rogers, M. (2002). Classical and technological convergence: beyond the Solow–Swan growth model. *Oxford Economic Papers*, 54(3, July), 369–385.

Kalecki, M. (1971). *Selected Essays on the Dynamics of the Capitalist Economy, 1933–1970*. Cambridge: Cambridge University Press.

Kaltenbrunner, A. and Painceira J. P. (2017). Subordinated financial integration and financialization in emerging capitalist economies: the Brazilian experience. *New Political Economy*, 23(3). doi: 10.1080/13563467.2017.1349089.

Lazonick, W. and O'Sullivan, M. (2000). Maximizing shareholder value: a new ideology for corporate governance. *Economy and Society*, 29(1), 13–35.

McKinnon, R. (1973). *Money and Capital in Economic Development*. Washington, DC: The Brookings Institution.

Solow, R. M. (1963). *Capital Theory and the Rate of Return*. Amsterdam: North-Holland.

Steindl, J. (1952). *Maturity and Stagnation in American Capitalism*. New York: Monthly Review.

UNCTAD (n.d.). The top 100 non-financial MNES from developing and transition economies, ranked by foreign assets, different years. *UNCTAD/Erasmus University data*. Retrieved from https://unctad.org/Sections/dite_dir/docs/wir2005top100_en.pdf, accessed 20 March 2020.

PART I

Post crisis new capital movement trend

1. Financial geography and the 'social reality of finance': aspatial or 'real space' analyses of financial crises?

Gary Dymski and Nicole Cerpa Vielma

In 2015, the Global Network on Financial Geography (www.fingeo.net) was formally launched in Oxford. Dariusz Wójcik, the cofounder of this network, summed up the academic rationale for 'financial geography' as follows: 'The view of finance in economics became as detached from the social reality of finance, as some financial practices … became detached from society. Social scientists in turn neglected money and finance assuming it was taken care of by economists' (Wójcik, 2017). That is, when social scientists have focused on space and its implications, they have ignored the monetary realm; and when economists have discussed that realm, they have ignored 'the social reality of finance'.

Wójcik's comment clearly takes aim at efficient-market-based financial economics: the explanatory sand-castles aimed at retaining empirical relevance at micro-market scales even while the steadily rising volume of financial crises since the 1980s demonstrates their explanatory limits. But his observations can be extended to the complementary blind-spots he identifies. In particular, his term 'social scientists' classifies economists who do not isolate financial practices from 'social reality' as 'social scientists', not economists. No offence is intended by this geographer's telling distinction, and none is taken. This contrast reveals that just as some economists use narrow criteria for what counts as 'economics', non-economists sometimes wear blinkers about what economics is. And while many economists have broken out of this methodological cul-de-sac while remaining 'economists', very few of them have worked explicitly with 'space' in ways that most geographers would recognize.

A self-conscious field of financial geography can provide the necessary terrain for interdisciplinary exchange between economists and geographers who want to work on 'the social reality of finance'. But closing this gap will require some adjustments on both sides. Geographers, on their side, must see that the analytical conventions used in mainstream economics are well within the boundaries of the discipline. Economists, in turn, must develop much clearer ideas about the boundaries and possibilities of spatial analysis in economics. We argue here that economists hoping to establish interdisciplinary dialogues about the 'social reality of finance' must do two things: first, accept the importance of the geographic dimension; second, concede that economics is differentiated, as a social science discipline, by its analytical entry-points, not by the epistemological superiority of its insights. We illustrate our argument by exploring several economic models of financial crises in developing countries. The modelling conventions that guide mainstream models rule out both social factors and 'real space', just as they rule out the 'real time' approach used in Post-Keynesian economics. Bringing in 'real time' and 'real space' requires breaking with these conventions.

This chapter is divided into four sections. Section 1.1 argues that answering Wójcik's critique will require an economics that takes a 'real space' approach, parallel to the 'real time' framework that has helped to shape Post-Keynesian economics. Section 1.2 sets out some iconic models by economists of inherently spatial phenomena – the recurrent cross-border financial crises that have afflicted the global economy since the 1980s. These examples show how the mainstream toolkit invisibilizes key aspects of financial crises. Section 1.3 sketches out a 'real time/real space' approach to cross-border financial crises. This shows how this financial geography perspective can bring the 'social reality of finance' more firmly within the explanatory boundaries of economics and geography. Section 1.4 briefly sketches the main conclusions of this chapter.[1]

1.1   'REAL TIME' AND 'REAL SPACE' ANALYSIS AND THE PROBLEM OF SOCIAL POWER

What is required to build a spatial analysis incorporating the 'social reality of finance'? The first strand of Wójcik's critique, that economists treat financial phenomena as aspatial, applies both to models of high-speed trading and derivatives markets in hyper-space and to models of financial processes that incorporate no geographic dimension. A *necessary* condition is recognizing processes or events that unfold in different spaces. This immediately implies that the agents involved are heterogeneous. This can be established very simply by assuming that everything doesn't happen in the same place, and it is costly to move from one location to another. For example, Townsend (1983) uses this assumption to explain the use of money.

More is needed, though, to incorporate the 'social reality of finance'. The situation of spatially separated agents maximizing utility through exchange is reversible: it has no social dimension. A *sufficient* condition for bringing in 'social reality' is to specify that agents separated in space have location-specific differences in their choice sets or resources. So location is not reversible, and conveys either more options or fewer. This division can take many forms – two sides of the tracks, global North and global South, and so on. It immediately conveys differences in social power, which is inherent in differential constraints or choices. Analyses can be termed 'real space' when they incorporate non-reversible space with one or more social dimensions.

An analogy to this idea of 'real space' is available in the 'real time' perspective that underpins one of the several strands of Post-Keynesian economics (Hamouda and Harcourt, 1988). Shackle (1974) and Davidson (1978) led the way in demonstrating how the concept of liquidity preference introduced by Keynes implied the centrality of 'real time' in economic dynamics. Economic agents confront 'real time' when they have to make decisions in the face of irreducible uncertainty – and not simply probabilistic risk – about the outcomes that may result. This leads to a major emphasis in Post-Keynesian economics on the need to stabilize the macroeconomic environment and aggregate spending streams, as this minimizes disturbances in beliefs and disruptions in the confidence required to make irreversible investment and consumption decisions.

'Real time' analysis differentiates Post-Keynesian approaches to financial and macroeconomic analysis from mainstream models, which do not allow for fundamental uncertainty.

'Real space' is an independent dimension, which in turn is missing from most mainstream and Post-Keynesian writing (Dymski and Kaltenbrunner, 2021). When time is 'real', the unforecastable unknown itself affects human decisions in the present; when space is 'real', what can and cannot be done depends on factors beyond physical distance itself.

Some Post-Keynesian work does incorporate 'real space' analysis. A prime example is the work of Dow (1987) on the differences between the functioning of banking systems in a national economy's core and peripheral regions. She argues that the periphery is subject to credit starvation in periods of financial distress – as a consequence, levels of financing, liquidity, and growth differ in time and across time. This finding rests implicitly on the differential social power of core and periphery, which can be traced to differences in spatial resource endowments and in market access.

Note that 'real space' analysis thus requires references to physical realms that are divided in some manner by borders. Processes or the movement of entities then differ according to whether they are contained inside a border, exist outside of it, or cross it. Note as well that borders exist at different spatial scales – regions, nations, cities, neighbourhoods, even streets. Most economic analysis that works with given spatial layers – nation-states, or city-regions, etc. – uses these as foundational analytical units; for example, one might read that 'Mexico took on foreign lending'. Geographers, by contrast, see spatial layers as sites of social processes. Lefebvre (1991), in his foundational analysis, discusses the 'production of space' (or 'social space') (ibid., p. 67) through 'spatial practices' (ibid., pp. 16–18). Any given spatial layer contains actors and objects connected through 'upward' and 'downward' linkages to larger and smaller spatial areas via purchases and sales, rights and obligations, permissions and denials. Soja referred to the '*spatiality* of human life' as 'thirdspace', accompanying the '*historicality* and *sociality*' (Soja, 1996, p. 3) of lived experience.

Economists' and Geographers' Approaches to Power

This brings us to the problematic of power. One challenge in overcoming the gap identified by Wójcik is that economists view power through the lens of market transactions, and geographers through the lens of social relations more broadly. For economists, power involves mechanisms that either redistribute gains and losses outside of market transactions, or situations in which one party to a market transaction has inferior alternatives and thus cannot bargain freely over terms and conditions of the contract achieved. As Bowles (2006, p. 256) puts it, power accrues to the party on the 'short' side of the market. Power is little discussed, in any case, especially by mainstream economists, who use Walrasian general equilibrium as their analytical reference point, and prefer explanations that meet the Occam's Razor criterion – deviating as little as possible from the ideal of agent choice based on utility maximization (Dymski, 2014).

Some geographic work follows this market-centred approach. Cohen's *The geography of money* (1998), referenced below, defines the root of financial power as national governments' 'monopoly control over the issue and management of their own money' (Cohen, 1998, p. 4). But since 'currencies increasingly are employed outside their country of origin, penetrating other monetary spaces ... power has been redistributed not only between states but, even more important, from states to market forces. ... authority must be shared with other market agents, in particular the users on the demand side of the market' (ibid., p. 5).

So the approach of Cohen – an international political economist – stays within the 'market power' conception. Many geographers take a broader approach. For example, Lefebvre (1991) argues that capital exerts power over the production of space, and indeed is hegemonic over space. Soja also uses this terminology: 'Hegemonic power ... actively *produces and reproduces difference* as a key strategy to create and maintain modes of social and spatial division that are advantageous to its continued empowerment and authority' (Soja, 1996, p. 87). Richard Peet's *The geography of power* covers similar ground to that of Cohen, but follows the approach of his fellow geographers:

> With the term 'geography of power' I refer to the concentration of power in a few spaces that control a world of distant others. My argument is that a new kind of economic power system has arrived on the world scene. Power has increasingly been accumulated at the global level by governance institutions – the G7/G8, the European Union, the Bretton Woods Institutions and the United Nations. (Peet, 2013, p. 1)

Peet's subsequent discussion focuses on global finance capital, 'the influence of capital markets on the making of global development policy by government and governance institution' (ibid., p. 35), and the revolving door between Wall Street and government, *inter alia*. But these are the insights of a geographer writing geography. Can such open discussions of power as one aspect of the 'social reality of finance' be encompassed within economics?

1.2   MAINSTREAM ECONOMIC MODELS OF FINANCIAL CRISES AND GLOBAL IMBALANCES

Since the 1980s, mainstream macroeconomic models have been held to the same explanatory standard that previously pertained only to microeconomic models: the economist building a model must demonstrate how the observed result follows from the rational choices of one or more individual agents in a representative market setting. This reflected a shift away from the macroeconomic models that had prevailed since World War II, which had featured the structural characteristics of sectors of the economy and largely ignored rational choice questions, which were considered microeconomic issues. The downfall of the older generation of models coincided with the chaotic macroeconomic and geo-economic events of the 1970s. The moment was ripe for the long-brewing methodological critique of Keynesian macroeconomics by Robert Lucas and his New Classical associates. This new orthodoxy insisted on models of rational behaviour under rational expectations. This section sets out two illustrative models that conform with these mainstream conventions.

In the early 1980s, recession and skyrocketing interest rates took hold across the world, and led first Mexico and then other Latin American nations to default on their cross-border loans.[2] While economists such as Diaz-Alejandro (1984) pointed to structural dimensions of the global economy and of Latin America, building a mainstream model required answering a different question: how to explain the Latin American debt crisis while conforming with the 'rational agent' requirement imposed by the macroeconomic reformation? One defensible approach was to model the lender–borrower relation as involving a principal–agent problem because of asymmetric information: lenders don't know how borrowers will perform once they receive loans, and thus face potential loss from this 'moral hazard'. This became the dominant explanation of the Latin American debt crisis (Eaton et al., 1986). The borrower country, conceptualized as a unitary agent, compares the gains from repaying and from defaulting, and rationally defaults when the penalty for defaulting is set too low.

While this model purports to explain loan defaults across space, it is aspatial – space plays no role. This model is also asocial. It ignores the diverse agents interacting at multiple spatial scales prior to default – the companies unable to pay, the governments stepping in, the workers shouldering the higher public debt burden. Instead, the borrower is conceived as a unitary agent, a 'country'. While it clashed with the actual chronology and specifics of the case, this model proved durable. Krugman (1998) used it to argue that the root cause of the East Asian crisis of 1997 was a rampant moral hazard in Asia's state-controlled banking systems. This same model has been deployed in explanations of the Eurozone and subprime crises (Dymski, 2014).

Our second example is the 'shortage of safe assets' explanation of the Great Financial Crisis. In Fall 2008, Caballero et al. (2008, p. 1) explained: 'The current financial crisis has its origins in global asset scarcity, which led to large capital flows toward the United States and to the creation of asset bubbles that eventually burst.' Caballero and Krishnamurthy (2009, p. 1) elaborated further:

> A key structural factor behind this [2008] crisis is the large demand for riskless assets from the rest of the world. In this paper we present a model to show how such demand not only triggered a sharp rise in U.S. asset prices, but also exposed the U.S. financial sector to a downturn by concentrating risk onto its balance sheet. … capital flows into the U.S. are mostly non-speculative and in search of safety. … In other words, as global imbalances rise, the U.S. increasingly specializes in holding its 'toxic waste'.

This model is aspatial and asocial, as was the moral-hazard model of debt crises; replacing that model's borrower/lender binary is a safe-asset country/risky-asset country binary, in a stripped-down setting: the model has neither a banking nor a financial sector. In this case, the globally peripheral countries have not exploited a poorly solved principal–agent problem, but compensated for their own nations' inability to create safe assets by overbidding for US safe assets, leading through portfolio effects to excessive risk migrating to US financial markets and generating a bubble there.

As Dominguez (2008, p. 56) put it: 'This ambitious paper … seeks to explain, in one model, all that is wrong in the global economy. The culprit is underdeveloped financial markets in emerging Asia and the oil producing countries. U.S. fiscal and monetary policies play no role.' Its description of the facts of the case is wrong, as was the moral-hazard debt-crisis model. Federal Reserve economists Bertaut et al. (2011) have shown that it was European investors, not developing economies, that accounted for the vast majority of cross-border asset-backed securities purchases in advance of the 2008 crisis. Nonetheless, Caballero and his co-authors have doubled down, arguing that 'the supply of safe assets has not kept up with global demand. The reason is straightforward: the collective growth rate of the advanced economies that produce safe assets has been lower than the world's growth rate' (Caballero et al., 2017).

Aspatiality and Atemporality in Mainstream Models of Global Processes

More examples of mainstream models of cross-border crises or processes could readily be found; but these two are sufficient to demonstrate the pattern. The moral-hazard and safe-asset explanations rest on thinly specified models with incomplete representations of even the processes they are explaining.

The moral-hazard model of the Latin American crisis denotes the borrower as the sovereign – a misrepresentation. The 'borrower' in this model, the sovereign nation, was not originally part of the credit-market transaction with the overseas lender. Financial structures within the borrower countries are ignored, as is the commodity-price decline. Krugman's model of the East Asian crisis blames crony-capitalism – the provision of credit to borrowers in affected East Asia countries on the basis of clientelism – ignoring the social and institutional basis of these very nations' high growth rates. Quite simply, establishing a moral-hazard dilemma on the basis of a binary principal–agent relationship is the simplest – Occam's Razor – path to an argument rooted in agent incentives and optimization; the historical and institutional context is a distraction. The safe-asset argument, in turn, ignores other processes that could explain the systematic inflow of capital into the US, such as deindustrialization and financial deregulation in the 1980s.

'Real space' – the fact that all events unfold in interconnected spatial sites or across spatial borders – and 'real time' – the context-dependent impact of the uncertain future on liquidity preference – are completely absent. While these models pertain to agents and instruments separated in space, space plays no role. And because of the aspatiality of the constructs, which places all parties within the model on an imaginary even playing field, power differentials are invisibilized. Another dimension of aspatiality is that the multi-scalar social and political context of the nation-states in question receives no attention. Economic dynamics at the regional and global scales larger than the borrower and safe-asset seeking nations are ignored, as are economic and social dynamics within these nations. The fact that cross-border constraints have to be met – and indeed, are part and parcel of the flows highlighted in the 'search for safe assets' story – is ignored, as are the implications of those cross-border constraints for the net direction of flows. Regarding 'real time', all payoffs are well-defined in the moral-hazard model. In the 'shortage of safe assets' model, the nature of 'safe' versus 'risky' assets is not discussed at all; the problem of running for safety itself, which motivates the model, is described as a matter of optimal portfolio allocation. Uncertainty and asymmetric power are hiding in plain sight, but never discussed.

1.3   FINANCIAL POWER IN GLOBAL SPACE

The reason to make space for financial geography in foundational discussions of the political economy of financial processes, outcomes, and systems is that there are different stories to be told than can be reached while working within the confines of models disciplined by concerns about Occam's Razor distancing from general equilibrium.

In this section, we will sketch out the bare bones of a 'real time', 'real space' analysis encompassing the two global scenarios covered in Section 1.2 – the occurrence and consequences of sovereign debt crises, and the driving forces of global imbalances. Instead of highlighting developing-economy wealth owners' search for safe assets, we focus attention on structural factors that have led developing-economy sovereign nations to endure financially fragile – risky – structural positions. And instead of considering why those sovereigns are such reluctant payers, we consider structural pressures compromising their ability to pay.

This change of perspective requires that we include within our analytical focus not just the nation-state level, highlighted in the models covered in Section 1.2, to the global architecture of power in finance. This short section shows how an alternative to the economic models summarized in Section 1.2 can be replaced via a financial geography that encompasses real time and real space. 'Real time' here connotes more than the situation of the decision-maker facing uncertainty. The decisions made across the face of the nation and, indeed, the world, lead to flows of goods and services and to the accumulation or decumulation of wealth in each period of time. The location of every decision-maker in the world, and the resources at her command, affects their options and their power. And power resides in some locations, not in others. So a 'real time', 'real space' approach, to be fully expressed, has to be historically informed and institutionally grounded, and conscious of the distribution of power.

In the suggestive sketch set out in this section, we first delineate the origin and shape of financial power at the global scale, deployed to establish rules of the game; then we turn to nation-states inside or seeking to enter the global core; and finally we consider the situation of nation-states in the periphery. These are, to summarize crudely, zones of control, of dominance, and of submission. Our focus in every one of these spheres is to consider in what power consists.

Power in Finance at the Global Spatial Scale

At the core of the core of global finance, even years after the end of the Bretton Woods system, are the United States and its too-big-to-fail megabanks. This position was achieved via a series of radical policy measures that remade a regulated system that was losing customers to the money and bond markets by the end of the 1970s. Ending geographic segmentation and deregulating banking instruments and product-lines, together with an extended bank merger wave (Dymski, 1999), fed new capital into the financial system and bolstered the importance of the country's money-centre banks. These large banks' attempts to replace lost customers by opening new markets, including Latin America and East Asia, led first to a financial crisis (as noted above), but then to the emergence of too-big-to-fail megabanks in the US from the mid-1980s onwards.

Then and subsequently, the US Federal Reserve demonstrated the capacity and willingness to support its national-champion banks; and it showed its resolve as a lender-of-last-resort in a series of financial panics from the 1980s onwards: backstopping the money-centre banks that had overlent to Latin America and to the 'oil patch' region of the US; the 1987 stock-market crash; the Mexican Tesobono crisis of 1994–1995; the 1997 East Asian financial crisis; the 1998 Long-Term Capital Management collapse and the 1998 Russian financial crisis; the bursting of the IT bubble in 2000. Had there been any doubts about whether the US Federal Reserve could, by issuing its own currency as needed, satisfy 'flight to safety' impulses in a crisis-prone world, these were laid to rest.

From 1980 onwards, the current-account deficit grew, and the capital-account surplus along with it. The growing willingness of global markets to hold dollars, encouraged by the Federal Reserve's steady hand, facilitated the steady inflow of capital; this provided financing for the growing federal-government deficit, and consolidated the permanence of the systematic US current-account deficit. The US used the 'exorbitant privilege' (Eichengreen, 2010) afforded it by the global dominance of the dollar to sustain and fund large budget and current-account deficits. The Treasury liabilities emitted to support these imbalances are held by central banks the world over.

With this stable neoliberal structure came positional power – the ability to define rules of the game.[3] Once the US had done so, other countries hastened to deregulate their financial systems. US housing finance was reshaped from a bank-based to a market-based credit system. The securitization process at the heart of this system began with safe, 'plain vanilla' mortgage loans, but by the 1990s expanded to riskier loans, including subprime mortgages. An interconnected network of shadow banks centred around megabanks and investment banks (Wójcik, 2012) grew to originate, service, and hold these loans. Again, overseas capital flowed in to secure its share. Much of this new system either has since the 1980s escaped or challenged regulatory oversight.

This was the system being put in place when the Latin American crisis unfolded, and that was solidifying its gains when empirical evidence of a hunt for 'safe assets' could first be detected. The global economic consequences of this system are made devastatingly clear in D'Arista's recent volume *All fall down* (2018). D'Arista shows that financial globalization creates a global pyramid, under the terms of which only the country at the top can stop panics when financial crises occur. She demonstrates, as suggested here, that problems of unchecked financial flows are reinforced by structural imbalances in current and capital accounts. Further, she shows that the persistent neoliberal-era US current-account deficit implies that developing-economies' holdings of US liabilities are supporting financialization globally, and increasing pressures that destabilize governments and increase the returns to global financial predation.

The 'real time', 'real space' dimensions are central to this evolving replacement system of finance. Location in space (and time) matters, in terms of what vector of forces are at work, and with what effect, across the face of the inhabited planet. And indeed, we might differentiate between different spaces and, in turn, agents' positions within those spaces. If one is not located at the centre of the system, it matters greatly for financial dynamics and differential power both whether one is located in the core or periphery, and in turn where one is positioned, whether in the core or periphery.

Nation-States in the Global Financial Core

Beyond the hegemonic dollar, which nations are in the global financial core? Cohen observes that governments that maintain 'monetary monopoly' over payments systems accrue four powers: 'political symbolism, seigniorage, macroeconomic management, and insulation from external influence' (Cohen, 1998, p. 119). Cohen's monetary monopoly, however, establishes only territorial integrity, not the viability of national finance beyond its own boundaries.

There are three possible projections of financial power outside a nation's own boundaries. The first is the ability to emit a currency that other nation-states willingly hold. The test of this lies in global currency reserve holdings. The International Monetary Fund (IMF) lists the holdings of only eight nations' currencies in its published registry: this is a small club. Dollar holdings far exceed those of the euro, which in turn vastly outstrip those of the UK pound and Japanese yen, with Chinese renminbi holdings even farther behind. Beyond the even smaller global reserve holdings of Canadian and Australian dollars and of Swiss francs, this club has no other members.

The second power arises when a given nation's currency is used in contracts outside its own borders. An example arises when one nation's currency is used to finance investment outside its national borders. When this is done recurrently, this nation's legal practices and business service firms can shape the cross-border financial processes in which they participate. Kaltenbrunner and Lysandrou (2017) show that virtually no nations' currencies now challenge the dominance of the US dollar in this regard. A third power is the capacity to provide third-party financial services to foreign buyers. The best example here is the City of London, whose foreign-currency and offshore bond markets are world leaders, almost a century after the British pound lost its central place in the global monetary system.

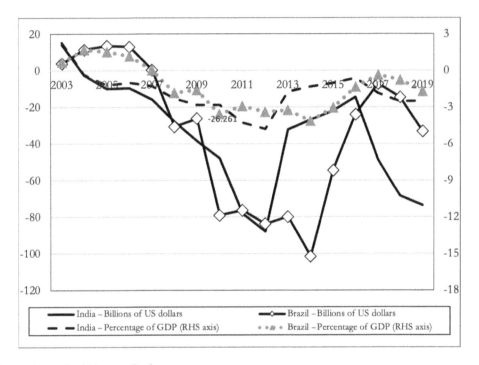

Source: International Monetary Fund.

Figure 1.1   Two measures of current-account balance, India and Brazil (2003–2019)

Projections of any of these three cross-border powers is sufficient to qualify a nation for the global financial core. Membership in the core entails two benefits. First is guaranteed safety: nations in the core maintain very low reserves; they do not fear systematic speculative attack – speculators know their central banks can emit domestic money (reserves) at will, without reserve. The US, Germany, France, and the United Kingdom – home nations of aggressive, globally active megabanks that have attracted the close scrutiny of the Financial Stability Board – have reserve totals substantially lower than those of non-core nations with smaller income levels. The second benefit to core nations is that, precisely because they are immune to speculative attack, they can host financial firms that can take stakes in other nations' systems and/or engage in zero-sum speculation with external parties. This can be considered offensive power; it has enabled these core nations' largest banks to expand aggressively, to sizes sometimes surpassing the GDP levels of their home nations.

Nation-States in the Global Financial Periphery

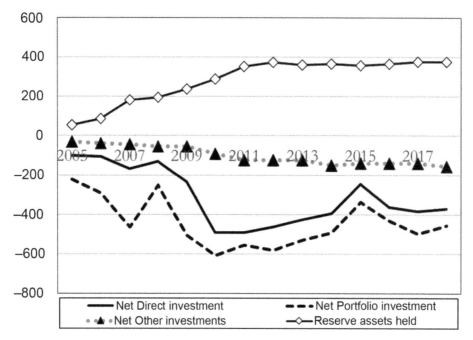

Source: International Monetary Fund.

Figure 1.2   Net international investment position, India (2005–2018) (billions of US$)

A nation is classified in the global financial periphery when it does not maintain 'monetary monopoly' over its own territory and/or when it lacks any of the three cross-border powers detailed above. To fail both the former and latter tests, of course, puts a nation in the deep core of the periphery. A nation that lacks any cross-border power but retains monetary monopoly is vulnerable to attack by financial firms based in nations in the financial core. Further, such a nation is more vulnerable to 'sudden stop' crises (Dymski, 2019), especially if it depends on a flow of financing from external lenders.

   An examination of the cross-border accounts of many developing economies, including India and Brazil, reveals that despite having current-account deficits, these countries are over-borrowing so as to build up their stocks of currency reserves. Protection from attack – the power to be left alone – is a key motive for many developing nations. To see this graphically, first consider Figure 1.1, which shows that both countries' current-account balances shifted from positive to negative in the global financial crisis period, recovering somewhat thereafter. The inescapable logic of cross-border balances is that a nation's current account deficits

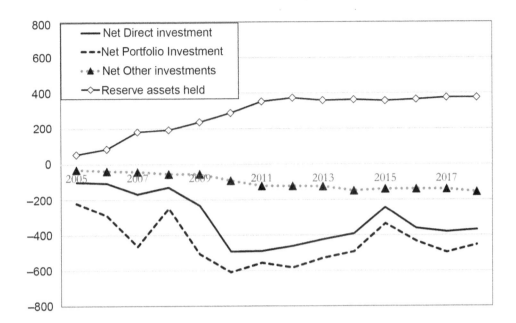

Figure 1.3   Net international investment position, Brazil (2005–2018) (billions of US$)

(resulting in net outflows of domestic currency chasing foreign goods and services) must be financed either by an inflow of foreigners' savings (such as foreign direct investment) or by spending down its stock of foreign reserves. The implication of Figure 1.1 is thus that foreign savings should be increasing or reserves declining, or both.

Figures 1.2 and 1.3 provide the evidence for the capital-flow side of this equation by summarizing the net investment position of these two countries in the same time-frame. Net investment position is positive when a nation's wealth-owners net purchases of foreign assets exceeds foreigners' purchases of domestic assets (and vice versa). So net investment position should be negative for both India (Figure 1.2) and Brazil (Figure 1.3). It is, in both cases, for three categories of net investment (portfolio, direct, and other). The anomaly is that in both countries, reserve assets held rise systematically throughout the 2005–2018 period depicted. As noted, reserves should remain constant or be reduced when the current account balance is negative. But both countries have, to the contrary, amassed systematically more holdings of foreign currencies. They have, in effect, over-borrowed so as to protect themselves from speculation.

Financial fragilities arise for nations lacking financial power. The asymmetric power of core nations vis-à-vis peripheral nations – immunity from speculative attack – constitutes a severe danger for the latter. Countries whose currencies have begun to enter open global markets are under most threat. To offset that disadvantage, a peripheral country may take action by enhancing its defensive power. Defensive power can take several forms. One is to impose inward capital controls. This move may be ruled out by prior action put in place after IMF intervention in the wake of a previous financial crisis. A second form of defensive power is the build-up of excess stocks of foreign-currency reserves.[4]

1.4   CONCLUSIONS

This chapter has argued for the importance of establishing a financial geography that can offer counter-analyses to mainstream economists' aspatial models of spatial processes. Comparing economists' models of imbalances and crises with spatial analyses focused on asymmetrically distributed economic power illustrates why financial geography is needed. Economists' models are disciplined by their fealty to rational behaviour and to their own version of Occam's Razor. These pre-commitments make it difficult or impossible to introduce important institutional and historical elements into their models; as we have seen, this often leads to models that are descriptively wrong or partial, and that ignore history rather than heeding its lessons.

We have made three interlocking arguments about how financial geography can provide the discursive space for meeting these goals. First, non-economists (especially geographers) must expand their own criteria for what counts as economics, to include the richer palate of methodologies and perspectives that draws many economics to the practice of heterodox – not mainstream – economics. Second, economists – especially heterodox economists – must more explicitly recognize the importance of 'real space' – the spatial dimension – in their analyses. It is often, as noted, hiding in plain sight in discussions of power, inequality, stratification, and so on. Third, economists, geographers, sociologists, and other social scientists must be willing and able to either work with terms that are accessible to those outside their own specialty fields, or to work as translators. In sum, constructing a financial geography that is fit for the purposes designated here is, at heart, a bridge-building exercise.

Some final reflections on Wójcik's inadvertent dismissal of the heterodoxy in his use of the term 'economist' are pertinent in suggesting the way forward. The question is, in asking geographers to redefine 'economics' more widely, so as to encompass that discipline's heterodoxy instead of just its mainstream 'core', are we suggesting that 'anything goes'? In effect, are we asking geographers focusing on financial geography to have a conversation with a category of economics that is an empty set? The answer is, 'no, but it's complicated'.

The fact that what binds 'heterodox' economists together is their opposition to mainstream orthodoxy is a well-worn observation, usually expressed as a joke. But after acknowledging this joke, it is important to dig into its deeper meaning, which has changed over time. Post-Keynesian economists engaged in a lengthy debate three decades ago, discussed in Hamouda and Harcourt (1988), about whether those identified as Post-Keynesian economists shared a particular set of core methodological and conceptual commitments. The one concept agreed on by all was that aggregate demand feeds back on and co-determines output levels. Even Keynesian uncertainty was not an essential concept for some varieties of Post-Keynesianism: indeed, the importance of the hyphen between 'Post' and 'Keynesian' even became the object of debate. The recent effort by Marc Lavoie (2015) to compile the key findings and methods of Post-Keynesian economics begins with a long discussion of the different 'schools' of Post-Keynesian thought.

But the core of the old joke – the rejection of the notion that economic theory should be based, to the extent possible, on the optimizing behaviour of individual or representative agents coordinating their activity through market exchange – actually is the definitive unifying thread. To deny this is to pose, for oneself, the question of how to organize a coherent set of ideas about how the provisioning system fits into and interacts with the broader social world outside of it. Throughout this chapter, the term 'economy' and not 'political economy' has been used to designate this system. The term 'political economy' has its uses, in acknowledging that economic relations cannot be defined independent of the political context in which they exist, whether 'democracy', 'socialism', 'fascism', or other alternatives. But the arrangements for provisioning also have a social context, and an ecological one.

Parallel debates to those that have preoccupied Post-Keynesian economists about their common identity have gone on, and will continue, for Marxian economists, for institutional economists, and for others. Arguably the core commitment of feminist economics – that every agent is gendered, and this matters in economic behaviour, organization, and outcomes – necessitates a positionality outside the core of the mainstream. The same logic applies to ecological economics. This brings up a key point about 'heterodox economics' itself. This term has emerged in the past quarter-century (Lee, 2009; Carpintero, 2013) precisely because of the flowering of work outside the mainstream. Beyond the old joke, Dymski (2014) has pointed out that this resurgence is linked to various social and political movements – for women's rights, for racial equality, for ecological sustainability, for reduced inequality, and so on. There can be no expectation of uniformity in economic heterodoxy, because its membership is multiple, and the research it stimulates makes points that are pertinent from different points of criticality about existing society.

The critical move designated herein for economists is to embrace 'real time'; this is shorthand for identifying with core elements of Post-Keynesian economics, on one hand; but accepting 'real time' and the associated insight that aggregate demand 'matters' does not require self-designation as a Keynesian or Post-Keynesian. Parallel to 'real time' here has been the centrality of 'real space'. There are certainly domains of geographic theory where space is defined in an abstract way, shorn of any links to social relations; the literature on size-ordering of cities comes immediately to mind, as does the literature on geospatial mapping. That said, the frameworks used by those who practise what might be termed 'abstract geography', for our purposes here, in no way play the role in geography that the core mainstream model does in economics. It would arguably be impossible to locate a conceptual point of reference in geography that is equivalent to the general economic equilibrium in economics. This has liberated geography, as a discipline, from stark designations about whose work is 'serious' and whose is not.

There is, however, something about contending a power centre within the economics discipline that defends the priority of the market over and against 'society' that has been productive for heterodox economists. It generates bonds of solidarity. The struggles to build heterodox insights in economics, as tortured and multiple as they have been, do bring practitioners together. The journey is never individual; for one has to identify and join in with other heterodoxy working on similar problems or methods to oneself. This opens up a ready space for collaborative discussion between heterodox economists and economic geographers, in particular, as the latter often feel their work is undervalued and overlooked in policy discourse.

But this sense of being excluded from a mainstream narrative that, despite the good intentions of those who accept its methodological premises, can bind geographers and heterodox economists in what should be the defining purpose of financial geography. In the absence of an effective counter-narrative, the consequences of global financial power go unremarked, even unseen. Financial geography can fill this gap. Spatialized representations of power can capture some of the key financial dynamics of our time. Space is not unitary and does not follow one repeating pattern. Societies in 'real space' encompass tableaus of exploitation at many different spatial – and temporal – scales. These points are, in many cases, well known already to geographers; but they are absent in the narratives and models of economics that drive discussions of policy alternatives. Efforts to redress the imbalance of global spatial power must begin with efforts to rebalance the governing analyses of its drivers and consequences.

NOTES

1. This chapter builds on insights developed in Dymski and Kaltenbrunner (2021) and in Dymski (2021). Some of Section 1.3, and some sentences in Section 1.4, are drawn from the latter paper.
2. Dymski (2019) provides a comprehensive review of international financial crises since 1980.
3. A nation can be considered fully hegemonic in financial terms when its currency establishes the level at which all other currencies in the global system exchange, and when its rules for financial-market activity set the standard for all other nations' rules. A country is partially hegemonic when it defines rules of financial market activity that other nations imitate or follow.
4. ECB (2006) defines such holdings as indicating a 'precautionary motive'; but this term is ambiguous, insofar as it could refer to a nation's need for currency because of its own miscalculations (as when one of its export goods' prices collapsed) or to an external attack (or a sudden withdrawal of external lending).

REFERENCES

Bertaut, C.C., L.P. DeMarco, S.B. Kamin and R.W. Tryon (2011). ABS inflows to the United States and the global financial crisis. *Journal of International Economics 88*(2), 219–234.
Bowles, S. (2006). *Microeconomics: Behavior, institutions, and evolution.* Princeton: Princeton University Press.
Caballero, R.J., E. Farhi and P.-O. Gourinchas (2008). Financial crash, commodity prices, and global imbalances. *Brookings Papers on Economic Activity*, Fall, 1–55.
Caballero, R.J., E. Farhi and P.-O. Gourinchas (2017). The safe assets shortage conundrum. *Journal of Economic Perspectives 31*(3), Summer, 29–46.
Caballero, R.J. and A. Krishnamurthy (2009). Global imbalances and financial fragility, NBER Working Paper No. 14688. Cambridge, MA: National Bureau of Economic Research.
Carpintero, O. (2013). When heterodoxy becomes orthodoxy: Ecological economics in *The New Palgrave Dictionary of Economics. American Journal of Economics and Sociology 72*(5), 1287–1314.
Cohen, Benjamin J. (1998). *The Geography of Money.* Ithaca: Cornell University Press.
D'Arista, J. (2018). *All Fall Down: Debt, deregulation, and financial crisis.* Cheltenham, UK and Northampton, MA, USA: Edward Elgar Publishing.
Davidson, P. (1978). *Money and the Real World.* London: Palgrave Macmillan.
Diaz Alejandro, C.F. (1984). Latin American debt: I don't think we are in Kansas anymore. *Brookings Papers on Economic Activity 2*, 335–403.
Dominguez, K. (2008). Comment. *Brookings Papers on Economic Activity* (2), 56–60.
Dow, S. (1987). The treatment of money in regional economics. *Journal of Regional Science 27*, 13–24.
Dymski, G. (1999). *The Bank Merger Wave: Economic causes and social consequences of financial consolidation.* New York: M.E. Sharpe.
Dymski, G. (2014). Neoclassical sink and heterodox spiral: Political divides and lines of communication in economics. *Review of Keynesian Economics 2*(1), 1–19.
Dymski, G. (2019). Post-war international debt crises and their transformation. In J. Michie (ed.), *The Handbook of Globalisation* (pp. 103–118). Cheltenham, UK and Northampton, MA, USA: Edward Elgar Publishing.

Dymski, G. (2021). Financial geography, imbalances and crises: Excavating the spatial dimensions of asymmetric power. In J. Knox-Hayes and D. Wójcik (eds), *The Routledge Handbook of Financial Geography* (pp. 510–531). Cheltenham, UK and Northampton, MA, USA: Edward Elgar Publishing.

Dymski, G. and A. Kaltenbrunner (2021). Space in Post-Keynesian monetary economics: An exploration of the literature. In B. Bonizzi, A. Kaltenbrunner and R.A. Ramos (eds), *Emerging Economies and the Global Financial System: Post-Keynesian analysis*. London: Routledge.

Eaton, J., M. Gersovitz and J.E. Stiglitz (1986). The pure theory of country risk. *European Economic Review 30*(3), 481–513.

Eichengreen, B. (2010). *Exorbitant Privilege: The rise and fall of the dollar and the future of the international monetary system*. Oxford: Oxford University Press.

European Central Bank (ECB) (2006). The accumulation of foreign reserves. *Occasional Paper Series, 43*. Frankfurt: European Central Bank.

Hamouda, O. and G.C. Harcourt (1988). Post Keynesianism: From criticism to coherence? *Bulletin of Economic Research 40*(1), 1–33.

Kaltenbrunner, A. and P. Lysandrou (2017). The US dollar's continuing hegemony as an international currency: A double-matrix analysis. *Development and Change 48*(4), 663–691.

Krugman, P. (1998). What happened to Asia? *Working Paper*. MIT Department of Economics.

Lavoie, M. (2015). *Post-Keynesian Economics: New foundations*. Cheltenham, UK and Northampton, MA, USA: Edward Elgar Publishing.

Lee, F. (2009). *A History of Heterodox Economics*. New York: Routledge.

Lefebvre, H. (1991). *The Production of Space*. London: Blackwell.

Peet, R. (2013). *The Geography of Power: Making global economic policy*. London: Zed.

Shackle, G.L.S. (1974). *Keynesian Kaleidics*. Edinburgh: Edinburgh University Press.

Soja, E.W. (1996). *Thirdspace: Journeys to Los Angeles and other real-and-imagined places*. Oxford: Blackwell.

Townsend, R. (1983). Financial structure and economic activity. *American Economic Review 73*(5), 895–911.

Wójcik, D. (2012). The end of investment bank capitalism? An economic geography of financial jobs and power. *Economic Geography 88*(4), 345–368.

Wójcik, D. (2017). What on earth is financial geography? *Global Network on Financial Geography*. Retrieved from http://www.fingeo.net/.

2. The transmission mechanism of financial crisis to developing countries: why the 'global financial crisis' wasn't global

Jan Toporowski

The 2008 financial crisis in the US, followed by crises in Europe, gave rise to considerable discussion about its impact on developing countries. The situation itself was novel because previous international financial crises, the Third World Debt Crisis of the 1980s and the emerging market crises of the 1990s, spread from developing or emerging markets, so that developing countries were incriminated and affected from the start. In the 2008 crisis, the developing countries, for once, were not in the room when the crisis broke. Given the immense range of economic circumstances and exposure to international financial markets among the developing countries, the manner in which they were affected was inevitably going to be more complex and indirect than in previous crises.

Current economic theory gave little guidance as to how the crisis was going to impact upon the developing countries. This is partly because the starting point of mainstream economic theory is optimisation based on setting policy parameters that will secure internal and external equilibrium for a given country. It is more realistic to use a stock-flow analysis that places developing countries within a given structure of international economic and financial flows which are largely determined by expenditures in rich countries. Within this framework, international assets and liabilities are largely determined by the history of past market disequilibria, rather than saving or portfolio preferences.

In this framework of international assets and liabilities, and the resulting cash flows from assets to finance liabilities, a key role is played by the common monetary standard of international finance, namely the US dollar. As with any other currency, there are three aspects of this standard that have a bearing on the international financial system. There is, first of all, the rate of interest. Until the 2008 crisis, this was the only aspect of the US dollar that was considered by monetary policymakers. The second aspect is the exchange rate of the US dollar which, in an international credit system, is by no means the rate at which borrowing in US dollars can be converted into borrowing in any other currency. This is because of a third aspect of an international currency, namely its liquidity, or ease of conversion into other currencies. Recent Post-Keynesian theorising points to a 'hierarchy' of currencies according to their respective liquidity. However, this hierarchy is not stable. Behind it lies a complex structure of American business, which is further explained in the next section, and whose international monetary effects come through two institutional mechanisms. The first is the US current account balance, which shows the amount of 'free' (i.e., unborrowed) US dollars going into the international monetary system in any given period. The second is the willingness of US banks to create credit (advance loans) against the security of other currencies. The latter has developed into a complex international system of foreign exchange swaps that now underpin not only the international monetary system, but also the domestic money markets of many supposedly monetarily 'sovereign' countries, for example, the European Monetary Union. In Latin America, a particular part is played by swaps of US dollars against the Mexican peso.

A consequence of this is the dependence of the international financial system on the monetary cycle in the United States. As argued below, this cycle is steered by monetary policy that is orientated towards domestic US considerations and not the liquidity and financial requirements of developing countries and emerging markets.

2.1   US CORPORATE HEGEMONY

Monetary economists conventionally attribute the dominant role of the US dollar in international monetary arrangements to certain monetary properties which the dollar is supposed to possess. Accordingly, the US dollar is supposed to be a superior medium of exchange, store of value and unit of account in ways that are intrinsic to the dollar, rather than intrinsic to the systems of production and distribution organised by the corporations that dominate the international economy. In fact, the dollar is superior because it is the domestic currency of those corporations, the unit of account in which they conduct their bookkeeping, the currency in which they hold their most important liquid assets (bank deposits), and the currency in which they finance their balance sheets.

The financing of corporate balance sheets needs liquid capital markets. This liquidity is provided by the American government through government debt: risk-free bonds that make good security against which banks will advance credit. At the start of the twenty-first century, the international financial system is effectively an indirect US Government Bond Standard, in which the US dollar acts as a standard of value for all other currencies, and is held because it is directly convertible into US government bonds. The inter-bank money markets of the industrialised countries, through which banks are supposed to manage their liquidity, have effectively been replaced by foreign exchange swaps secured on good American assets (mostly US government bonds) (Shirakawa 2020).

Along-side the system of corporate finance is the system of international debt, which again is mostly in dollars and requires a permanent flow of dollar payments to countries that export to the United States. The nearest alternative international currency, the euro, cannot take over as a reserve currency because a more or less balanced trade account does not allow the Eurozone to supply the rest of the world with the amounts of 'free' (i.e., unencumbered by borrowing) euros necessary to finance trade. Moreover, the ruling policy doctrine in the European Union remains hostile to government bond issues on a scale and liquidity that would be necessary to back a global reserve currency. Much the same applied to the other aspirant to global currency status, the Chinese renminbi, whose use in international transactions is largely as an instrument to keep reserves within the Chinese central bank.

In this international financial system, the means of payment for international transactions are not US dollar banknotes, backed by the US government through the US Comptroller of the Currency who signs those banknotes, but commercial bank credits backed by bank loans to firms and governments. (Private individuals do not borrow in any significant amounts from international banks.) Thus international banking has its counterpart in an international debt system, mostly in US dollars, whose net debtors are largely smaller and poorer countries, because larger and richer countries can finance more of their needs with internal debt rather than borrowing from abroad.

Finally, crucial to the current structure of international trade and finance is the location in the US of the main markets for the commodity exports on which depends the foreign trade of most developing countries. Those commodities are therefore priced in US dollars.

2.2   THE VULNERABILITY OF THE DEVELOPING COUNTRIES

These features of international finance and trade combine to make developing countries extraordinarily vulnerable to the financial crisis that broke out in the US in 2008. Had that economy succumbed to debt deflation (reduced expenditure in an effort to repay debt), imports into the US would have been reduced, and with that the supply of 'free' dollars to the rest of the world would have diminished. In the event, the US trade deficit, which had peaked in 2006 at around $750bn, and dropped to $380bn in 2010, subsequently recovered to over £600bn in 2018 and 2019. The other industrial countries, which are the main suppliers to the US, still have large domestic markets and are therefore less exposed than developing countries to a fall in their exports. China in particular has concentrated on expanding its domestic market. Europe, which fell into crisis over government debts has overall experienced economic stagnation, rather than reduced demand for imports from the developing world (the deflation in southern Europe has been less significant for the European Union as a whole). For the developing countries a brief reduction in their exports to the US was exacerbated by an equally brief fall in commodity prices. This is what signalled to many observers at the time that the American financial crisis was going to be a global one, which would hit hard at the poorest countries on the globe (see te Velde 2008). However, commodity prices recovered quickly, and rose to new cyclical peaks around 2014. The terms of trade of many developing countries were further improved by an almost 30% appreciation of the US dollar in foreign exchange markets since the crisis started. This wholly unexpected appreciation has surprised many observers still thinking in terms of a foreign exchange market determined by rational portfolio calculations of varying degrees of risk-aversion. But the appreciation was entirely rational in the context of an indirect US Government Bond Standard.

From the point of view of trade, the principal beneficiaries of this improvement in the terms of trade of developing countries were countries in Africa, reliant upon commodity exports while importing mostly from Europe. However, the trade benefits have been off-set by the effects of the dollar appreciation on the foreign debts of developing countries that are the principal net debtors in the international financial system. Nearly two thirds of all international debt is denominated in US dollars and its value has therefore risen along with the appreciation of the dollar. The US is of course the largest net international debtor in the world. But, because the international financial system uses an indirect US Government Bond Standard, the US government can borrow abroad in dollars, servicing that borrowing in the same way that it finances its domestic debt.

The situation of countries in Latin America is, however, different. This is overwhelmingly a dollar sphere of influence, whose countries pay for their imports largely in dollars, because they import from the United States, or they import from neighbouring countries that invoice their exports in dollars. Both Mexico and Brazil buy around half of their imports from the

United States. However, Latin America has benefitted least from the trade deficits of the United States, which have directed this 'free' flow of net trade payments to East Asia, rather than to the countries south of the Rio Grande.

Africa was well-placed to ride out the crisis of 2008: Debt forgiveness, under the Highly Indebted Poor Countries Initiative and the Multilateral Debt Relief Initiative, in the later 1990s and the early years of this century, reduced the foreign borrowing of most African countries below 50% of GDP. As central banks in the rich countries reduced interest rates to zero, and even below, international bond markets recovered their 'appetite for risk' allowing governments in developing countries to borrow at rates of interest below 10% (Toporowski 2018). However, most countries in Latin America were unable to benefit from debt forgiveness under these initiatives because their per capita income disqualified them. Argentina's almost permanent foreign debt crisis has effectively shut down the transmission mechanism of crisis to that country. However, other countries, like Mexico, Brazil and Chile, remain exposed to the extent of their borrowing in US dollars.

2.3   THE COMMODITY PRICE SUPER-CYCLE

The dependence on commodity exports exposes governments in developing countries to what is sometimes called the *commodity price super-cycle*, that is the movement of prices of raw materials in the international markets in which those materials are traded. Crude oil prices may be taken as a proxy for such prices (commodity prices, on the whole, tend to move together in similar directions).

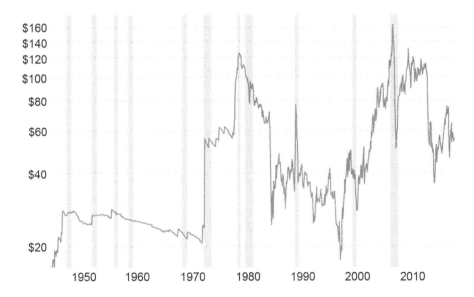

Source: Macrotrends.

Figure 2.1   Crude oil prices since 1945

The price of crude oil since 1945 is shown in Figure 2.1 and it reveals why traders refer to variations in that price as a 'super-cycle'. There is obviously a first cycle, from 1945 through to the oil price 'shock' of 1973, with a peak at the time when the Korean War placed great demand in the markets for raw materials and energy. A second cycle was initiated by the 1973 oil price shock, and ended at the end of the 1980s, or the 1990s. A final boom and fall in prices started in the late 1990s, and broke after 2014. It is since 2014 that alarms have been raised, with increasing urgency, over the security of the foreign borrowing of governments in the poorer developing countries that are most dependent on commodity exports.

Commodity prices are important for developing countries not only because of their effect on those countries' terms of trade and, hence, the trade balances that determine governments' ability to accumulate foreign currency reserves, as a hedge against international economic instability, and to service foreign debt. Commodity prices are also a key leading indicator of portfolio and foreign direct investment (FDI) into developing countries. Most foreign direct investment in the world takes place between the industrialised and newly industrialised countries, that is in the northern hemisphere between Europe, North America and East Asia. However, between a third and a half of global foreign direct investment goes to developing countries. As Figure 2.2 shows, the 2008 financial crisis had a significant, but only temporary, effect on foreign direct investment. By 2010, FDI to developing countries exceeded pre-crisis levels, and continued to rise slowly, before falling away from 2014. Portfolio investment, arguably more directly affected by the failure in American capital markets in 2008 than FDI, shows no falling away in the wake of that crisis. But the fall in commodity prices in 2014 was anticipated by portfolio disinvestment and was followed by volatile flows to the developing countries.

It should, however, be borne in mind that, unlike commodity exports, only part of foreign direct investment actually provides convertible currency revenue to governments in developing countries with debts in such currencies. Foreign direct investment consists of two elements: greenfield investment, in which infrastructure, premises and equipment are installed for future productive purposes, for example, port facilities and mining or oil extraction equipment; and mergers and acquisitions, in which existing productive or revenue-generating capacity is purchased by a foreign owner. Only the latter is actually paid for in foreign currency to a company's owner resident in a developing country. A common example, that featured prominently in the notorious structural adjustment programmes of the International Monetary Fund in the 1980s and 1990s, is a government 'privatising' a state-owned business. However, such sales have usually followed periods of underinvestment in the capacity of the privatised business. New owners typically reduce the purchase price of a state undertaking by the value of the required repair and re-equipment. Any actual repair and re-equipment is bought in from abroad. Similarly, in the case of greenfield investment, much of the equipment is bought in from already industrialised countries. FDI therefore provides relatively little foreign currency for developing countries (see endnote 3).

The problematic nature of foreign direct investment as a source of foreign exchange is well illustrated in the case of Angola, in Africa, where the government has received payment for oil exports to China in the form of foreign direct investment. Such construction projects may have an important use-value in the domestic economy. But the Angolan government cannot service its foreign currency borrowing with projects of foreign direct investment.

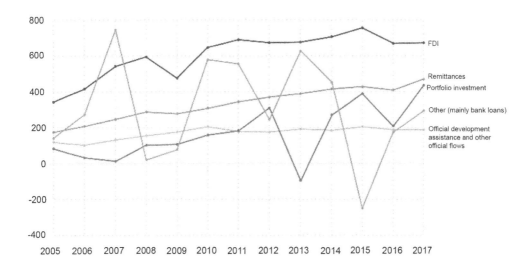

Source: UNCTAD World Investment Report 2018.

Figure 2.2   Sources of external finance, developing economies (2005–2017) (billions of US$)

2.4   THE INTERNATIONAL MONETARY CYCLE

The reason for using the term 'super-cycle' for fluctuations in commodity prices is that these price cycles are significantly longer than the standard business cycle in the advanced industrialised countries, whose currencies, in particular the US dollar, are borrowed when developing country governments resort to foreign borrowing. The business cycles of those advanced industrialised countries effectively determine interest rates in those countries. So, in the case of the United States, its rate of interest, and effectively the base rate over which other governments abroad borrow in US dollars, is set in accordance with the business cycle in the United States.

As is apparent from Figure 2.3, the monetary cycle in the United States is much shorter than the commodity super-cycle. The monetary cycle, ranging from 5 to 10 years, reached a peak around 1980, when the then Chairman of the Federal Reserve, Paul Volcker attempted to rein in price inflation in the United States using a restrictive monetary policy that caused interest rates to rise substantially, and thereby precipitated the international debt crisis of 1982. As that crisis indicates, the major debt crises of developing countries are formed by the interaction of the commodity price super-cycle and the monetary cycle in the United States.

Comparing the two cycles, it should be noted that the commodity price super-cycle is longer than the US monetary cycle because international prices of raw materials are essentially 'demand-determined' prices, and the demand for those raw materials comes predominantly from the industrialised countries. The demand from those countries is unstable and follows the construction and fixed capital investment cycle in each of those countries. Taken together, this

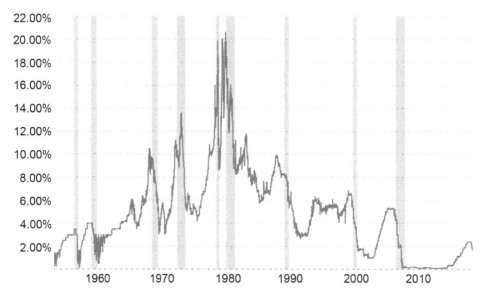

Source: Macrotrends.

Figure 2.3   The US federal funds rate

demand is rather more stable than it is in each country individually (in the aggregate different cycles in various countries tend to 'average out'). Super-imposed on these industrial country cycles has been the long industrialisation of China, which tends to give an upward trend to commodity prices.

A comparison of Figure 2.3 with Figure 2.2 also shows that there is little connection between foreign direct investment and the rate of interest in the United States, as might be indicated by the Wicksellian orthodoxy that is currently guiding monetary policy in most countries. High interest rates before the 2008 crisis were associated with rising, rather than falling FDI, while the reduction of interest rates to near zero to stem the crisis made little impact on FDI.

2.5   THE DYSFUNCTION IN INTERNATIONAL DEBT MARKETS

The dysfunction in the international debt markets arises because the commodity price super-cycle and international monetary cycle, driven by monetary policy in the United States, do not coincide in a way that allows for effective cash flow management of dollar borrowing outside the United States. By contrast, US monetary policy periodically operates in a *counter-cyclical* way, in relation to commodity prices because of the impact of developing country debt on those prices. When foreign debt exceeds a certain threshold, or when high interest rates raise the cost of servicing that debt, commodity exporters will sell off stocks of commodities to generate means of payment, and price cartels, such as OPEC break down. This accelerates the fall in commodity prices. The coincidence of falling commodity prices and rising interest rates was a notable feature of the 1982 crisis referred to above. In such periods the perceptions of participants in international debt markets make foreign debt management even more problematical, as governments find that they cannot refinance their external borrowing at all, or only at an exorbitant cost.

The distortion in market perceptions has been well illustrated since the crisis of 2008, when the monetary authorities in the United States and Europe have loosened monetary policy to an unprecedented degree, to deal with the economic crisis that affected those economies. Immediately after the crisis, the countries of the developing world were in the middle of a commodity boom that by and large meant that the developing countries were not affected by the crisis. However, commodity prices turned down in 2014, as new commodity supplies came on stream (in the energy market this was combined with the new technologies for extracting oil and shale gas) and the growth of aggregate demand in the world's largest economies started to slow down. However, this was just as monetary authorities in the United States and Europe began to signal their desire to 'normalise' monetary policy by raising interest rates and ceasing the quantitative easing that has made the international money markets so liquid. The Eurobond markets that had readily refinanced African government's debt, have since become reluctant to issue on behalf of those governments.

Underlying these difficulties has been a long-standing problem of illiquidity in the world's capital markets that goes back to the 1990s, when the global shift towards funded pension schemes reached maturity. The first sign of this was the bursting of the dot.com bubble in 2000. The 'Greenspan response' to this was a period of low interest rates that exaggerated the benefits of lending to emerging markets. Although short-term rates in the US were rising again by 2005, longer-term rates of interest for US government bonds stayed at their lowest levels since the 1960s (despite record US government borrowing). The 2008 crisis was followed by the 'Paulson–Bernanke response' of quantitative easing, effectively flooding the international money markets with liquidity (Toporowski 2020).

This liquidity spread further into the international monetary system by a system of foreign currency swaps, mostly with the financially advanced countries, but including also the central banks of Japan, South Korea, Singapore, Brazil and Mexico.[1] Ostensibly designed to relieve liquidity pressure among commercial banks funding themselves through foreign exchange swaps, the currency arrangements have reinforced these funding mechanisms and hence also a general shortage of the highly rated long-term dollar bonds that serve as security for foreign exchange swaps. In this way the funding mechanisms help to maintain low yields for US government bonds.

2.6   CHANNELS OF CRISIS TRANSMISSION

This account of the impact of the 2008 crisis on developing suggests three channels through which financial crisis has been channelled to developing countries and emerging markets. These are a *financial* channel through illiquidity in balance sheets, causing debt crises; a *monetary* channel, when exchange rates change the value of external liabilities; and an *export* channel, if the value of exports falls below the value required to maintain production and service external debt.

The financial channel is perhaps the most complex and obscure of these channels because it involves not only the geographical and currency distribution of debt, but also because it requires consideration of the time profile of payments required by the set of debt commitments at any one time. Here, an important distinction needs to be made between gross and net debt, and the currency of the debt. The government and residents of the United States together owe more to residents of other countries than is owed by any other nation on the planet. However, the residents of the United States also have more foreign assets than the residents of any other country. This allows corporations in the United States that own most of these foreign assets to engage in balance sheet transactions to ensure that payments due on liabilities are made, regardless of developments in the income and expenditure flows from current production and exchange of goods and services. The currency of the debt is important. Virtually all American foreign liabilities are in US dollars. This means that the US government and corporations can 'hedge' their foreign liabilities with domestic as well as foreign assets (the latter are mostly in foreign currencies).[2]

In their turn, those US liabilities held by foreign residents constitute the reserves of the international monetary system. Those reserves are reinforced by the domestically held highly rated assets that are used as collateral in the various foreign exchange swap agreements that increasingly fund the domestic money markets of the rich countries and emerging markets.

In the international financial system, the developing countries stand out for having large deficits between the foreign liabilities of their governments and residents, and their foreign assets. The former is made up of the borrowing in foreign currencies of those countries' respective private sectors and governments. The latter is largely made up of those governments' foreign currency reserves. A recent development in the financial channel of crisis transmission to the developing countries, has been the rapid rise of foreign indebtedness in the private sectors of developing countries (Bonizzi and Toporowski 2018), encouraged by an irrepressible, but nonetheless fallacious, conviction among development economists that low saving rates in developing countries somehow hold back their development, and therefore such countries need loans from rich countries. This conviction has been embraced with enthusiasm by international bankers keen to find borrowers who will pay higher rates of interest than may be charged in rich and overbanked countries.[3]

A second channel is the *monetary channel*, through the markets in which the developing countries' currencies are exchanged for the currencies in which they borrow abroad. Here again many economists have tended to exaggerate the benefits that may be obtained for exports from devaluing the currency of the country producing the exports. In the case of commodity exports, as noted above, these have their prices determined in international markets in accordance with global levels of demand. In this situation, currency devaluation results in the producer receiving more of the domestic currency for a given dollar value of exports. In theory, this should give the producer a greater incentive to produce more. But this incentive is weakened by the conditions under which most developing country exports are produced. Raw material exports are subject to decreasing returns, while manufactured goods have their export incentive off-set by the rising cost of imports.

But this argument over exports overlooks a much more fundamental problem for countries with foreign currency debts. For them, monetary policy does not provide any solutions. Depreciation of the developing country's local currency against the dollar, to raise the domestic value of exports, increases the domestic cost of external debt financing. Pegging to the dollar holds external financing costs constant, but leaves the country exposed to reduced US dollar commodity export prices. Lowering the cost of foreign currency in local currency (i.e., appreciation) reduces export earnings, and encourages imports.

Third, there is the *export channel*, which makes developing countries dependent on the level of demand in developed markets. As noted above, this is especially prominent in the case of commodity exports, whose prices are largely determined by levels of demand in the industrialised countries. It is true that demand in those countries has stagnated since the 2008 crisis. But this did not have much impact on commodity prices until 2014, and terms of trade actually benefitted after that crisis from the stronger dollar, in relation to the currencies of non-American industrialised countries (Europe, East Asia) from which developing countries import. Although the COVID crisis is global as a health emergency, it is through the export channel that it will affect the developing countries.

Prior to the 2008 crisis, the developing countries had done well out of the combination of a weak dollar and high commodity prices. Since then weaker commodity prices have been, to some degree, off-set by the appreciation of the US dollar. But that appreciation has also driven up the value (relative to the value of exports) of those countries' foreign debts, just as exports to the US are falling. This is the point at which the 2008 crisis put financial pressure on poorer countries.

2.7 INSTITUTIONS AND POLICY

Since the outbreak of the international debt crisis in 1982, financial stability, or instability, has been an essential feature of monetary and financial policy discussions. The crisis of 1982 exposed developing countries and emerging markets as weak links in the international monetary and financial system. Thereafter, development economists and Keynesian sympathisers focused on capital account controls as the essential protection for developing countries against unstable (usually short-term or speculative) international capital flows (see Akyüz 1993, 2013, Diaz-Alejandro 1985, Kregel 2015, Singh 1997). This chapter suggests that there is more to the crisis transmission mechanism than simply unstable capital flows. Behind them lie the commodity price super-cycle and the international monetary cycle that is guided by the monetary policy of the US Federal Reserve. These factors explain the vulnerabilities of developing countries in the international financial system as well as why the 'global financial crisis' of 2008 was not global.

Even before the COVID crisis, many governments in developing countries faced the threats to the sustainability of their debt and fiscal positions from low or falling commodity prices, bringing with them slower economic growth, reduced foreign direct investment, lower revenue for governments, demands for higher government expenditure and therefore widening fiscal deficits. However, the pandemic, and policy reactions to it in the rich countries have, temporarily at least, removed fears of a contraction in the liquidity of international financial markets as central banks in Europe and North America move to 'normalise' their monetary policy by ceasing, or reversing, their quantitative easing policies and raising interest rates. This, together with the movement for debt relief grants may make it easier to roll over existing foreign borrowing. Temporarily too, the urgency of the medical pandemic has alleviated some of the populist pressures in Europe and North America to reduce official aid to developing countries.

However, in the longer term, to prevent the deterioration of their fiscal and debt position, governments of developing countries need to rebalance their institutions and policy framework in order to avoid the economically, politically and socially destabilising effects of external crises. Capital controls are inadequate to prevent such crises, and would not block the monetary or export channels of transmission. An adequate policy menu must start with fiscal policy that as far as possible seeks to support cash flows in the economy by maintaining existing (non-financial) expenditure in those economies, in order to prevent a deflationary reinforcement of the reduction in FDI that is already taking place. Where possible, governments should expand public investment, in particular in infrastructure and housing where welfare and economic benefits are large, but import costs are small. Failure to do this will reduce economic growth. Any fiscal imbalances need to be addressed by increasing taxation.

In developing countries, a common consequence of any rise in employment is an increase in the prices of food and basic necessities, that then concentrates the accumulation of money in the hands of local farmers and property-owners and, in the case of the modern sector of the economy, in the accounts of multinational companies. Primary fiscal deficits and trade surpluses then add to the accumulations in these monetary 'sumps'. They are a cause of financial instability in large part because most developing countries lack the financial markets to tie up this liquidity in financial instruments in the domestic currency. The accumulations then drain out of the economy into foreign, convertible currencies, or do so abruptly when alarms are raised about the prospect of inflation (devaluing the local currency). In the case of foreign-owned funds, this alarm typically arises when companies or funds perceive, or expect, macroeconomic imbalances: a combination of fiscal deficits and trade deficits. However, it should be emphasised that it is not these macroeconomic imbalances themselves that directly cause such capital flight. The capital flight cannot take place without monetary accumulations. In extreme cases, such capital flight can give rise to 'dollarisation', as holders of liquid assets convert those assets into foreign currency, and then proceed to use that foreign currency in their transactions between each other. Such capital flight undermines the exchange making foreign borrowing more expensive. It is in part through *domestic* accumulations of liquidity that the export channel contributes to financial instability regardless of capital controls. It is worth noting that such financial instability arises from *domestic* accumulations of liquidity, to which the export channel may contribute. Such financial instability may therefore arise regardless of capital controls.

An important aspect of the policy framework required to meet the challenge of international financial instability due to the respective cyclical movements in commodity prices and international illiquidity, is debt management. Wherever possible, governments should be financing their deficits in domestic currency markets through the issue of financial obligations at the longest possible maturity. Domestic currency debt has the advantage that it is 'hedged' by a government's assets and income in that same currency: government assets in foreign currencies consist overwhelmingly of their foreign currency reserves. While such reserves may be large enough to manage current commitments on total (private and public) foreign debt, they may not be large enough in the event of capital flight, or a need to roll over short-term debt. Second, a government can manipulate the terms of domestic currency borrowing, where it sets interest rates, or through operations along the yield curve, if markets are sufficiently developed.

Third, the issue of domestic obligations helps to keep the monetary accumulations in an economy tied up in domestic financial markets, and therefore less prone to capital flight. When the central bank issues domestic currency reserves against the value of the new foreign currency reserves, it will often sell domestic currency bonds to 'sterilise' the increase in the money supply. An unfortunate aspect of the move towards inflation-targeting in the policy frameworks of central bank in developing countries is that it treats capital flows as manageable by means of interest rate differentials. Yet the implied conditions of interest rate parity, or even covered interest rate parity have very little empirical support. Moreover, it has become very apparent since the 2008 crisis that financial stability requires more active use of open market operations by central banks, to manage the liquidity of debt markets.

By contrast with domestic debt, foreign currency debt easily becomes a burden on a country's earnings from exports, in conditions of the commodity price super-cycle, in particular as those earnings are threatened by low commodity prices. It should be emphasised that it is not only government foreign currency debt that poses this threat, but also private sector foreign currency debt. Unless the private sector has assets abroad, its foreign currency debt payments are a claim on the foreign currency reserves of a government that cannot be refused without causing a currency devaluation that can dramatically increase the domestic resource costs of government foreign currency debt. Moreover, where governments are weak or have limited domestic political legitimacy, taxation to service foreign borrowing, or the conditions under which external loans are given, become a target of political opposition. Taxation and political reform come to be regarded as foreign impositions, weakening the political authority necessary for effective governance.

The ultimate challenge at this stage of the international financial and commodity cycles that is weakening the financial systems of developing countries, and their ability to withstand shocks in the international financial system is the absence of an institutional mechanism that could convert foreign currency debt into domestic debt. The matter is made more urgent in view of the appreciation of the US dollar, by approximately 20% since 2014, when commodity prices started to fall. On the one hand this appreciation has off-set the decline in export commodity prices, which are priced in dollars. On the other hand, however, since most developing country foreign debt is denominated in US dollars, the increase in the foreign exchange value of that currency has also increased the domestic resource cost of that debt.

In the financially advanced countries this conversion of foreign currency debt into domestic currency debt is readily effected and has even been institutionalised in foreign exchange swaps markets. The Bretton Woods institutions, the IMF and the World Bank, have under fairly strict conditionality, participated in arrangements for refinancing government foreign debt in emerging markets and developing countries, and finally in the writing off of foreign debt since the Highly Indebted Poor Countries Initiative in 1996. But this refinancing has remained in foreign currencies, rather than converting the debt into domestic currency debt. The difference is important because, as indicated above, domestic currency debt is more manageable by governments, and its issue contributes to financial development in a way that foreign currency debt does not. Among larger emerging markets (for example in Mexico between 1989 and 1994) such a conversion of government debt into domestic currency debt was made possible by a favourable conjuncture in the international financial markets and portfolio capital inflows. However, many developing countries do not have capital markets on such a scale as to absorb such a manoeuvre. In any case, such a conversion through the capital markets transfers government foreign debt to the private sector, making that sector even more vulnerable to the depreciation that inevitably follows the reduction in investment that accompanies this kind of expansion in indebtedness. This is an important reason why the arrangements for such conversion need to be done in a multilateral official framework. But with the decline in support for international initiatives by the key issuer of international financial reserves, the government of the United States, there is little prospect that such a facility will emerge, let alone that it will be ready for the next developing country debt crisis.

In the absence of such a mechanism, an effective and perhaps simpler substitute would be Kalecki's proposal for the financing of developing country trade deficits with long-term debt (Kalecki 1946), and ensuring that such debt facilities remained available to developing countries through the extended downturns in the commodity price super-cycle. This should be accompanied by a regime of stable exchange rates, which would facilitate the conversion of foreign currency debt into domestic debt.

A further supportive and stabilising mechanism could be the extension of the US Fed's currency swap arrangements to developing countries beyond the small number of emerging markets that currently have these arrangements. It may legitimately be objected that such arrangements reinforce the hegemony of the United States and its corporations in the international financial system, and make that system vulnerable to political direction from the President of the United States (notable recent examples have been the sanctions against Iran and China). A more positive contribution may be made by European institutions (for example, the European Investment Bank, or even the European Central Bank), whose multilateralism is less vulnerable to unilateral political direction.

2.8   CONCLUSIONS

The mechanism that transmits crisis to developing countries is a complex one that includes financial, monetary and export channels. These channels are associated with a commodity price super-cycle that determines not only the inflows of revenues from exports but also flows of foreign direct investment into developing countries. In the wake of the 2008 crisis these channels were largely dormant with the quantitative easing undertaken by the key central banks in the industrialised countries, and the continuation of high commodity prices that also drew investment into those commodity export activities. The downturn in those prices after 2014 was eased by continued international monetary expansion. However, this may have just postponed the outbreak of financial crisis in the developing world. More permanent stabilisation may be obtained from reducing fluctuations in commodity prices and resuming economic growth in Europe and North America, to maintain flows through the export channel, encouraging greater reliance on domestic financial resources, and stabilising exchange rates. This was where many critics from developing countries, and their sympathisers, started at Bretton Woods.

NOTES

1. The swap arrangements with the Banco de Mexico go back to 1994, and were established, along with similar arrangements with the Bank of Canada, under the North Atlantic Framework Agreement.
2. The balance sheet of the foreign assets and liabilities of the residents of a given country is known as the International Investment Position of that country. The balance between assets and liabilities is known as the Net International Investment Position. For the United States, this data is published by the Bureau of Economic Analysis. However, it should be pointed out that this data is distorted to an unknown extent by the 'off-shoring' domestic assets and liabilities in tax havens, so that foreign assets are exaggerated by the assets of American residents kept in tax havens, which assets turn out to be claims on US corporations.
3. More correct is the view of Rosa Luxemburg, that the rich countries need to indebt poor countries in order to monetise the surpluses produced in the rich countries. See Luxemburg 1951, Chapter xxx.

REFERENCES

Akyűz, Y. (1993). Financial Liberalisation: The Key Issues. *UNCTAD Discussion Paper 56.*

Akyűz, Y. (2013). *The Financial Crisis and the Global South: A Development Perspective.* London: Pluto Press.

Bonizzi, B. and Toporowski, J. (2018). Sovereign Debt Sustainability. In *'Sub-Saharan Africa' in United Nations Conference on Trade and Development Debt Vulnerabilities in Developing Countries: A New Debt Trap? Volume I: Regional and Thematic Analyses.* New York and Geneva: United Nations, pp. 15–51.

Diaz-Alejandro C. (1985). Good-Bye Financial Repression, Hello Financial Crash. *Journal of Development Economics*, 19, 1–24.

Kalecki, M. (1946). Multilateralism and Full Employment. *Canadian Journal of Economics and Political Science*, 12(3), 322–327.

Kregel, J. (2015). Emerging Market Economies and the Reform of the International Financial Architecture. *Levy Economics Institute of Bard College*, Public Policy Brief No. 139, New York.

Luxemburg, R. (1951). *The Accumulation of Capital.* London: Routledge and Kegan Paul.

Shirakawa, M. (2020). The Foreign Currency Swap Market: A Perspective from Policy-Makers. In A. Stenfors and J. Toporowski (eds.), *Unconventional Monetary Policy and Financial Stability: The Case of Japan.* Abingdon, UK: Routledge, pp. 28–37.

Singh, A. (1997). Financial Liberalisation, Stock Markets and Economic Development. *Economic Journal*, 107(May), 771–782.

te Velde, W. (2008). The Effects of the Global Financial Crisis on the Developing Countries and Emerging Markets – Policy Responses to the Crisis. *Comment* Overseas Development Institute, December.

Toporowski, J. (2018). Fiscal Policy and Debt Sustainability in Africa. Report Addis Ababa: United Nations Economic Commission for Africa, October.

Toporowski, J. (2020). Financialisation and the Periodisation of Capitalism: Appearances and Processes. *Review of Evolutionary Political Economy*, 1(2), 149–160.

3. Foreign direct investment, inequality, and macroeconomic stability on the eve of the COVID-19 crisis

Hanna Szymborska

The Global Financial Crisis (GFC) in 2007–2008 has fundamentally changed the landscape of international financial flows. It resulted in an estimated 15% decline in global foreign direct investment (FDI) flows (UNCTAD 2009), driven primarily by a massive drop in flows into and out of developed economies. These trends can be understood from the perspective of both increased macroeconomic uncertainty in the Global North during the GFC as well as monetary policy implemented by the Federal Reserve and the European Central Bank to mitigate the crisis. Nevertheless, the share of direct investment inflows in GDP continued to rise relative to the GDP share of portfolio investment between 2003 and 2016, and the size of FDI inflows has outweighed portfolio flows in the majority of developing countries (Calderon et al. 2019; IMF 2020).

Loose monetary policy measures and low interest rate environment in developed countries after the GFC have led to an increase in capital flows to the developing world. But these capital flows proved to be remarkably volatile in response to changing attitudes towards monetary policy and trade policy in the Global North, and to perceptions of political and economic instability in the host countries in the Global South (Caceres et al. 2017; UNCTAD 2019). Rollback of the post-GFC quantitative easing program by the Federal Reserve in 2014 induced a decline in capital inflows to developing countries. A further pressure has been exerted by the revival of protectionism in trade policy among key players in the global economy since the mid-2010s, most notably in the USA (ibid.).

The COVID-19 crisis has hit developing economies against the backdrop of weak aggregate demand, sluggish recovery from the GFC, and mounting levels of external debt, particularly in Latin America and sub-Saharan Africa. Numerous countries in the Global South face the threat of a particularly acute economic downturn due to lasting interruptions in global supply chains in result of the pandemic, low commodity prices, and restricted domestic policy space owing to strict conditionality of accessing international financial assistance. Early evidence suggests that the pandemic has led to a massive halt in global FDI flows, particularly in terms of FDI inflows to developing countries (UNCTAD 2020a).

While the patterns of global FDI flows have faced substantial changes since the GFC, less is known about their impact on income distribution in the parent and the host countries. Economic policies rooted in the mainstream paradigm assert that FDI contributes to reducing inequality through improvements in productivity and, thereby, wages. However, while existing research on the distributional effects of FDI since the GFC is scarce, prior evidence suggests that the characteristics of FDI and its emphasis on expanding exports in host countries are more often than not associated with rising inequality. The GFC led to a brief decline in income inequality within countries, but the top income shares in many countries have swiftly returned to their rising trend since the 1980s, against a steady expansion of the FDI stock relative to GDP.

This chapter examines the impact of the recent trends in FDI on different measures of income inequality. Insufficient data availability and heterogeneity of institutional conditions across countries pose a challenge to quantitative analyses of the distributional effects of FDI since the 2008 GFC. In this context, the chapter reviews the existing empirical literature on the topic and reports descriptive statistics on FDI, inequality, and macroeconomic stability for a panel of developed and developing countries, with particular emphasis on regional disparities. The original contribution of this work is to conduct a comprehensive overview of the distributional impact of FDI after the GFC against the backdrop of institutional changes in the global economy, taking into account multiple dimensions of income inequality.

The chapter is structured as follows. Section 3.1 revisits the link between FDI and the export-led growth model, examining its implications for inequality and macroeconomic stability after the GFC and in the context of the COVID-19 crisis. Sections 3.2 and 3.3 analyse the impact of FDI on global inequality and inequality within countries respectively. Section 3.4 concludes.

3.1   PATTERNS OF FDI FLOWS AND THE EXPORT-LED GROWTH MODEL

The measure of FDI that is most commonly used in empirical studies is in terms of stocks rather than flows, often relative to the value of GDP. Flows of FDI refer to the value of FDI-related transactions conducted in a given year, while stocks record the value of FDI accumulated over the reference period. In 2019, the value of the GDP share of inward FDI across the regions of the world was the highest in Europe at 61.4% and Northern America at 45.1%, followed by Latin America and the Caribbean at 41.9% and sub-Saharan Africa at 36.2% (UNCTAD 2020b). The ratio was the lowest in Eastern and South-eastern Asia at 27.5% and Southern Asia at 12.8%. That year, the value of the GDP share of outward FDI was the highest in Europe at 68.5%, Northern America at 40.3%, and Eastern and South-eastern Asia at 31.9%, and it was the lowest in sub-Saharan Africa at 15.5%, Latin America and the Caribbean at 14.8%, and Southern Asia at 4.3% (ibid.).

The GFC led to a moderate fall in the share of inward and outward FDI stock in GDP around the world between 2007 and 2008. Since then, the GDP shares of both inward and outward FDI stocks have been rising steadily in all regions of the world. Between 2008 and 2019, the increase in the GDP share of inward FDI stock was the largest in North America, Latin America and the Caribbean, and Europe, growing at a compound annual rate of 8.2%, 6%, and 5.9% respectively (author's calculations based on UNCTAD 2020b). In the same period, the GDP share of outward FDI stock expanded at a particularly rapid rate in sub-Saharan Africa and Latin America and the Caribbean, increasing at a compound annual rate of 8.4% in the former region (with a peak of 22.5% in 2017) and 6.9% in the latter region (ibid.).

It is often argued that measuring FDI as stocks over GDP presents a more long-term perspective into the structural features of FDI activity in host and parent countries (Wacker 2013). Nevertheless, calculation of FDI stocks is not straightforward as it requires an assumption of how the value of the accumulated flows changes over the reference period (ibid.). In this context, analysis of FDI flows allows to capture how dynamics of the global economy as well as exchange rate movements, and unexpected events influence the patterns of FDI activity in the short term. In contrast to the GDP share of FDI stocks, the ratio of FDI inflows to GDP fell on average[1] across the regions of the world between 2008 and 2018, at an annual compound rate over 7% in Europe, approximately 5% in sub-Saharan Africa and Northern America, 3% in Asia, and 1.3% in Latin America and the Caribbean (author's calculations based on UNCTAD 2020b).

Figure 3.1 shows the patterns of regional distribution of FDI flows around the world since 2006. As seen in panel A of Figure 3.1, the share of FDI inflows to Northern America and Europe plummeted from nearly 70% in 2006 to less than 40% in 2018, except for a short revival in 2015 and 2016, which corresponds to the period of rising interest rates in the USA. This has been paralleled by an increase in the developing countries' share of global FDI inflows between 2007 and 2014, driven primarily by inflows into Asia. Additionally, Latin America has recently recorded the highest share of net FDI inflows in GDP among developing and emerging economies at over 3% in 2019, compared to around 2% or less in sub-Saharan Africa and East Asia (World Bank 2020). Panel B of Figure 3.1 shows that developing countries, primarily in Asia, also accounted for an increasing share of global FDI outflows in this period. Asia's share of global FDI outflows rose from just under 20% in 2006 to over 50% in 2018.

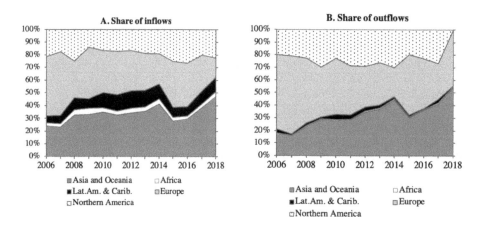

Source: Author's calculation based on UNCTAD (2020b).

Figure 3.1   *Trends in regional distribution of FDI flows*

FDI is primarily oriented towards fostering domestic production capacity through promoting exports, industrial upgrading, and knowledge transfers (Narula and Driffield 2012). A key rationale for openness to FDI flows is to boost economic growth by taking advantage of foreign demand and technology. Attracting FDI to increase exports, and integration into the global economy more broadly, have been seen as vital steps towards achieving sustainable development. The export-led growth model has been actively promoted by the United Nations 2030 Agenda for Sustainable Development. For instance, the Sustainable Development Goal (SDG) 17.11 aims to "significantly increase the exports of developing countries … with a view to doubling the least developed countries' share of global exports …" (United Nations 2015). The expansion of exports in developing countries is envisioned in an environment of free trade, especially in global agricultural markets (see SDG 2.b, ibid.).

Together with adoption of the export-led growth model in a developing country context, FDI is argued to generate knowledge spillovers and attract financial resources in excess of what is domestically available. SDG 10.b explicitly encourages "official development assistance and financial flows, including foreign direct investment, to … in particular least developed countries, African countries, small island developing States and landlocked developing countries" (ibid.). Investment in developing economies as part of FDI is typically conducted by large private multinational corporations (MNCs). MNCs are usually headquartered in developed countries, although FDI flows between developing countries (the so-called South–South FDI) have been on the rise since the GFC (see Amighini and Sanfilippo 2014).

Despite such strong support for openness to capital markets, international trade, and FDI advocated by the global community, the causality between FDI and GDP growth is ambiguous and likely runs both ways (see Sumner 2008 for an overview). Inward FDI can increase economic growth by raising export revenues and improving domestic productivity levels. But given that it is middle- and high-income countries rather than low-income or least-developed economies that account for the majority of global FDI activity, some argue that high GDP growth also attracts FDI. Moreover, the quality of domestic economic institutions has been argued to play a critical role in a country's ability to extract the benefits of FDI (Buchanan et al. 2012).

Furthermore, it has been pointed out that FDI may have less impact on the domestic productive capacity than is typically asserted. This is because a large portion of profits from FDI is repatriated to parent countries (where MNCs are headquartered), while loosening of regulatory measures that is often undertaken to attract inward FDI undermines the country's ability to realise the benefits of FDI inflows (Sumner 2005). In addition, FDI activity may lead to crowding out of domestic private investment if it is concentrated in industries with few linkages (see Mayer-Foulkes and Nunnenkamp 2009), and it can also exacerbate the financing gap in developing countries if FDI requires imports of expensive machinery and equipment, and when high royalties and management fees are charged by the MNCs to the host country.

According to available evidence, the increase in the GDP share of FDI stocks in the Global South since the GFC has been associated with an expansion in the absolute export volume, particularly in South Asia, East Asia and the Pacific, and Latin America and the Caribbean, expanding at a compound annual growth rate of 5.6%, 3.8%, and 2.4% respectively between 2008 and 2018 (author's calculations based on UNCTAD 2020b). However, the size of exports relative to GDP has declined somewhat, falling between 2008 and 2018 at an annual rate of 2% in Asia, nearly 3% in sub-Saharan Africa, and 0.1% in Latin America and the Caribbean (ibid.).[2] This has been accompanied by a continued deterioration in the current account balance in many developing countries after the GFC. Between 2008 and 2018, current account deficits deepened in absolute terms in South Asia (from -1.4% of GDP in 2008 to -2.1% in 2018), sub-Saharan Africa (from -0.04% to -2.3%), and Latin America and the Caribbean (from -1% of GDP to -1.8%), while the relative size of the current account surplus in East Asia became smaller, falling from 5.5% of GDP to 1.9% (World Bank 2020). This has been matched by opposite trends in the current account balance in the Global North, namely a reduction in the post-GFC current account deficit in North America, from -4.1% of GDP in 2008 to -2.4% in 2018, and a shift from a current account deficit of -1.3% of GDP in 2008 to a current account surplus of 2% in 2018 in the European Union (ibid.).

The increase in current account deficits in sub-Saharan Africa and Latin America has been paralleled by an increase in their external debt obligations. Between 2008 and 2018, the service on external debt as a proportion of GDP rose at a compound annual growth rate of 7.5% in sub-Saharan Africa and 5% in Latin America and the Caribbean, reaching 3.8% and 5.6% of GDP respectively in 2018 (author's calculations based on World Bank 2020). In the same period, the external debt-service-to-GDP ratio also increased in China, at a compound annual rate of 9%, standing at 1.7% of GDP in 2018, while in South Asia the ratio declined slightly, reaching 2.3% in 2018 (ibid.). The capacity to repay external debt has been further eroded by a relative fall in foreign reserves. Between 2008 and 2018 all of the above regions experienced a fall in the size of their foreign reserves relative to the size of their external debt stocks. The decrease was particularly large for China, where the ratio of foreign reserves to total external debt fell at a compound annual growth rate of 11% between 2008 and 2018, to the value of 161.5% in 2018, and in sub-Saharan Africa, where the ratio declined at a compound annual growth rate of 7.3% in these years, reaching 33.2% in 2018 (author's calculations based on World Bank 2020).

Deepening balance of payments problems pose a grave challenge for developing countries in dealing with the COVID-19 crisis because they restrict the capacity of these countries to finance the fiscal stimuli needed to mitigate the economic downturn. Furthermore, the health-care systems in many countries in the Global South and the state's capacity to invest have been systematically weakened by decades of structural adjustment programs that underlined access to multilateral financial assistance from the International Monetary Fund (IMF) and the World Bank (Saiz 2020). In response to the pandemic, these organisations have encouraged introduction of debt moratoria and suspension of bilateral debt repayments for developing countries (Laskaridis 2020). However, these steps have been accompanied by continued calls to "implement structural reforms to … create confidence that the recovery can be strong" in an effort to "foster markets" in countries with "excessive regulations, subsidies, licensing regimes, trade protection" (Malpass 2020). These attitudes further dampen the prospect of a sustainable and equitable recovery from the COVID-19 crisis in the Global South.

In sum, the period after the GFC was associated with a sustained accumulation of FDI stocks relative to GDP around the world, an increased importance of FDI flows into and between developing countries and a rise in the export volume in the Global South, particularly in Asia. Nevertheless, in the decade since 2008 the relative size of both FDI inflows and exports as a share of GDP decreased on average in the regions of the developing world. The international financial position of many countries in the Global South deteriorated, owing to accumulation of external debt, relative declines in foreign reserves, widening current account deficits, and restricted capacity to conduct fiscal and monetary policy in countries receiving multilateral financial assistance. These patterns can be understood against the backdrop of changing institutional conditions in the global economy, especially the trajectory of monetary policy implemented in the USA, rising sentiments towards trade protectionism, and commitments of United Nations 2030 Agenda for Sustainable Development to further integrate developing countries into the international trade and capital flows. In this context, the following section examines the patterns of global inequality.

3.2   IMPACT ON GLOBAL INEQUALITY

The impact of inward FDI on inequality between countries is not clear *a priori* as FDI activity is typically driven by profitability motives rather than by goals of social justice. On the one hand, if inward FDI brings about improvements in productivity it may result in wage increases in the host country (TeVelde 2004). If wages are responsive to changes in productivity, then higher levels of inward FDI may contribute to convergence across countries. On the other hand, FDI may increase income inequality between countries for reasons discussed in the previous section, namely repatriation of profits, high fees and royalties charged by MNCs, and potentially negative impacts on the foreign reserve gap. Moreover, if FDI activity focuses on capital-intensive production, it may generate little employment gains in the host country.

Recent debates in the inequality literature tend to disagree about the direction of change in the patterns of global inequality. Lakner and Milanovic (2016) argue that inequality between countries has fallen in recent decades, finding that between 1988 and 2008 gains in income (in real PPP terms) were the largest for the middle classes in developing countries, particularly in Asia, even though income growth rates were modest in sub-Saharan Africa and for the middle classes in the Global North. Convergence is also established by Kharas and Seidel (2018) for the period 1993–2013.

However, others argue that the fall in global inequality has been much less impressive, and that the global distribution of income has actually become more polarised since the 1980s. Hickel (2017) points out that the findings of convergence between countries are driven disproportionately by economic growth in China, while the share of global income accruing to sub-Saharan Africa has been systematically falling. Existing evidence indicates that there were persistent wage differentials between countries before the GFC (Hemmer et al. 2005). After the GFC, some developing countries have experienced faster expansion of GDP per capita since 2008 compared to developed economies. According to World Bank data, GDP per capita in the region of East Asia and the Pacific as well as in South Asia grew at the fastest average rate of nearly 5% per year between 2008 and 2018 (author's calculations based on World Bank 2020). In contrast, GDP per capita in sub-Saharan Africa and in Latin America expanded on average at approximately 1% per year in the same period, and a similar growth rate is recorded for GDP per capita in Europe and North America (ibid.).

Additionally, Hickel argues that studies of convergence tend to focus on the relative aspect of inequality. When absolute inequality is considered, global income distribution has become substantially more unequal since the 1960s (Hickel 2017). Moreover, Alvaredo et al. (2017) find that the global top 1% income share rose from 16% in 1980 to over 20% in 2016, peaking at 22% in 2007, while the income share of the global bottom 50% experienced a relatively much smaller increase in this period.

In this context, FDI has arguably contributed to reinforcing the persistent core–periphery dynamics in the global economy through repatriation of profits and exacerbation of external debt problems in the Global South, thus deepening global inequality (Hickel 2017). Furthermore, the potentially beneficial effects of FDI on productivity and wage growth may become increasingly difficult to realise as the link between labour compensation and productivity growth has been systematically weakened since the 1980s, with wage growth lagging behind productivity growth in several developed countries (OECD 2018).

Econometric studies of the relationship between FDI and income convergence tend to find mixed effects of FDI on inequalities between countries. Gopinath and Chen (2003) find that net FDI stock is associated with a convergence of wages across countries with different levels of development. Income convergence is also established by Choi (2004) for a panel of countries, and by Dunne and Masiyandima (2017) for countries in the region of the Southern African Development Community. Conversely, Mayer-Foulkes and Nunnenkamp (2009) find that in the USA FDI contributes to convergence only among high-income regions, and a similar finding is estimated for Europe by Völlmecke et al. (2016). Moreover, Demir and Yi (2018) establish that FDI has no significant effect on productivity growth in a panel of countries between 1990 and 2012 irrespective of the direction of FDI flows and sector, and hence doesn't act to close productivity gaps between the host and the parent country.

Overall, existing evidence on the relationship between FDI and global inequality is not decisive. While certain parts of the developing world, namely Asia, have seen their per capita incomes increase rapidly, other regions of the Global South, in particular sub-Saharan Africa, have not experienced much slower income gains. The extent to which FDI flows have contributed to these patterns is not explicit, and the empirical association has not been extensively studied by the existing literature. In many aspects, it is likely that FDI flows have facilitated the reproduction of inequalities in the global economy, although some beneficial effects of FDI inflows on productivity may have also supported income gains in the rapidly growing regions of the developing world.

3.3   IMPACT ON INEQUALITY WITHIN COUNTRIES

Research on the effects of FDI on within-country inequality is more extensive than evidence of FDI's impact on global inequality. Existing studies analyse both groups of countries and individual economies over time, focusing primarily on the period before the GFC. In reviewing the findings of this body of work, we distinguish between the effects on functional income distribution and personal income inequality within countries.

Functional Income Distribution

Functional income inequality analyses the distribution of national income between factors of production, namely labour and capital. FDI is likely to influence the share of national income accruing to labour and capital income through its impact on export expansion and the involvement of MNCs in the domestic economy. In theory, FDI inflows may raise the labour share of national income if they increase productivity and lead to strong employment creation in sectors with many linkages. On the other hand, FDI inflows may exacerbate functional income inequality by promoting interests of a small group of local factory owners and managers, thus increasing the capital share of national income.

Existing evidence on the empirical association between FDI inflows and labour share in the host country is limited. Early studies using panel data find that inward FDI from developed countries exacerbates functional income inequality in developing economies (Harrison 2005; Decreuse and Maarek 2015). Onaran and Stockhammer (2008) find a positive short-run impact of FDI on wages in Central and Eastern Europe in high-skilled and capital-intensive sectors, but this effect turns negative in the long run. Additionally, Stockhammer (2017) establishes a negative association between globalisation (measured by trade openness) and wage share in a panel of developed and developing economies, while Onaran and Galanis (2012) find that openness to international trade is associated with a more profit-led regime of aggregate demand. These findings suggest that FDI flows may put a downward pressure on wages in an attempt to increase the capital share of income. Moreover, given the issues of capital-intensity highlighted in the previous section, there are serious challenges that may prevent this beneficial impact of FDI inflows on the wage share from being realised.

Furthermore, FDI outflows are also likely to influence functional income distribution in the MNC's parent country. Jia et al. (2018) find a negative correlation between labour share and outward FDI in the case of China, although the association turns positive if FDI activity is focused on technology or resource seeking. Corlett (2016) argues that liberalisation of international trade, and, indirectly, outflows of foreign investment have contributed to worsening of within-country inequality in developed countries, as wage growth of low- and middle-income workers has been dampened by competition with low-paid workers in the Global South.

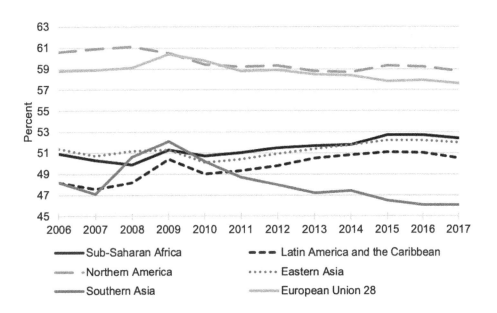

Source: Author's own calculation based on ILO (2020), modelled estimates, July 2019.

Figure 3.2   Labour income share (% of GDP)

To relate the existing evidence to the situation after the GFC, Figure 3.2 presents trends in the labour share across regions of the world. In the majority of regions, the labour share of national income increased briefly during the Great Recession. However, between 2008 and 2018 the share declined in North America and the European Union, as well as in South Asia. With the exception of the latter region, the labour share of national income rose in other parts of the developing world between 2008 and 2015. Nevertheless, the wage share has stagnated since 2015 in Eastern Asia, and fell slightly in sub-Saharan Africa and Latin America. While this data does not directly relate these trends to changes in FDI flows, the period of reduced FDI inflows after 2015 is paralleled by decreasing labour share in some of the regions of the developing world.

In sum, existing research suggests that FDI flows are often associated with deteriorating functional income distribution in both host and parent countries, although this likely varies across sectors. The relationship between the labour share of GDP and FDI flows since the GFC has not been clear-cut. Nevertheless, data presented in this section reveals systematic declines in the wage share since the mid-2010s. This poses a major challenge to trade policy in developed and developing economies alike and puts into question how FDI flows should be used in order to mitigate the concentration of national income in favour of capital.

Personal Income Distribution

In contrast to functional income distribution, personal inequality captures income disparities between individuals or households in an economy. It also allows to examine the heterogeneity of experiences within the group of workers. FDI may contribute to personal income inequality by generating disparate gains in wages across sectors of the domestic economy, especially between high-skilled and low-skilled workers (see Feenstra and Hanson 1997). Specifically, FDI is likely to lead to faster income increases for workers in modern sectors, especially in high-value added industries, compared to low-paid workers in the primary sector and low-value added manufacturing. Moreover, since FDI activity tends to be concentrated in urban centres, it may exacerbate regional inequality between urban and rural workers.

Available evidence in the literature focuses on the period preceding the GFC. Gopinath and Chen (2003) estimate that inward FDI deepens wage inequality in developing countries. Basu and Guariglia (2007) find that an increase in the share of net FDI inflows in GDP is associated with a higher Gini coefficient of income for a panel of developing countries. A similar finding is established by Choi (2006) for a panel of countries with different levels of development. Lin et al. (2013) estimate that the direction of the relationship between FDI and inequality depends on human capital, so that FDI reduces inequality up until a certain threshold of human capital, but exacerbates it thereafter. Similarly, Bumann and Lensink (2016) find that the distributional impact of FDI depends on the level of financial depth, estimating a widening effect of FDI on income inequality at low levels of private credit to GDP. Moreover, looking at wage inequality, Figini and Görg (2011) establish that the distributional effects of inward FDI differ across the level of development between 1980 and 2002, with a positive impact on wage inequality in developing countries and a negative (i.e. inequality-reducing) effect in developed countries. In a similar period, Herzer and Nunnenkamp (2013) estimate a non-linear impact of inward FDI on income inequality for a panel of European countries and find a positive effect in the short run that turns negative in the long run. A widening impact on inequality of inward FDI in the long run is also established for a panel of Latin American countries by Herzer et al. (2014).

Couto (2018) is one of few econometric studies providing evidence for a panel of countries for more recent years. She estimates that a higher share of inward FDI stocks in GDP typically increases inequality (measured by the Gini index of disposable income) in a panel of countries at different income levels between 1990 and 2013. Nevertheless, the study establishes that

Table 3.1   Pre-tax national income shares by income group

	Top 1%		Top 10%		Middle 40%		Bottom 50%	
	Value in 2016	Change, 2008–16	Value in 2016	Change, 2008–16	Value in 2016	Change, 2008–2016	Value in 2016	Change, 2008–2016
Asia (excl. Middle East)	16.3%	-0.88%	47.5%	-0.03%	40.3%	+0.41%	12.2%	-1.17%
Europe[1]	10.8%	-0.18%	35.7%	+0.1%	45.3%	-0.05%	19%	-0.06%
Latin America	27.9%	-0.68%	55.4%	-0.2%	32.4%	+0.14%	12.2%	+0.59%
North America	20.2%	+0.43%	47.1%	+0.47%	40.4%	-0.18%	12.5%	-1.08%
Sub-Saharan Africa	19.9%	-0.18%	54.4%	-0.1%	33.4%	+0.22%	12.2%	-0.12%

Source: Author's own calculation based on World Inequality Database 2020.
Note: [1]The values for Europe are given for 2017. Change is calculated in terms of a compound annual growth rate between 2008 and 2016 (2017 for Europe).

the estimated distributional impact of FDI depends on the level of development, but that the shape of the relationship is not unambiguous. FDI is found to reduce income inequality in least developed countries and in middle-income countries, but raise it in lower-middle-income countries and in high-income countries. No significantly different effect is found for the period after the GFC. Another study by Bogliaccini and Egan (2017) for a panel of countries between 1989 and 2010 establishes that sector matters for the distributional impact of FDI and that the inequality-increasing effects of FDI tend to be higher in the services sector. Furthermore, focusing on Africa, Kaulihowa and Adjasi (2018) estimate a non-linear empirical relationship between FDI and inequality for a panel of African countries between 1980 and 2013, but find that on average FDI reduced inequality in the sample.

Table 3.1 presents data on trends in personal income inequality measured by the Gini coefficient of disposable income and the share of inward and outward FDI stock in GDP since the GFC. As comprehensive information on the Gini index is only available at the country level, a selection of countries is provided for each region analysed. In the majority of countries shown, the Gini index has declined since 2008, although the magnitude of the fall tends to be small. In Latin America, the largest decrease is recorded for Argentina between 2008 and 2017 and Ecuador from 2008 to 2018, albeit at only around 1%. In sub-Saharan Africa, changes in the Gini index have been marginal, oscillating between -0.3% and 0.2% for countries analysed. Similar patterns are observed for countries in Asia, with the largest declines recorded in China (by 0.6% between 2008 and 2017) and in Thailand (0.5% between 2008 and 2018), while South Korea experienced a 0.5% rise in the Gini index from 2008 to 2017. In European and North American countries, the Gini index rose by 0.2% in France and Germany, and by 0.4% in the USA between 2008 and 2017, but it fell by a very small margin in Canada and the UK. The observation of small variations in the Gini index for income since the GFC across countries complicates any causal analyses between the patterns of FDI flows and changes in personal income distribution. There are several explanations for this. First, estimates of the Gini index are typically based on individual-level microdata, which are prone to missing observations across individuals and over time. To minimise any potential measurement errors, missing information is imputed, which introduces uncertainty to the precise magnitudes of the estimates. In this context, the estimated values of the Gini index are known to usually change only gradually from one year to another (Solt 2020:13). This issue is particularly visible in the

Standardised World Income Inequality Database (Solt 2019), from where the income inequality measure reported in Table 3.1 is sourced, as that dataset performs additional quantitative adjustments in order to provide standardised and internationally comparable measures of the Gini indices based on various data sources containing different definitions of income and varying number (and type) of observations (Solt 2020).

The other explanation of the lack of a clear empirical relationship between the Gini index and FDI relates to the methodological flows of the Gini index as a measure of income distribution. Despite its widespread use in the literature, the Gini coefficient is a controversial measure of inequality. On the one hand, the index is comparable across different population sizes and satisfies a range of other desirable properties (Cowell 2009). On the other hand, changes in the Gini coefficient are overly sensitive to transfers between observations in the middle of the distribution (Solt 2020). Consequently, the index may not provide an accurate picture of inequality if the latter is driven by changes at either the top or the bottom of the distribution. This is problematic as much of the increase in income inequality in recent decades has been caused by extreme concentration of income at the top of the distribution (see Piketty 2014).

To provide an alternative insight into the changes in personal income inequality after the GFC, Table 3.2 illustrates trends in the shares of national pre-tax income accruing to individuals in the top 1%, the top 10%, the middle 40%, and the bottom 50% of the income distribution. The use of a measure of income before taxes complements the analysis of inequality in disposable income presented in Table 3.1. Apart from North America, the share of the top 1% in pre-tax income declined slightly in all of the analysed regions between 2008 and 2016 (which is the latest available datapoint in the dataset). In these years, the decrease in the top 1% was relatively the largest in Asia and in Latin America (though it remains small in absolute terms). Similarly, the top 10% share of national income decreased modestly in Asia, Latin America, and sub-Saharan Africa. However, with the exception of Latin America, falling top income shares in these regions have not been matched by gains in the national income share for the bottom 50% of the distribution. Asia and North America recorded the largest declines in the bottom 50% share, which decreased at a compound annual growth rate of over 1.2% and 1.1% respectively between 2008 and 2016. Nevertheless, in Asia, as well as in Latin America, it was individuals in the middle 40% of the income distribution who saw an increase (albeit modest) in their income share. This is consistent with the finding of the falling Gini indices in the selected countries in these regions shown in Table 3.1. Meanwhile, in North America and in Europe, it was the top 10% who experienced a rise in their share of national income.

Based on data presented in Table 3.1, there appears to be no clear empirical relationship between changes in the Gini coefficient and the share of FDI in GDP in the countries and regions shown. Nevertheless, analysis in Table 3.2 provides insight into how national income was distributed across income groups in the years after the GFC. Contrary to the assertions of mainstream economic policies, the lack of visible improvements in the bottom 50% share of income in the majority of analysed regions signals that expansion of the GDP shares of inward and outward FDI stock has not been associated with substantial improvements in incomes for the lowest and low-to-middle income earners. Conversely, increases in the share of FDI stock in GDP have been paralleled by redistribution of income towards the top 10% in North America and Europe, and the middle 40% in Asia and Latin America. This suggests that the FDI activity after the GFC may have served to mainly advance the interest of local capitalist and managerial classes in these regions, with a potential exception of Latin America.

Table 3.2   Trends in the Gini index and FDI stock in selected countries

	Gini index	Gini index, % change from 2008	Inward FDI stock, % GDP 2019	In. FDI stock GDP share, % change 2008–19	Outward FDI stock, % GDP 2019	Out. FDI stock GDP share, % change 2008–19
Latin America						
Argentina	37.5 (2017)	-1.3%	15.4%	-2.6%	9.7%	1.9%
Brazil	46.9 (2018)	-0.3%	35.3%	7.9%	12.4%	4.4%
Chile	44 (2017)	-0.4%	95.2%	4.8%	46.8%	6.4%
Ecuador	42 (2018)	-1.0%	18.2%	-0.1%	N/A	
Mexico	41.3 (2018)	-0.7%	49.7%	6.3%	18.2%	11.2%
Sub-Saharan Africa						
Ethiopia	33.4 (2015)	0.2%	26.2%	5.6%	N/A	
Ghana	43.5 (2016)	0.2%	58.7%	15.2%	0.8%	12.9%
Rwanda	50.4 (2016)	-0.2%	25.6%	14.7%	1.2%	14.3%
Sierra Leone	40.3 (2016)	-0.3%	47.9%	8.5%	N/A	
Zimbabwe	46.8 (2016)	-0.1%	22.4%*	-0.8%*	2.5%*	-4.6%*
Europe and North America						
Canada	30.7 (2018)	-0.1%	59.8%	3.7%	95.4%	7.9%
France	29.5 (2017)	0.2%	32.1%	4.8%	56.7%	5.3%
Germany	29.1 (2017)	0.2%	25%	0.2%	45%	3.2%
United Kingdom	33.1 (2018)	-0.2%	73.6%	8.1%	69.2%	2.0%
USA	38.2 (2017)	0.4%	43.9%	9.1%	35.8%	5.0%
Asia						
China	40.9 (2017)	-0.5%	12.4%	3.8%	14.8%	12.6%

Capital movements and corporate dominance in Latin America

	Gini index	Gini index, % change from 2008	Inward FDI stock, % GDP 2019	In. FDI stock GDP share, % change 2008–19	Outward FDI stock, % GDP 2019	Out. FDI stock GDP share, % change 2008–19
Korea, Rep.	32.7 (2017)	0.5%	14.3%	4.3%	26.5%	9.9%
Singapore	38.5 (2017)	-0.3%	469.3%	6.3%	305.8%	5.7%
Thailand	39.7 (2018)	-0.6%	46.9%	3.4%	25.4%	19.4%
Vietnam	34.6 (2018)	-0.1%	61%	3.5%	4.2%	18.7%

Source: Author's own calculations, based on Solt (2019) and UNCTAD (2020).
Notes: Change from 2008 calculated as compound annual growth rate. "Data for the ratio of FDI stock to GDP in Zimbabwe is given for year 2018.

Note that the above conclusion is not based on any conditional estimations of the empirical relationship between these variables – this task is left to future research. However, it is notable that the patterns of inward and outward FDI as a share of GDP are highly diverse across countries, particularly in terms of the pace of increase. This suggests that analyses of the distributional effects of FDI are likely to be specific to a particular country's institutional context. In this light, future research will aim to conduct a more focused analysis of the impact of FDI on personal income inequality in a specific country context.

In sum, existing evidence on the impact of FDI flows on within-country inequality is inconclusive. The literature on functional income distribution tends to find that FDI inflows (outflows) are associated with a deterioration in the labour share of national income in host (parent) countries. However, the effect of FDI inflows on personal inequality differs across countries analysed, depending on the level of development, institutional conditions, and time frame studied. Descriptive analysis of the top and bottom income shares suggests that since the GFC and apart from Latin America, FDI may have benefitted primarily capitalists and managers, rather than poorer workers. While the literature typically focuses on the period before the GFC, limited data availability means that there are not yet any definite patterns observed between the measured of within-country inequality and changes in FDI activity. Nevertheless, substantial disparities remain in terms of the gains in income between factors of production and across the distribution of income in the majority of analysed regions. In the context of the COVID-19 crisis, these persistent inequalities highlight the need to evaluate the likely distributional effects of any future FDI projects as an integral part of their impact assessments.

3.4   CONCLUSION

The chapter discussed the distributional effects of FDI since the GFC. Its original contribution is to provide a comprehensive overview of the existing state of knowledge on FDI's impact on different measures and concepts of inequality between and within countries, complementing it with the analysis of descriptive statistics of inequality and FDI across regions of the global economy after the GFC.

The relationship between FDI and income inequality since 2008 is complex and remains mainly theoretical as preliminary analysis of the available data did not reveal any systematic patterns between the different measures of income inequality and changes in FDI. Nevertheless, rising size of inward and outward FDI stock relative to GDP has failed to counteract deepening global inequality, as evidenced by persistent disparities in the growth of GDP per capita across developing countries.

In terms of within-country income inequality, in the most recent years the labour share of national income has deteriorated, although functional income distribution was more favourable to labour in the immediate aftermath of the GFC. Moreover, apart from Latin America, rising share of FDI stock in GDP has not been paralleled by increases in relative income share for the bottom 50% since the GFC, suggesting that FDI activity may have benefited primarily local capitalists and managers in the top 10% and the middle 40% of the income distribution, depending on the region analysed.

Issues with data availability and caveats in measuring inequality inhibit any direct causal conclusions regarding the distributive impact of FDI since the GFC at this stage. Furthermore, the analysis in this chapter suggests that the empirical relationship in question is likely to depend on a country-specific institutional context.

Future work will undertake a more extensive and country-specific econometric analysis of the impact of FDI on different aspects of inequality after the GFC. Nevertheless, the chapter discussed strong theoretical rationale suggesting that inward and outward FDI carries important direct and indirect implications for global inequality as well as for wages and inequality in parent and host countries, which may not be easily reflected in statistical estimations. The persistence of unequal gains in income between and within countries that was documented in this chapter testifies to this observation. For this reason, the potential distributional impact of FDI needs to be closely scrutinised in both developing and developed countries in order to strive towards an inclusive and sustainable recovery from the COVID-19 crisis.

NOTES

1. Note that the trends in the export-to-GDP and FDI inflows-to-GDP ratios have varied across individual countries within regions, see Table 3.1 in this chapter.
2. According to UNCTAD data, between 2008 and 2018 the regional export-to-GDP ratio increased only in the European Union.

REFERENCES

Alvaredo, F., Chancel, L., Piketty, T., Saez, E. and Zucman, G. (2017). The elephant curve of global inequality and growth (Working Paper). *WID World*, 2017(20).

Amighini, A. and Sanfilippo, M. (2014). Impact of south–south FDI and trade on the export upgrading of African economies. *World Development*, 64, 1–17.

Basu, P. and Guariglia, A. (2007). Foreign direct investment, inequality, and growth. *Journal of Macroeconomics*, 29(4), 824–839.

Bogliaccini, J.A. and Egan, P.J.W. (2017). Foreign direct investment and inequality in developing countries: Does sector matter? *Economics & Politics*, 29(3), 209–236.

Buchanan, B.G., Le, Q.V. and Rishi, M. (2012). Foreign direct investment and institutional quality: Some empirical evidence. *International Review of Financial Analysis*, 21, 81–89.

Bumann, S. and Lensink, R. (2016). Capital account liberalization and income inequality. *Journal of International Money and Finance*, 61(C), 143–162.

Caceres, C., Goncalves, C., Lindow, G. and Sher, G. (2017). Capital flows to Latin America: Prospects and risks. *Dialogo a Fondo*. Retrieved from: https://blog-dialogoafondo.imf.org/.

Calderon, C., Chuhan-Pole, P. and Kubota, M. (2019). Drivers of gross capital inflows: Which factors are more important for sub-Saharan Africa? (Working Paper). *Policy Research, WPS 8777*, Washington, DC: World Bank Group.

Choi, C. (2004). Foreign direct investment and income convergence. *Applied Economics*, 34(10), 1045–1049.

Choi, C. (2006). Does foreign direct investment affect domestic income inequality? *Applied Economics Letters*, 13(12), 811–814.

Corlett, A. (2016). Examining an elephant: Globalisation and the lower middle class of the rich world. Resolution Foundation Report. Retrieved from: https://www.resolutionfoundation.org/.

Couto, V. (2018). Does foreign direct investment lower income inequality? New evidence and discussion on the role of service offshoring (Captive Centers). *Conference of the Latin American Network for Research on Services (REDLAS)*, 13–14 September 2018, Buenos Aires, Argentina.

Cowell, F.A. (2009). *Measuring Inequality*, LSE Perspectives in Economic Analysis. Oxford: Oxford University Press.

Decreuse, B. and Maarek, P. (2015). FDI and the labor share in developing countries: A theory and some evidence. *Annals of Economics and Statistics*, 119(120), 289–319.

Demir, F. and Yi, D. (2018). Bilateral FDI flows, productivity growth, and convergence: The north vs. the south. *World Development*, 101, 235–249.

Dunne, J.P. and Masiyandima, N. (2017). Bilateral FDI from South Africa and income convergence in SADC. *African Development Review*, 29(3), 403–415.

Feenstra, R. and Hanson, G. (1997). Foreign direct investment and relative wages: Evidence from Mexico's maquiladoras. *Journal of International Economics*, 42(3–4), 371–393.

Figini, P. and Görg, H. (2011). Does foreign direct investment affect wage inequality? An empirical investigation. *The World Economy*, 34(9), 1455–1475.

Gopinath, M. and Chen, W. (2003). Foreign direct investment and wages: A cross-country analysis. *Journal of International Trade & Economic Development*, 12(3), 285–309.

Harrison, A. (2005). Has globalization eroded labor's share? Some cross-country evidence. *MPRA Paper 39649*. University Library of Munich.

Hemmer, H.R., Krueger, R. and Seith, J. (2005). Foreign direct investment and income inequality revisited. In El-Shagi, M. and Ruebel, G. (eds), *Aspects of International Economics*. Wiesbaden: Deutscher Universitaetsverlag, pp. 97–115.

Herzer, D. and Nunnenkamp, P. (2013). Inward and outward FDI and income inequality: Evidence from Europe. *Review of World Economics*, 149(2), 395–422.

Herzer, D., Huehne, P. and Nunnenkamp, P. (2014). FDI and income inequality – evidence from Latin American economies. *Review of Development Economics*, 18(4), 778–793.

Hickel, J. (2017). Is global inequality getting better or worse? A critique of the World Bank's convergence narrative. *Third World Quarterly*, 38(10), 2208–2222. doi: 10.1080/01436597.2017.1333414.

ILO (2020). *ILOSTAT Database*. Retrieved from: https://ilostat.ilo.org/data/.

IMF (2020). *Balance of Payments Statistics*. Retrieved from: https://data.imf.org.

Jia, N., Han, Y., Peng, K. and Lei, H. (2018). FDI and labour share of home-country: Empirical evidence from micro data of Chinese enterprises. *Economic Research-Ekonomska Istraživanja*, 32(1), 1320–1335. doi: 10.1080/1331677X.2019.1628652.

Kaulihowa, T. and Adjasi, C. (2018). FDI and income inequality in Africa. *Oxford Development Studies*, 46(2), 250–265.

Kharas, H. and Seidel, B. (2018). What's happening to the world income distribution? Global Economy & Development at Brookings (Working Paper) 114.

Lakner, C. and Milanovic, B. (2016). Global income distribution: From the fall of the Berlin Wall to the Great Recession. *World Bank Economic Review*, 30(2), 203–232.

Laskaridis, C. (2020). Debt moratoria in the global south in the age of coronavirus. *Developing Economics*. Retrieved from: https://developingeconomics.org/.

Lin, S.C., Kim, D.H. and Wu, Y.C. (2013). Foreign direct investment and income inequality: Human capital matters, *Journal of Regional Science*, 53(5), 874–896.

Malpass, D. (2020). Remarks by World Bank Group President David Malpass on G20 finance minister's conference call on COVID-19. *World Bank*. Retrieved from: https://www.worldbank.org/.

Mayer-Foulkes, D. and Nunnenkamp, P. (2009). Do multinational enterprises contribute to convergence or divergence? A disaggregated analysis of US FDI. *Review of Development Economics*, 13(2), 304–318.

Narula, R. and Driffield, N. (2012). Does FDI cause development? The ambiguity of the evidence and why it matters. *European Journal of Development Research*, 24(1), 1–7.

OECD (2018). Decoupling of wages from productivity: what implications for public policies? *OECD Economic Outlook*, Issue 2.

Onaran, O. and Galanis, G. (2012). Is aggregate demand wage-led or profit-led? National and global effects. ILO Conditions of Work and Employment Series no. 40.

Onaran, O. and Stockhammer, E. (2008). The effect of FDI and foreign trade on wages in the Central and Eastern European Countries in the post-transition era: A sectoral analysis for the manufacturing industry. *Structural Change and Economic Dynamics*, 19(1), 66–80.

Piketty, T. (2014). *Capital in the Twenty First Century*. Cambridge, MA: Harvard University Press.

Saiz, I. (2020). Time for a rights-based global economic stimulus to tackle COVID-19. *Center for Economic and Social Rights*. Retrieved from: https://www.cesr.org/.

Solt, F. (2019). The Standardized World Income Inequality Database. *Harvard Dataverse*. Retrieved from: https://doi.org/.

Solt, F. (2020). Measuring income inequality across countries and over time: The Standardized World Income Inequality Database. *Social Science Quarterly*. Retrieved from: https://github.com/fsolt/swiid/blob/master/paper/updating_swiid.pdf.

Stockhammer, E. (2017). Determinants of the wage share: A panel analysis of advanced and developing economies. *British Journal of Industrial Relations*, 55(1), 3–33.

Sumner, A. (2005). Is foreign direct investment good for the poor? A review and stocktake. *Development in Practice*, 15(3/4), 269–285.

Sumner, A. (2008). Foreign direct investment in developing countries: Have we reached a policy 'tipping point'? *Third World Quarterly*, 29(2), 239–253.

TeVelde, D.W. (2004). Foreign direct investment and income inequality in Latin America: Experiences and policy implications. In TeVelde, D.W. (ed.), *Foreign Direct Investment; Income Inequality and Poverty*. London: Overseas Development Institute, pp. 16–62.

UNCTAD (2009). Assessing the impact of the current financial and economic crisis on global FDI flows. UNCTAD/DIAE/IA/2009/3 Report.

UNCTAD (2019). *World Investment Report 2019*. Retrieved from: https://unctad.org/en/PublicationsLibrary/wir2019_en.pdf.

UNCTAD (2020a). *World Investment Report 2020*. Retrieved from: https://unctad.org/en/PublicationsLibrary/wir2020_en.pdf.

UNCTAD (2020b). *UNCTADStat Database*. Retrieved from: https://unctadstat.unctad.org/EN/.

United Nations (2015). *Transforming our World: The 2030 Agenda for Sustainable Development*, A/RES/70/1.

Völlmecke, D., Jindra, B. and Marek, P. (2016). FDI, human capital and income convergence: Evidence for European regions. *Economic Systems*, 40(2), 288–307.

Wacker, K.M. (2013). On the measurement of foreign direct investment and its relationship to activities of multinational corporations. European Central Bank, Working Paper #1614.

World Bank (2020). *World Development Indicators*. Retrieved from: https://databank.worldbank.org/.

World Inequality Database (2020). Retrieved from: https://wid.world.

4. Pension funds and domestic debt markets in emerging economies

Jennifer Churchill, Bruno Bonizzi and Annina Kaltenbrunner

The East Asian Financial Crisis forced the international policy community to take the risks of financial liberalisation in emerging economies (EEs) seriously. Currency and maturity "mismatches" were seen to have introduced grave fragility to the balance sheets of banks and firms, opening the way for a currency crisis to induce a financial and economic event of regional proportions (Corsetti, Pesenti and Roubini 1999; Sharma 2003). This chapter focuses on two contemporary interrelated policy debates that emerged from these experiences: first, the need to create local currency domestic bond markets (LCBMs), and second, the need for institutional investors, including private pension funds, to form the dependable, patient demand within them.

Consensus regarding the benefits of LCBMs and patient investors has only grown stronger in the light of the Global Financial Crisis. There has been a coordinated policy drive by the transnational and regional economic and financial organisations (G20 Finance Ministers and Central Bank Governors 2011; World Bank Group 2012; IMF 2013; The World Economic Forum 2016) to encourage and enable, in particular, domestic local currency *private* bond markets, and a growing focus on the need for *domestic* private institutional investors to participate in those markets. In this manner, domestic pension policy has been drawn into the debate, with the privatisation of pension delivery gaining a renewed focus. Importantly, this pivot towards the importance of domestic investors reflects disappointing results in relation to the stability of investment from international institutional investors. We present our own explanation as to why international investors have not proven to be the key to financial stability: ultimately, the behaviour of foreign pension funds is determined by the nature of their liabilities, which are embedded in the conditions of their home economy (Bonizzi and Kaltenbrunner 2019). The problem of achieving stable sources of finance is not however necessarily solved by growing the domestic investor base, and reducing the proportion of state or corporate debt held by foreigners. External vulnerability may be reduced, but the behaviour of domestic pension funds is also more complex than previously allowed (Bonizzi, Churchill and Guevara 2020). This can be seen from the wide divergence in outcomes from pension reform, both in terms of pension fund holdings of domestic corporate debt (indicating their role in supporting development of the market), and – fundamentally – their success in providing adequate retirement provision.

This chapter is divided into four sections. Section 4.1 traces the development of policy on the development of LCBMs following the 1997 East Asian Financial Crisis, and the Global

55

Financial Crisis. Section 4.2 reviews some regional experiences in market development. This is followed by a section (4.3) that considers these experiences in light of an understanding of the behaviour of international and domestic pension funds, drawn from our prior research. The conclusion (section 4.4) offers some alternative policy directions that are deserving of more consideration.

4.1   POLICY DEBATE

A prominent argument within the literature exploring the causes of the East Asian currency and banking crisis is that the success of capital account liberalisation depends on domestic institutional and regulatory factors (Corsetti, Pesenti and Roubini 1999). In terms of regulation, it was evident that more could be done to oversee and direct the behaviour of banks to limit risk-taking to more "acceptable" levels. A more significant suggestion however, was that the external vulnerability and financial system fragility in affected countries was partly due to the absence of domestic debt markets and a lack of diversity in the domestic currency instruments in which foreign capital could invest – a lack of appropriate institutions. In Thailand, foreign capital inflows had been channelled into equity or real estate leading to unsustainable asset price inflation – partially due to a lack of other appropriate investible assets (Sharma 2003). At the same time, domestic banks had sourced capital from international financial markets. This meant that the balance sheets of banks were exposed not only to maturity but also to currency mismatches, meaning that the reversal in capital flows and resulting devaluation of the exchange rate badly affected net worth. Once crisis hit the banks, finance dried up for corporations that might otherwise have been able to turn to the debt markets: there was no "spare tyre". Financial liberalisation, therefore, should be undertaken only with the appropriate additional policies to develop domestic capital market institutions.

Borrowing in a foreign currency is seen as a key mechanism through which financial instability can be introduced by states and/or firms in emerging economies but is not necessarily a matter of choice. The inability of emerging economies to borrow in their own currency has been termed "original sin" (Eichengreen and Hausmann 2005), with the fault arising systemically from the organisation of global finance, only partly determined by the characteristics of the debtor country. This line of theorising also points to the benefits of creating local currency domestic bond markets, with instruments across all maturities. With long-term capital markets, it was thought, it would be possible to draw patient capital from the institutional investors and other cash-pools in the advanced economies into emerging economies and so address maturity and currency issues together. Patient foreign portfolio inflows into long-term debt markets, rather than being formed of hot speculative and destabilising flows, could match foreign direct investment in terms of commitment. Bond flows could be preferable to FDI, given that they did not result in the loss of control of domestic firms through foreign acquisitions.

The pathway to this institutional growth was understood to first involve the development of the public debt market. The state offers instruments over a range of maturities establishing a yield curve. This was expected to facilitate the development of a private debt market. On the demand side were international pension funds that had the capacity to hold longer-term assets, in addition to the desire to diversify their portfolios further by holding more emerging market assets. On the supply side, beyond the state, were the domestic firms struggling to raise affordable finance. This high cost of finance for domestic firms has been recognised as a problem across the spectrum of literature; in the financialisation literature for example, one consequence of operating within the global finance setting – beyond dealing with volatile exchange rates – is argued to be that emerging economies are often forced to keep interest rates high (Bonizzi 2013), with the consequence that bank lending can be very expensive. This high cost of domestic finance can explain much of the demand for the cheaper foreign denominated debt prior to the Asian crisis.

Post-Global Financial Crisis

The Global Financial Crisis heralded a new era of volatile, destabilising capital flows in emerging economies. After a short lag, where questions of "decoupling" were hopefully raised, capital began flowing out at unmanageable speed and volume, only to return as the easy monetary policy adopted in the US and elsewhere led investors to reverse their actions, overwhelmed by concerns over funding and future liquidity levels in the absence of growth assets in their portfolios. Evidence emerged suggesting that the large participation of foreign pension funds and institutional investors did not act as a stabilising force during the retrenchment (Hofmann, Shim and Shin 2020a, 2020b).

In this context, the G20 came together at the Cannes Summit to agree an "action plan" to further support the development of LCBMs, as part of a strategy to build "resilience against the transmission of capital flow shocks, as well as helping provide finance for development" (G20 Finance Ministers and Central Bank Governors 2011: 1). The Action Plan articulated the role of LCBMs in increasing financial stability through their role in reducing "contagion effects across financial markets and spill-overs into the real economy" and noted that "as international investors strive for broader diversification of their portfolios, EMDE financial assets will become increasingly attractive. Therefore, EMDE authorities need to prepare for this development" (ibid.: 1). This new policy initiative was in reality just a more centrally coordinated push for the same policies being promoted prior to the Global Financial Crisis, with the only significant change being the admissibility of capital account management techniques, at least as a last resort option to curb excess capital inflows. However, a key concern in this latest incarnation of debt market promotion was the lack of progress in the majority of emerging economies in developing deep, liquid *private* debt markets with a range of instruments across the broad maturity spectrum. Furthermore, achieving this was increasingly presumed to require "efforts to develop the domestic investor base" (ibid.: 1).

The 2011 Action Plan noted the inadequacy of help available to emerging and developing countries to take the steps necessary to establish institutional change and committed to addressing this issue by coming up with a way of measuring where a country stands in terms of the development trajectory and where there may be weaknesses or bottlenecks that could be prioritised in future reforms. All organisations that were already looking into this area were urged to work in a coordinated manner on this goal. In 2013, the IMF published a diagnostic framework following collaboration between itself, the World Bank, the EDRB and the OECD (IMF 2013). Diagnosing the institutional situation of any country consisted in considering six key components of development: "the macroeconomic framework, composition and needs of the issuer and investor base, primary and secondary market structures and related market dynamics, regulatory and legal frameworks, and market infrastructure" (ibid.: 1). Key indicators were mapped to these categories. Action to improve on the investor base could include "a debt management strategy aimed at gradually lengthening the maturity structure of public debt and creating benchmarks for pricing reference" so as to "meet the needs of institutional investors (e.g., pension funds or insurance companies), thus attracting different types of investors and deepening the market" (ibid.: 15).

The World Economic Forum also entered the debate, through its *Accelerating Capital Markets Development in Emerging Economics Initiative*, established in 2014. The Forum published a White Paper in 2016, that made recommendations seeking to "broaden the investor base" by, amongst other things, lowering the "actual and perceived risks of participating in the market for domestic and international investors" (The World Economic Forum 2016: 5). Demand from international investors was being held back for some reason, begging the question whether there was anything more that could be done to make investment more attractive, for example by reducing risks. A multi-agency "report-back" on the 2011 action plan, led by the IMF, proposed areas for action creating new appropriate instruments (IMF 2016). A link was drawn to the infrastructure needs of emerging markets. Infrastructure was argued to be ideal for pension funds due to matching pension fund long-term liabilities whilst reducing inflation exposure. New thinking in terms of "guarantee structures" and "credit risk enhancement instruments" were seen as necessary to make instruments acceptable to funds, alongside "direct engagement of government and multilaterals" (ibid.: 15).[1] In terms of domestic demand, the report argued for the relaxing of regulations regarding asset allocation for insurance and pension funds, whilst the World Economic Forum argued that further deregulation would help develop the capital markets more generally, using Colombia as an example: "Colombia subjects pension funds to relative profitability rules, which require funds to achieve rates of return above a prescribed minimum. These minimum return requirements limit risk differentiation and have created herd-like behaviour" (The World Economic Forum 2016: 11).

The IMF "report-back" found overall progress to date on domestic investor base and private market development underwhelming. Emerging market institutional investors had growing assets under management, but remained significantly less important than local banks. Furthermore these assets were still largely in government debt. In line with this, the Bank for International Settlements (BIS) published in 2019 a working paper "Establishing viable capital markets". Distinctly more rhetorical in nature than the "Cannes summit" publications, the paper bemoaned the "vestiges of financial repression" running through emerging economies, referring also to regulations regarding asset holdings by institutional investors, and to "paternalism" in relation to management of stock prices (BIS 2019). On the supply side, the paper noted that what growth there was in capital markets in emerging economies has been "somewhat flattered by issuances from state-owned firms and companies with large insider holdings" (ibid.: 1); in other words, progress to date was located in China and Brazil. This paper also, therefore, sought further focus on creating a domestic investor base through the "greater financialisation of household savings" (ibid.: 3) alongside a general promotion of "greater respect for market autonomy" (ibid.: 44). The paper noted that "many of the EMEs with the largest corporate securities markets relative to GDP, including Chile, Korea and South Africa, also have larger private pension, insurance, and/or mutual fund sectors" (ibid.: 28). The paper claimed that these investors "can be effective in providing long-term funds and are less likely to exacerbate volatility by selling into short-term corrections" (ibid.: 28).

4.2   REGIONAL EXPERIENCES

Emerging Asia

Prior to this global policy debate, several concrete measures to develop capital markets had been undertaken by emerging economies. At the end of 2002, ASEAN + 3 (Southeast Asian Nations (ASEAN), the People's Republic of China, Japan, and the Republic of Korea) launched the Asian Bond Markets Initiative (ABMI). The purpose of this Initiative was to develop bond markets, with a specific focus on LCBMs, and to "promote regional financial cooperation and integration to strengthen financial stability and reduce the region's vulnerability to the sudden reversal of capital flows" (Asian Development Bank 2017: 5). Another Asian Development Bank (ADB) publication highlighted institutional capacities in Hong Kong and Singapore:

> (i) government bond yield curves extending up to 10 years, which are used as a reliable basis for pricing corporate bonds; (ii) efficient market infrastructure; (iii) sound regulatory environment; (iv) good secondary market liquidity; (v) liberal tax treatment of bonds; (vi) diverse issuer profile (consisting of triple-A rated supranational agencies, multinational corporations, and local corporations); and (vii) strong commitment by the authorities to develop and foster the domestic debt markets. In addition, bond markets in both countries are open to foreign investors, with hardly any restrictions and reporting requirements. (Fabella and Madhur 2003: 6)

Seeking to emanate this success, several countries set out on a process of institutional upgrade. During the initial phase (2002–2007), a period in which there was significant capital inflow into the region, action was taken to build the infrastructure needed to support and boost the supply and demand for local currency bonds in a number of ways. Settlement systems were promoted, and domestic credit rating agency capacity increased. The dissemination of key information was organised through a specially designed website (www.AsianBondsOnline .adb.org). In many cases the Initiative was pushing on an open door; Malaysia, for example, had taken steps since the late 1980s to grow its capital markets, with the central bank supporting development of the government and housing-backed (Cagamas) bond secondary markets through the setting up of principle dealer and auction systems (Adhikari et al. 1999; Rethel 2010; Hardie and Rethel 2019). Subsequently Malaysia adopted a ten-year Capital Market Masterplan in 2001.

The Republic of Korea had also adopted a Capital Market Promotion Act back in 1968 and the Bank of Korea (BOK) facilitated development through, for example, introducing a settlement system. The proportion of corporate debt to total debt peaked at over 60 per cent by the 1980s, but sterilisation measures to counter inflationary risks from inflows started to bring this proportion down (Asian Development Bank 2018). Despite progress, it was concluded that "institutional flaws in financial markets amplified the crisis" (ibid.: 3) and therefore the Republic of Korea was still very much part of the initiative, with aspirations to increase market transparency, increase the number of participants and adopt "international standards".

The most notable development, however, has been in China, and also Thailand (see Figure 4.1). Focusing on China, both economic and financial systems have undergone radical transformation since 1979, yet remain distinct to those of neighbouring countries. Processes of decentralisation pushed economic power outwards from central to local government, and towards State Owned Enterprises (SOEs), while at the same time a strong central grip was

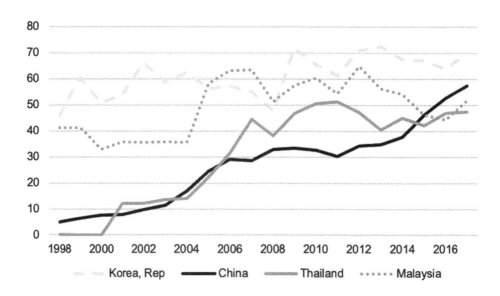

Source: The Global Financial Development Database, World Bank.

Figure 4.1   Outstanding domestic private debt securities to GDP %, Asia

maintained on banking. Rapid development sparked demand for huge extensions of credit, and as quantity was the focus over quality, the result was a high incidence of non-performing loans, many of which were subsequently written off. The process of loan extension and write off – particularly at the point of the Asian crisis – lacked transparency, leading to accusations of incomprehensibility and fragility across the banking system akin to, if not worse than, what was seen in the worst affected countries. However, because China had not liberalised its capital account fully, it was almost entirely spared from the crisis, holding strong against devaluation and in fact making significant contributions to the IMF loans for neighbouring countries in crisis (Sharma 2003).

China was not spared, however, from internal pressure to reform its financial system (ibid.). Many changes have been made to bring banking to some level of comparability with international standards. New state development banks form part of a push to more clearly delineate between state-directed investments and investments made on the basis of bank evaluation by "commercial" banks, in the name of increasing efficiency in capital allocation. To clean up balance sheets and establish some level of capital adequacy, non-performing loans have been transferred to special institutions, and programmes of recapitalisation have been undertaken. At the same time, and relatedly, there have been big steps taken to create bond markets (Aglietta and Maarek 2007). An end to monetary financing of the state first led to booming large sovereign debt markets, and subsequently corporate markets have also taken off. State presence is felt on both sides of the market, through links with those firms able to issue debt, and with the banks able to hold it.

The measures across the region have been matched by significant, if not regular, market growth. The Deputy Governor of the Bank of Japan, making the keynote speech to the Asia Securities Industry and Financial Markets Association (ASIFMA) annual conference 2019, noted that:

> Asia's capital markets have experienced remarkable growth since the Asian financial crisis in the late 1990s. Asia's share of global stock market capitalization soared from 1 percent in 2000 to 15 percent in 2017. Notably, the amount outstanding in local currency bond markets in Asia as a share of GDP in 2018 increased to more than double that in 2000. Obviously, the rapid expansion of Asian economies has driven the growth of the capital markets in the region. At the same time, the collective efforts of market participants, policy makers, and regulators both at national and regional levels have contributed to market liberalization and enhancement of market infrastructures in Asia. (Amamiya 2019)

Importantly, these developments occurred without a substantial privatisation of pension systems. South Korea, for example, partly funded its national pension system, which has grown to be the third largest pension fund in the world, but remains under state direction, and also retains a defined benefit scheme for the majority of its population, ensuring some level of retirement income adequacy. In China institutional investors, such as pension funds, have played a minor role to date, with the main purchaser of its booming bond markets being banks, and the main issuers being SOEs: 82 per cent of the corporate debt market was SOE debt in 2018 (Molnar and Lu 2019). The role of pension funds is expected to grow in the near future – in fact one reason put forward for growing private bond markets is to provide suitable assets for emerging pension and insurance funds which are expected to deliver welfare to replace the "iron bowl" system of welfare provision via SOEs (Aglietta and Maarek 2007; Zhu and Walker 2018). In this way, causation is turned on its head in the Chinese context, with the egg coming before the chicken. These funds, however, will still not be private institutions: the majority of Chinese Pension assets are managed by the National Council for Social Security Fund, a State institution which manages an increasing proportion of the assets for the public retirement system, which has also been receiving share transfers of several Chinese SOEs (KPMG 2020).

Latin America

The experience of Asia presents commonalities but also important differences to the policy agenda in Latin America. The Inter-American Development Bank commissioned research eventually published as the 2008 book *Bond Markets in Latin America: On the Verge of a Big Bang?* (Borensztein et al. 2008a). The authors presented the benefits of market development and documented the recent divergent experiences of countries in the region (see Figure 4.2).

As elsewhere, the benefits of LCBMs were seen as the reduction of currency mismatches arising from borrowing in the major international currencies, and also a reduction in the impact of banking crises on the broader economy: "The corporate bond market plays a key role in the financial system, providing cheap and stable financing for large, well-established corporations, leaving banks to specialize in lending to borrowers for which information asymmetries are greater" (Borensztein et al. 2008b: 1).

The Chilean fixed-income market around 2008 was similar in size to Korea's, following several phases of financial reform after 1973. According to Braun and Briones, "[f]inancial

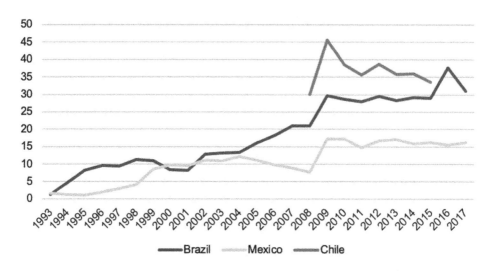

Source: The Global Financial Development Database, World Bank.

Figure 4.2   Outstanding domestic private debt securities to GDP %, Latin America

repression reached a peak" under disposed President Allende (Braun and Briones 2008: 153) and new thinking saw early measures to "free" interest rates from taxation as well as broad privatisation of the banking sector. The 1980s saw the introduction of private funded pensions, as an outright replacement for state pension provision and thus with mandated worker contributions. A banking crisis was followed by new prudential laws regarding for example reserve requirements, throwing some sand in the banking system and creating demand for government short term securities. Bankruptcy laws were also updated. During the 1990s capital controls were removed and a floating exchange rate was adopted. In addition, the state voluntarily started aiming for structural surpluses. Braun and Briones saw this in particular as a key catalyst for growth; public debt was considered to have been "crowding out" the issuance of corporate bonds. In the 2000s new regulations continued to support general capital market growth, with adjustments to the rules on asset allocation for institutional investors, tax reductions on capital gains and measures to enable assets to be used as collateral. Chile has also been commended for achieving macroeconomic stability. Mexico, despite having taken steps to build a domestic investor base through pension reforms, had relatively little development. Castellanos and Martinez posited that up to 2001 "the unstable conditions of the Mexican economy since the introduction of a formal private debt market in 1982 seem to have constantly hindered its development" (Castellanos and Martinez 2008: 63).

    In Brazil, Leal and Carvalhal-da-Silva presented their case study findings as to why in a country where the public debt market was "one of the most liquid and sophisticated among emerging markets" (Leal and Carvalhal-da-Silva 2008: 188) the private market was still relatively small. Their conclusion was that the latter outcome was in fact the consequence of the former, arguing that the "federal government's gargantuan financing needs induce it to pass regulation favoring its own debt to the detriment of the development of the corporate financing market" (ibid.: 210). These regulations included, for example, asset allocation rules for institutional investors, and the role of treasury debt in meeting capital adequacy requirements. Survey results found firms complaining about the cost of issuance, whilst on the demand side, institutional investors had concerns over secondary market liquidity, incomplete establishment of a yield curve and lack of confidence in the bankruptcy framework. However, we can note here looking at Figure 4.2 that Brazil has developed further following the publication of this study, and now stands out as a regional performer.

Drawing on Experience: Some Inconvenient Truths?

Three themes have emerged in the contemporary (post Global Financial Crisis) policy literature, reviewed in section 4.1, regarding what is deemed necessary for success in developing local currency corporate bond markets: first, there is the need for macroeconomic stability – which in many cases is taken to primarily mean tackling rates of inflation; second, developing a domestic investor base, most obviously by privatising pension provision; and third, limiting state expenditure to avoid "crowding out" of the market by large state issuance.

We argue, however, that it is difficult to trace these lessons of best practice back to the actual experiences of countries, especially in the emerging Asia region, as reviewed in section 4.2. Take first the question of the possibility of "crowding out" of the bond markets by the state: this is the suggestion that private bond markets may be being held back where states are issuing too much debt at attractive interest rates. In the case of Chile for example, above, we saw the argument that fiscal austerity was key in enabling the private bond market to flourish. However, it should be noted that Chile is rather an outlier in terms of the reduced size of its outstanding domestic public debt securities to GDP (see Figure 4.3), and therefore there are few grounds for drawing a universal lesson in this regard. On the contrary, developed public sector bond markets are very often a pre-condition for deep private-sector bonds.

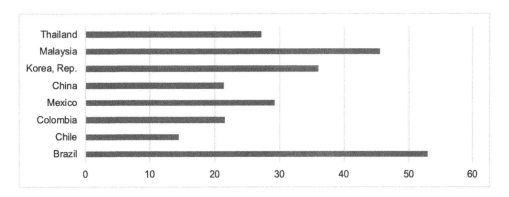

Source: The Global Financial Development Database, World Bank.

Figure 4.3   *Crowding out*

Second, on the question of the proper role for domestic pension funds and other institutional investors, and the possible need to privatise pension systems in order to create the demand required for market development, there does not seem to be clear evidence of a positive relationship. While Korea may have large pension funds, these are state-run. In Brazil and especially in China, bond market development has proceeded with a limited engagement of private pension funds. Again, the experiences of Chile – an outlier – seem to be being put forward as the "one true path" to the end goal of LCBM development without an adequate argument for this position.

Finally, and relatedly, the most contemporary policy contributions seem to seek to bypass or radically reduce the role of the state as a catalyst and guiding hand in the development of evolutionary institutional change in the financial system. But to discount the role of the state in the vast majority of successful cases seems, to us, to be a rewriting of history. In China, Korea and Brazil, the coordinating force of state participation, either through state banks, state investment funds and/or state led enterprises has been fundamental to market development. In our view, the expectation of success in the absence of state participation depends on a false understanding of the determinants of private pension fund behaviour.

4.3   CRITICAL COUNTERVIEWS

In this section we link our theories explaining the behaviour of both foreign and domestic pension funds to this question of whether either foreign or domestic institutional investors are necessary or sufficient for the growth of local currency domestic private bond markets. We argue that the behaviour of foreign funds is ultimately determined by the nature of their liabilities, which are embedded in the conditions of the home economy. As such, the ability of these funds to follow through with patient and stabilising investment abroad is undermined. Where funds are openly adopting liability-driven investment, emerging market assets form part of their growth portfolio, which is structurally volatile and open to more active management. Therefore, even if emerging economies are able to ostensibly reduce currency risk by issuing local currency debt, when the holders of that debt are still largely foreign investors, the currency risk has simply been shifted, not removed altogether. This explains why we have seen what is being termed as "new forms of external vulnerability" (Kaltenbrunner and Painceira 2015) or "original sin redux" (Hofmann, Shim and Shin 2020b) especially during the "taper tantrum" of 2013, and in response to Covid-19, where emerging economies have seen large adjustments in domestic asset prices and the exchange rate despite relatively sound domestic economic conditions.

To understand the behaviour of domestic funds it is helpful again to revisit historical experience. Across the Latin America region and in parts of Central and Eastern Europe – where similarly timed pension reforms created large private domestic funds – there have been different trajectories in terms of asset holdings, caused not only by differences in regulation concerning asset allocations, but more fundamentally by structural factors including distinctions in the variety of capitalism in each country, and by financial subordination. This has meant that pension funds have hit upon a lack of investible domestic assets, and have instead shifted to holding, for example, more foreign assets. These experiences are raising the question of the sequencing necessary to achieve deep, liquid markets.

Foreign Pension Funds: Liability-Driven Investment and New Forms of External Vulnerability/Original Sin Redux

Eichengreen, Hausmann and Panizza (2003) argued that one determinant of currency mismatch was what they termed "original sin" – the difficulty/impossibility for some countries of borrowing from foreign investors in their own currency – a difficulty lying systemically with the organisation of global finance, rather than being somehow the fault of the country in question (Eichengreen, Hausmann and Panizza 2003). As discussed above, enticing foreign institutional investment into emerging economy LCBMs was considered to be sensible by the international community, and one way to reduce original sin, because in addition to being very large cash-pools, institutional investors such as pension funds are also thought uniquely able to invest long-term. Unlike banks with their short-term deposit liabilities, pension commitments are supposedly stable and predictable, and allow for strategies of buying and holding assets over a number of years.

However the experience of the Global Financial Crisis and the subsequent taper tantrum and Corona crisis have showed that despite the rising participation of foreign institutional investors in domestic bond markets in emerging economies, these countries are still subject to massive capital retrenchments and gyrations in asset prices and exchange rates – largely independent of domestic economic conditions. Our view is that this is due to the structural vulnerabilities created by emerging economies' integration into a (spatially) structured and hierarchic international monetary and financial system. Our theory of investor behaviour invalidates the arguments behind the current push for market development as a source of financial stability, which relies on the above characterisation of institutional investors as patient capital.

In Bonizzi and Kaltenbrunner (2019) we argue that structural developments specific to the advanced economy (AE) setting have led to a particular form of liability-driven investment by AE institutional investors. The asset allocation decisions of institutional investors are dependent on the condition of their liabilities – investors seek to hold portfolios that match their liabilities as much as possible. However, a perfect match is only possible at a certain point of maturity and in reality, funds are divided into two distinct categories – those assets that match liabilities, and those that are chosen for growth, with the size of each of these components dependent on factors such as the maturity of the fund, and the funding level. The liabilities of institutional investors depend on spatially contingent factors relating to institutions, regulations and macroeconomic developments in AE. Given this, there is no way for emerging market assets, given their own spatially specificity and "subordinate position in the spatially uneven international financial and monetary system" (ibid.: 422), to match AE investor liabilities. As a consequence, allocations to emerging markets are made in the growth side of the portfolio. These investments are volatile, and are only marginally determined by "fundamentals" in the recipient countries.

Bonizzi and Kaltenbrunner argue that this framework accounts for both the growth in emerging market inflows by AE pension funds and insurance companies following the Global Financial Crisis and their large retrenchments during moments of international market turmoil. Equity market inflation in advanced economies, caused in part (and somewhat ironically) by the growth of institutional investor inflows, ceased at the turn of the century, and equity prices fell calamitously. Partial recovery in prices was again lost with the Global Financial Crisis, while at the same time, quantitative easing combined with commitments to fiscal restraint undermined yields on government bonds. Liabilities are valued by discounting future cashflow commitments using interest rates, so at this point the value of liabilities was being pushed up by the dropping rates at the same time that increased life expectancy was increasing estimations of cashflow commitments. Funding deficits emerged. The only way to close these gaps was through allocating more assets to the growth part of the portfolio. Emerging economy assets were considered ideal for this growth portfolio given their higher returns but also their improvement in macroeconomic fundamentals at the time and apparent diversification benefits.

However, these allocations are re-assessed actively, and capital has been withdrawn whenever conditions changed in the advanced economies, as seen in the 2013 taper tantrum, and in the outbreak of Covid-19. As highlighted in Kaltenbrunner and Painceira (Kaltenbrunner and Painceira 2015) and more recently by the BIS (Hofmann, Shim and Shin 2020a, 2020b) with the concept of "original sin redux", whereas the participation of foreign investors in local currency bond markets reduces the currency mismatch (original sin) of domestic agents, it shifts that same mismatch from the borrower onto the lender. This opens a mechanism where a currency depreciation reduces the value of assets when converted into home currency. Linking this to the analysis above, where emerging market assets are held in the growth component of institutional investor portfolios, depreciation induces sell-offs which can be discerned in higher emerging economy bond spreads. In support of this hypothesis, it is notable that "EMEs with higher shares of foreign ownership in local currency bond markets have experienced significantly larger increases in local currency bond spreads" (Hofmann, Shim and Shin 2020a: 2).

The significance of this explanation is that it undermines the suggestion that somehow, the development of local currency bond markets with the participation of supposedly long-term and patient foreign institutional investors will be enough to address financial instability arising from the subordinate position of emerging markets in the global financial system. The resulting policy conclusion of the BIS is to continue developing local currency bond markets, but do so with a stronger participation of domestic long-term investors, that is, pension funds. This conclusion echoes what was already a tenet of the earlier version of "original sin"; the pathway to absolving this sin relied on "privatizing social security systems to generate a broad constituency of domestic investors opposed to the manipulation by sovereigns of domestic debt markets" (Eichengreen and Hausmann 1999: 36). As the next section shows, drawing on our collaborative work on Colombia and Peru (Bonizzi, Churchill and Guevara 2020), not even that policy recommendation is a panacea to achieve stable source of financing for EMEs.

Domestic Pension Behaviour

The proceeding arguments might all be marshalled in favour of the contemporary policy agenda focus on the necessity of creating a local investor base. However, the empirical evidence presented about the diverging experience of Asia vis-à-vis Latin America should raise doubts about the merits of developing private funded pensions. Despite a much more explicit promotion of private pension funds, on the whole Latin American capital markets remain underdeveloped, and more prone to foreign-induced financial instability. This is despite significant containment of inflation and state expenditure.

Explaining this involves recognising that domestic pension fund behaviour can also be affected by an economy's position of subordinate financial integration. In a study into Peru and Colombia, Bonizzi, Churchill and Guevara (Bonizzi, Churchill and Guevara 2020) focus on structural factors shaping pension fund demand. The "extraversion" of the productive structure "leaves capital markets peripheral to financing domestic companies and limits public sector borrowing", holding down the supply of bonds being issued. At the same time, subordinate financial integration has led to a growing presence of foreign investors in domestic financial markets, adding pressure to demand. This leaves capital markets peripheral to the dynamics of the economy. In these circumstances, domestic institutional investors have turned to foreign financial investments, and to new asset classes. Pension funds in these countries have adopted more sophisticated asset allocations and investment practices including turning to derivatives (Cardozo Alvarado et al. 2015). Most importantly, AFPs (Administradora de Fondos de Pensiones) have been crucial in developing the demand for an "alternative" asset class, a phenomenon common to pension funds in advanced economies (Bonizzi and Churchill 2017). These assets comprise mainly of private equity and infrastructure funds, and to a smaller extent hedge funds (Bonizzi, Churchill and Guevara 2020). Therefore, in the context of subordination, pension privatisation and lack of state involvement have hindered rather than promoted the development of stable local bond markets.

A further concern has to be raised at this point: namely the ability of private pension systems to adequately provide income for retirees. Failure to do this efficiently has, in some cases, led to a (partial) reversal of pension privatisation. The trajectory of Poland in particular rewards scrutiny. In Poland, as in several Latin American countries, radical pension reform was undertaken before the turn of the century shifting pension provision to private funds, with contributions from certain categories of workers mandated by law. As elsewhere, this move was taken partly to reduce fiscal pressures on the state, and partly to develop a domestic investor base (Raddatz and Schmukler 2008), as "the presence of a stable domestic investor base that includes institutional investors is thought to contain yields and foster stability in bond prices and yields" (Andritzky 2010). However, Poland has quite radically changed direction, whilst retaining a similar goal of reducing its requirement for foreign capital.

Following the pension reforms of the 1990s, institutional investors in Poland, including pension funds, quickly became the second largest investor in the Treasury bond market. This development was linked to Poland's ability to weather the 2007–2008 crisis relatively well, where "high investment outlays made by the public sector played an important stabilizing role … [in replacing] … the reduction of investment by the private sector … [and helped] … to sustain internal demand" (Janc, Jurek and Marszalek 2013). Public sector debt "rose by more than 50% between 2007 and 2011" (ibid.). Nonetheless, private pension funds were widely seen to be performing poorly, particularly in relation to their high fees and disappointing returns. Aided by a court ruling that the funds were technically public bodies – due in large part to the mandatory nature of their contributions – a re-nationalisation was undertaken by the PO (Civic Platform) government in 2013. Government bonds were retired, and foreign assets put in the demographic reserve fund (demographic reserve fund FRD). Despite this change in direction, the Public Finance Sector Debt Management Strategy 2017–2020 was still centred around an aspiration to reduce the foreign currency denominated State Treasury debt to less than 30 per cent, and with it the foreign holdings of all state debt. Given that of the domestic holdings, pension funds now held a small proportion of domestic state treasuries, this goal was to be achieved through the domestic banking sector. The state banking sector in particular has been growing in size and aspiration over this timeframe. According to the Commission's 2019 Country Report on Poland, the state "controls about one third of the banking sector, as well as the biggest insurance company" (European Commission 2019). These developments, disparagingly summarised by the FT as a "rush to banking sector socialism" (Miszerak and Rohac 2017), are promoted more optimistically by agents of the state itself.[2]

4.4   CONCLUSIONS

Acknowledging the determinants of the actual rather than the desired behaviour of pension funds – which are often, it must always be remembered, private financial institutions – raises questions concerning the feasibility and/or desirability of the policies being adopted in the name of local currency bond market development, especially given the risks this poses on the provision of adequate retirement income for a country's population. The countries that have achieved most notable growth in their domestic local currency corporate debt markets – for example China and Brazil – have not done so primarily on the back of private domestic investor demand. It has been state banks that have been pivotal in providing a stable growth of demand, and state-led enterprises pivotal in providing a stable growth of supply of bonds underlying market development.

More broadly, the questions regarding the overall benefits of private bond market development remain, in our view, open. From a post-Keynesian perspective, where investment leads savings rather than the opposite, it does not make sense to think of development as being held back where there is a lack of access to international capital, beyond the balance of payment constraint. The argument behind the requirement made on countries to liberalise their capital accounts in recent decades is therefore undermined. Given liberalisation, and the consequences it has on interest rates and exchange volatility for emerging and developing countries due to their subordinate position, it is easy to see why the development of local currency sovereign and corporate debt markets is appealing. However, the argument has not yet convincingly been made that would demonstrate that market-based finance with full capital account liberalisation ("financialisation") enables development as efficiently and safely as a banking system (including state-led development banks) (Scherrer 2017).

NOTES

1.   This connects with another transnational policy discourse under the title of Maximising Finance for Development. This project promotes methods of creating "blended finance" – combining state and multilateral development finance with private international finance – institutional investors, thought to have long-term horizons and lots of cash to invest – for projects working to meet the Sustainable Development Goals (SDGs).
2.   An advertising feature distributed by the FT claims that the institutions in which the state is taking a large part of or total control (e.g. PKO Bank Polski, and the Polish Development Fund (PFR)) are playing a prominent role in "industrial modernisation". Poland is described here as "a dynamic economy that plays to its strengths and knows where it is going" with the ambition to "narrow the economic gap between it and its western neighbour by 2030" (Hesse 2016).

REFERENCES

Adhikari, R., Edwards, D., Hoschka, T., Mundle, S., Oh, S., Rana, P., Shimomoto, Y., Siregar, R., Speck, P., Subramaniam, R., and Cuong, V.V. (1999). Rising to the Challenge in Asia: A Study of Financial Markets: An Overview. *Asian Development Bank, 1* Manila, Philippines.

Aglietta, M. and Maarek, P. (2007). Developing the Bond Market in China: The Next Step Forward in Financial Reform. *Economie Internationale, 111*, 29–53.

Amamiya, M. (2019). Development of Asia's Capital Markets: Roles and Challenges Keynote Speech, *ASIFMA Annual Conference 2019*, 10 October. https://www.bis.org/review/r191010b.htm (Accessed: 9 January 2021).

Andritzky, J.R. (2010). Government Bonds and Their Investors: What Are the Facts and Do They Matter? *IMF Working Paper WP/12/158.* https://www.imf.org/external/pubs/ft/wp/2012/wp12158 .pdf (Accessed: 26 August 2020).

Asian Development Bank (2017). The Asian Bond Markets Initiative: Policy Maker Achievements and Challenges. *Asian Development Bank.* https://www.adb.org/publications/asian-bond-markets -initiative (Accessed: 26 August 2020).

Asian Development Bank (2018). ASEAN+3 Bond Market Guide Republic of Korea. *Asian Development Bank.* https://www.adb.org/publications/asean3-bond-market-guide-2018-republic-korea (Accessed: 26 August 2020).

BIS (2019). Establishing Viable Capital Markets: Report Submitted by a Working Group Established by the Committee on the Global Financial System. https://www.bis.org/publ/cgfs62.htm (Accessed: 24 August 2020).

Bonizzi, B. (2013). Financialization in Developing and Emerging Countries. *International Journal of Political Economy, 42*(4), 83–107.

Bonizzi, B. and Churchill, J. (2017). Pension Funds and Financialisation in the European Union. *Revista De Economia Mundial, 46*, 71–90.

Bonizzi, B., Churchill, J. and Guevara, D. (2020). Variegated Financialisation and Pension Fund Asset Demand: The Case of Colombia and Peru. *Socio-Economic Review*, mwaa033, https://doi. org/10.1093/ser/mwaa033.

Bonizzi, B. and Kaltenbrunner, A. (2019). Liability-Driven Investment and Pension Fund Exposure to Emerging Markets: A Minskyan Analysis. *Environment and Planning A: Economy and Space, 51*(2), 420–439.

Borensztein, E., Cowan, K., Eichengreen, B. and Panizza, U. (eds.) (2008a). *Bond Markets in Latin America: On the Verge of a Big Bang?* Cambridge, MA; London: The MIT Press.

Borensztein, E., Cowan, K., Eichengreen, B. and Panizza, U. (2008b). Building Bond Markets in Latin America. In Borensztein, E., Cowan, K., Eichengreen, B. and Panizza, U. (eds.), *Bond Markets in Latin America: On the Verge of a Big Bang?* (1–29). Cambridge, MA; London: The MIT Press.

Braun, M. and Briones, I. (2008). Development of the Chilean Corporate Bond Market. In Borensztein, E., Cowan, K., Eichengreen, B. and Panizza, U. (eds.), *Bond Markets in Latin America: On the Verge of a Big Bang?* (151–185). Cambridge, MA; London: The MIT Press.

Cardozo Alvarado, N., Rassa Robayo, J.S. and Rojas Moreno, J.S. (2015). Caracterización del mercado de derivados cambiarios en Colombia, *ODEON, 9*, 7–79. doi: http://dx.doi.org/10.18601/17941113.n9 .02 (Accessed: 9 January 2021).

Castellanos, S.G. and Martinez, L. (2008). Development of the Mexican Bond Market. In Borensztein, E., Cowan, K., Eichengreen, B. and Panizza, U. (eds.), *Bond Markets in Latin America: On the Verge of a Big Bang?* (51–89). Cambridge, MA; London: The MIT Press.

Corsetti, G., Pesenti, P. and Roubini, N. (1999). What Caused the Asian Currency and Financial Crisis? *Japan and the World Economy, 11*(3), 305–373.

Eichengreen, B. and Hausmann, R. (1999). Exchange Rates and Financial Fragility. *National Bureau of Economic Research.* https://ideas.repec.org/p/nbr/nberwo/7418.html (Accessed: 24 August 2020).

Eichengreen, B. and Hausmann, R. (eds.) (2005). *Other People's Money: Debt Denomination and Financial Instability in Emerging Market Economies.* Chicago and London: University of Chicago Press.

Eichengreen, B., Hausmann, R. and Panizza, U. (2003). Currency Mismatches, Debt Intolerance and Original Sin: Why They Are Not The Same and Why It Matters. NBER Working Paper Series. *National Bureau of Economic Research (NBER)*. https://www.nber.org/papers/w10036 (Accessed: 26 August 2020).

European Commission (2019). *Country Report: Poland*. https://ec.europa.eu/info/sites/info/files/file _import/2019-european-semester-country-report-poland_en.pdf (Accessed: 26 August 2020).

Fabella, R. and Madhur, S. (2003). Bond Market Development in East Asia: Issues and Challenges. *ERD Working Paper Series No. 35*. https://www.adb.org/publications/bond-market-development-east-asia -issues-and-challenges (Accessed: 26 August 2020).

G20 Finance Ministers and Central Bank Governors (2011). *G20 Action Plan to Support the Development of Local Currency Bond Markets*. G20. https://www.mofa.go.jp/policy/economy/g20_summit/2011/ pdfs/annex03.pdf (Accessed: 26 August 2020).

Hardie, I. and Rethel, L. (2019). Financial Structure and the Development of Domestic Bond Markets in Emerging Economies. *Business and Politics*, 21(1), 86–112.

Hesse, C. (2016). Polish Pension Fund Reform: Getting Away With a Black Eye. *EME Strategy Report 7 July 2017, Joh. Berenberg, Gossler & Co. KG* distributed commercially by *Financial Times*.

Hofmann, B., Shim, I. and Shin, H.S. (2020a). Original Sin Redux and Policy Responses in Emerging Market Economies during the COVID-19 Pandemic. In Djankov, S. and Panizza, U. (eds.), *COVID-19 in Developing Economies* (353–361). VOX EU CEPR. https://voxeu.org/content/covid-19-developing -economies (Accessed: 2 January 2021).

Hofmann, B., Shim, I. and Shin, H.S. (2020b). Emerging Market Economy Exchange Rates and Local Currency Bond Markets amid the Covid-19 Pandemic. *Bank for International Settlements*. https:// www.bis.org/publ/bisbull05.htm (Accessed: 31 July 2020).

IMF (2013). *Local Currency Bond Markets – A Diagnostic Framework*. http://www.oecd.org/daf/fin/ public-debt/Local-Currency-Bond-Markets-Diagnostic-Framework-2013.pdf (Accessed: 26 August 2020).

IMF (2016). *Staff Note for the G20 IFAWG Development of Local Currency Bond Markets Overview of Recent Developments and Key Themes*. IMF. https://www.imf.org/external/np/g20/pdf/2018/061518 .pdf (Accessed: 26 August 2020).

Janc, A., Jurek, M. and Marszalek, P. (2013). Studies in Financial Systems No 7 Financial System in Poland. *Financialisation, Economy, Society & Sustainable Development (FESSUD) Project*. http:// fessud.eu/wp-content/uploads/2012/08/Poland-Studies-July-2013.pdf (Accessed: 26 August 2020).

Kaltenbrunner, A. and Painceira, J.P. (2015). Developing Countries' Changing Nature of Financial Integration and New Forms of External Vulnerability: The Brazilian Experience. *Cambridge Journal of Economics*, 39(5), 1281–1306.

KPMG (2020). China Pensions Outlook: Looking Ahead after a Year of Change. https://assets.kpmg/ content/dam/kpmg/cn/pdf/en/2020/03/china-pensions-outlook-looking-ahead-after-a-year-of-change .pdf (Accessed: 11 January 2020).

Leal, R.P.C. and Carvalhal-da-Silva, A.L. (2008). Development of the Brazilian Bond Market. In Borensztein, E., Cowan, K., Eichengreen, B. and Panizza, U. (eds.), *Bond Markets in Latin America: On the Verge of a Big Bang?* (185–217). Cambridge, MA; London: The MIT Press.

Miszerak, M. and Rohac, D. (2017). Poland's Rush to Banking Sector Socialism. *Financial Times*, 30 June.

Molnar, M. and Lu, J. (2019). State-Owned Firms behind China's Corporate Debt *Economics Department Working Papers No. 1536 OECD*. https://www.sipotra.it/wp-content/uploads/2019/03/ State-owned-firms-behind-China-s-corporate-debt.pdf (Accessed: 11 January 2021).

Raddatz, C. and Schmukler, S.L. (2008). Pension Funds and Capital Market Development: How Much Bang for the Buck? *World Bank*. https://openknowledge.worldbank.org/handle/10986/6308?locale -attribute=en (Accessed: 24 August 2020).

Rethel, L. (2010). Financialisation and the Malaysian Political Economy. *Globalizations*, 7(4), 489–506.

Scherrer, C. (ed.) (2017). *Public Banks in the Age of Financialization*. Cheltenham, UK; Northampton, MA, USA: Edward Elgar Publishing.

Sharma, S.D. (2003). *The Asian Financial Crisis: Crisis, Reform and Recovery*. Manchester and New York: Manchester University Press.

The World Economic Forum (2016). *Accelerating Capital Markets Development in Emerging Economies: Country Case Studies*. The World Economic Forum. http://www3.weforum.org/docs/WEF_accelerating-capital-markets-development-in-emerging-economies.pdf (Accessed: 26 August 2020).

World Bank Group (2012). *Supporting the Development of Local Currency Bond Markets: Interim Report on Implementing the G20 Action Plan on the Development of Local Currency Bond Markets*. https://documents.worldbank.org/en/publication/documents-reports/documentdetail/2757814 68335977188/supporting-the-development-of-local-currency-bond-markets-interim-progress -report-on-implementing-the-g20-action-plan-on-the-development-of-local-currency-bond-markets (Accessed: 26 August 2020).

Zhu, H. and Walker, A. (2018). Pension System Reform in China: Who Gets What Pensions? *Social Policy & Administration, 52*(7), 1410–1424.

5. The distribution of dividends of multinational banks operating in Latin America

Mimoza Shabani

Since the 1990s foreign bank participation has increased significantly in Latin America. The presence of foreign banks in host countries, particularly in emerging markets, has been well documented in the literature, suggesting that foreign banks are more efficient in developing countries (Demirguc-Kunt and Huizinga 1998; Claessens et al. 1998). Indeed, foreign banks can increase competition which could lead to lower interest rates for borrowers (Levine 1996) and promote economic growth. Foreign banks could indeed be in a better position to provide credit, and hence boost domestic investment in host economies, at a lower rate than domestic banks mainly due to the support they receive from their parent bank.

On the other hand, foreign banks can be in a better position to cherry-pick their customers hence leaving other banks bearing the risk of the rest of the customers. Therefore, a higher share of foreign banks in the market reduces the profitability of domestic banks (Claessens et al. 1998). Indeed, profitability plays a decisive role for banks setting up overseas operations and, overall, foreign banks tend to outperform domestic banks in host countries. This could suggest that the earnings of multinational banks could leave the host country in the form of dividend repatriation and hence leave little for re-investment (Gonzalez 2013). However, the repatriation of profits, in the form of dividends, of foreign banks is not well documented in the literature.

This chapter adds to the literature on international banking by analysing some of the activities of multinational banks that operate in countries in Latin America through foreign subsidiaries. Using bank-level data on all multinational banks that operate in Argentina, Brazil, Chile, Colombia, Mexico and Peru, this chapter presents evidence on dividends paid to the shareholders of the parent company. The findings suggest that dividend payments in most countries in Latin America have been rather volatile over the last few years. When looking at the dividend payout ratio, the analysis suggests that, on average, foreign banks that operate in Mexico, Brazil and Chile pay a higher proportion of their earnings in dividend to the shareholders of their parent banks. Furthermore, this chapter argues that macroeconomic conditions in host countries could help explain the dividend repatriation of foreign banks.

The analysis begins with a brief overview of the foreign banks that operate in the six Latin American countries. Given the crucial role banks play in the economy by means of providing the necessary credit to companies to finance their investment opportunities we examine the lending portfolio of these banks that reside in the selected countries. The last section of the chapter discusses the dividend repatriation activities of the multinational banks discussing the implication of this on the economies of host countries.

5.1 AN OVERVIEW OF BANKING SECTORS AND DATA DESCRIPTION

We obtain information on foreign subsidiaries of multinational banks that operate in Latin America, namely Argentina, Chile, Mexico, Brazil, Peru and Colombia, from the BankFocus database. Our sample includes all foreign subsidiaries[1] that are at least 50 percent owned by the parent bank and hence the parent has a controlling stake. We consider only banks with at least one foreign subsidiary in each Latin American country. For those banking groups that have more than one subsidiary in each country, the consolidated banking group is considered.

We also obtain information on all available domestic banks in each Latin American country. We further distinguish between privately owned and state-owned domestic banks. We consider a bank to be state-owned if the government owns at least 50 percent of the shares.

In total we have 103 foreign-owned banks and 129 domestic banks. Figure 5.1 shows the size of the banking sector for each country as a share of GDP. Brazil has the largest banking sector, by asset, relative to the GDP over the period 2013–2019.[2] Chile, on the other hand, seems to have exceeded Brazil's level with the country's banking assets accounting for 123 percent of GDP, as of 2019. That is a significant increase from the 2013 levels of nearly 84 percent. Similarly, Colombia is associated with higher banking sector size over the period, increasing from 26 percent to 60 percent of GDP in 2019. However, the reverse can be observed for Peru's banking sector showing a slightly lower share of its banking assets relative to GDP. The size of the Mexican banking sector, however, seems to have remained almost constant, accounting for, on average, 43 percent of GDP.

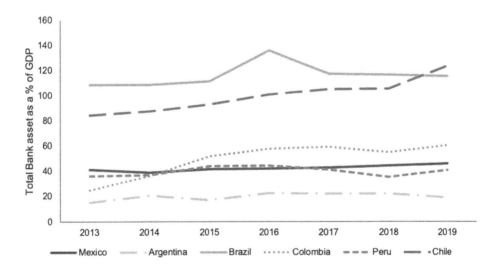

Notes: Total assets are obtained from the financial statements available from BankFocus. GDP is obtained from World Bank and is in current prices.
Source: BankFocus and World Bank, author's calculation.

Figure 5.1   *Total banking assets as a share of GDP*

Foreign bank participation has also been stable over the last few years in Mexico, as evident in Figure 5.2. The share of foreign bank assets to total banking sector assets in Mexico accounts for around 70 percent. Peru is another Latin American country for which the share of total bank assets held by foreign banks is high, accounting for more than 50 percent of total banking sector assets. Conversely, Brazil has the lowest foreign bank participation with banking assets held by foreign-owned banks being 15 percent of the total bank assets. Foreign bank participation increased significantly during the 1990s in Brazil, however by mid-2000 they retreated, the reason being, amongst other things, the low profitability of the sector (Fachada 2008).

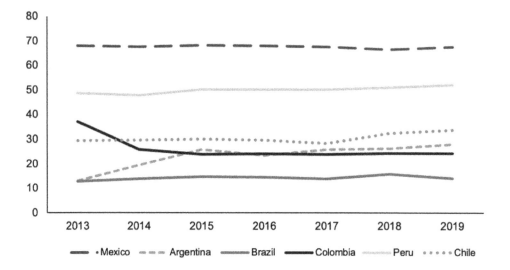

Source: BankFocus, author's calculation.

Figure 5.2   Share of banking assets held by foreign-owned institutions

Whilst financial development is argued to promote economic growth (King and Levine 1993)[3,4] the overall size of the financial system, in particular the banking sector, received much attention during the financial crisis of 2007–2009. However, the evidence is mixed in the sense that the crisis highlighted that countries with large banking sectors relative to the size of the economy, such as Iceland, faced similar banking distress in the aftermath of the crisis, as those countries with relatively smaller banking sectors such as Italy and Greece. Hence whilst the overall size of the banking sector as a share of the economy might not be a source (or indicator in increasing the vulnerability) of bringing about a financial crisis, Kakes and Nijskens (2018) suggest that some indicators of banking sector size could be a source of financial fragility. They find a positive correlation between various variables such as credit volume, bank leverage, non-deposit funding and the market share of the largest banks operating in the sector, and financial distress. They add to the literature considering the possible negative relationship between finance and growth. A large banking sector that exceeds beyond a certain level could indeed turn this relationship negative or insignificant (Easterly et al. 2000; Cecchetti and

Kharroubi 2012; Bijlsma et al. 2018). On the other hand, the financial fragility could arise given the nature of the financial sector being inherently unstable (Kindleberger 1978; Minsky 1992).

Attention has also been given to the size of individual banks operating in a given economy (Davies and Tracey 2014, Laeven et al. 2014) as a possible source of financial instability. Large banks tend to be highly leveraged and rely more on wholesale funding which could make them more vulnerable to financial risk. For instance, focusing on foreign-owned institutions that operate in Mexico, BBVA Bancomer accounts for nearly 22 percent of the market share, by asset size. This is followed by Citibanamex and Santander, both having a near-13 percent market share. HSBC and Scotiabank are at the top of foreign bank participation in Mexico, albeit with a much smaller market share, ranging between 5 percent and 7 percent of the total banking sector assets. Argentina's banking sector share of the economy is smaller than the other selected Latin American countries, accounting for nearly 20 percent, with Santander dominating the market. Its asset size accounts for just over 12 percent of total bank assets. This is followed by BBVA with nearly 9 percent of the market and HSBC having nearly 65 percent of total banking sector assets. Looking at Table 5.1, it can be seen that loan-to-deposit of foreign bank operating in Mexico has increased slightly over the period between 2013 and 2019, suggesting that the reliance of non-deposit funding has increased. However, the wholesale funding ratio of these banks seem to have declined since 2013. Domestic banks, on the other hand, seem to be more reliant on wholesale funding, which is significantly higher than foreign banks. A possible explanation for this could be that parent banks provide funds to their subsidiaries via the internal capital markets (De Haas and Van Lelyveld 2014). Mexican domestic banks also seem to have a higher leverage ratio than foreign banks but are less profitable.

Santander also dominates the Brazilian banking sector as a foreign bank having 10 percent of the total banking sector assets. JP Morgan and BNP Paribas on the other hand have a 1 percent combined market share of total banking assets. As discussed above, foreign bank participation in Brazil is relatively small with domestic state-owned banks dominating the sector. In particular, Itau Unibanco, Banco Bradesco, Banco do Brazil, Caixa and BNDES have more than 75 percent of the total banking sector assets. Out of the top five domestic banks in Brazil, three, namely Caixa, Banco do Brazil and BNDES, are state-owned banking institutions. Similar to the case of Mexico, foreign banks operating in Brazil rely less on wholesale funding but are much less profitable than domestic banks. Perhaps lower growth opportunities and volatile economic conditions[5] could be an explanation for the relatively low foreign bank participation in the Brazilian banking sector. Santander is also a significant bank in Chile and Peru, accounting for nearly 20 percent of the total banking assets in the former but with a much smaller share in Peru, having only a 1.4 percent share in total banking assets. In Peru, nearly 16 percent of banking assets are held by Scotiabank, a Canadian bank. Scotiabank also operates in Peru with a significant market share by asset size, accounting for more than 13 percent of total assets.

Foreign banks that operate in Peru seem to be more profitable than domestic banks, despite having similar wholesale funding ratios in 2019, as Table 5.1 depicts. In the period between 2015 and 2017, their reliance on wholesale funding was lower than domestic Peruvian banks. However, foreign banks in Peru seem to be more leveraged than domestic banks. Foreign banks in Peru play an important role in providing credit in the economy, supplying more than

65 percent of the total credit. However, the credit volume seems to be funded by loans issued in the domestic market, as reflected in the higher loan-to-deposit ratio associated with foreign banks, which is higher than that of the domestic banks.

5.2   LENDING PORTFOLIO AND DIVIDEND REPATRIATION

The banking system plays a key role in providing credit for investment opportunities and thus contributing to economic growth. The argument in favour of emerging economies opening to foreign bank ownership is indeed that these banks increase the funding available to domestic investment projects as well as contribute to the overall supply of credit in the economy (Dages et al. 2000). However, the literature on credit supply to small businesses suggests otherwise. Indeed, Berger et al. (2001), using a rich dataset containing income and balance sheet statements of 61,295 Argentinean firms for 1998, find that foreign bank lending to small businesses tends to be significantly lower than larger ones. Similarly, Clarke et al. (2005), using bank level data over the mid-1990s for Argentina, Chile, Colombia and Peru, find that foreign banks lend less to small businesses than domestic banks.

Due to data limitations, this study cannot distinguish loans to businesses by business size, but it can observe the contribution of foreign banks in lending to different sectors in the economy. Table 5.1 exhibits that foreign banks in Mexico do indeed provide more credit than domestic banks. Around 69 percent of the total loans in the economy were provided by foreign banks in 2019. Foreign banks also outperform domestic banks in all loan categories such as mortgages, consumer and corporate loans. Therefore, foreign-owned banks play a vital role in the Mexican economy in supplying credit to both households and corporations. The Peruvian economy also benefits from foreign banks that reside in the country with around 65 percent of the loans being made by them in 2019. Foreign banks also dominate the mortgage market, providing more than 90 percent of total mortgages, increasing significantly from 66 percent in 2013. Foreign banks also provide the vast majority of corporate loans, accounting for more than 90 percent.

In the other four countries, namely Argentina, Brazil, Colombia and Chile, it can be observed that the supply of credit is mainly provided by domestic banks rather than foreign banks. In the case of Chile, nearly 40 percent of mortgages, consumer loans and credit to corporations are provided by foreign banks. These contributions are smaller in the case of Argentina, for which it ranges between 30 percent and 36 percent. Foreign banks located in Brazil provide only nearly 11 percent of total credit in the economy. However, the contribution in each loan category tends to be rather volatile over the period 2013–2019. Credit to corporations increased from nearly 22 percent in 2013 to nearly 35 percent in 2015–2017 and then decreased again in 2019.

Dividend Repatriation

Whilst the foreign operations of banks in Latin America have been well documented in the literature, little is known about the dividend payments of those banks to the main stakeholders, in our case the parent bank. Banks expand internationally by setting up branches or subsidiaries. Subsidiaries are in effect a separate legal entity in which the parent bank can have a large stake, or wholly own it. Therefore, and especially in the case in which it is wholly owned by the

Table 5.1   *Banking indicators of domestic and foreign-owned banks*

Brazil

	2013	2015	2017	2019
Domestic banks				
Loan-to-deposit	1.84	2.06	1.70	1.46
Deposit-to-asset	0.26	0.24	0.26	0.29
Leverage	14.68	14.87	12.30	11.36
Wholesale funding	0.45	0.48	0.45	0.43
ROE	17.85	18.97	14.59	18.76
Foreign banks				
Loan-to-deposit	1.57	1.73	1.36	1.29
Deposit-to-asset	0.13	0.21	0.23	0.24
Leverage	23.72	11.95	11.10	12.76
Wholesale funding	0.17	0.43	0.37	0.32
ROE	0.25	0.78	0.98	1.49

Mexico

	2013	2015	2017	2019
Domestic banks				
Loan-to-deposit	1.15	1.18	1.01	1.14
Deposit-to-asset	0.40	0.41	0.44	0.41
Leverage	11.45	10.90	11.80	10.47
Wholesale funding	0.52	0.49	0.44	0.49

Colombia

	2013	2015	2017	2019
Domestic banks				
Loan-to-deposit	1.05	1.16	1.20	1.20
Deposit-to-asset	0.59	0.56	0.58	0.57
Leverage	7.77	9.21	8.25	7.98
Wholesale funding	0.23	0.25	0.23	0.24
ROE	12.50	16.24	11.77	14.54
Foreign banks				
Loan-to-deposit	0.91	1.04	1.03	1.04
Deposit-to-asset	0.77	0.66	0.67	0.65
Leverage	11.68	10.76	10.93	10.45
Wholesale funding	0.12	0.19	0.20	0.20
ROE	14.62	13.26	9.37	11.55

Peru

	2013	2015	2017	2019
Domestic banks				
Loan-to-deposit	0.69	0.89	0.95	0.65
Deposit-to-asset	0.64	0.53	0.55	0.62
Leverage	5.97	6.66	6.91	6.76
Wholesale funding	0.16	0.28	0.27	0.18

Argentina

	2013	2015	2017	2019
ROE	11.42	10.37	13.73	13.52
Foreign banks				
Loan-to-deposit	1.01	1.03	1.03	1.06
Deposit-to-asset	0.43	0.44	0.47	0.47
Leverage	9.41	9.97	9.89	9.46
Wholesale funding	0.27	0.25	0.21	0.21
ROE	15.72	13.64	17.19	18.45
Domestic banks				
Loan-to-deposit	1.10	0.85	0.80	0.72
Deposit-to-asset	0.45	0.54	0.59	0.61
Leverage	9.96	9.36	9.36	9.13
Wholesale funding	0.42	0.31	0.24	0.20
ROE	26.25	30.03	18.91	25.02
Foreign banks				
Loan-to-deposit	2.10	0.79	0.85	0.68
Deposit-to-asset	0.63	0.68	0.69	0.68
Leverage	7.79	8.61	9.29	8.41

Chile

	2013	2015	2017	2019
ROE	10.52	11.16	7.23	12.28
Foreign banks				
Loan-to-deposit	0.91	1.05	1.09	1.15
Deposit-to-asset	0.69	0.61	0.63	0.59
Leverage	8.80	9.02	7.13	7.40
Wholesale funding	0.17	0.19	0.15	0.18
ROE	14.87	16.70	13.30	14.22
Domestic banks				
Loan-to-deposit	1.10	1.12	1.10	1.20
Deposit-to-asset	0.63	0.61	0.62	0.55
Leverage	13.55	13.91	13.10	14.12
Wholesale funding	0.22	0.24	0.24	0.27
ROE	17.02	15.75	14.31	13.56
Foreign banks				
Loan-to-deposit	1.37	1.33	4.98	1.45
Deposit-to-asset	0.54	0.53	0.15	0.46
Leverage	10.58	12.02	37.80	14.83

	2013	2015	2017	2019
Wholesale funding	0.15	0.09	0.14	0.12
ROE	26.89	24.70	16.85	41.96

	2013	2015	2017	2019
Wholesale funding	0.29	0.26	0.09	0.28
ROE	15.58	13.74	10.17	14.59

Notes: Loan-to-deposit is equal to the share of gross loans and advances to customers to customer deposits, Leverage is calculated as the ratio of assets to equity, Wholesale funding represents the share of wholesale funding to total assets, ROE is computed as a share of net income to shareholders' equity.

Table 5.2   Share of foreign bank lending (%)

Country	Year	Total loans	Mortgage loans	Consumer loans	Corporate loans
Mexico	2013	66.91	86.9	92.8	75.6
	2015	66.60	86.6	90.7	74.1
	2017	69.37	88.4	89.0	82.7
	2019	69.18	89.4	85.5	84.3
Argentina	2013	28.41	4.8	26.8	28.7
	2015	29.18	9.1	27.7	33.0
	2017	30.40	11.4	31.8	37.5
	2019	29.15	24.2	31.5	36.3
Brazil	2013	5.7	1.6	11.9	21.8
	2015	11.4	30.0	6.9	35.8
	2017	10.2	24.8	5.9	34.4
	2019	10.7	30.6	26.5	22.7
Colombia	2013	26.9	41.2	17.3	29.8
	2015	24.1	33.3	15.1	37.9
	2017	23.9	32.7	16.5	33.2
	2019	24.2	25.0	25.7	26.9
Peru	2013	57.8	66.1	32.6	88.0
	2015	58.5	68.0	36.6	90.0
	2017	57.9	69.3	37.0	86.4
	2019	65.3	92.2	41.1	96.0
Chile	2013	30.88	45.9	38.6	31.3
	2015	30.73	45.4	39.8	31.8
	2017	30.31	34.5	40.3	38.2
	2019	34.06	39.4	39.8	39.1

Notes: Total loans represent the share of gross loans and advances of foreign-owned banks to total gross loans and advances. Mortgage, consumer and corporate loans represent the share of each loan category of foreign institutions to the total.

parent bank, any profit that is generated in host countries where foreign subsidiaries operate is distributed to the parent company partly in a form of dividend repatriation. We have mainly included those subsidiaries that are wholly owned by a bank headquartered outside the legal jurisdiction in which the subsidiary operates. Dividend payments made to the shareholders of the parent bank[6] are reported in the financial reports available from BankFocus.

Overall, we find that bank dividend payments in the countries selected are rather volatile.[7] This is consistent with the dividend payments in Emerging Markets reported by the Henderson Group.[8] According to this study, the region reported an increase by more than 10 percent in dividend payments as of the end of 2019, with Brazil being the main contributor of our selected six Latin America countries, with a total of over $2.3 billion dividend payments paid in the first quarter of 2019. This was followed by Chile, Mexico and Colombia. The Henderson Group also reports that the financial sector, with banks being the most significant group, is the largest contributor to the overall world dividend payouts.

Looking at the dividend repatriation of foreign-owned banks operating in Latin America, we can observe that banks located in Brazil and Mexico have made the largest dividend payments during the last decade, as seen in Figure 5.3. Indeed in Mexico, as of 2019 foreign banks distributed a total of $3.5 billion in dividends to the shareholders of the parent bank. BBVA Bancomer, which is a Spanish-owned bank, paid a total of $1.9 billion, followed by Citibanamex with nearly $850 million. Banco Santander paid nearly $550 million and HSBC Mexico around $107 million. Over time however, the dividend distribution has been rather volatile, increasing in 2012 and then falling sharply in 2014, with both Banco Santander and Citibanamex reducing their dividend payments significantly, reflecting the decline in economic activity, as measured by GDP, in the period between 2014 and 2016.

Banco Santander was the main contributor of dividend payments of foreign subsidiaries operating in Brazil, in 2019. Out of the nearly $3 billion dividend payments made by foreign-owned banks, Banco Santander paid nearly $2.7 billion in dividends. Santander is also the main contributor of total dividend payments in Peru, accounting for nearly 70 percent of all payments with nearly $500 million. Other banks that operate in Peru paying dividends to their parent stakeholders are HSBC and Scotiabank. Overall Peru has seen a steady increase in total dividend payments since 2010. Scotiabank and Santander also operate in Peru and Colombia and are the main foreign banks that make and distribute dividends to their parent stakeholders. Looking at the dividend paid relative to the net income generated by foreign banks in Table 5.3 Brazilian banks have a high payout ratio, with nearly 74 percent as of 2019. However, this is lower than in the previous years for which that ratio reached 85 percent in 2013. Even though foreign-owned banks located in Mexico have made the highest dividend payments, as discussed above, in proportion to income earned they fall behind those banks located in Brazil. A possible explanation of this could be that given the economic recession Brazil experienced in the period between 2014 and 2016, see Table 5.4a, foreign banks seem to repatriate a large proportion of their income in the form of dividends to their parent bank rather than reinvest in the affiliate. Foreign banks in Chile and Colombia, whilst having similar payout ratios in 2019, paying 60 percent of their earnings in dividends to their shareholders, over the years have been seemingly dominated by foreign Colombian banks. Indeed, those banks operating in Colombia have paid dividends that have exceeded 80 percent of their earnings, reaching 84 percent in 2017. Argentina and Peru have also rather volatile dividend payout ratios, as depicted in Table 5.3. Argentinian operating banks have decreased their dividend payments significantly from

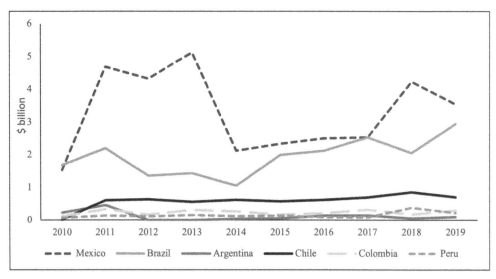

Source: BankFocus, author's own calculations.

Figure 5.3   Total dividend payments

2017, with the ratio falling from nearly 22 percent to 8.5 percent in 2019. The reverse can be observed in the case of Peru, for which banks have more than doubled their dividend payout ratio, increasing from 18 percent in 2017 to around 39 percent in 2019. Whereas in 2018 more than 80 percent of earnings of Peruvian foreign-owned banks were distributed in the form of dividends to the shareholders, leaving less than 20 percent to re-investment.

Overall, these findings suggest that whilst Mexico's foreign-owned banks have distributed a higher amount of dividend payments to their parent bank shareholders, when taking into account the total amount relative to the total earnings, Brazilian banks seem to pay more and keep less for re-investment. Indeed, on average over the 2013–2019 period Brazilian foreign-owned banks have repatriated more than 75 percent of their earnings in dividends to their parent bank. This is followed by those foreign banks located in Chile which pay more than 65 percent of their earnings. Argentinian banks on the other hand seem to pay less dividends as a share of their earnings to the shareholders, paying only 11 percent, suggesting that a large proportion of their earnings is kept for future investment.

The income of foreign-bank institutions generated in host countries can either be reinvested in the company or, as discussed above, repatriated[9] to the home country and hence to the parent company. The above discussion has focused on a micro-insight analysis of foreign banks dividend repatriation. The amount that banks decide to reinvest, from a micro-perspective, depends on the profitability opportunities that host countries offer. However a macro-perspective analysis would also help to understand the determinants of dividend repatriation and reinvestment of earnings in the affiliate in the host country.

Tables 5.4a and 5.4b include information of various macroeconomic indicators for the six selected countries. The volatility of Mexican dividend payments, as discussed above, reflects the country's rather turbulent economy. During this period, foreign direct investment (FDI) has also fluctuated, declining significantly from $48 billion to nearly $33 billion in 2019, as

Table 5.3   *Dividend payout ratio*

Country	2013	2014	2015	2016	2017	2018	2019
Mexico	91.0	47.3	52.5	62.9	47.4	65.7	48.7
Brazil	85.0	67.8	81.0	91.3	77.5	53.6	73.9
Argentina	-	4.1	6.9	20.2	22.3	7.3	8.5
Chile	56.2	55.4	74.5	67.5	59.8	79.9	60.5
Colombia	59.5	49.4	38.0	42.4	84.2	41.0	60.5
Peru	41.6	33.0	30.7	20.2	18.3	80.8	39.2

Notes: There is no data available for Argentina in 2013. Dividend payout ratio is computed by the share of dividends paid to net income.
Source: BankFocus, authors' own calculations.

shown in Table 5.4b. Greenfield investment has also decreased steadily since 2013, suggesting the amount of investment projects in new companies in Mexico fell considerably, given the unfavourable economic conditions. When looking at the amount of dividend repatriation relative to greenfield investment[10] announced in 2013, it can be observed from Figure 5.4, that this ratio was 14 percent. This indicates that 14 percent of the income generated from the FDI inflows leaves Mexico in the form of dividend repatriation. However, in 2014 the share of dividend payment to greenfield investment fell drastically to nearly 6 percent. This could imply that foreign banks reinvested more in the affiliate, rather than repatriate to their parent bank in the home country. This finding is in line with the above discussion that foreign-owned Mexican banks had a lower dividend payout ratio, declining from 91 percent in 2013 to around 47 percent in 2014, as shown above in Table 5.3. In other words, banks paid a lower share of their income to the shareholders of their parent banks in dividends. However the proportion of repatriation to the inflow of greenfield investment increased again in the last two years of the analysis.

Exchange rate movements can also affect the repatriation of earnings of foreign companies. A depreciation, or the expectation of future currency depreciation, of the host country currency would dampen the amount of repatriation and hence leave more available for reinvestment in host countries (Lundan 2006). The amount of dividend repatriation also reflects the depreciation of the Mexican currency. Indeed, the depreciation of the currency from 2013 is associated with a lower amount of dividend repatriation. However, the same cannot be observed for other countries such as Brazil and Argentina. For example, whilst the Brazilian currency has overall depreciated since 2013, as depicted in Table 5.4a, dividend repatriation has increased dividend payment. Moreover, foreign-owned banks in Brazil pay a higher proportion of their income in dividends to the shareholders of their parent bank, as discussed above. Similarly, dividend payments do not seem to be affected by the country's currency exchange rate. As shown in Figure 5.4 the share of dividend payments to greenfield investment for Argentina increased for the period between 2014 and 2017, a period of great economic uncertainty for the country. Therefore, banks would be discouraged to reinvest in the host country's established affiliate. The Chilean economy has also been rather volatile for the period 2013–2019, with GDP growth rate falling significantly in 2014 and only slightly recovering in 2018, declining again in 2019. During this period, Chilean banks were associated with a high dividend payout ratio, and a higher proportion of dividend payments in relation to greenfield investment, as shown in Figure 5.4. This would suggest that indeed foreign banks located in Chile reinvested less in the economy, and repatriated higher dividends to finance investment in their home country.

Table 5.4a   Macroeconomic conditions

	2013	2014	2015	2016	2017	2018	2019
				Argentina			
Real GDP	2.41	−2.51	2.73	−2.08	2.67	−2.48	−2.16
Exchange rate	90.38	74.45	86.22	71.24	75.54	61.84	54.79
FDI inflows	9.821.7	5,065.3	11,759.0	3,260.2	11,516.9	11,872.9	6,244.4
FDI outflows	890.0	1,920.5	875.2	1,786.5	1,155.6	11,556.9	1,573.8
Greenfield investment	5,054	3,248	2,551	11,761	4,187	6,615	4,115
Lending interest rates	17.15	24.01	24.92	31.23	26.58	48.52	67.26
				Brazil			
Real GDP	3.0	0.50	−3.55	−3.28	1.32	1.32	1.14
Exchange rate	90.22	89.31	74.62	79.27	86.36	77.24	75.83
FDI inflows	59,089.3	63,845.9	49,961.4	53,700.4	66,584.9	59,802.4	71,989.3
FDI outflows	−478.2	−3,261.2	−11,642.8	−5,900.8	19,040.4	−16,335.6	15,515.3
Greenfield investment	21,448	15,592	16,740	10,212	9,643	15,412	30,814
Lending interest rate	27.39	32.01	43.960	52.10	46.92	39.08	37.48
				Chile			
Real GDP	4.05	1.77	2.30	1.71	1.19	3.95	1.05
Exchange rate	101.74	92.29	90.44	92.17	95.73	97.13	92.17
FDI inflows	21,683.5	22,848	20,490.6	12,103.9	6,519.0	7,020.7	11,437.4
FDI outflows	9,361.4	12,090.9	15,542.5	6,769.8	5,525.5	278.2	7,937.5
Greenfield investment	10,889	4,762	9,288	5,352	4,556	7,498	8,703
Lending interest rate	9.26	8.10	5.51	5.59	4.55	4.18	–

Note: Exchange rate is the Real Broad Effective Exchange Rate, Index 2010=100.
Source: Real GDP Growth and Lending interest rate obtained from World Development Indicators database; Exchange rate is obtained from Federal Reserve Bank of St Louis; FDI inflows, outflows and Greenfield investment obtained from UNCTAD.

5.3   CONCLUSION

This chapter has analysed some of the activities that multinational banks undertake in the six selected Latin American countries, in the recent years. Foreign bank entry in Latin America has been the focus of wide research studies in the past two decades. However, little focus has been given to the profit distribution of these subsidiaries to the parent bank. The implications of which are not only the outflow of funds out of the host country but also the disadvantages it posits for using the funds for future investment and hence continuing to contribute in the economy in which banks operate.

Table 5.4b   *Macroeconomic conditions*

	2013	2014	2015	2016	2017	2018	2019
				Colombia			
Real GDP	5.13	4.50	2.96	2.09	1.36	2.52	3.32
Exchange rate	101.18	97.50	81.08	79.33	82.98	83.52	78.60
FDI inflows	16,210.0	16,169.0	11,724.0	13,848.0	13,836.7	11,535.1	14,493.1
FDI outflows	7,652.0	3,899.0	4,218.0	4,517.0	3,689.60	5,126.3	3,214.3
Greenfield investment	11,903	2,772	2,482	2,767	3,088	5,672	6,772
Lending interest rates	10.99	10.87	11.45	14.65	13.69	12.11	11.77
				Mexico			
Real GDP	1.35	2.80	3.29	2.91	2.12	2.14	−0.15
Exchange rate	102.00	101.19	90.92	79.30	81.34	81.33	84.15
FDI inflows	48,207.4	30,434.0	35,351.6	30,989.4	34,165.0	34,745.7	32,921.2
FDI outflows	15,490.1	6,910.8	10,663.0	481.7	3,919.2	7,712.0	10,227.9
Greenfield investment	36,495	35,673	24,808	25,830	27,588	27,033	27,859
Lending interest rate	4.25	3.55	3.42	4.72	7.34	8.08	8.48
				Peru			
Real GDP	5.85	2.38	3.25	3.95	2.52	3.98	2.15
Exchange rate	105.36	104.05	104.03	103.34	106.64	104.67	107.07
FDI inflows	9,826.0	3,929.9	8,314.0	6,739.1	6,860.5	6,487.9	8,891.9
FDI outflows	492.3	1,106.8	189.1	1,156.0	500.1	19.2	896.4
Greenfield investment	6,453	4,965	909	3,798	4,195	6,444	13,095
Lending interest rate	18.14	15.74	16.11	16.47	17.05	–	–

Notes: Exchange rate is the Real Broad Effective Exchange Rate, Index 2010=100. Data for Lending interest rate for 2019 is missing due to data unavailability.
Source: Real GDP and Lending interest rate obtained from World Development Indicators database; Exchange rate is obtained from Federal Reserve Bank of St Louis; FDI inflows, outflows and Greenfield investment obtained from UNCTAD.

Using bank-level data on a total of 103 foreign-owned banks and 129 domestic banks, this chapter provides an overview and comparison of the activities in each country. The Brazilian banking sector's share of the economy is the highest out of the six countries. This is followed by Chile and Peru. However, when looking at foreign bank participation, for which the analysis is restricted to including only those subsidiaries that are 50 percent or more owned by the parent bank, Mexico has the highest proportion of foreign bank participation. It is worth noting here that even though Brazil has a large banking sector characterized with low foreign bank

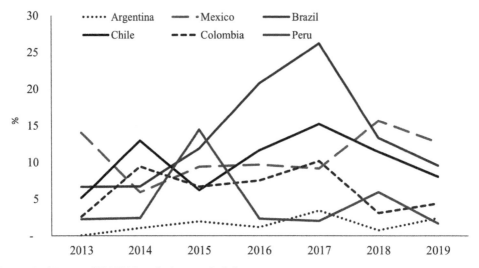

Source: BankFocus and UNCTAD, author's own calculations.

Figure 5.4   Dividend payment to greenfield investment ratio

participation, the sector is dominated by state-owned banks. Chile, on the other hand, does not have a large proportion of state-owned banks operating; the role of the country's main bank, namely the Banco Estado, has been found to have acted as a stabilizer in the financial crisis of 2007–2009 by issuing higher levels of credit necessary in the economy (Biron et al. 2019). Meanwhile, those foreign banks that operate in Chile pay a relatively large amount of their earnings in dividends to the shareholders of their parent bank. However, Chile is second after Brazil, with foreign banks having the highest payout ratio of the six countries under consideration.

Foreign banks in Mexico provide more credit than domestic banks and distribute more dividends than their peers operating in the other Latin America countries. However, when considering the earnings of these banks in Mexico, on average over the period 2013–2019 they tend to pay more dividends, hence hindering their investment in their host country's economy. Colombia, on the other hand, has a lower foreign bank participation but also a relatively high payout ratio, with more than half of their earnings being distributed to shareholders in the form of dividends. Argentina and Peru exhibit lower dividend repatriation.

Lastly, the evidence suggests that dividend payments reflect the economic conditions in which foreign banks operate. Indeed, the analysis suggests that when macroeconomic conditions in host countries are gloom or highly volatile, both of which increase uncertainty levels, banks seem to repatriate a larger amount of their earnings to their country rather than reinvest in the host countries where they operate.

ACKNOWLEDGEMENT

I thank Ali Hassan for his research assistance. I am also grateful for comments and suggestions received from Eric Owusu Boahen and other participants during the STAMP session on Globalisation in Questions at the UEL Summer Research conference.

NOTES

1. BankFocus may not provide information on all banks that operate in each country.
2. The sample period reflects the data availability for each bank. For instance, the data is limited for the period pre-2013.
3. See also Levine (2005) for a discussion of the literature on the role of finance on economic growth.
4. King and Levine (1993) provide an empirical analysis on the finance–growth nexus in support of Schumpeter's (1911) views on the role banks have on economic development.
5. The Brazilian economy was in a deep recession from late 2014 until 2016.
6. The Financial Statement of banks report on the dividends paid to the shareholders of the parent company which are the main stakeholders and the non-controlling interest which are the minority stakeholders. However, such distinction is not available on BankFocus and hence we are assuming that the large amount of dividend payment is made to the shareholders of the parent company.
7. For more information see Henderson 2020, Edition 26, https://cdn.janushenderson.com/webdocs/JHGDI+Ed+26+Report+_Global.pdf.
8. Henderson Group publishes the Henderson Global Dividend Index which has been recorded since 2009. It measures the progress global banks make in paying their investors, calculated in US dollars and can be broken down by regions, industries and sectors.
9. Earnings repatriation can be realized through dividend payments, interest payment or royalties. Due to data limitations this study only uses dividend payments as a proxy for income repatriation of foreign-bank institutions that operate in the six selected Latin American countries.
10. Data on the announced greenfield project includes all industries in the country. There is no data available for greenfield investment by industry in each country.

REFERENCES

Berger, A., Klapper, L. and Udell, G. (2001). The ability of banks to lend to informationally opaque small businesses. *Journal of Banking and Finance*, 25(12), 2127–2167.
Bijlsma, M., Kool, C. and Non, M. (2018). The effect of financial development on economic growth: a meta-analysis. *Applied Economics*, 50(57), 6128–6148.
Biron, M., Cordova, F. and Lemus, A. (2019). Banks' business model and credit supply in Chile: the role of a state-owned bank. BIS Working Paper, No. 800.
Cecchetti, G.S. and Kharroubi, E. (2012). Reassessing the impact of finance on growth. BIS Working Paper No. 381.
Claessens, S., Demirguc-Kunt, A. and Huizinga, H. (1998). How does foreign entry affect the domestic banking market? World Bank Discussion Paper. Retrieved from http://worldbank.org.
Clarke, G., Cull, R., Martinez Peria, M.S. and Sanchez, S. (2005). Bank lending to small businesses in Latin America: does bank origin matter? *Journal of Money, Credit and Banking*, 37(1), 83–118.
Dages, B.G., Goldberg, L. and Kinney. D. (2000). Foreign and domestic bank participation in emerging markets: lessons from Mexico and Argentina. *FRBNY Economic Policy Review*, 6(3), 17–36.
Davies, R. and Tracey, B. (2014). Too big to be efficient? The impact of too big to fail factors on scale economies for banks. *Journal of Money, Credit and Banking*, 46(1), 219–253.
De Haas, R. and Van Lelyveld, I. (2014). Multinational banks and the global financial crisis: weathering the perfect storm? *Journal of Money, Credit and Banking*, 46, 295–326.
Demirguc-Kunt, A. and Huizinga, H. (1998). Determinants of commercial bank interest and profitability. World Bank Policy Research Working Paper 1900.

Easterly, W., Islam, R. and Stiglitz, J. (2000). Shaken and stirred, explaining growth volatility. The World Bank, mimeo.

Fachada, P. (2008). Foreign banks' entry and departure: the recent Brazilian experience. *Banco Central Do Brazil*, Working Paper Series No. 164.

Gonzalez, J. (2013). Foreign banks in Mexico: is there a reason to worry? World Bank blog. Retrieved from: https://blogs.worldbank.org/allaboutfinance/foreign-banks-mexico-there-reason-worry.

Kakes, J. and Nijskens, R. (2018). Size of the banking sector: implications for financial stability. *DeNederlandsche Bank*, Occasional Studies, Volume 16-6.

Kindleberger, C.P. (1978). *Manias, panics and crashes: a history of financial crises*. Basic Books, New York.

King, R.G. and Levine, R. (1993). Finance and growth: Schumpeter might be right. *Quarterly Journal of Economics, 108*(3), 717–737.

Laeven, L., Ratnovski, L. and Tong, H. (2014). Bank size and systemic risk. IMF Staff Discussion Note, 14/04.

Levine, R. (1996), Financial development and economic growth: views and agenda. *Policy Research Working Paper Series 1678*, World Bank.

Levine, R. (2005). Finance and growth: theory and evidence. In P. Aghion and S.N. Durlauf (eds.), *Handbook of Economic Growth* (Vol 1A, Chapter 12, 865–934, edition 1). Elsevier, North Holland.

Lundan, S.M. (2006). Reinvested earnings as a component of FDI: an analytical review of the determinants of reinvestment. *Transitional Corporations, 15*(3), 35–66.

Minsky, H.P. (1992). The financial instability hypothesis. The Levy Economics Institute of Bard College. Working Paper No. 74.

Schumpeter, J.A. (1911). *The theory of economic development*. Harvard University Press, Cambridge, MA.

6. The unique development of non-financial corporations in Latin America

Noemi Levy-Orlik and Jorge Alonso Bustamante-Torres

Cross-border capital movements modified the dominant capitalist mode of production, imposing financial complex relations that transformed big corporation organizations and profit appropriation. In this context, financial variables acquire outstanding importance, particularly the rate of interest and the rate of exchange (unrelated to real variables) along with prices of financial instrument that, altogether, assume a leading role on the mechanisms of profits distribution.

In this chapter we discuss the impact of international capital movements on big non-financial corporations, analysing the volume and composition of foreign direct investment (FDI), including its effects on Latin American and Caribbean (LAC) economies, including the non-financial corporations originated in the region, named *multilatinas*, in order to assess whether overcapitalization practices are similar to multinationals centred in developed countries.

FDI inflows to the LAC region initiated in the late 1980s and the beginning of the 1990s, promoting the process of financialization in the region and, more importantly, laid the grounds for *multilatinas* development, unfolding overcapitalization practises, based on different strategies.

We should warn readers that complex financial relations in big non-financial corporations have a long history, whose first manifestations are traced to the "Companies Laws" in England and the United States (Ireland 2010; Blankenburg 2012) in the late 19th century, from where two different theoretical explanations emerged. The mainstream view argues that capital market guarantees efficient intermediation via "correct prices" that reflects real returns of the productive capital; in which financial systems are neutral, that is, do not modify the value of enterprises or production activity. The heterodox vision, on the other hand, assumes that the financial market modifies the big corporation's valuation, and prices are structurally incorrect (productive and more importantly financial), on the basis of which profit appropriation extends to the circulation sphere and modifies the distribution of profits. This process imposed oligopolistic capitalist structures, imposing unequal profit appropriations, differentiated credit access, and financial costs that, altogether, enabled big enterprises consolidation (Kalecki 1954; Steindl 1945).

This chapter is organized in three sections. Section 6.1 contains an extremely brief account of the rise of big corporations, highlighting its relationship with capital market developments, followed by an abbreviated discussion of the main theories that related these two issues. Section 6.2 discusses how capital movement took place from the 1990s onwards, looking at FDI movements at a global and regional level and in specific Latin America and Caribbean countries, including regional classification of big corporations, followed by a balance sheet analysis of the more representative corporations of Brazil, Chile and Mexico. Finally, in Section 6.3 the conclusions are put forward.

6.1 LARGE COMPANIES: BACKGROUND AND THE THEORETICAL EXPLANATIONS OF THEIR INTERACTION WITH CAPITAL MARKETS

Big Companies Background

Blankenburg (2012) and Ireland (2010) place the first reference of big corporations with the *commenda*[1] (12th century), followed by regulations to limit risks on semi-public entities (monasteries and traded guilds) that operated on the basis of commonly held property. A second impulse was the issuance of privileges to certain companies to operate in sectors or regions (i.e., colonies, 16th and 17th centuries). A third drive is linked to Unincorporated Public Limited Companies, operating de facto as limited liability entities, which prompted the Bubble Act in England (1720) as the result of the first financial bubble – South Sea Bubble. This was followed by the development of common law companies that prohibit stock trading between unincorporated joint stock companies. This arrangement dominated during the industrial revolution.[2]

The establishment of big companies occurred in the second half of the 19th century as a result of the acts of free incorporation (not tied to Royal Charters or Parliamentary acts) and limited liability, based on the concept of "natural persons" (United States) and companies' ownership separation from its administration (the Salomon case, 1896, England[3]).

Another important building concept that consolidated the formation of modern stockholder companies was the extension of the figure of limited responsibility to the establishment of legal property rights of financial intangibles. This made possible the dissociation between legal rights property of "things" from its responsibilities and obligations, creating a legal status that contained financial instruments, which accomplished the definitive separation between property and company management. Financial instruments' legal status facilitated the relationship between large companies and capital markets without putting at risk shareholder's wealth, but laid the foundations for speculative activities, expanding return appropriation to the circulation sphere, that is, capital markets. These changes were not free of critical judgements. Berle and Means (1933) criticize the joint stock companies on the basis of inefficiency and possible embezzlement; on the same token, Mill, Marshall and Robert Peel (industrialist and Prime Minister) argued that unjust privileges could emerge from joint stock companies (Blankenburg 2012, p. 195).

After the Second World War, mainly due to the 1929 crisis, capital markets' operations were reactive-limited and thereby shareholder's companies' growth was on the basis of financial speculation; but this situation changed in the last decades of the 20th century, at the onset of globalization, in the light of the increased activity of financial markets that revived the shareholder companies along with their treasury departments. In this period, the concept of limited liability was again changed, giving way to new privileges to enterprises other than (listed) shareholding corporations, such as limited liability partnerships (LLPs) and the so-called limited liability companies (LLCs). The new privileges shift to tax advantages and lower partnership disclosure requirements, excluding taxes from partnership, thereby "LLPs extend limited liability to the limited partners (the equivalent of owner partnerships/shareholders)" (ibid., p. 197). While LLCs constitute a hybrid between LLPs and fully quoted limited corporations, it removed the ceiling on the number of partners/shareholders allowed to be active in the management of the company, facilitating business owners' tax avoidance, while fully enjoying the advantages of limited liability.

From the above discussion it can be highlighted that the big transformation of the capitalism system of the 19th century set up new legal corporations' forms of organization, from where emerged new "rentiers" that, in the third part of the 20th century, led a "rentier revolution" (Smithin 2018) and brought back financial complex relations to economic activity, reactivating capital markets, and the second biggest financial crisis (2008), still unresolved as the 2020 crisis witnesses.

The Conventional Analysis of Investment Finance

The mainstream view assumes that savings are a precondition of investment, which implies that current present needs have to be postponed to maximize total consumption (Woodford 2003; Wicksell 1893/1954). Saving is determined by a relative price that equates intertemporal consumption between the present and the future; and the rate of interest is a real variable, representing a volume of goods, whose consumption is deferred to the future, which thereby denotes the opportunity cost between consuming today or saving. From this argument is developed the intertemporal utility maximization concept, in which savings is a residual variable, determined by the rate of interest. On the other side, firms are deficit units that expand income and profit through using their own savings or accessing other people's savings, which means that the higher marginal productivity (incorporated in investment capital) is shared with savers. Hence, the rate of interest is determined by savings and investment.

A financial system is a space of intermediation that puts in contact surplus agents (consumers) with deficit units (firms); which means that free market forces, based on the assumption of flexible prices, distribute production factors in the most efficient way, and each production factor will be remunerated in accordance with their productivity, including investment finance costs. A firm's finance (banks advances and financial non-bank institutions liquidity) is structurally neutral, determined by its capital marginal productivity and the firm's value (Modigliani and Miller 1958);[4] and marginal productivity of capital depends on specific entrepreneurial activity. Thereby dividends and interest on shares, bonds, and all types of debts, include risks, and are related to specific productive sectors in which firms operate and take equal free risk asset, within a financial investor portfolio.

Under the assumption of complete financial markets,[5] returns of different forms of finance are perfect substitutes since highly rentable financial instruments require risk compensation of equal proportions; and perfect arbitrage equal returns from different sectors and activities. The volume of finance is set by the equality of costs and marginal productivity, portrayed by the value firms, and the share price is not modified by the financial structure (proportion of different types of debts and shares within a financial structure). Although, finance through debts has fiscal advantages and thereby is considered a better strategy than shares (Modigliani and Miller 1958).

In this context, price shares and firms' values in different sectors are the most reliable indicators of capital profitability; and returns among different industries are socialized by dividend payments and financial services interest rates; given a certain level of information and perfect arbitrage, the market shares price is the most reliable indicator of capital productivity, risks and firm's value.

The assumptions put forward by Fama (1991) are more flexible. He assumes that shares prices don't fully adjust to changes of profits (response speed is lower because of incomplete information availability, and precisely the level of information determines whether the efficiency of a financial market hypothesis is strong, semi-strong or weak).[6] However, share prices continue to be a firm's most trustworthy indicator (Tobin and Brainard 1977) since, throughout time, false prices are corrected.[7] In this discussion, a key point is that the higher the price of shares represents higher profitability and finance access.

Neo-Keynesians put forward an alternative explanation under the heading of asymmetric information (Stiglitz 1988). According to them debt structures are relevant information for financial agents because higher indebtedness can be associated with higher default risk, which may affect firms' value, through price shares. Financial market operates via credit and share rationing reducing firms' finance, under the headings of adverse selection, moral risks and monitoring costs (Stiglitz 1988, Jensen and Meckling 1976). Financial market scores the debt structure of firms that are expressed via the fluctuations of price shares and credit adverse selection; from where it is argued that the restriction of finance is due to asymmetric information and *sticky* prices that, altogether, prevents the financial and productive markets from being emptied.

Under this view, credit and stock markets take place through intermediation mechanisms between surplus agents whose savings are operated by investors through financial investment portfolios. Moreover, financial markets (stock and bank) socialize productivity gains by financial instruments that compensate finance for its contribution to capital marginal productivity.

The Heterodox Explanation of Capital Market and Big Corporation Relationships

The starting point of the interaction between capital market and big corporations is subjected to the dominant institutional organization, and the rejection of the capital scarcity assumption in big corporations; and the dominant causality goes from investment to savings, without rejecting that capital availability is distributed among alternative production projects or that financial capital is channelled to the stock market and they are used to finance production; but available capital can be wasted in unnecessary productive and administrative projects or conspicuous expansions (Toporowski 2012). Non-financial corporations operate on the basis of diversified portfolios, in which are included financial and productive physical capital (Steindl 1990; Dallery 2009; Minsky 1975).

Big corporations are usually in surplus and acquire financial instruments to increase their share; which creates net excess flows into capital markets along with financial inflation (deflation) that modifies productive cycles. In periods of financial inflation, productive activity (investment) expands and economic growth increases (boom period), which are reverted when financial flows into financial markets cease to increase; financial prices deaccelerate, productive activity slows down and corporation financial flows shrink, giving way to an economic downturn; and if corporation inflows are smaller than their debt commitments, debt deflation takes place, and an economic crash might occur.

In the late 1960s developed countries experienced an industrial crisis which revived mergers and acquisitions operations that restored corporation profits. Capital markets were deregulated (mainly in Great Britain and the United States), institutional investors reappeared that, on the whole, strengthened financial mechanisms of profit appropriation, regardless of economic activity, unleashing economic cycles combined with higher corporation capitalization value. Deregulation along with economic globalization deepened in the 1990s, extending mergers and acquisitions to all developed economies, via foreign direct investment, including emerging and developing economies, at the end of the 20th century. Hence, Latin America and the Caribbean was included in this new arrangement at the beginning of the 21st century, and from the second quinquennium of 2000s, Latin American big corporations internationalized.

From this follows that joint stock firms consolidated, and overcapitalization processes developed, taking place in a process of excess financial instruments issuance (bonds and shares) in relation to financial commitments and commercial needs. Big corporations retained liquidity, blocking capital market financial flows for the optimal redistribution of capital. In addition, the excess capital retained by big corporations limited how capital markets were supposed to function to attain the highest possible economic growth, giving way to financial speculation.

Economic historians refer to two events of overcapitalization that, although they differ, preceded (and originated) the financial crashes at the beginning of the 20th and 21st centuries. The first overcapitalization experience was discussed by Marshall, Lavington, Hobson and Veblen (referred to in Toporowski 2012) and is associated with financial investors watering down companies stocks to increase their commissions. Dividend stocks shrank, corporations were confronted with lower profits, and were unable to guarantee higher yields of their financial instruments, and even of their productive projects. This process was initiated at the end of the 19th century and extended to the beginning of the 20th century and was interrupted by the 1929 financial crash. Kalecki (1937), based on the first overcapitalization period, proposed the "principle of increasing risk", where he argued that firms have limited and differentiated access to liquidity, which is followed by business cycles.

At the end of the 20th century the process of overcapitalization re-appeared along with institutional investors (i.e., pension and investment funds, insurance companies) concentrating large volumes of liquidity that were channelled to the financial market to increase their capitalization value, increasing financial instruments' demand. Toporowski (2000, 2012) argues that institutional investors' priorities are to augment investment portfolio yields in corporations in which they operate, and this process differs from the previous overcapitalization period, in that the excess capital inflow to the financial markets, which came along with financial inflation, took place from retaining capital shares. Thereby financial gains accrued from selling financial instruments and the cost burdens were passed from the sellers to the buyers. Financial costs dropped and the share yields could be settled by the financial gains of the corporation's financial instruments.

Under these circumstances the mainstream theory of equilibria doesn't hold since shares issuance exceeds industrial and entrepreneurs' finance needs, accruing excess liquidity in the form of bank deposits, foreign currency and commercial paper, thereby corporation profits stemmed from their excess liquidity.[8] In this institutional arrangement, an enterprise's collateral increases so does their lending capacity, along with a higher business credit grade that, in turn, reduces credit costs and, altogether, the firm's external debt expands. The increased corporation liquidity took place through mergers and acquisitions and balance sheet restructuration.

However, big corporation treasury activity takes place mainly in multinational centres, from where it follows that there they have strategical control that determines production and multinational consumption. And, property right acquisitions (intangible assets) enter the scene because they guarantee cash flows via the control of higher levels of market participation and selling rights in specific markets that come along with the control of product innovation.[9] These financial activities reduce new investment risks and strengthen financial inflation.

The above arguments partially explain the different financial bubbles that have led to economic crashes, from where it is derived that financial organization based in complex financial relations (also known as financialization) induces overcapitalization, that comes along with higher levels of indebtedness, which initially are settled by financial gains, derived from financial inflation.

The big limitation is that financial inflation is finite and after reaching a certain level, prices of financial instruments decrease (because of uncertain expectations), which leads to financial instability, whose main results are large concentrations of income and wealth in multinationals, low salaries, stagnation of productive investment, labour precarization and pauperization that, altogether, stagnates economic growth.

6.2 THE FINANCIALIZATION OF THE MEXICAN ECONOMY: FDI MOVEMENTS, ITS COMPOSITION AND LARGE COMPANIES GROWTH STRATEGIES

FDI Inflows and Outflows and Mergers and Acquisitions by Buyers and Sellers

FDI movements in the last three decades have been extremely large and global, including all the capitalist regions, specifically developing countries and Latin America and the Caribbean (LAC). Between 1990 and 1999 (named as the globalization period) FDI inflows worldwide increased six-fold, and LAC became an important receiver of these resources. In the next decade (2000–2009, the trans-nationalization era for developing economies) FDI movement stagnated at the worldwide level, less so in developing countries, including LAC, with no important changes after the Global Financial Crisis of 2008. Looking at some specific countries of LAC, during the period of globalization, Brazil attracted the largest volume of FDI inflows, which can be explained in terms of its size and robust economic growth, followed by Peru and Chile. In the following decade, Peru, Chile and Colombia maintained FDI capital inflows, with no perceptible change after the 2008 crisis, see Table 6.1 – lower right quadrant.

FDI inflow movements concentrated in developed countries showing a downward trend from the second decade of the 21st century, while in developing economies continued the positive trend, which means that these economies increasingly continued to be FDI inflow receivers. This was the case of the LAC region during the 1990s in the light of the financial market globalization, which increased even more after the 2008 crisis. FDI inflows to LAC in terms of countries, taking into account their size (FDI/GDP), situate Chile in the first place, showing an upward trend in the next three decades, followed by Peru and Colombia, with relatively lower coefficients in Brazil and Mexico (first quadrant on the left). The latter can be explained due to the higher economic diversification, development banks in Brazil, and public companies in Mexico. Finally, Argentina attraction of FDI inflows slowed down due to the successive different political upheavals in the last thirty years, see Table 6.1. From the above, we can point out that FDI flows to LAC affected all the countries, regardless of their size.

Looking at FDI outflow movements, as would be expected, they concentrate in developed countries with declining trends, while in developing economies, particularly in LAC, they show an upward trend, although their volumes were extremely low (Table 6.1, first quadrant on the right). This implies that the financial opening brought along financial instability, especially in LAC, where the first neoliberal financial crises took place (Mexico, December 1994) that spread out throughout the LAC region, and moved later to other developing countries, until it broke up out in the US.

An important element that explains large companies' expansionary strategy is operations related to mergers and acquisitions (M&A), including developing economies. For the first time in history large companies originating in developing countries were created, based on capital from the region. Thus, the novelty of capital movements is that developing countries exported capital to the rest of the world.

The first aspect to note in the FDI movements is that M&A by sales with respect to capital inflows (capital imports) and M&A by buyers with respect to capital outflows (capital exports) were dominant in developed countries and, even though developing countries also used M&A as a means of expansion, and more importantly, from the 1990s, these coefficients doubled, especially after the second decade of the 21st century; in developing countries M&A by buyer was twice as big as M&A by seller. This behaviour was replicated in LAC at smaller scales, Chile being leader of this phenomena, see Table 6.1, second quadrant, left and right.

Finally, the ratio of FDI with respect to Gross Fixed Capital Formation (GFCF) was relatively high in Latin America in relation to developing countries and especially with respect to developed countries, see Table 6.1, third left quadrant. This is due to the extreme structural weakness of the LAC domestic capital goods production sector. Chile has the higher ratio of the region, especially from the first decade of the 21st century, followed by Peru and Colombia, and Brazil, Argentina and Mexico occupy the last places; this is because in the first group of countries the productive sector is less diversified and led by exports of the primary sector. This condition doesn't apply to Mexico because of the "maquila" nature of its business organization and the extractive export sector (oil) remained under state control, until 2013. In Brazil, the FDI/GFCF ratio doubled in relation to Argentina, because the former remained a more diversified economy, and only from the first decade of the 21st century the Brazilian extractive export sector acquired importance, and public banks retained importance in financing growth.

Latin American Large Companies

In the light of the above information, large companies in developing and LAC countries showed and accelerated growth, although their size is comparatively smaller in relation to multinationals of developed countries, and their growth took place through external markets.

Based on UNCTAD data of the 100 largest companies in developed countries,[10] the companies' size (measured in assets) increased four-fold between 1993 and 2018, sales expanded 2.5 times, and employment increased 1.4 times. Between the periods of 1993–2000 and

Table 6.1   *Capital movement global, regional and by countries*

	1990/99	2000/09	2010/18	1990/99	2000/09	2010/18
	FDI inflows/ total inflows			**FDI outflows/ total outflows**		
Developed countries	68.4	64.8	51.7	89.0	85.8	66.9
Developing countries	30.6	31.6	44.4	10.7	12.3	29.7
Latin America and Caribbean	9.1	7.9	11.0	1.1	1.6	2.2
Argentina/GDP	2.6	2.2	1.9	0.5	0.4	0.2
Brazil/GDP	1.4	2.7	3.1	0.1	0.6	0.0
Chile/GDP	4.7	6.4	6.8	1.3	2.8	4.3
Colombia/GDP	2.1	3.5	4.0	0.3	1.0	1.5
Mexico/GDP	1.9	2.8	2.7	0.0	0.5	0.9
Peru/GDP	3.1	3.6	4.1	0.1	0.1	0.2
	M&A purchasers/ FDI inflows			**M&A purchasers/ FDI outflows**		
Developed countries	86.57	87.26	88.19	87.1	84.9	81.7
Developing countries	9.05	8.84	8.68	12.4	13.2	18.9
Latin America and Caribbean	2.69	2.64	2.67	7.7	2.5	5.7
Argentina	0.19	0.19	0.19	1.7	0.5	0.1
Brazil	0.02	0.02	0.05	0.6	0.5	0.6
Chile	0.79	0.79	0.71	1.3	0.8	1.0
Colombia	0.00	0.00	0.00	0.5	0.7	0.2
Mexico	0.19	0.23	0.24	0.3	0.4	0.4
Peru	0.01	0.01	0.01	1.3	0.7	0.5
	FDI inflows/ GFCF			**FDI movement by periods**		
World				6.6	1.0	1.0
Developed countries	4.8	9.1	8.9	6.6	0.6	0.8
Developing countries	7.6	11.1	8.1	6.7	2.7	1.1
Latin America and Caribbean	10.4	15.1	15.0	9.3	2.0	0.9
Argentina	16.2	13.8	11.3	5.7	1.1	1.1
Brazil	7.5	14.9	16.5	33.2	2.4	0.8
Chile	18.9	29.0	31.7	7.4	3.1	0.5
Colombia	8.5	17.9	16.3	4.9	2.6	1.7
Mexico	10.8	13.7	11.7	6.9	1.5	1.2
Peru	15.4	18.8	17.8	19.7	10.4	0.7

Note: GFCF – Gross Fixed Capital Formation.
Source: Own calculations based on UNCTAD database. http://unctad.org/en/pages/DIAE/World%20Investment
%20Report/Annex-Tables.aspx.

2008–2018, the share of external assets to total assets expanded 2.8 times, external sales
to total sale increased two-fold, and external employment to total employment increased
1.2 times. This implies that the assets and sales growth was based on the domestic markets,
applying to a lesser extent to the employment expansion. The average of the transnationality
index[11] of the 100 largest companies of developed countries, between 1993 and 2018, grew 13

points (it averaged 52 points between 1993 and 2000, 62 points between 2001 and 2007, and 65 points between 2008 and 2017).

The size of large companies of developing and emerging countries[12] is remarkably smaller compared to developed countries (difference over 1:200) with a growth rate less vigorous. The average size of companies (measured by assets) between 2008 and 2017 increased 2.7 times, and sales and employment expanded 1.9 times. In addition, the ratio of external assets to total assets averaged around 30% between 2008 and 2009, not very different from the multinational ratio during the 1990s, with the particularity that it remained relatively unchanged in the second period (2010–2017). The ratio of sales and external employment to their totals was much higher than those of developed countries' multinationals (46%, 40%, respectively). Regarding the transnationality index, it did not vary significantly between 2008–2009 and 2010–2017 (it averaged around 50 points), which implies that large companies in developing countries entered into the global economy with high external variables (sales and employment).

Finally, it should be highlighted that the participation of Latin American large companies in the 100 largest corporations of developing and emerging countries is very insignificant. Argentina and Chile had one company between 2008 and 2017; Brazil, three and four companies at the beginning between 2008 and 2014, increasing to five and six from 2015. Mexico is the country with the largest number of companies, with four firms between 2008 and 2014, and seven from 2015. In terms of assets, sales and employment, Mexican corporations, on average, are the largest, although Mexico is not among the main FDI capital importers or exporters. Lastly, Mexico's transnationality index is markedly higher than Brazil and Chile due to the maquiladora nature of its companies.

Large Companies' Ownership by Ownership and Stock Market Linkage

A more detailed analysis of large company development in LAC, with information from the 500 largest companies in the region (America Economia[13]), between 2000 and 2014, on average, shows that Brazil has the largest number of big firms (204), followed by Mexico (160), which might be explained by the size of these economies (they represent 39% and 26% of the total GDP of LAC, respectively, for the period 2000–2018). Chile occupies the third place in company numbers (50) although it represents only 4.6% of regional GDP,[14] followed by Colombia (27) and finally Peru has 17 companies (with just 3.6% of regional GDP).

The number of companies with stock market presence is higher in Chile (60%), followed by Brazil (49%) and Peru (48%), while in Mexico and Colombia companies have low capital market participation, see Table 6.2. These data, in part, explain the higher capitalization volumes of the Chilean and Brazilian stock market, the rise of the Peruvian capital market and the relatively stagnated Mexican capital market. According to the type of property, national private companies dominate the region (Table 6.2), although foreign private companies in Chile and Peru represent around half of national private companies in those countries (Table 6.2).

From the above discussion it can be highlighted that large foreign corporations are listed in local stock market exchanges, while large domestic-based private companies are present in their home stock exchanges, since it's their way of access to foreign finance and thereby to internationalize; more discussion in the next section. In fact, in Mexico, 90% of the companies listed in the local stock exchange are of domestic origin, followed by Chile (80%), Brazil and

Table 6.2   *Big enterprises in selected countries of Latin America (by type ownership, number and size, 2000–2004)*

	Argentina	Brazil	Chile	Colombia	Mexico	Peru
Number of big enterprises by country						
Total	36	204	50	27	160	17
Not listed in Stock Exchange	25	104	20	23	107	9
Listed in Stock Exchange	12	100	30	4	54	8
Private Nationals	16	119	35	13	112	8
Not listed in Stock Exchange	10	52	12	11	63	5
Listed in Stock Exchange	6	68	24	2	48	4
Foreign Private	21	68	15	10	42	9
Not listed in Stock Exchange	16	45	10	10	38	4
Listed in Stock Exchange	5	24	7	1	4	5
State owned	0	17	0	4	7	1
Not listed in Stock Exchange	0	8	0	3	6	1
Listed in Stock Exchange	0	9	0	1	1	0
Total asset/GDP						
Total	23	65	134	43	82	23
Not listed in Stock Exchange	11	17	39	30	44	5
Listed in Stock Exchange	12	48	95	13	38	18
By type of enterprises with respect to total assets						
Not listed in Stock Exchange	47.3	26.2	28.9	70.1	53.9	20.0
Private Nationals	37.8	15.4	12.7	24.5	26.8	9.7
Foreign Private	9.4	6.1	5.7	16.2	4.1	6.4
State owned	0.2	4.8	10.5	29.3	23.0	3.8
Listed in Stock Exchange	52.7	73.8	71.1	29.9	46.1	80.0
Private Nationals	21.5	35.2	46.7	5.0	33.2	31.7
Foreign Private	25.3	11.8	24.4	0.6	1.9	44.8
State owned	5.8	26.7	0.0	24.3	11.0	3.5

Note: For 2002 and 2017 there is no information available.
Source: Own calculations, based on America Economia "Las 500 empresas más grandes de America Latina".

Colombia. However, there are still a significant number of companies that are not related to local stock markets.

Looking at the ratio of assets of large companies to GDP in each of the countries analysed, Chile has the highest coefficient, mainly from companies listed in the local stock market, followed by Mexico and Brazil, with the particularity that in these economies the proportion of non-listed company assets is higher, while Colombia, Argentina and Peru occupy distant places (see Table 6.2). By type of ownership, the average number of assets listed on the stock exchange are national private companies; and highlights a proportion of assets of national private companies that are not listed on the stock exchange, which explains the stock markets' reduced development across the region, with the exception of Chile.

Brazil, Chile and Mexico Large Corporations: Balance Sheets Analysis

In this section, Latin American large companies located in Brazil, Chile and Mexico are studied through their financial statements. Our objective is to characterize their profit and debt strategies via their assets and liabilities structure, highlighting how their balance composition affects the indicators of profitability, liquidity and solvency. This analysis is based on large non-financial corporations that operate in the productive and service sectors, owned by domestic capital, listed in their respective stock markets. Our aim is to determine these companies' overcapitalization dynamics and the characteristic forms that unfold this phenomenon in the region.

An initial observation is that large non-financial companies don't operate through the domestic credit markets, although their local stock exchange is used to acquire transparency, and in this way they show adherence to international standards.[15] The main advantage of developing countries corporations' access to international bank credit and financial market liquidity is financial cost reduction, with the disadvantage that economic activity is exposed to exchange risks that, however, can be neutralized through hedging practices (options and futures). Nonetheless financial speculation has become an important option for domestic non-financial corporations since international markets are deeper and broader.

A second observation is that external market access for Latin American big corporations helps them to internationalize their operations via mergers and acquisition of developing and developed countries' established corporations, through purchases of new companies, leaving their operation unchanged. In this context, the purchase of intangible assets, which are property rights (patents, trademarks, franchises, among others) guaranteed big corporations' profit by increasing the sphere of influence and market control, with lower risks. Despite the fact that intangible asset purchases generate rights over specific brands, these operations retain its financial character, since they are tradeable at any time (so long as secondary markets are deep), without becoming a central activity of the acquired corporations. In this regard, several studies of the Mexican economy reveal that it became a marked characteristic of Latin American corporations in the financialized period (Domínguez 2015; Gómez 2018; Bustamante 2018). Thus, this growth strategy has been reproduced in the large companies' dynamics of Brazil and Chile, obviously with certain nuances.

The balance sheet and income statement of the listed non-financial corporation of the three countries analysed are presented in Table 6.3. The information source is the *Database of Economatica* and the figures are presented in aggregate values based on the set of companies of Chile, Brazil and Mexico (127 companies for Brazil; 63 for Chile; and 66 for Mexico) and the time period extends from 2000 to 2017. In general, we confirm that in the sample of large companies studied there are overcapitalization practices, which is deduced from their growth and profit strategies.

Five characteristics are observed from the indicators presented in Table 6.3. First, in the three countries analysed, their ratio of debts to productivity is rising, which means that debts are above the finance investment needs, represented by the indicator of total liabilities to physical assets (stock of physical capital), which is very noticeable in Brazil and Mexico.

Second, the Chilean large corporations, unlike Mexican and Brazilian, show a more dynamic growth in their asset current account. If this indicator is compared to the acid test (above unity in Chilean corporations), it follows that the formers obtain higher returns from their increased liquidity. In other words, the creation of higher liquid resources above short-term financial obligations is a profitable practice. The solvency ratio confirms this finding since this ratio for the Chilean firms is above Mexican and Brazilian firms, reaching values above two, during several years, which is reflected in the average of the period sample.

Third, in the three countries analysed the productive investment has diminished and its counterpart is the expansion of non-physical investment. It is important to note that non-physical investment includes non-current investment that covers long-term financial assets, investment in related companies, investment in subsidiaries, intangibles, and other property rights. In order of priority, Brazilian corporations stand out for deploying this strategy, representing this item 35% of total assets at the end of the period, followed by Mexico and Chile (32% and 28%, respectively).

Fourth, the debt indicators in Mexican and Brazilian corporations show that long-term debt increases over short-term debt, which is consistent with large international multinational corporations' trends (Hattori and Takáts 2015). However, Chilean corporations have a contrary movement. On the other hand, the solvency and debt-on-property ratios deteriorated during that period, showing the greatest risk in Brazil (with average solvency ratio oscillating around 0.7 to 0.6) while Chilean average ratios for the same period are three times higher.

Finally, the return on equity (ROE) and return on assets (ROA) ratios indicates that profitability decreased from the 2008 crisis, reaching the lowest level in 2017. This reflects the growing weakness of the dominant profit–growth–indebtedness strategy. It should be highlighted that the Mexican companies, although their profitability has a decreasing trend, their level is higher than Brazilian and Chilean counterparts.

The particular overcapitalization strategies followed by Latin American corporations show two important features. The first is related to the internationalization process which has been implemented through mergers and acquisitions and via purchases of strategic intangible assets that became key mechanisms to control and centralize profits in different markets and industries. That strategy is achieved by accessing the international financial markets and the increasing financial inflation of their shares, common stocks and debt collateralization. Second, it is clear that physical capital accumulation decreased and that affected significantly the level of employment and the income concentration in the region. It seems that financial gains through cash management via treasury department administration are not as dynamic and effective as in multinational corporations; although Chilean corporations may be the exception.

In general terms, it is clear that this strategy margin has been narrowed due to the increasing indebtedness and the decreased profitability trend of these indicators. The continuity of this strategy will depend on the recovery of the globalized export model, which is unlikely in light of the supply shock caused by the worldwide 2020 economic lockdown. and the persistent trade war between China and the United States. This, however, can open a stage of capital reorganization among different sectors and a new selection of non-financial corporation winners.

6.3   CONCLUSIONS

One of the fundamental pillars of large corporation development was set in the 19th-century corporate laws of the United States and England, with the creation of stock companies with limited responsibilities. The direct effect on the dynamics of large non-financial corporations

Table 6.3   *Big corporation consolidated balance sheet and income statement of Chile, Brazil and Mexico, selected indicators (%) (2000–2017)*

Country	Year	2000	2009	2017	Mean 2000–2008	Mean 2008–2017
Mexico	CA/TA	29.7	31.5	29.5	31.0	30.5
	NCA/TA	70.3	68.5	70.5	69.0	69.5
	FA/TA	53.9	41.9	38.2	48.3	39.5
	NCANF/TA	16.4	26.7	32.3	20.7	30.0
	Acid Test Ratio[1]	0.9	1.0	0.9	0.9	1.0
	Solvency[1]	1.9	1.8	1.6	1.9	1.7
	DTE[1]	1.1	1.2	1.6	1.2	1.4
	TL/FA	96.4	130.7	160.2	112.5	149.4
	CL/TL	44.1	40.9	38.5	43.2	40.5
	NCL/TL	55.9	59.1	61.5	56.8	59.5
	ROE	9.3	12.7	10.4	11.6	11.1
	ROA	4.5	5.7	4.0	5.4	4.6
Chile	CA/TA	17.7	25.6	29.8	22.4	29.6
	NCA/TA	82.3	74.4	70.2	77.6	70.4
	FA/TA	68.5	53.7	42.6	65.2	46.9
	NCANF/TA	13.8	20.7	27.6	12.4	23.6
	Acid Test Ratio[1]	0.9	1.3	1.0	1.1	1.1
	Solvency[1]	2.0	2.0	1.7	2.1	1.9
	DTE[1]	1.4	1.1	1.5	1.1	1.4
	TL/FA	73.5	91.2	135.4	72.1	117.4
	CL/TL	30.2	33.4	44.3	33.6	42.7
	NCL/TL	69.8	66.6	55.7	66.4	57.3
	ROE	4.9	10.6	5.2	8.0	8.7
	ROA	1.8	4.6	2.0	3.5	3.5

Country	Year	2000	2009	2017	Mean 2000–2008	Mean 2008–2017
Brazil	CA/TA	30.7	44.3	25.3	36.9	31.4
	NCA/TA	69.3	55.7	74.7	63.1	68.6
	FA/TA	49.4	33.4	39.5	41.6	37.1
	NCANF/TA	19.9	22.2	35.2	21.5	31.5
	Acid Test Ratio[1]	1.0	1.1	0.5	1.0	0.7
	Solvency[1]	0.6	0.7	0.62	0.62	0.61
	DTE[1]	1.4	2.4	1.7	1.8	1.7
	TL/FA	114.6	201.6	157.3	152.1	168.0
	CL/TL	52.7	47.0	29.1	48.9	36.5
	NCL/TL	47.3	53.0	70.9	51.1	63.5
	ROE	10.7	13.4	5.3	12.9	7.6
	ROA	4.4	3.8	1.9	4.5	2.7

Notes: CA (Current Assets); NCA (Not Current Assets); FA (Fixed Assets); NCANF (Not Current Assets Not Fixed); TA (Total Assets); E (Equity); TL (Total Liabilities); CL (Current Liabilities); NCL (Not Current Liabilities); ROE (Return on Equity); ROA (Return on Assets). [1] Levels.
Source: Own calculations on Economatica database.

was unprecedented access to liquidity in financial markets that enabled overcapitalization practices, creating capital in excess, used to trade financial securities and increase their profit appropriation in the circulation sphere (M-M'[16]).

Unlike the conventional theory, which assumes that firms stand out for being deficit agents that finance their investment spending in the financial markets, overcapitalization is a condition where liquidity restrictions are loosened, but financial speculation can also modify profit distribution. Moreover, processes of overcapitalization have preceded and originated the financial crashes of the early 20th and 21st centuries, respectively.

Overcapitalization can effectively reduce financial costs via stock market operations since financial inflation can settle debt payments commitments. The key variable is the inflation of financial price instruments that, as long as it's positive, ensures the debts payments, from financial gains accrued in the circulation sphere. This process annuls the conventional theory equilibrium discussion since instead of capital scarcity there is liquidity in excess and there is no mechanism available for financial markets to distribute efficiently financial savings between borrowers. Corporations' collateral financial values go up, credit ratings improve, and their financial access to banks credits and market liquidity rise, giving way to very unstable conditions, which is higher debts at lower costs.

The industrial crisis in developed countries, in the third part of the 20th century, saw an increase in capital movement, mainly through M&A (initially in industrial countries) followed by financial market deregulation in the United States and Great Britain, along with the strengthening of institutional investors that enhanced profit appropriation mechanisms in the financial market, unlinked to the productive activity that combined business cycles with increased capital valorization of big corporations. The financial deepening and deregulation, followed by an extensive economic globalization was extended to all economies, via FDI. This process included developing economies from the last years of the 20th century, fortifying in Latin America and the Caribbean since the first years of the 21st century.

It should be noted that FDI inflows mainly concentrated in developed economies, increasing by six times in the 1990s, and LAC became important recipients of these inflows. During the 2000s, global FDI inflows stagnated within developing countries, being less affected than the LAC region and more importantly FDI inflows increased after 2008 Global Financial Crisis.

In terms of FDI outflows, these are dominant within developed countries, with increasing participation of developing countries, including LAC, although its volumes are very small. In this framework LAC large non-financial corporations emerge, which internationalize through mergers and acquisitions, but still these corporations are marginal at the international level. In spite of some Latin American corporations which have consolidated in the international rankings, their international operations are not very linked to their domestic operations. Another important feature is that these corporations, although they are listed in their local stock markets, they operate mainly through the financial centres.

Finally, the financial indicators of the Brazilian, Mexican and Chilean corporations suggest that during the period of analysis these entities underwent overcapitalization processes through their internationalization growth strategies, specifically mergers and acquisitions and strategic intangible asset purchases, that altogether boost the financial value of their assets as well as growing indebtedness, resulting in a deterioration of their solvency indicators. This took place within a context of declining physical capital asset accumulation, affecting negatively employment and increasing income concentration. A major shortfall of the overcapitalization strategy of Latin American corporations is that financial gains through cash management were not as successful as for developing countries' multinationals. Chile shows a slightly different performance that needs to be analysed further.

We can conclude that the space of manoeuvre of the overcapitalization strategy followed in Latin American economies has been narrowing since the 2008 Global Financial Crisis, since all the corporations studied show a growing tendency of their debt structure coupled with decreasing profitability ratios, which will further deteriorate due to the supply shock generated by the Covid-19 pandemic.

NOTES

1. The *commenda* was an early form of a limited commercial partnership that differentiates between a general (or travelling) partner which has managerial control of the enterprise and fully assumes the risks, and a passive (or sleeping) partner who provides a share of the capital required for the enterprises and is liable only to the extent of this financial investment, Blankenburg (2012, p. 193).
2. The mainstream argument that capital market issued long-term finance for enterprise development during the early stages of capitalism is false. Ireland (2010, citing Cameron) reaffirms that internal funds were the main firm's financial source at the beginning of capitalism, because of the modest capital requirements of most industries.
3. The Salomon case is a landmark UK company law case, in which the House of Lords' unanimous ruling was to uphold firmly the doctrine of corporate personality, as set out in the Companies Act 1862, so that creditors of an insolvent company could not sue the company's shareholders for payment of outstanding debts, see Blankenburg (2012).
4. In the conventional model, internal finance or profits from previous periods are not considered, because they assume that in each period production factors are paid in accordance with their contribution to global productivity, until profits are exhausted (economic surplus is not compatible with "normal earnings").
5. The concept of complete markets, applied to the financial sphere, is when saver needs are aligned to investors requirements, and an ample variety of financial instruments are available, with different

risks, returns and temporality. The main issue is that through demand and supply, the financial market is emptied and this means that at equilibria finance demand equals to financial portfolio of savers and potential investors.

6. Financial market information generally operates with past information (weak hypothesis), public information (semi-strong hypothesis) and may lack private information (strong hypothesis).

7. This view denies the occurrence of financial bubbles because it assumes that mathematical expected returns on assets conditioned by past returns are equal to zero.

8. Excess liquidity payments take place if liquid capital returns are above the necessary cost for holding liquidity in excess.

9. Intangibles and property rights are obtained through mergers and acquisitions that belong to the asset structure of the corporation acquired. However, they can also be acquired individually through financial purchase operations with other companies via start-ups or spin-offs from related or non-related companies. These operations have a decisive effect on the control of key innovations in the technical–scientific paradigm or even on the innovations or the property rights to control monopolistic gains. Its financial character is revealed by the effect that its control generates on expected profits and financial inflation. In addition, these assets are tradeable at any moment in accordance with the financial and competitive strategical adjustment of big corporations.

10. Calculation based on "The world's top 100 non-financial TNC, ranked by foreign assets", different years, UNCTAD/Erasmus University data, https://unctad.org/Sections/dite_dir/docs/wir2005top100_en.pdf.

11. UNCTAD calculates the "Transnationality index" as the average of the foreign assets of three indexes: foreign assets to total assets, foreign sales to total sales and foreign employment to total employment.

12. Calculation based on "The top 100 non-financial MNES from developing and transition economies, ranked by foreign assets", different years, UNCTAD/Erasmus University data, https://unctad.org/Sections/dite_dir/docs/wir2005top100_en.pdf.

13. Source: https://www.americaeconomia.com/revista.

14. The calculation was made with the GDP of each country as a percentage of LAC GDP, it doesn't take into account deductions and depreciations of produced assets or natural resources depletion. Source: World Bank national accounts data, and OECD National Accounts data files NY.GDP.MKTP.CD.

15. For example, their attachment to OECD corporate government principles.

16. Taken from the Marxian Scheme of Money M, and Money of Altered Value M'.

REFERENCES

Berle, A.E. and Means, G.C. (1933). *The Modern Corporation and the Private Property*. New York: The Macmillan Company.

Blankenburg, S. (2012). Limited liability. In Toporowski, J. and J. Michell (eds), *Handbook of Critical Issues in Finance* (191–200). Cheltenham, UK and Northampton, MA, USA: Edward Elgar Publishing.

Bustamante, J. (2018). Financiarización, financiamiento y estrategias de crecimiento de las grandes empresas en México. In Levy, N. (ed.), *Financiarización y Crisis de las estructuras productivas en países en Desarrollo*. México: Facultad de Economía-UNAM.

Dallery, T. (2009). Post Keynesian theories of the firm under financialization. *Review of Radical Political Economics*, 41(4), Autumn.

Domínguez, C. (2015). Financiarización y las corporaciones no financieras de México: un análisis a partir de la estructura de sus activos, pasivos e ingresos, 1996–2013. In Levy, N., C. Domínguez and C. Salazar (eds), *Crecimiento Económico, Deudas y Distribución del Ingreso: Nuevo y Crecientes Desequilibrios* (303–304). México: Facultad de Economía-Instituto de investigaciones económicas-UNAM.

Fama, E. (1991). Efficient capital markets: II. *The Journal of Finance*, 46(5), December.

Gómez, G. (2018). Endeudamiento de la empresa privada en México en la crisis financiera mundial. In Levy, N. (ed.), *Financiarizacion y Crisis de las estructuras productivas en países en Desarrollo* (333–368). México: Facultad de Economía-UNAM.

Hattori, M. and Takáts, E. (2015). The role of debt securities markets. *Bank for International Settlements (BIS)*. BIS Paper No. 83c, November.

Ireland, P. (2010). Limited liability, shareholder rights and the problem of corporate irresponsibility. *Cambridge Journal of Economics*, 34(5).

Jensen, M. and Meckling, W. (1976). The theory of the firm: managerial behavior, agency cost and ownership structure. *Journal of Financial Economics*, 3.

Kalecki, M. (1937). The principle of increasing risk. *Economica New Series*, 4(16).

Kalecki, M. (1954). *Entrepreneurial Capital and Investment, Theory of Economic Dynamics: An Essay on Cyclical and Long-Run Changes in Capitalist Economy*. London: Routledge.

Minsky, H. (1975). *John Maynard Keynes*. New York: Columbia University Press.

Modigliani, F. and Miller, M. (1958). The cost of capital, corporation finance and the theory of investment. *The American Economic Review*, 48(3).

Smithin, J. (2018). *Rethinking the Theory of Money, Credit, and Macroeconomics: A New Statement for the Twenty-first Century*. London: Lexington Books.

Steindl, J. (1945). *Small and Big Business: Economic Problem of the Size of the Firms*. Oxford: Basil Blackwell.

Steindl, J. (1990). *Economic Papers 1941–88*. New York: Palgrave Macmillan.

Stiglitz, J.E. (1988). Why financial structure matters. *Journal of Economics Perspectives*, 2(4), Winter.

Tobin, J. and Brainard, W.C. (1977). Asset markets and the cost of capital. *Cowles Foundation,* Paper 427.

Toporowski, J. (2000). *The End of Finance: Capital Market Inflation, Financial Derivatives and Pension Fund Capitalism*. London: Routledge.

Toporowski, J. (2012). Overcapitalisation. In Toporowski, J. and J. Michell (eds), *Handbook of Critical Issues in Finance* (270–273). Cheltenham, UK and Northampton, MA, USA: Edward Elgar Publishing.

Wicksell, K. (1893/1954). *Value Capital and Rent*. London: George Allen & Unwin.

Woodford, M. (2003). *Interest and Prices: Foundations of a Theory of Monetary Policy*. Princeton, NJ: Princeton University Press.

PART II

Non-financial corporations and economic growth

7. Capital flows, the role of non-financial corporations and their macroeconomic implications: an analysis of the case of Chile

Esteban Pérez-Caldentey and Nicole Favreau-Negront[1]

7.1   INTRODUCTION

Since the adoption of a free market/neoliberal model in the early 1970s, Chile has embarked on a policy of trade and financial liberalisation as a means to promote growth and development.[2] The key policy actions in trade have included significant reduction in tariffs and non-tariff barriers, and the signing of free trade agreements with more than twenty-five commercial partners comprising more than 94% of its total trade.

The process of trade opening was complemented by financial liberalisation. This was initially seen as a component of the progressive liberalisation of the interest rate structure, the privatisation of commercial banks in the hands of the government, the reduction of barriers to entry into the financial system and the creation of a private pension system. In the early 1970s the government passed the Law-Decree 600, which governs foreign investment regulations in the country. Foreign investors are granted national treatment and "allowed to hold up to 100% of the equity of a firm in the vast majority of the sectors" (WTO, 2009).[3] Foreign investors are also granted the right to reinvest or repatriate liquid profits.[4]

As with the trade opening process, financial liberalisation was partially suspended during the financial crisis of the 1980s but then restarted accompanied by better and more rigorous banking supervision practices. Despite the implementation of capital controls in the 1990s, bilateral treaties (in particular, the bilateral treaty with the United States) committed the country to the free transfer of capital.

The arguments supporting financial liberalisation are couched in "real" terms and are very similar to those put forward for trade liberalisation. Indeed, both draw on the same principle, that of allocative efficiency, and the arguments for financial liberalisation are in fact an extension to trade in assets of the classical arguments of the gains in international trade. Using the standard neo-classical growth model proponents of financial liberalisation argue that financial liberalisation and more precisely capital account liberalisation improves the efficiency in the international allocation of resources. As put by Henry (2007: 887–888):

> In the neoclassical model, liberalizing the capital account facilitates a more efficient allocation of resources and produces all kinds of salubrious effects. Resources flow from capital abundant developed countries, where the return to capital is high. The flow of resources in developing countries

reduces their cost of capital, triggering a temporary increase in investment and growth that permanently raises their standard of living.

An analysis of the balance of payments for Chile, its main components (the current and financial accounts) and of its determinants tells a very different story. The current account of the balance of payments has been traditionally in a deficit position and in the aftermath of the Global Financial Crisis (2008–2009) has widened significantly with no evidence of mean reversion. In an accounting sense, the current account deficit has been balanced with growing capital inflows.

However, accounting identities are not the same thing as functional relationships. Financial inflows are not external savings that "finance", in any sense of the word, economic activity in the domestic Chilean economy. And the Chilean economy does not run current account deficits because domestic spending is greater than domestic savings.

The evidence shows that both the current and financial accounts are driven by finance. The deficit in the current account is explained to a great extent by profit repatriations of the non-financial corporate sector. Financial inflows are driven by short-term capital inflows both in terms of portfolio flows and foreign direct investment flows (FDI). Intercompany loans which are a significant part of FDI behave like portfolio flows. In turn, financial inflows are determined by the financial position of the non-financial corporate sector.

The available evidence shows that the non-financial sector has liquidity constraints and is overleveraged. Chile is the second most indebted emerging market economy in the world after China. In the first quarter of 2020, Chile's total debt stood at 226% of GDP (IIF, 2020). The bulk of Chile's debt is concentrated in the private sector and roughly half of the country's debt is held by the non-financial corporate sector. In addition, the non-financial corporate sector has witnessed a decline in its levels of profitability.

This chapter examines the relationships between capital inflows and the non-financial corporate sector. It argues that capital inflows do not respond to the financing needs of the real economy but rather to the fragile financial position of the non-financial corporate sector. The chapter is divided into seven sections. Following the introduction, the second section questions the mainstream "real" approach to the balance of payments and explains its dominance by financial factors. The third section analyses debt in the non-financial corporate sector. The fourth section links the behaviour of the balance of payments, and more specifically capital flows, to that of the non-financial corporate sector. The fifth section provides an analysis of the debt issues of the non-financial corporate sector and its main characteristics. Section six argues that the characteristics of the debt issues reflect a vulnerable and fragile financial position of the non-financial corporate sector. Section seven concludes.

7.2   THE MAINSTREAM APPROACH AND FINANCIAL DOMINANCE OF THE BALANCE OF PAYMENTS

The mainstream approach to the balance of payments is articulated around two interrelated propositions. The first sustains that the balance of payments whether analysed from the current account or the financial (capital) side responds to the behaviour of real variables.

One of the most illustrative expositions is the intertemporal approach to the balance of payments.[5] The intertemporal approach to the balance of payments analyses the external sector by postulating two representative agents in two different countries (C1 and C2).

Both differ in terms of endowments. C1's endowment is greater than C2. That is, C1 is richer than C2. As well, the richer agent (C1) has a slower future income stream than the poorer agent (C2). Moreover, the richer agent (C1) has a lower demand for current consumption than the poorer agent (C2). Finally, the richer agent (C1) has a lower marginal product of capital (higher capital to labour ratio) relative to the poorer agent (C2).

Both have well-behaved utility functions and pursue utility-maximising behaviour. As a result, given their differences both agents can benefit by "smoothing" their streams of future consumption. There arises an exchange between both in the form of a credit market that can lead to mutual beneficial gains. The richer country (C1) gives up some of its current consumption against greater future consumption. Conversely, the poorer country (C2) increases its current consumption by borrowing from the richer agent (C2), backing the borrowing by greater future income.

Once the analysis of exchange between both countries is worked out, financial flows can be introduced (as outside money) in the analysis and in this way, it is made consistent with the analysis in "real" terms.[6]

The second proposition asserts that the current account is a result of an imbalance between domestic investment and savings. In other words, a current account imbalance reflects increased expenditure over savings ($I > S$) which implies that restoring equilibrium to the balance of payments requires an increase in savings in order to avoid a contraction of economic activity due to a reduction in investment. This second proposition follows the logic of the first one, a current account disequilibrium resulting from "excess" spending at home is sustainable only to the extent that the economy in question is able to attract capital flows to "finance" its imbalance. The line of causation goes from the current account to financial flows. This obviously has major implications for domestic policy since it sets the stage for conservative fiscal and monetary policies. The external financing of a budget deficit requires "credibility" and good behaviour on the part of the government in order to avoid a downgrade in its credit rating that could impair its access to capital markets at an acceptable cost. Similarly, monetary policy is driven by interest parity considerations, hence the predilection for inflation targeting over other monetary frameworks.

The Chilean case is a perfect illustration that shows that these propositions fail to hold in the real world. The evidence provided by an analysis of the balance of payments, and in particular the current account and that of the financial (capital) flows shows that since the Global Financial Crisis (2008–2009) the current account has exhibited a trend towards an increasing imbalance and that this imbalance reflects to a great extent the behaviour of the balance on income account, that is profit repatriation. Empirical evidence available shows that the current account which had posted a current account surplus from 2003 to 2007, registered a deficit in 2008 reaching US\$6.7 billion and this grew to US\$10.9 billion in 2019.

The decomposition of the current account in its different components including the balance of goods and services, transfers and income account (which consists mainly of profit repatriations) shows that the only consistent negative item is the income account. In fact, if the income account was excluded from the current account, the latter would yield a surplus. Between 2009 and 2019 the merchandise and services balance averaged US\$5.9 billion. For its part, the income account averaged US\$-12.2 billion. On the financial side of the balance of payments, the evidence shows that since the Global Financial Crisis short-term inflows predominate

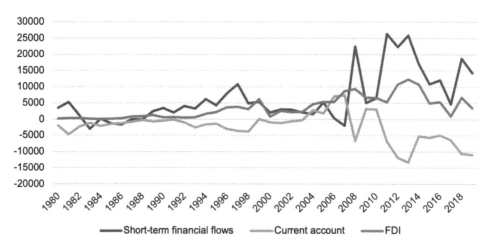

Source: On the basis of IMF (2020).

Figure 7.1   *Chile: evolution of the current account of the balance of payments,*
                  short-term capital flows and FDI (1980–2019) (millions of US dollars)

(Figure 7.1). On average between 2008 and 2019, short-term flows amounted to US$14.2 billion, that is twice the value of FDI for that period (US$7.1 billion).

As we will argue below, a major driving force underpinning the evolution of short-term portfolio flows (and also FDI flows) is the behaviour and financial situation of the non-financial corporate sector. More precisely, short-term financial flows respond to the state of indebtedness and that of the balance sheets of the non-financial corporate sector. A feasible hypothesis that explains the evolution of the balance of payments and of its components (since the Global Financial Crisis), is that the state of the balance sheets of the non-financial corporate sector determined the evolution of financial flows, which in turn determined the behaviour of the current account, in part due to its effects on the profit repatriation and thus the income account.

This explanation places financial rather than real factors at the centre of both domestic and external activity and stability. In a word, finance "rules the roost". At the same time this explanation reverses the traditional causality between the current and the financial accounts of the balance of payments. Finally, this approach also sustains that macroeconomic analysis cannot be limited to the analysis of aggregate magnitudes and must somehow escape the "vice of consolidation" (Kennedy, 1960, p. 568) and dig deeper into the behaviour of sectors and agents, particularly in a context such as that of Latin America and Chile, where concentration of the means of production and finance are so important to understand its pattern of growth and development.

7.3   DEBT IN THE NON-FINANCIAL CORPORATE SECTOR

Since the Global Financial Crisis, the bond market has become a major source of finance of real economic activity in developed and developing economies. The bond market has partly

Table 7.1   *Chile: cross border loans and international debt flows to the economy in the aggregate and non-financial corporate sector (2001q1–2015q4) (millions of US dollars)*

Debt flows and loans	2001q1–2008q4	2010q1–2015q4
International debt flows to the non-financial corporate sector	599.6	4,875.0
Cross-border bank loans to the non-financial corporate sector	1,923.9	633.1
Total bonds	993.0	8,324.4
Total loans	3,198.4	998.1

Source: IMF (2020).

replaced the role that cross-border bank lending had before the start of the crisis in international finance.

This is explained in part by the loss of profitability of global banks, its restructuring and regulation. But, it is also important to mention that the importance of the bond market as a source of finance in developing countries is also explained by the "increased risk appetite and search for yield" by international investors (Tendulkar and Hancock, 2014) and this was driven, to a great extent, by QE policies and low rates of return on assets in the developed world. This also provided favourable conditions for increased demand (jointly in part by high commodity prices and favourable exchange rate levels at least until 2014) for external finance.

Chile has not been aliened to this trend. Moreover, in the case of Chile, the non-financial corporate sector has been the most active sector in the international bond market.

From 2001q1 to 2008q4, the year prior to that during which the effects of the Global Financial Crisis started to be felt in Latin America and Chile, the volume of loans exceeded bond flows by a factor of 3 to 1. A similar situation is registered with the cross-border loans and bond flows in the case of the non-financial corporate sector (see Table 7.1). The Global Financial Crisis reversed this situation and between the first quarter of 2010 and the last quarter of 2015 bond flows surpassed cross-border loans by a factor of roughly 8 to 1 at the economy-wide level and for the case of the non-financial corporate sector.

As a result, the stock of debt of the non-financial corporate sector increased in line with the expansion of bond flows. The available evidence encompassing the period from March 2007 to March 2020 shows that its outstanding debt increased from US$8.9 to 55.4 billion representing 71.2% and 120% of GDP, while government and household increased from 9.3% to 33.1% and 29.1% to 50.3% of GDP respectively These sectors show a more stable behaviour, maintaining a moderate growth trend. In comparison with other countries, Chile's non-financial corporate sector has one of the highest stocks of outstanding debt of emerging market economies. In fact, the level of indebtedness of the Chilean non-financial sector is only surpassed by that of China (102% and 159% of GDP for Chile and China respectively).

7.4   THE LINKAGE BETWEEN THE DEBT OF THE NON-FINANCIAL CORPORATE SECTOR AND CAPITAL FLOWS

The fact that the non-financial corporate sector finances its operations in the international bond markets provides a critical linkage between indebtedness and capital flows. Indeed, the rise in

*Table 7.2   Chile: gross debt inflows and stock corporate debt outstanding (1980–2019)
(millions of US dollars)*

	1980–1990	1991–2000	2001–2010	2011–2019
Gross debt inflows	-9.7	466.4	1,548.9	6,926.7
Corporate debt	34.4	2,090.5	8,807.9	34,569.4

Source: On the basis of IMF (2020), FRED (2020) and BIS (2020).

indebtedness has been accompanied by an increase in gross portfolio inflows. Gross portfolio inflows expanded from US$-10 million on average during the period 1980–1990, to 466, 1,549 and 6,927 million for the periods 1991–2000, 2001–2010 and 2011–2019. This was the result in the expansion of outstanding stock of corporate debt which expanded by US$34, 2,090, 8,808 and 34,569 million for the same periods (see Table 7.2).

Since the Global Financial Crisis (2008–2009), gross debt inflows which are tied to non-financial corporate debt have tended to systematically out space gross debt outflows so that they constitute a net injection of liquidity into the economy. As Figure 7.2 illustrates, net debt inflows amounted to US$89,516 billion for the period 2000–2005 on average, turned negative in the 2006–2010 period (US$-117,155 billion) and increased dramatically in the period 2011–2019 reaching US$484,320 million.

In addition, the evidence also indicates that gross debt inflows have become an important source of finance, not only for the non-financial corporate sector but also for the Chilean economy in the aggregate. For the period 2011–2019, gross debt inflows represented 54.4% of FDI and 78.2% of gross portfolio inflows.

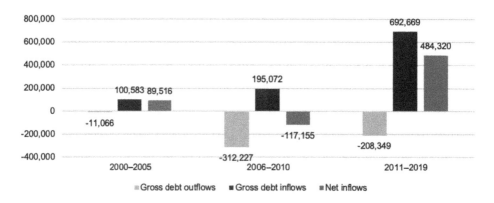

Source: On the basis of IMF (2020).

*Figure 7.2   Chile: gross debt outflows, gross debt net inflows and net debt inflows
(2000–2019) (millions of US dollars)*

An additional overlooked factor that underscores the importance of gross debt flows as a determinant of the financial account of the balance of payments and thus its dependency on the vicissitudes of the financing needs of the non-financial corporate sector is the fact that foreign direct investment not only includes equity (green field) investment but also intercompany loans.

FDI is founded upon a strategic long-lasting interest between a firm residing in a host country and a direct investor residing outside the firm's host country. By convention, the criterion to establish a long-lasting interest is provided by a benchmark of an ownership by the direct investor of at least 10% of the voting power of the firm. This benchmark provides the direct investor with a significant degree of influence in the management of the firm (OECD, 2008; Wacker, 2013).

Any capital transaction falling within the 10% or more benchmark is thus considered an FDI transaction. On this basis a difference can be drawn, between equity, re-invested earnings and intercompany loans: whereas as equity capital can constitute an FDI relationship in the sense that it can provide 10% of more of the voting power of a firm. Re-invested earnings and intercompany loans are characterised as FDI once a FDI relationship has been established (Wacker, 2013).

Intercompany loans as a percentage of total FDI (equity and intercompany loans FDI) for the period ranging from September 2007 to May 2016: During this period the share of inter-company loans in FDI increased from 2% to 50% of the total, reflecting the fact that FDI does not necessarily respond to long-term considerations or fundamentals but rather to the financial position of the firms in the non-financial corporate sector.[7]

7.5 THE DEBT PROFILE OF THE NON-FINANCIAL CORPORATE SECTOR

The number of Chilean firms that issue bonds in the international capital market is a very small subset of the existing number of firms. According to a recent survey there are roughly 14,172 large firms in Chile.[8] According to different sources (including Bloomberg, Dealogics, the Commission for the Financial Market of Chile (CMF) and the Chilean Internal Revenue Service (SII)) the number of firms that make available their balance sheets, financial position and financial results is roughly between 425 and 562 firms (for the period 2010–2019). Available data for the period running from 2014 to 2019 show that the number of bond-issuing firms reached only 44 firms in total out of which 28 belonged to the non-financial corporate sectors. In other words, the number of issuing firms represents 0.2% of the total number of large firms and between 7% and 11% of the number of firms that make their data available.

However, due to the oligopolistic structure of the Chilean economy, the firms that issue bonds in the international market account to more than 30% of total assets and more than 40% of the share of expenditure on fixed assets and long-term investment.

An analysis of the international debt issues for Chilean firms for the period 2014–2019 and its comparison to the issues of the economic sectors, the financial and government sectors, yield important insight on the financial position and vulnerability of the non-financial corporate sector. The analysis shows three important facts (see Table 7.3).

First, for the said period, the non-financial corporate sector issued fewer bonds than the financial sector (63 versus 90 bond issues). However, the total value of the debt issues of the non-financial corporate sector largely exceeds those of the financial sector and those of the government (US$39.4, 16.2 and 22.6 billion).

Table 7.3   Selected debt issue indicators for non-financial corporate sector, financial sector and general government (2014–2019)

Sectors	Non-financial corporate sector	Financial sector	General government
Number of debt issues	63	90	21
Value of debt issues (US$ billion)	39.4	16.2	22.6
Coupon rate (percentage)	4.7	2.6	2.5
Number of years to maturity	17	8	14
Issues in $US (percentage of total)	96	30	44

Source: On the basis of Dealogic and LatinFinance (Bonds Database). Financial sector corresponds to "Financial and insurance activities".

Second, the cost of the debt is higher for the non-financial corporate sector. The coupon rate (the annual interest rate on the value of the bond issue) in the non-financial corporate sector is 4.7% versus 2.6% and 2.5% for the financial and government sectors.

Third, the number of years to maturity of the bond issues of the non-financial sector is longer term than those of the financial and government sectors (17, 8 and 14 years respectively). On the one hand, greater number of years to maturity of bond issues lessens the liquidity and eventually insolvency risk that arises with short-term debt.

On the other hand, debt issues with greater years to maturity enhances the interest rate risk and the exchange rate risk. As is well known, the present value of a bond varies inversely with the rate of interest and the capital gain of loss derived from a change in the rate of interest is multiplied by the number of years to maturity. This means that as the years to maturity increase the interest rate sensitivity of a bond, or to put it another way, the interest rate risk increases. The interest rate risk can be compounded by changes in the exchange rate (exchange rate risk). The exchange rate risk for the non-financial corporate sector in the case of developing countries and Chile is high since this sector is generally exposed to currency mismatches. In the case of Chile available evidence for the years 2007 and 2014 shows that the net foreign-currency assets relative to exports (a proxy for currency mismatch) in the private corporate sector has trended up increasing from -20.6% to -58.7%, owing mainly to the behaviour of the non-financial corporate sector (Chui et al., 2016, 2018).

Moreover, the exchange risk is concentrated on the variations in the United States dollar. The international bond market issues are mainly denominated in US dollars for the non-financial sector whereas for the financial sector and government they are more diversified. In the case of the non-financial corporate sector, 97% of the bond issues are denominated in US dollars whereas 70% and 54% of the bond issues of the financial sector and the government are denominated in other currencies.

Exchange risk is enhanced by the fact that, as in the case of other Latin American and developing countries, firms in the corporate sector, including financial and non-financial firms, tend to operate with currency mismatches (Borio, 2019). In addition, available evidence for the period 2007–2014 indicates that currency mismatches have increased. In the case of Chile, the net foreign currency assets of firms in the corporate sector as a percentage of exports (a proxy for currency mismatches) decreased from -20.6% in 2007 to -58.7% in 2014 (Chui et al., 2016). Moreover, a more in-depth analysis reveals that this widening mismatch is mainly explained by the non-financial corporate sector (Chui et al., 2018).

7.6   A FINANCIAL ANALYSIS OF THE NON-FINANCIAL CORPORATE SECTOR

In order to complete our argument, we assess whether the rise in capital inflows is driven to a great extent by how the non-financial corporate sector responds to production requirements or to purely financial motives. To this end, we analyse the financial situation of firms that issued bonds in the international capital markets and whether the proceeds of these bonds were used for the formation of gross fixed capital.

The financial situation of the bond-issuing firms was assessed using three criteria: liquidity, solvency and profitability. The liquidity of firms was measured using the quick ratio (QR). Solvency was captured using the leverage ratio, the interest coverage, and the relationship between short-term debt and total debt. Finally, profitability was estimated using the rate of return on equity (ROE) and net profit margin (NPM).

The QR reflects a company's ability to pay its short-term obligations. It considers only the most liquid assets (less inventories assets) as a measure of a company's ability to meet its short-term obligations. Liquidity ratios equal to a value of one are traditionally considered to mean that companies are able to meet their short-term obligations and liquidity ratios whose values are below one are an indicator of the opposite.

Solvency ratios such as debt-to-equity ratio (i.e. leverage) measure a company's ability to meet its long-term obligations. Solvency ratios show the extent to which a company relies on indebtedness to finance its productive activity.

There is no established leverage threshold. Leverage ratios can exhibit a very high variance because these depend on both cyclical factors and also on country size, levels of development and type of productive activity. Following Gebauer et al. (2017) and Pérez-Caldentey et al. (2019), the leverage threshold was set at 0.8.

Gebauer et al. (2017) estimated the average leverage ratio (0.48) for the period 2005–2015 for a set of 618,000 companies operating in Italy, Spain, Portugal, Greece and Slovenia. The authors also established an overleverage 0.80–0.85 threshold interval. Pérez-Caldentey et al. (2019) applied the same methodology for a sample of 279 companies in Argentina, Brazil, Chile, Peru and Mexico and set the overleverage threshold at 0.81. Overleverage refers to a situation where the increase in debt and in investment are negatively correlated. That is, a firm issuing a bond in the international capital market uses the proceeds for other purposes than those of investing. For example, a firm uses the proceeds of a bond issue to increase its liquidity holdings in order to avoid a cash shortage or insolvency.

The interest coverage ratio index (earnings before interest and interest-divided taxes) is another measure of solvency. It is an indicator of how easily a company can pay interest on its debt and the extent to which a company relies on short-term debt to pay its obligations. As in the case of leverage there is not an established threshold for the interest coverage ratio. However, as in the case of the quick reason, a value of one can be used as a threshold to determine the financial strength of a firm's balance.

The third indicator used to gauge solvency is the ratio of short-term to total debt. A value of 0.5 is used as a threshold. Values above 0.5 imply that a firm can face cash constraints and may not be able to meet its debt obligations (at least the interest payments).

*Table 7.4   Percentage average of bond issuing firms in the non-financial corporate
sector in financial fragility position (2009–2016)*

Financial Indicators	Value
Liquidity Ratio	45.6
Interest coverage ratio	27.2
Leverage	96.9
Short-term to total debt	9.1
ROE	77.2
NPM	76.4

Source: On the basis of Bloomberg (2019).

Finally, for profitability, no specific criteria are used. Rather, the main issue is whether profitability (using ROE and NIM) increased or decreased. The base for comparison is the period
2009–2010.

In order to determine the strength/vulnerability of the financial situation of debt-issuing
firms, we identified the percentage of firms that are above the thresholds for the quick-ratio
(QR), leverage, and short-term to total debt. We also obtained the percentage of debt-issuing
firms that have registered a decline in the rate of return on equity (ROE) and the net profit
margin (NPM).

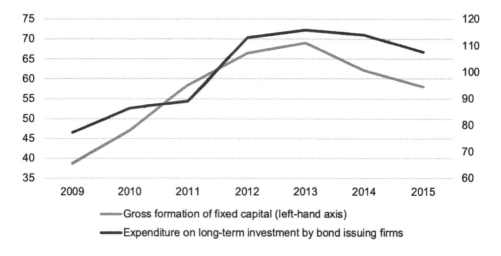

Notes: The expenditure on long-term investment and gross fixed capital formation is expressed in current dollars.
But the latter refers to value added which explains the difference in current dollars between both magnitudes.
Source: On the basis of Bloomberg (2019) and Central Bank of Chile (2020).

*Figure 7.3   Chile: evolution of expenditures of international bond issuing firms on
long-term investment and gross fixed capital formation (2009–2015) (billions
of US dollars)*

The results show that the most vulnerable aspects of firms' finances are both liquidity and solvency measured by the leverage ratio. Table 7.4 shows that close to half of the firms that issued bonds in the international capital markets have a liquidity ratio below one and that roughly all of these firms are overleveraged. Also, the results show that 77.2% and 76.4% of all bond-issuing firms witnessed a decline in profitability according to the rate of return on equity and the net interest margin (ROE and NIM).

Greater access to external finance does not imply increased expenditure on investment. Available empirical evidence for the period 2009–2015 shows that firms' expenditure of long-term investment increased between 2009 and 2012 and decreased thereafter. The evidence also shows that the investment behaviour of bond-issuing firms mimics the evolution of gross fixed capital formation of the economy in the aggregate (Figure 7.3).

This is no fortuitous coincidence. Large firms (and thus the largest of the large, that is the firms that issue bonds in the international capital market) account for the lion's share of investment. To illustrate this point, a sample of 279 large Chilean companies was divided into one hundred groups of equal intervals and the percentage of long-term investment concentrated by each group was estimated. The results show that the first three groups (the first, second and third percentiles) concentrate the bulk of the investment The results show that the first, second and third percentile companies account for an average of 30%, 56% and 70% of gross fixed capital formation.

7.7   CONCLUSIONS

This chapter argues that, contrary to the conventional wisdom of mainstream economics, the behaviour of the balance of payments and more specifically that of the capital/financial account is explained by financial and not real factors. Moreover, the chapter argues that this behaviour does not reflect the interactions of the economy in the aggregate but that it is rather sector specific. The evolution of the capital account is explained by the rising importance of the international bond market and by the financial position of the non-financial corporate sector, and more precisely, by a minority of firms that issue debt in the international capital markets.

The analysis shows that the financial position of the international bond issuing firms is rather vulnerable and fragile. Roughly more than half of these firms have liquidity constraints, while the majority are overleveraged and show declines in profitability. Under these conditions the international bond market is not a source of finance of real activity, rather a means through which these firms can guarantee their financial survival. International bond-issuing firms use the liquidity obtained in the internal bond market to buffer up their balance sheet rather than use it to finance investment. Indeed, the existing literature shows that beyond a given leverage threshold, firms tend to increase their cash and liquid assets and reduce investment. The decline in profitability strengthens the inverse relationship between debt and investment.

This analysis provides important insights for macroeconomic analysis. There is an urgent need to integrate not only the financial with real factors (in mainstream economics this integration exists only in terms of market imperfects, such as information asymmetries) but also to integrate the micro with the macroeconomic dimension. In countries such as Chile and in general in Latin America, production, in the same way as finance, is highly concentrated. As a result, macroeconomic outcomes reflect the actions and choices of a few economic agents.

And as a result, a complete and full macroeconomic analysis requires an understanding of how these agents act and interact. In other words, macroeconomics must also escape the vice of consolidation (Kennedy, 1960) if it is to provide useful guidance for the design of economic policy.

NOTES

1. The opinions here expressed are the authors' own and may not coincide with the institutions with which they are affiliated.
2. These include an initially implicit and then explicit fiscal rule to ensure a pattern of sustainable expenditures and deficits in line with the structural factors of the Chilean economy. The fiscal rule not only was viewed as a means to expand the fiscal space but also to ensure a high external credit rating. Similarly, the country progressed towards a flexible exchange rate regime, to reduce the possibility of currency crises and create a buffer of stocks to absorb negative external shocks. Greater exchange rate flexibility allowed the country to implement monetary policies with a greater degree of autonomy. A free-floating exchange rate regime jointly with operational and instrument independency of the central bank were two main components of a full-fledged inflation targeting regime. This monetary framework provided the required credibility and reputation to pursue and ensure price and nominal stability. According to the WTO (2015) the average tariff rate in Chile is 6% (in 1973 it was 103%).
3. The exceptions include coastal shipping, air transport and the communications media (WTO, 2015).
4. According to the latest WTO Policy Trade report of Chile (2015): "Since 1974, most of them have invested in the country under DL No. 600. Up to 2011, a total of US$82,021 million (56.5% of Chile's gross capital inflow) entered Chile through this mechanism. Nonetheless, in recent years DL No. 600 has lost ground to Chapter XIV of the Central Bank's Compendium of Foreign Exchange Regulations, owing to factors such as the removal of exchange controls by the central bank in 2001, the incorporation of investment disciplines in the free trade agreements, Chile's admission to the OECD in 2010, and more recently the tax reform introduced through Law No. 20.780."
5. See Obstfeld and Rogoff (1996); see Art. 10.8 of the Free Trade Agreement between Chile and the United States (WTO, 2009).
6. In this type of model, the main role of the external sector is to smooth out consumption over time. Increases in actual over permanent domestic income, result in positive transitory income which can be saved and invested abroad to earn a higher rate of return than if invested domestically. Contrarily, when actual income falls below permanent income and transitory income becomes negative, the level of consumption is maintained by increasing imports and foreign borrowing. Whatever the ultimate outcome, actual consumption is always maintained at a level consistent with that of permanent income, and capital is always allocated to its most profitable (efficient) use.
7. The data are the authors' own computations on the basis of IMF (2020).
8. The distinction between different firm size levels is based on the volume of turnover. Micro-enterprises have turnover of less than 2,400 UF, small firms have turnover ranging between 2,400 and 25,000 UF, medium sized firms have a turnover ranging between 25,000 and 100,000 UF. Large firms have a turnover that exceeds 100,000 UF. The UF (Unidad de Fomento) is a unit of account that is indexed to price variations to maintain the purchasing power of the value of contracts and assets denominated in UF. As of 28 February 2017 the value of one unit UF was equivalent to 26,392.09 Chilean pesos.

REFERENCES

BIS (2020). Debt statistics. *Bank for International Settlements*. Geneva: BIS.

Bloomberg. (2019). Bloomberg data. Retrieved from www.bloomberg.com.

Borio, C. (2019). Monetary policy frameworks in EMEs: inflation targeting, the exchange rate and financial stability. BIS Annual Economic Report 2019. *Geneva, Bank for International Settlements (BIS)*. Retrieved from https://www.bis.org/publ/arpdf/ar2019e2.pdf.

Central Bank of Chile (2020). *Base de Datos Estadísticos Cuentas Nacionales*. Santiago. Retrieved from https://si3.bcentral.cl/siete/.

Chui, M., Kuruc, E. and Turner, P. (2016). A new dimension to currency mismatches in the emerging markets: non-financial companies. *BIS Working Paper*, No. 550.

Chui, M., Kuruc, E. and Turner, P. (2018). Leverage and currency mismatches: non-financial companies in the emerging markets. *Special Issue: Global Trade Policy 2018*, 41(12). The World Economy. Retrieved from http://wileyonlinelibrary.com/journal/TWEC.

FRED (2020). Economic data. *Federal Reserve Bank of St. Louis*. Retrieved from https://www.stlouisfed .org/.

Gebauer, S., Setzer, R. and Westphal, A. (2017). Corporate debt and investment: a firm level analysis for stressed euro area countries. *ECB*, Working Paper Series No. 2101. Frankfurt am Main: European Central Bank.

Henry, P.B. (2007). Capital account liberalization: theory, evidence and speculation. *Journal of Economic Literature*, 45(4), 887–935.

IMF (2020). International financial statistics. *IMF*. Retrieved from https//www.imf.org.

Institute of International Finance (IIF). (2020). Global debt monitor. Sharp spike in debt ratios. 16 July.

Kennedy, C. (1960). *Money in a Theory of Finance* by J.G. Gurley and E.S. Shaw. *Economic Journal*, 70(279), 568–569.

Obstfeld, M. and Rogoff, K. (1996). *Foundations of International Macroeconomics*. Cambridge: MIT Press.

OECD (2008). *Benchmark Definition of FDI*. Fourth Edition. Paris: OECD.

Pérez Caldentey, E., Favreau Negront, N. and Méndez Lobos, L (2019). Corporate debt in Latin America and its macroeconomic implications. *Journal of Post Keynesian Economics*, 42(3), 335–362.

Tendulkar, R. and Hancock, G. (2014). Corporate bond markets: a global perspective. *IOSCO Research Department*. Retrieved from https://iosco.org/.

Wacker, M.C. (2013). On the measurement of foreign direct investment and its relationship to activities of multinational corporations. *European Central Bank*, Working Paper Series No 1614 / November 2013.

World Trade Organization (WTO). (2009). Chile. Trade policy review. Retrieved from https://wto.org/.

World Trade Organization (WTO). (2015). Chile. Trade policy review (Report No. 5). Retrieved from https://wto.org/.

8. Foreign direct investment in the Mexican steel industry

Samuel Ortiz-Velásquez[1]

The steel industry is a strategic and global industry, due to the simple fact that steel is an essential input in almost all investments in fixed capital and in durable consumer goods. This means that we are dealing with a vertically integrated industry forward with crucial activities such as construction, metalworking, capital goods, energy, military and because certain segments (mainly rolling steel products) are incorporated as suppliers for the global automotive and aerospace value chains.

In Mexico, this steel industry is an extension of the global industry since the segments with the highest profit generation are controlled by multinational companies (MNCs). Such industrial organization makes it possible to warn that, surely, in investment decision making in the Mexican steel industry, microeconomic and institutional factors may be more significant than traditional macroeconomic factors. Moreover, this suggests that a correct reading of the determinants of investment in the steel industry should go beyond macroeconomic theory, to rely on theories of industrial organization and foreign direct investment (FDI).

The objective of this chapter is to examine the incentives for investment in the Mexican steel company, at the industry and company level. For this, the chapter is divided into five sections. Section 8.1 addresses the characteristics of the world steel company with emphasis on the China–United States trade dispute and the United States–Mexico–Canada Agreement (USMCA). This is relevant, considering that global changes impact the behaviour of investment in the Mexican steel company. Section 8.2 contains a theoretical and empirical discussion of the determinants of physical investment, based on Marxist, post-Keynesian, industrial organization and FDI approaches. Section 8.3 describes an analysis of the industrial organization of the steel industry in Mexico with emphasis on investment. Section 8.4 examines the factors affecting such an investment at the industry and company level, based on the results of the Economic Census (EC) 2019 and the case studies on the foreign subsidiaries Tenaris Tamsa, Ternium, Gerdau-Corsa and TIM. The last section contains the conclusions and introduces some recommendations aimed at ensuring that the Mexican steel industry can take advantage of the new regional integration with the UMSCA.

8.1 THE STEEL INDUSTRY IN THE WORLD

Main Processes and Products

The industry is made up of five typical phases: mining, production, casting, rolling, and finished products (CEPAL, 2009). The first one provides the raw materials: coking and iron ore in the form of fines, pieces, and pellets. In the second phase two technological routes are identified: integrated and semi-integrated plants. In the former, the dominant pattern is the production of Basic Oxygen Furnace (BOF) by the combination of iron and coking in large plants. The latter uses Electric Arc Furnace (EAF) to produce steel through scrap metal, this route is more compact, modern, and sustainable.

In the third phase the steel is cast and transformed into slabs to produce flat laminates or into billets for long laminates and seamless tubes. Integrated plants predominate in the former, semi-integrated plants predominate in the latter. In the fourth phase, the steels are transformed into final products. Both flat and long laminates are subdivided into carbon laminates and specialty laminates. Sheet metals, coils and tinplate stand out in flat carbon laminates, while in the special plants the stainless ones stand out. In the long carbon laminates, concrete bars, wire rod, bars, profiles, rails, and seamless tubes stand out; while in the special long laminates, bars, wire rod and seamless tubes stand out. In the fifth phase, the finished product plants are usually smaller in size with high added value; there are plants for welded tubes, wire drawing and "laser welded custom forms".

International Trends

The steel industry has had two booms since the end of World War II. The first occurred during 1950–1975 with an average annual growth in its production of 5%. It was due to reconstruction efforts, the expansion of infrastructure in developed countries, as well as public investment efforts in Latin America (LA) (CEPAL, 2009). The second occurred during 2001–2008 which was reflected in a growth rate of 6.8%, fuelled by a growing demand from China.

The international crisis of 2008–2009 caused a reduction in the demand for steel due to the slowdown in the construction industry in the United States and Europe, giving way to a new negative cycle that continues to this day and which is characterized by excess capacity and oversupply of labour in China. At present, China accounts for three quarters of the growth in world crude steel production and produces one out of every two tons of steel in the world. Meanwhile, the United States has significantly reduced its share of world production. The following sections delve into the industrial organization of the main global players: The United States and China.

The Steel Industry in China

The steel industry in China grew at an average annual rate of 11.6% between 2000 and 2017 (NBSC, 2018), stimulated by the accelerated modernization and urbanization process in that country. The construction industry is the main buyer of steel, followed by industries that are intensive in steel consumption and with significant state financing, such as the automotive industry (Popescu et al., 2016).

The industry has been actively supported by the Chinese public sector at different levels: through subsidies (land use, public services, environmental protection), preferential credit policies, price controls for raw materials, lax regulations in environmental matters, cash donations through "special funds", and others (Steel Industry Coalition, 2016).

It is a concentrated, capital-intensive industry run by large state-owned companies. In fact, 7,712 steel companies reported revenues above 20 million yuan in 2017. Of these, two out of three are private and control 21.53% of the capital stock, while 4.77% of the companies are public and control the 53.26% of the capital stock in the branch (NBSC, 2018).

Chinese steelworks have been vertically integrated backward with the world by seeking resources to secure raw materials (mainly iron ore) to cope with rising domestic demand. The 2005 China Iron and Steel Industry Development Policy underlined the need for greater collaboration with foreign mines through cross-border joint ventures, mergers and acquisitions (M&A), in order to establish bases of iron ore supply abroad (Huang and Tanaka, 2017).

The Steel Industry in the United States

For the U.S. Department of Commerce (USDC), steel is a matter of national security and considers that it has been threatened by imports (USDC, 2018). While domestic production falls, imports rise to supply growing domestic demand. In fact, in 2018, the American industry reported a trade deficit of $16.96 billion; tube and pipe products, flat steel and semi-finished products were the main drivers of the deficit. Canada, Mexico, Korea and Brazil are the main partners of the United States with a 56% share in trade, with Mexico being the only generator of surplus, particularly in flat and long steel (GTA, 2020).

Seven companies are considered as part of national security as they serve as prominent suppliers to the arms industry. They are a mix of private companies with national and foreign capital and were responsible for almost 80% of American steel production (GSTM, 2018). Nucor Corporation, United States Steel Corp., Steel Dynamics INC., AK Steel Corporation and Commercial Metals are private companies with national capital that accounts for more than two thirds of the national steel production. The foreign companies are ArcelorMittal and Gerdau North America and together they produced 14.63% of the national steel production.

Steel in the China–United States Tariff Dispute and the New USMCA

To reactivate the American industry and increase its competitiveness, the USDC suggested that imports should shrink to a level that should, in combination with "good management", allow domestic mills to operate at 80% or more of their capacity (USDC, 2018). This would be achieved by raising the tariff on all steel imports to at least 24%.[2] In response to the USDC, since 2017 the tariff rate applied by the United States to steel imports went from zero to 12.01% in 2019 (U.S. Census Bureau, 2020).

The USMCA went into effect on 1 June 2020, containing new regional value content provisions for certain sectors, with the intention of encouraging greater use of steel and aluminium products produced in North America. The sectors affected include automotive products, certain steel products, and steel-intensive products. Chapter 4 of the USMCA contains new rules of origin specific to automotive goods, which seek to raise regional content in the auto-parts automotive industry. In this regard, article 4-b.6 indicates that a passenger vehicle, light truck, or heavy truck, will be original only if, during the previous year, at least 70% of the purchases of steel and aluminium, by the producer of the vehicle in North America, are original (SE, 2020). On the other hand, in the Modifying Protocol, Mexico achieved that, for the steel to be considered originating, all the steelmaking processes must occur in the region, including the initial smelting and with a seven-year term for its implementation. This was considered an achievement for Mexico given that, as will be discussed in the subsequent sections, only three companies located in Mexico produce structural steel for the automotive industry.

Implications for the Steel Industry in Mexico

The imposition of tariffs shows that steel exports to the United States fell at a rate of 9.1% between 2017 and 2019, but American crude steel production rose from 81.6 to 86.6 million metric tons (mmt), this is the maximum expansion in seven years (GTA, 2020). China has been the biggest loser, since the 22.1% increase in the tariff was accompanied by a fall of almost 13% in its exports to the United States, while Brazil and Mexico appear as the most dynamic suppliers in the American market, with rates growth of 5% and 2.6% respectively (GTA, 2020).

On the other hand, the new rules of origin for automotive goods are likely to reaffirm the trend described. Indeed, steel producers in the United States expect the new rules to lead to higher production, employment, and wages in their country, as well as higher demand for steel from the automotive industry in Mexico (USITC, 2019). This is considering that Mexico has a deficit in structural steel for the automotive industry, mainly with the United States. Indeed, in 2019 Mexico's structural steel trade totalled 5.306 million dollars and the United States participated with 55.29%; the trade deficit reached 4.331 million dollars and the United States participated with 45.29% (GTA, 2020).

Before addressing the behaviour of investment at the industry and company level in the Mexican steel industry, it is pertinent to review the determinants of private investment from a theoretical perspective. This will be discussed in the next section.

8.2   DETERMINANTS OF PRIVATE INVESTMENT: THEORY AND EMPIRICAL EVIDENCE

Microeconomic Determinants

Private investment (national and foreign) depends primarily on the rate of return expected by investment agents. In turn, the expected rate of return (business profit rate "bp" to be more precise) is influenced by factors that can be ordered based on the following analytical framework taken from Valenzuela-Feijóo (2006).[3]

The business profit rate (defined as the business profit to equity ratio) depends on factors that operate in: (i) the sphere of production, through the rate of profitability (g) (equation 8.3), which depends positively on the exploitation rate (p), on the participation of variable capital in total capital (V/K) and on the period of rotation of variable capital (n_v); (ii) the sphere of demand (equation 8.2), reflected in the behaviours of the operating rate (or) or degree of use of installed capacity, which is closely related to the variable degree of monopoly (k); (iii) the financial sphere (equation 8.1), through the leverage coefficient (d) or the ratio of capital borrowed to equity, and the interest rate (i). In formal terms we have:

$$bp = or(1+k)g + d\left[or(1+k)g - i\right] \tag{8.1}$$

$$g_1 = or(1+k)g \tag{8.2}$$

$$g = p(V/K)(n_v) \tag{8.3}$$

The internationalization of MNCs through FDI in countries with a lower level of development is fundamentally guided by factors such as degree of monopoly (k), demand (or) and production (g). In this regard, the degree of monopoly (k) is the manifestation of market power and this refers to the ability of an industrial branch (especially dominant companies) to achieve a higher or lower rate of return than the average (Valenzuela-Feijóo, 2014b). In turn, (k) depends on barriers to entry and concentration at branch level, to the extent that both barriers to entry and concentration at branch level, increase the market power of MNCs. The evolution of demand (the accelerator) can be reflected in the operating rate (or), if we assume a linear relationship between it and the rate of return, a decrease in demand is reflected in a drop in "or" and "bp" (see equation 8.2). In other words, the dynamics of demand affects profitability by modifying the degree of use of installed capacity.

The eclectic paradigm or OLI helps to order the factors that affect "k", "or" and "g". This paradigm indicates that MNCs are established when three advantages are present (Dunning and Lundan, 2008): ownership (O), localization (L) and internalization (I).

The O advantages are barriers to entry that favour concentration and derive from the market power held by MNCs, ultimately manifesting themselves as a higher degree of monopoly (k). Dunning classified O benefits into two types: asset and transactional. The former is based on the superior technological capacity and size of foreign subsidiaries, which allows them to obtain economies of scale, capital intensity, operate with low unit costs and develop technologies. They are also associated with intangible assets, such as management techniques and organizational skills (Narula and Driffield, 2012), as well as property rights, non-codifiable knowledge, and finance and marketing expertise. The latter refers to the superior ability of MNCs to govern and coordinate a network of assets located in different countries (Dunning and Lundan, 2008).

The L advantages refer to the resources available in certain places such as natural resources, labour, infrastructure, and market size. Such resources can be ordered based on the motivations of FDI in the recipient territories: (i) Coverage of the domestic market through the search for markets; (ii) reduction of production costs through efficiency-seeking projects; (iii) access to raw materials and labour force through resource search projects; and (iv) acquisition of strategic assets (Dunning and Lundan, 2008). In particular: market search (e.g. market size) can be captured in the demand factor measured through "or"; the search for strategic assets that increasingly takes the form of cross-border M&A is captured in "k"; the search for resources (e.g. workforce) and efficiency (reduction of production costs) are factors that impact the business profit rate through "g" (see equation 8.3).

The analytical framework described does not mean that there are no causal relationships among the determining factors of "bp", thus, the variables "or", "k", "d" and "i" are closely linked. For example, in a crisis situation manifested in a decline in global demand, the adverse impact on the business profit rate can be partially offset by an increase in the degree of monopoly, since crises also favour an increase in industrial concentration levels. Let us add, in the face of a high debt ratio, a rise in the interest rate combined with a decrease in the g_1 rate can reinforce the fall in the business profit rate (Valenzuela-Feijóo, 2014b).

Macroeconomic and Institutional Determinants

The macroeconomic policy can impact the corporate profit rate through "or" and "d". Indeed, despite the fact that a competitive exchange rate can stimulate foreign sales of exporting companies and this has a positive impact on their profitability through the accelerator, it also negatively impacts it by making the imported component of investment and intermediate consumption more expensive; in the end the net effect of the accelerator on investment can be negative. Public spending generates external economies (through public investment in infrastructure, health, education, etc.) and, as it complements private investment, it becomes an additional stimulus to global demand and therefore boosts business investment through the accelerator. On the other hand, considering the existence of preferential access to credit based on the size of the company, the availability of financial resources to the private sector is a determinant of investment for smaller companies. This does not mean that investment in smaller companies is insensitive to interest rates, but rather that its impact occurs indirectly through external financing.

The development of companies goes hand in hand with the formation of collaboration networks (formal and informal) between companies and institutions (public and private) related to industrial conglomerates (Esser et al., 1999). On this basis, a correct model of industrial policies (meso-political) must seek a strategic collaboration between the private and public sectors with the aim at jointly discovering the most relevant obstacles to investment and determining which interventions are most likely to eliminate them (Rodrik, 2007).

The previous items are relevant because they warn that a correct reading of the determinants of private investment must be disaggregated and multilevel or systemic. Thus, it must start from an analytical framework that involves factors of a micro, meso, macroeconomic and global nature, which affect particularly companies and industrial branches. This approach is identified in the conceptual and empiric literature (Dunning and Lundan, 2008; Narula and Driffield, 2012; Perri and Peruffo, 2016; Dussel-Peters, 2007 and 2018; Ortiz-Velásquez, 2015; CEPAL, 2018). Thus, for example, while certain macroeconomic determinants such as the real exchange rate, the levels of public investment and the availability of credit may be relevant to explain the permanence of smaller local companies in the market, the investment of the large company seems to respond predominantly to microeconomic profitability criteria.

Empirical Evidence for Mexico

The empirical evidence available for Mexico shows that, in general, an expanding domestic market, abundant and cheap credit, a competitive exchange rate, and a high coefficient of public investment in infrastructure, are counted as fundamental incentives for investment decision making (Ortiz-Velásquez, 2015; López-Gallardo, 2016). However, an examination of 220 industrial classes shows that, in those oriented to the national market and predominantly smaller in size, the systematic variable that explains investment is the demand for their products, while the exchange rate had a negative impact. In the export-oriented classes, the evolution of international demand (reflected in US exports) determined investment (predominantly made up of FDI), while domestic sales and the exchange rate did not result significantly (Ortiz-Velásquez, 2019).

Concentrating the discussion on FDI, in a recent document (Ortiz-Velásquez and Gordillo-Olguín, 2020), 18 empirical studies on the determinants of FDI published between 2002 and 2018 were observed: (i) ten of them addressed the problem from the macroeconomic field; (ii) six examined the issue at the federal entity level using the aggregate data of state FDI; (iii) two dealt with the issue based on economic activities. It is striking that the systematic variable that determines FDI in Mexico in a macro, meso and territorial scope is the size of the market. Exports, trade openness and productivity have shown positive signs; the economically active population (EAP) and physical infrastructure had a positive association, while labour costs showed a negative association.

As for the steel industry, the work of Cano-Gutiérrez (2018) points that innovation strategies, geographic location and environmentally sustainable practices are factors that determine the level of international competitiveness in 35 MNCs participating in the Mexican steel industry. On the other hand, CEPAL (2009) highlights that the steel companies in Latin America sought to benefit from the positive cycle of steel in the world, from the size of the market and from the privatization and deregulation process of the 1990s.

In an environment dominated by aggregate econometric studies on national and foreign private investment in Mexico, which in general do not contribute to improving the understanding of the factors that influence investment decision making in steel companies and branches, it is necessary to move towards an approximation at the company level. In section 8.3, a group of systemic determinants of foreign investment are examined at the industry and company level, closely following the analytical framework developed in this section.

8.3   THE STEEL INDUSTRY IN MEXICO

Industry-Level Features

The steel industry in Mexico is made up of 950 establishments that represent 0.16% of the manufacturing establishments but concentrate 11.16% of the capital stock and 4.59% of the profits of Mexican manufacturing (Table 8.1). It is an industry with high participation of foreign capital, superior market power (reflected in its concentration levels and the high natural barriers to entry), high rate of return and high investment coefficient.

Between 2008 and 2018, the industry increased the number of economic units, but as can be seen in Table 8.1, the increase in establishments occurred in the least concentrated segments with the lowest barriers to entry (pipes, poles and other products). This explains that the average size of the establishment did not change over time. FDI was the most dynamic indicator with a growth rate of 14%, being the segments of steel complexes, and tubes and poles the most dynamic in attracting FDI. It is striking that fixed investment did not react with the same speed as FDI, which reveals that the expansion strategy of companies participating in the steel complexes and tubes and poles segments was based on cross-border M&A.

The steel industry observed, between 2008 and 2018, a drop in the profitability rate, which did not stimulate investment. The fall in the profitability rate was explained basically by demand problems reflected in a slow expansion of the product, the contraction of exports, greater competition from imports and the fall in the operating rate. Let us add, the increase in market power in the steel complex segment was insufficient to offset the drop in industrial profitability.

Table 8.1   Mexico: indicators of the steel industry (2008–2018)

| | | | Mining | | | | Steel industry | | | |
| | National (total) | Manufacturing (total) | | | | Steel complexes | Casting | Steel rolling and finished products | | |
			Total	Coal mining	Iron mining		Primary slabs and ferro-alloys	Pipes and poles	Other iron and steel products	Foundry melding of iron and steel parts
Values in 2018 a /										
Economic units (number)	4,800,157	579,828	950	65	28	8	17	173	399	260
Average size of establishment (ratio) b /	6	11	113	132	300	2,847	244	98	73	65
FDI coefficient (%) c /	6.1	9.4	22.5	0.0	-6.0	41.9	0.0	17.6	20.5	5.5
Concentration index 8 (%) d /	40.18	57.07	81.60	97.08	93.60	100.00	93.91	59.91	49.47	77.22
Capital density (thousands of pesos)	427	457	3,094	1,051	1,805	10,126	2,360	789	1,363	787
Labor productivity (thousands of pesos)	41	37	265	82	235	940	248	78	119	92
Used plant capacity (%)	nd	81.1	83.4	nd	nd	75.7	89.6	75.6	82.7	78.4
Rate of return (%) e /	30.6	28.8	30.0	34.7	34.8	21.9	38.2	47.2	30.2	27.5
Investment coefficient f /	7.5	6.2	6.3	15.8	8.7	7.7	3.0	3.5	5.2	9.0
Percentage structure in 2018 a / g /										
Economic units	100.00	12.08	0.16	0.01	0.00	0.00	0.00	0.03	0.07	0.04
Total employed population	100.00	23.93	1.65	0.13	0.13	0.35	0.06	0.26	0.45	0.26
Profits	100.00	35.63	4.59	0.11	0.21	1.17	0.52	0.81	1.52	0.24
Gross census value added	100.00	31.99	4.40	0.13	0.20	1.44	0.42	0.64	1.32	0.25
Total stock of fixed assets	100.00	25.61	11.16	0.30	0.51	7.77	0.33	0.45	1.34	0.45
FDI	100.00	49.12	10.55	0.00	-0.13	6.45	0.00	1.20	2.89	0.15
Average annual growth rates (2008–2018) h /										
Economic units	2.6	2.9	5.1	1.9	7.2	-3.1	-0.6	11.0	7.0	1.8
Total employed population	3.0	3.4	4.8	-0.3	6.4	6.1	0.5	5.0	6.1	4.9
Average size of establishment	0.5	0.5	-0.3	-2.1	-0.7	9.5	1.0	-5.4	-0.8	3.0

	National (total)	Manufacturing (total)	Steel industry							
			Mining			Steel complexes	Casting	Steel rolling and finished products		
			Total	Coal mining	Iron mining		Primary slabs and ferro-alloys	Pipes and poles	Other iron and steel products	Foundry melding of iron and steel parts
Export	4.5	4.6	-3.3	-20.3	0.0	1.4	-23.1	-3.0	1.2	2.1
Import	3.7	2.4	2.6	-1.0	-3.7	2.7	4.3	2.2	6.6	1.4
Used plant capacity	nd	0.3	0.5	nd	nd	-1.3	-0.2	1.2	-0.1	-0.6
Gross census value added	2.3	2.2	0.7	-5.4	-5.1	1.5	7.9	-1.9	1.5	2.5
Rate of return	1.8	0.4	-2.1	0.8	-7.9	-5.0	7.7	-1.3	-1.0	-1.5
FDI	2.1	5.3	14.0	0.0	0.0	18.5	0.0	36.5	8.5	0.0
Gross fixed investment	1.5	2.4	0.5	-4.0	-9.8	12.0	2.5	-9.7	7.7	-6.3
Investment coefficient	-0.8	0.2	-0.2	1.4	-5.0	10.3	-5.0	-8.0	6.1	-8.6

Notes:
a. Original data expressed in current pesos.
b. Total employed population divided by number of establishments.
c. Foreign direct investment (FDI) divided by gross census value added.
d. Data for 2013. Totals (national, manufacturing and steel) are an average.
e. The rate of return results from dividing the income from the supply of goods and services, by the sum of the expenses for the consumption of goods and services, plus the remuneration, all minus 1.
f. Gross fixed investment divided by gross census value added.
g. The percentage structure of the steel industry is estimated with respect to total manufacturing.
h. Original data expressed in millions of constant 2013 pesos.
Source: Own elaboration based on data from the Economic Census of Mexico 2019 (INEGI, 2020).

The added value and the generation of profit are concentrated in the production and lamination segments (Table 8.1), each one shows a different industrial organization, effectively:

i. The steel complex segment operates in a concentrated market, with a high share of FDI, high barriers to entry and low profitability. In the last decade and with the help of foreign investment, the segment raised its concentration levels and barriers to entry, but the industry faced demand problems (reflected in a decrease in operation rate), which adversely impacted its profitability. However, physical investment expanded to 12%. This may indicate that, together with the demand problems, there was a reduction in the output–capital ratio, caused by a type of passive investment that requires a longer period of maturation and learning, during which the capital stock increases but not the product.

ii. The steel casting segment is made up of establishments mainly dedicated to the manufacture of slabs and billets. It is the second most concentrated segment, showing high barriers to entry, dominated by national investment, and having the highest profitability rate in the industry. In 10 years, the number of establishments went from 18 to 17, marginally increasing their average size and capital endowment per worker. The expansion of the capital stock was basically explained by national private investment. It is a segment that faces an expanding domestic market, all of which determined a growth in its profitability and expansion of its gross fixed investment.

iii. The rolling segment dedicated to the manufacture of other products (sheets, profiles, wire rod, cables, rods, angles, etc.) has, after the steel complexes, the highest relative share in profits and in FDI. It is the least concentrated segment, since eight establishments account for 49.47% of the capital stock. It also shows low barriers to entry and a high profitability rate. Low barriers to entry partly explain the significant increase in the number of economic units and the dynamism of FDI. It faces demand problems and an explosive growth in its imports, which explains the semi-stagnation of the profitability rate.

iv. In the foundry moulding of iron and steel parts, a wide variety of parts such as gaskets, nuts, pipes, valves, and so on are manufactured. It has the smallest average size of the establishment and national private investment predominates. With a total of 260 establishments that make up the segment, only eight control 77.22% of the capital stock. During the study period, the number of establishments and their average size increased. The contraction in profitability was guided by the abrupt decrease in the degree of use of installed capacity, which stood at 78.4% in 2018. All the above had an adverse impact on the expansion of gross fixed investment.

The following section delves into the factors that affect the profitability (and investment) of the steel industry at company level.

8.4   SYSTEMIC DETERMINANTS OF INVESTMENT IN FOREIGN AFFILIATES

The CE 2019 offers the results of the questionnaires applied to 579,828 manufacturing establishments. Its objective was to detect the problems that companies face to stay in the market. A global look indicates that the manufacturing establishments faced problems of an institutional nature, the most important being the perception of public insecurity; followed by microeconomic factors, mainly high industrial costs (raw materials, inputs, water services, electricity, etc.) and macroeconomic factors, mainly low demand (Table 8.2). Consistent with the revised theory, permanence in the market depends on the size of the establishment and the characteristics of the industry, as follows:

i.   The more than 543,000 micro-size manufacturing establishments add to the previous difficulties lack of credit. In contrast, the large establishments indicated predominantly microeconomic and institutional factors, such as high industrial costs, high tax burdens, insecurity, and excess paperwork. Meanwhile they did not face demand problems or lack of credit.
ii. The 1,378 establishments of the steel industry predominantly faced problems of public insecurity, while in the micro field, high industrial costs, high taxes, and unfair competition predominate. The 632 micro establishments faced not only institutional restrictions (such as public insecurity) and microeconomic ones (such as high industrial costs and taxes), but also they faced problems of demand and lack of credit. On the other hand, the medium and large-sized company faced predominantly microeconomic difficulties, where in addition to high industrial costs and taxes, there was little experience of the staff.

During the period November 2019 to January 2020, a set of semi-structured interviews and plant visits were carried out in the foreign subsidiaries Tenaris Tamsa, Gerdau Corsa and TIM as part of the activities of the institutional project DGAPA-UNAM-PAPIIT IA303118.[4] The objective of the field work was to understand from a more realistic perspective the factors that explain the expansion and/or permanence of foreign affiliates in Mexico. The issue is of the greatest relevance, considering that the MNCs participate in a concentrated industry and explain a significant part of the production, this means that the industry tends to reproduce their behaviour. In other words, if we understand the motivations that govern the investment behaviour of such global companies, we can understand the predominant factors that govern investment in the Mexican steel industry. Consistent with the theoretical and conceptual review contained in section 8.2, investment by foreign affiliates is due to a combination of global and systemic aspects, where microeconomic factors predominate. We delve into this in the following paragraphs.

Characteristics of the Companies

As discussed in section 8.3 (first part), the steel production segment in Mexico operates in a concentrated market, since eight companies account for 94.7% of the capital stock in the branch (INEGI, 2014) and practically 100% of the production in quantum. National private equity companies Altos Hornos de México (AHMSA), Deacero, Simec and Tyasa account for 46.13% of production. The rest is explained by the foreign subsidiaries ArcelorMittal, Ternium México (TM), Gerdau Corsa (GC) and Tenaris Tamsa (TT). In 2020 TM was ranked as the 40th most important company in Mexico (based on net income), followed by AHMSA which was ranked 80th and DeAcero ranked 96th (Expansión, 2020). TM is the most diversified company with 12 products while Tenaris Tamsa specializes in a high value product.

Even though the objective of the document is concentrated in the study of four foreign subsidiaries, it is convenient to stop for a moment at the national private company AHMSA, currently immersed in a corruption scandal. This is due to the fact that this case reveals the Mexican businessman profile, which is more concerned with achieving favours and/or privi-

Table 8.2   Mexico: firms' permanence problems in manufacturing and steel subsectors, according to the size of the firm (2018)

	Economic units (number)		Institutional		Microeconomic					Macroeconomic	
	Total	Economic units that did face problems	Public insecurity	Excess of government procedures to operate	High costs of raw materials, supplies or merchandise	High expenses in payment of services (electricity, water, telephone)	Unfair competition	High taxes	Employed population with little experience	Low demand for your goods or services	Lack of credit
Manufacturing	579,828	578,862	23.46	4.27	21.20	18.71	15.79	8.52	3.02	14.06	7.69
Micro a/	543,236	542,457	22.53	3.53	20.77	17.72	15.71	7.13	2.41	14.23	7.90
Little b/	24,247	24,063	37.46	12.59	27.06	30.60	19.02	25.43	11.47	12.28	5.82
Median c/	7,808	7,806	37.98	21.68	31.90	38.65	15.73	38.46	14.55	11.49	2.42
Big d/	4,537	4,536	36.20	18.52	23.81	39.46	8.09	32.87	11.46	8.27	0.90
Steel industry	1,378	1,378	33.53	12.99	26.05	25.47	13.50	24.02	9.80	16.55	5.81
Micro a/	652	652	37.73	7.06	18.87	19.17	12.27	16.26	5.21	19.02	9.51
Little b/	350	350	33.14	15.71	29.71	27.14	15.14	26.57	12.86	14.86	4.29
Median c/	240	240	31.25	26.67	38.33	35.42	15.42	37.92	15.83	13.75	0.83
Big d/	136	136	18.38	10.29	29.41	33.82	11.76	30.15	13.24	13.97	0.74

Notes: a. From 0 to 10 workers; b. From 11 to 50 workers; c. From 51 to 250 workers; d.e. 251 and more workers.
Source: Own elaboration based on data from the Economic Census of Mexico 2019 (INEGI, 2020).

leges from the political group in power, than in achieving a moderately scientific management style focused on production tasks (Valenzuela-Feijóo, 2014a).

Altos Hornos is the most important national private company in the Mexican steel industry, but currently faces a complex financial and operating scenario, which has affected its profitability, for example, in the first quarter of 2020, its net sales fell by 50% and its EBITDA fell by 646% (AHMSA, 2020). AHMSA's crisis is due to the seizure of all bank accounts of the company and its subsidiaries, derived from the arrest of the president of the board of directors, Alonso Ancira.

It should be remembered that its president received, apparently, millionaire bribes for the fraudulent sale of Agro Nitrogenados, a "junk" plant with 18 years out of operation, to Petróleos Mexicanos (PEMEX). The sale occurred in 2014 in the context of the "industrial policy" emanating from the 2013 Energy Reform; PEMEX paid 275 million dollars (md) for a plant valued at only 19.5 md. Currently, Alonso Ancira and Emilio Lozoya (former director of PEMEX) are facing legal proceedings. There has been speculation about the sale of AHMSA to Grupo Villacero of national capital and based in Monterrey, this would be great news for the Mexican steel industry, since AHMSA is the main producer of structural steel for the automotive industry and the one that has, therefore, the greatest potential to take advantage of the new USMCA rules of origin. If the operation is not carried out, there is a risk that, as with NAFTA, the benefits will be transferred to the MNC, since after AHMSA, the transnationals Ternium and ArcelorMittal are the only producers of structural steel.

The foreign subsidiaries Tenaris Tamsa and Ternium de México belong to the Italian-Argentine group Techint, the first operates in Veracruz and accounts for 5,728 direct jobs, the second operates predominantly in Nuevo León and accounts for 9,000 jobs; both together have a share of 40% of the employment generated in the production segment. For its part, Gerdau Corsa is a foreign subsidiary of the Brazilian group Gerdau, it has medium-sized plants in Hidalgo and the State of Mexico, accounting for approximately 15% of the occupation in the production segment.

Subsidiaries are strategic for their parent companies. Indeed: (i) Gerdau's national subsidiaries account for 49% of the group's installed capacity, followed by foreign subsidiaries operating in the North American region with 43% (US SEC, 2020); (ii) the Tenaris Tamsa complex is the most important of Tenaris, since 24.4% of the 23,000 employees it generates are located in Mexico and 23.73% in Argentina; and (iii) 44% of Ternium's 16,700 direct jobs are in Mexico, followed by Argentina with 27%.

The Tenaris Tamsa industrial complex is clearly vertically integrated forward with high-value segments and with significant investments since 2005. Currently it has a semi-integrated steelwork, three tube factories, an accessories factory, an automotive parts centre specialized in automotive components, a sucker rod factory, and three completion and service centres. On the other hand, in 2006 and 2010 they opened the Research and Development Centre and Tenaris University, respectively, which allow conducting research and testing in metallurgy and welding, the development of processes and mechanical solutions and a testing laboratory. In 2016, the test training centre was opened, which allows simulating drilling operations, representing an investment of 14 million dollars. It is the only company in Mexico that manufactures seamless tubes for deep waters and exports 80% of its production, of which 47% goes to the North American region. TT accounts for 100% of Mexican exports in this segment.[5]

On the other hand, Gerdau Corsa, and a segment of Ternium de México compete in the Mexican market in long rolled products, especially commercial structural profiles, and rods. Both companies show clear backward vertical integration, Gerdau Corsa being the less diversified. In recent years, both companies have made significant investments to generate greater ties with the automotive industry. Indeed, Gerdau Corsa inaugurated a semi-integrated plant in Ciudad Sahagún in 2015. For its part, Ternium inaugurated in 2013 the Ternium Industrial Center in Pesquería, to expand the range of products required by the automotive industry. Later, in 2018 they opened a laboratory (in Pesquería), to strengthen research in processes and products linked to industry 4.0.[6]

As discussed in section 8.3, first part, the lamination segment shows the lowest concentration levels of the chain and the smallest average size of the establishment. In fact, 10 companies would be responsible for more than 50% of branch production, five of them are national capital companies: Galvasid, Maquilacero, Zincacero-Villacero, Ladesa and Sigosa. The foreign subsidiaries are: Posco, Outokumpu Mexinox, Aceros Camesa, Signode and Trefilados Inoxidables de México (TIM). Unlike national private equity companies, foreign affiliates are in more than one demarcation generating more employment.

TIM is in Tlaxcala and was founded in 1999 as a national private equity company that was sold to a French group in 2001; later in 2004 it was acquired by the NOVAMETAL group based in Switzerland. TIM specializes in manufacturing 13 product lines, including: wire, specialty welds (stainless steel, nickel alloy, aluminium), and stainless-steel bars. The highest sale is generated by fine wire and for mechanical use, whereas solder is the product of greater value. Its high diversification in products allows it to position itself as a specialized supplier to a wide variety of industries: food, textile, chemical, automotive, aerospace, medical and energy, with automotive its main customer, accounting for 70% in sales.

Since 2009, the subsidiary invested in modern machinery such as drawing machines, furnaces, winders, and state-of-the-art measuring equipment. It also implemented training programs for the workforce, organizational improvements, and standardization and implementation of international regulations. All this allowed TIM to comply with international standards and customer specifications, rapidly diversifying its portfolio of domestic and foreign customers. This is reflected in several indicators: (i) an increase in productivity, from 900,000 pounds per month in 2009 to 2 million pounds in 2019 and reducing the workforce from 180 to 142 workers; (ii) a used plant capacity that fluctuates between 89 and 92%; (iii) TIM currently exports 50% of its production (in the past it was 100%), mainly to Europe, the United States, Central and South America, while they have acquired a greater presence in the local market along with other companies such as Bosch.

The Investment in Tenaris Tamsa, Ternium, Gerdau Corsa and TIM

Consistent with the analytical framework introduced in section 8.2, the following lines order the factors that explain the investment behaviours of foreign affiliates in four dimensions: global, macroeconomic, microeconomic, and institutional. Regarding the global dimension, the interviewees indicated that their investment is governed by profitability and that the latter are influenced by aspects such as:

i.   The evolution of world GDP and companies' main customer's product.
ii. Cost competition versus Chinese imports: in 2019 the average price of a metric ton of hot rolled roll was 1.7 times higher in Mexico compared to China (MEPS, 2019).
iii. Low profitability per se in the industry depends to a large extent on the evolution of international prices of metals such as nickel and is reflected in the full price, which in turn is mainly controlled by Asian companies. In short, the international competitive price or full price is made up of a base price that explains around 59% of the full price and an alloy surcharge that explains the remaining 41%; the latter seeks to protect the margins of the companies against the higher volatility in the price of alloying elements such as nickel.

In the macroeconomic sphere and consistent with the results of the 2019 CEs and the revised theory, investment in subsidiaries responds positively to the dynamics of the domestic market and the supply of qualified labour, while it responds negatively to public insecurity. On the other hand, the MNC did not face financing problems and the exchange rate did not function as a first-order variable, effectively:

i.   The privatization and deregulation processes of the 1990s motivated investment through transactions carried out in the form of cross-border M&A.
ii. The investment sought markets. In this regard, it should be remembered that Mexico is the most important steel market in Latin America and the second most important in North America.
iii. Given that the interviewed actors buy and sell in dollars, but pay salaries in local currency (pesos), the process of depreciation of the current exchange rate since at least 2002 has been favourable for them through reduction of labour costs, while not being affected by the increase in cost of imports.
iv. To finance their investment projects, companies predominantly resort to foreign loans (in the case of TIM) and/or issue debt instruments (TT and TM are listed on the stock exchange), since interest rates in Mexico are high, for example, TIM is financed through its holding company in Switzerland at a rate of 2.5%, compared to rates of 10% and 11% in Mexico.
v.   The growing problem of public insecurity is a factor that adversely impacts investment decisions, by increasing risk premiums.

In the microeconomic sphere, companies seek to increase profitability rates through different strategies:

i.   MNC trans-nationalization seeks to generate economies of scale, increase market power and therefore the margin, which is low in the industry.
ii. Some economic innovations at the product level open up investment opportunities, for example, the construction industry is witnessing an increasing replacement of concrete structures with steel structures, while the automotive industry is moving towards the development of lighter and more efficient fuel saver cars.
iii. To deal with the Chinese threat, companies have resorted to various strategies. The GC strategy is based on logistical advantages, linked to delivery times, waiting costs and

quality. TIM opted for a strategy of greater specialization and added value, moving towards stainless steel products aimed at a specialized market. Even though the specialized product is more expensive, TIM compensates through strategies of reducing delivery time and adapting to customer needs.

4. Since TIM imports 80% of the wire rod raw material from Italy, its import is subject to the payment of a 25% duty in the United States (section 232). In other words, the new USMCA does not benefit the company since it cannot declare the raw material as originating. Because of this, the company is working on a strategy that allows it to substitute imported wire rod for billet. With the billet, the company would have to carry out the rolling process to obtain wire rod; only then could it be declared as originating, and, in turn, it would allow TIM to export directly to the United States, without paying the duty.

5. Intangible investments in international certifications, R&D, supplier development, and workforce training have been fundamental components in improving productivity. For example, TT promotes the Metallurgical career together with the Universidad Veracruzana. It also develops, through Nacional Financiera, a supplier program to support them in obtaining quality and safety certifications. Ternium invested 29 million dollars in an educational program called "Roberto Rocca Technical School". Meanwhile, TIM has a worker training program, due to the lack of a qualified workforce.

The meso economic factors that explain investment in companies are concentrated in the following facts:

i.   NAFTA motivated companies to diversify their production and expand the market.
ii. The USMCA is a positive aspect and some MNCs are ready, so Ternium and Gerdau Corsa have invested in plants to develop and produce parts for the automotive industry.
iii. Temporary import programs for re-export (such as IMMEX and PROSEC) allow them to lower the cost of certain imported inputs.

8.5   CONCLUSIONS

The low investment coefficient is a structural feature that typifies the Mexican economy since the 1980s. Given the importance of investment as a determinant of output growth, the role of industrial policy should be based, according to Rodrik, on a strategic collaboration between the public and private sectors, with the aim at discovering the obstacles faced by investments and determining which interventions are most likely to eliminate them. Likewise, it must give priority to interventions in strategic industries in terms of vertical linkages backwards and forwards. In this regard, the steel industry fulfils this strategic role, in addition, due to its global nature, it has the potential to take advantage of the new regional industrial organization that is being developed through the USMCA and the growing US–China trade tensions.

Throughout this chapter, it has been shown that the Mexican steel company could be considered as an extension of the world steel company, since the MNC participates in segments with the highest profit generation. In general terms, the steel industry is a concentrated, capital-intensive industry, with high barriers to entry and high profitability, all of which restricts competition particularly for smaller companies. From this perspective, in the absence of an active industrial policy, the potential benefits expected from the new rules of origin for steel contained in the USMCA would be transferred, as it has traditionally happened, to the MNC.

At the segment level (mining, production, casting, rolling, and finishing) and company level, the analysis identified some obstacles faced by investment, as well as areas of intervention in industrial policy. Thus, for example, while 652 micro steel establishments participating predominantly in the rolling segment stated that public insecurity is a problem for their permanence in the market, while macroeconomic factors, such as low demand for their goods (the accelerator) and lack of credit, are the main restrictions they face. In contrast, the 136 large companies participating mainly in the production and casting segment and with a significant share of FDI, predominantly faced microeconomic constraints, such as high industrial costs (raw materials and inputs), high taxes and a labour force with little experience.

The foreign subsidiaries Ternium de México, Tenaris Tamsa and Gerdau Corsa predominantly participate in the steel complex segment, while TIM participates in the rolling segment. These companies stated that investment is governed by the profitability rate while some factors affecting the latter are: (i) market size, exports and competition from Chinese imports; (ii) degree of monopoly – given that it is an industry of scale – MNCs seek to increase their market power and margin, which is low per se; (iii) economic innovations developed in industries with which they are linked vertically forwards such as construction and automotive; (iv) various strategies aimed at facing competition with Chinese imports, dealing with section 232 in the United States, developing suppliers and training the workforce. Let us add, in coherence with the results of the economic censuses, that the depreciation of the real exchange rate and the domestic monetary policy (reflected in the interest rate) do not seem to affect the MNCs directly.

A correct design of industrial policy must aim at promoting investment in the rolling and finished segments, with features of low barriers to entry and low concentration of producers. Effectively:

i.   Considering that the rolling and finished segments are an intermediate link between production-casting dominated by large companies and among customers located in the construction, automotive and aerospace industries, production would not face demand problems, since it would take advantage of the dynamism of the export industry under the USMCA.

ii. It is essential to facilitate access to credit at preferential rates for these companies, as well as to protect, against increases in the exchange rate, companies indebted in dollars.

iii. Greater government spending on public security and infrastructure would stimulate investment by reducing the risk factor and would act as an additional stimulus to demand.

iv. Local and municipal governments can favour investment in such segments through a reduction in the procedures to register and operate a company, likewise, they can generate, in coordination with the leading multinational companies in the automotive and aerospace industry, supplier development programs (which requires training for smaller companies to obtain certifications). Also, considering that in the absence of a qualified workforce, the MNCs have chosen to develop training programs, such experience can be replicated with the support of local governments with the objective that the intervened segments do not face restrictions in the scope of labour supply.

NOTES

1. This research is a result of the project Las empresas chinas en la industria de autopartes y automóviles en México: condiciones actuales y perspectivas ante el Tratado México-Estados Unidos-Canadá (T-MEC) supported by DGAPA-UNAM-PAPIIT IA302620.
2. It was estimated that these tariffs would reduce steel imports from 36 to 13.3 million metric tons (mmt), raising domestic production from 81.9 to 90.6 mmt. With this, the rate of use of installed capacity would rise to 80% and the import coefficient would be reduced from 33.8% to 22% (USDC, 2018). As the rate of use of installed capacity is a determinant of product growth and, in turn, the latter is the systematic determinant of investment, the foundations would be laid for a reactivation of the industry.
3. A detailed discussion is found in Valenzuela-Feijóo (2006) and Ortiz-Velásquez (2015).
4. The section is based on an extensive literature review, interviews, and plant visits, between October 2019 and January 2020. The author thanks Lucas Da Rocha, Gerdau Corsa Civil Construction Sales Manager; Sergio Ramos Vázquez, Deputy Director General of TIM; Jesús Flores Ayala and Jorge Meneses, Institutional Director of International Trade Affairs and Manager of Tenaris Tamsa Institutional Relations respectively, for the interviews and the facilities granted during the visits to the Tenaris Tamsa industrial complex in Veracruz, the Gerdau Corsa plants located in Tultitlán Estado de México and Ciudad Sahagún Hidalgo and the TIM plant in Huamantla Tlaxcala. The author is solely responsible for the information contained in the chapter.
5. It should be remembered that Mexico is the fifth exporter of the subheading tubes, pipes, and hollow profiles for sea, with 1,167 million dollars and only below China, Japan, Germany, and Italy (GTA, 2020).
6. The fourth industrial revolution is based on the adoption of disruptive technologies by companies, for the progressive automation of their production processes, for example, additive manufacturing, artificial intelligence, internet of things (IoT), big data, robotics, quantum computing, nanotechnologies, autonomous vehicles, etc.

REFERENCES

Altos Hornos de México S.A. de C.V. (AHMSA). (2020). *Informe financiero trimestral*, 2020-I. AHMSA, Mexico.
Cano-Gutiérrez, José Antonio. (2018). *Factores que determinan la competitividad internacional de las empresas de la industria siderúrgica mexicana*. UANL, Mexico.
CEPAL. (2009). La inversión extranjera directa en América Latina y el Caribe. *CEPAL*.
CEPAL. (2018). Estudio económico de América Latina y el Caribe. Evolución de la inversión en América Latina y el Caribe: hechos estilizados, determinantes y desafíos de política. *CEPAL*.
Dunning, John H. and Sarianna M. Lundan. (2008). *Multinational Enterprises and the Global Economy*, Second Edition. Cheltenham, UK and Northampton, MA, USA: Edward Elgar Publishing.
Dussel-Peters, Enrique (ed.). (2007). *Inversión Extranjera Directa en México: desempeño y potencial una perspectiva macro, meso, micro y territorial*. Mexico: Siglo XXI Editores.
Dussel-Peters, Enrique. (2018). Cadenas globales de valor. Metodología, contenidos e implicaciones para el caso de la atracción de inversión extranjera directa. In Dussel Peters (ed.), *Cadenas Globales de Valor. Metodología, teoría y debates* (45–66). CECHIMEX-UNAM.
Esser, Klaus, Wolfgang Hillebrand, Dirk Messner and Jörg Meyer-Stamer. (1999). Competitividad sistémica Nuevo desafío para las empresas y la política. In Klaus Esser (ed.), *Competencia global y libertad de acción nacional. Nuevo desafío para las empresas, el Estado y la sociedad* (69–86). Caracas: Nueva Sociedad/Instituto Alemán de Desarrollo.
Expansión. (2020, July). *Las 500 empresas más importantes de México. Expansión*. Retrieved from https://expansion.mx/empresas/2020/07/15/estas-son-las-500-empresas-mas-importantes-de-mexico-2020.

Global Steel Trade Monitor (GSTM). (2018, July). *Steel Imports Report: United States*. International Trade Administration, Department of Commerce United States of America, September. Retrieved from https://legacy.trade.gov/steel/countries/pdfs/2018/q2/imports-us.pdf.

Global Trade Atlas (GTA). (2020, July). Retrieved from https://www.gtis.com/gta/default.cfm?login.

Huang, Xiaochun and Akira Tanaka. (2017, July). Industrial Organization of China's Steel Industry and the Restructuring of the Asia-Pacific Iron Ore Market. *Discussion Paper Series*, no. E-17-006 (Kyoto University).

INEGI. (2014). *Censos Económicos 2014. Características principales de las empresas del sector privado y paraestatal que declararon contar con participación de capital extranjero y realizaron actividades en 2013, según actividad y tipo de empresa*. INEGI, Mexico. Retrieved from https://www.inegi.org.mx/programas/ce/2014/default.html#Tabulados.

INEGI. (2020). *Censos Económicos 2019. Sistema Automatizado de Información Censal (SAIC)*. Retrieved from https://www.inegi.org.mx/app/saic/default.html.

López-Gallardo, Julio. (2016). *Tiempo de cambios. Las tres últimas décadas de la economía mexicana*. Mexico: UNAM.

MEPS. (2019). *MEPS Developing Markets' Steel Review*. UK: MEPS, March.

Narula, Rajneesh and Nigel Driffield. (2012). Does FDI Cause Development? The Ambiguity of the Evidence and Why it Matters. *European Journal of Development Research*, 24, 1–7.

NBSC. (2018). *China Statistical Yearbook 2018*. Retrieved from http://www.stats.gov.cn/tjsj/ndsj/2018/indexeh.htm.

Ortiz-Velásquez, Samuel. (2015). *Inversión en la industria manufacturera mexicana y sus determinantes mesoeconómicos: 1988–2012*. Mexico: Faculty of Economics, UNAM.

Ortiz-Velásquez, Samuel. (2019). El comercio exterior de México con Estados Unidos y China: efectos en la conducta de la inversión física de la industria mexicana. *Comercio Exterior* (Bancomext), 19 (July–September), 52–57.

Ortiz-Velásquez, Samuel and Jackelin Gordillo Olguín. (2020). La inversión en la industria siderúrgica en México: retos ante el T-MEC y China. In Maya Claudia (ed.), *Financiarización, Desarrollo y Cambios en América del Norte: Estructuras y Procesos*. Mexico: CISAN-UNAM (in process of publication).

Perri, Alessandra and Enzo Peruffo. (2016). Knowledge Spillovers from FDI: A Critical Review from the International Business Perspective. *International Journal of Management Reviews*, 18, 3–27.

Popescu, G., E. Nica, E. Nicolăescu and G. Lăzăroiu. (2016). China's Steel Industry as a Driving Force for Economic Growth and International Competitiveness. *Metalurgija*, 1(55), 123–126.

Rodrik, Dani. (2007). *One Economics, Many Recipes: Globalization, Institutions, and Economic Growth*. Princeton, NJ: Princeton University Press.

Secretariat of Economy of Mexico (SE). (2020). *Textos finales del Tratado entre México, Estados Unidos y Canadá (T-MEC)*. Retrieved from https://www.gob.mx/t-mec/acciones-y-programas/textos-finales-del-tratado-entre-mexico-estados-unidos-y-canada-t-mec-202730?state=published.

Steel Industry Coalition. (2016). *Report on Market Research into the Peoples Republic of China Steel Industry Part 1*. Final Report. Steel Industry Coalition, June 30. Retrieved from https://www.steel.org/~/media/Files/AISI/Reports/Steel-Industry-Coaliton-Full-Final-Report-06302016.

U.S. Census Bureau. (2020). *USA Trade Online*. Retrieved from https://usatrade.census.gov/.

US SEC. (2020). Forma 20-F. *Annual report pursuant to section 13 or 15(d) of the securities exchange act of 1934. For the fiscal year ended December 31, 2018*. Retrieved from https://www.sec.gov/Archives/edgar/data/1073404/000110465919018684/a19-2248_120f.htm.

USDC. (2018). *The effect of imports of steel on the national security. An investigation conducted under section 232 of the trade expansion act of 1962, as amended*, in U.S. Department of Commerce, Bureau of Industry and Security, Office of Technology Evaluation, 11 January. Retrieved from https://www.commerce.gov/sites/default/files/the_effect_of_imports_of_steel_on_the_national_security_-_with_redactions_-_20180111.pdf.

USITC. (2019). *U.S.–Mexico–Canada Trade Agreement: Likely Impact on the U.S. Economy and Specific Industry Sectors*. USITC, April. Retrieved from https://www.usitc.gov/publications/332/pub4889.pdf.

Valenzuela-Feijóo, José. (2006). *Ensayos de economía marxista*. Mexico: UAM Iztapalapa.

Valenzuela-Feijóo, José. (2014a). *México: estancamiento económico y descomposición social*. Mexico: CEDA.

Valenzuela-Feijóo, José. (2014b). *Teoría general de las economías de mercado: tomo II, funcionamiento y dinámica*. Mexico: Faculty of Economics, UNAM.

WSA. (2019). *Steel Statistical Yearbook 2018. World Steel Association*, November. Retrieved from https://www.worldsteel.org/en/dam/jcr:e5a8eda5-4b46-4892-856b-00908b5ab492/SSY_2018.pdf.

9. Excess international liquidity and corporate financing in Mexico: reflections from USA monetary policy of quantitative easing

Ximena Echenique-Romero

The United States real estate crisis of 2008 had a limited impact on the structure of corporate debt in Mexico. Our case study is America Movil, because it is one of the ten corporations with the highest sales volume in Mexico. Our main hypothesis is that the unconventional monetary policy implemented by the United States, known as Quantitative Easing, had a very limited effect on America Movil's financial schemes, as a result of their inefficient performance within the process of financialization of the global economy, a process characterized by the free movement of capital toward markets with high yields and low costs.

Our analysis focuses in particular on the theses of Eugene Fama (1970), who affirms that prices of financial assets reflect complete or full information, and therefore the capital market provides accurate signals for allocation of resources in the economy. Fama acknowledges that a scenario of efficient markets where asset prices fully reflect the information available (public and private) is unlikely. Therefore, since 1970, Fama identifies three alternate scenarios: weak efficiency (asset prices consider information from prior periods), semi-strong efficiency (asset prices contain all public information), and strong efficiency (asset prices represent privileged information). Fama even observes (1998) that there may be an overreaction or an underreaction to information affects prices of financial assets but that fact, and the three alternate hypotheses do not represent anomalies in efficient markets, but rather are consistent with such markets. Then, following the logic of efficient markets, movements of capital within financialization should respond to changes in the cost of capital estimated by the interest rate which represents the price of capital, added to the price of other assets, such as preferred shares, common shares, and bonds.

In this chapter we describe the determinants of international liquidity in the process of financialization to determine if the United States' policy of Quantitative Easing (hereinafter QE[1]) which has expanded international liquidity, affected corporate financing in Mexico. The question focused on determining through which channels QE impacted the debt structure of Mexican corporations. Thus, we can establish that the QE policy accentuated the interest rate differential between the United States and Mexico, with the result that lower interest rates in the former promoted indebtedness of Mexican corporations on the U.S. capital market, as in the case of America Movil. In particular, issuing bonds on the U.S. market became an attractive option for Mexican corporate capital. However, it should be underscored that the stock market has remained one of the primary engines of corporate financing in Mexico. This helps us trace a line of enquiry as to why the structure of corporate debt in Mexico is not sensitive to changes in the monetary policy of the United States.

In this sense, after this introduction, in the first and second sections we describe the theoretical framework of international liquidity and the investment portfolio, in order to link the variables involved in these economic models with corporate financing in Mexico. In the third section, we examine the details of QE policy, to determine whether it has affected the type of domestic corporate financing through its impact on the cost of capital defined by interest rates. Fourth, we analyze the case of America Movil, as one of Mexico's ten leading corporations by value of sales based on the ranking published by the magazine *Revista Expansion*.[2]

9.1   THE CAPITAL MARKET AND INTERNATIONAL LIQUIDITY

Domestic liquidity is made up by private and official liquidity. According to Landau (2011), the former has the following particularities: (i) it can produce indirect international effects, and (ii) it is cyclical around a growing tendency. Therefore, there is a close relationship between the creation of private liquidity and leverage, and also between destruction of liquidity and deleveraging. In parallel, central banks, through their regular monetary operations, create official liquidity, where, for periods of stress, emergency liquidity programs are implemented. Also, there are instruments which promote official liquidity in foreign currency, the first management of foreign currency reserves; the second swap lines; and the third facilities, such as FMI programs or Special Drawing Rights.

Analyzing domestic liquidity involves understanding the capital market. In Fama's words:

> [T]he primary function of the capital market is the allocation of the stock of capital in the economy. In general terms, the ideal is a market in which prices provide accurate signals for resource allocation. In other words, a market in which companies can make production and investment decisions and investors can choose between the values which ownership of corporate assets represent on the assumption that at any time prices "fully reflect" all available information. (Fama, 1970: 383)

Granting Fama's hypothesis that the efficiency of the capital market is linked to expected yields in the Capital Asset Pricing Model, in the second part we incorporate a portfolio model which takes three assets to establish a single price, to wit: the interest rate, which is the key variable which determines the composition of investment between money, short-term bonds, and stocks. For the time being, it is important to clarify that, in the capital market, the economic variables considered in the analytical framework of corporate financing include liquidity, credit, and investment. The performance of these three indicators is the result of economic relations which have developed in the process of financialization of the global economy, in a context where capital movements produced by an unconventional policy in a developed country, may affect the economic performance of developing countries. Reasons why an economy is affected by the economic policy decisions of a third country include, precisely, the impact of capital flows on interest rates, the exchange rate, and the rate of inflation, among other macroeconomic variables.

Capital flows are part of international capital mobility (hereinafter ICM), which is a key factor in the global economy because it influences: (i) different market prices (for example, interest rates, exchange rates, and asset prices); (ii) the size of public and private credit; (iii) direct and indirect investment; and (iv) the internal rate of return which determines the present value of investment projects. ICM responds largely to the indirect ratio of risk to yield, as the FMI methodology shows: capital-flows-at-risk. Strictly speaking, this process refers to the capital outlays achieved based on a predefined probability. This methodology incorporates the factors "push" and "pull," which refer to the elements of expulsion (from developed countries) and attraction (toward developing countries) of capital flows which have been present in developing countries both in the 1990s and in the first decade of the 21st century (Calvo, 1993). Both respond to the structural characteristics and political organization of nations, which consist of: (i) the growth of the financial sector; (ii) the opening of the capital account; (iii) the exchange rate regime; (iv) the quality of domestic institutions; and (v) the transparency of the central bank (Gelos et al., 2019: 7–8).

Within the dynamic of international capital mobility, we need to define international liquidity by identifying the variables on which it depends, and those it defines. In quantitative terms, two variables shape international liquidity: price (liquidity) and quantity (risk) (Landau, 2011). Also, international liquidity reports gross international capital flows (cross-border flows of credit and financial loans in foreign currency) and cross-border portfolio movements made by private banks. Technically, as explained in an extensive specialized literature (Cerutti et al., 2014; and Bruno and Shin, 2015), among indicators related to international liquidity we can include: cross-border claims on banks (as an alternative measure of international liquidity), Bloomberg Financial Conditions Indices, FRED Financial Stress Indices, Chicago Fed's National Financial Conditions Index, Kansas City Financial Stress Index, Saint Louis Financial Stress Index, and Systemic Stress Composite Indicator. The Bloomberg index is noteworthy for its international recognition.

In this chapter we will analyze changes in international liquidity through the FRED Financial Stress Indices,[3] which are freely accessible, acknowledging that those indices actually report on the impact of international liquidity on different rates of cost of capital. The index reflects an excess of liquidity from the first quarter of 2004, peaking in the fourth quarter of 2007 with a value of 6.55. This excess of liquidity continued for another two years; for example, in the second quarter of 2009, the index was 1.5635. These numbers coincide with the growth of liquidity in the United States. From 1997 to 2007, the U.S. liquidity ratio (monetary base plus reserves) as a percentage of GDP did not exceed 6.7%, but starting in 2008, the figure was in two digits. In 2013, the U.S. liquidity ratio as a percentage of GDP reached 22.42%. While the Large Scale Asset Purchases (QE) program went from representing 3.37% of the U.S. GDP in 2008 to 12.77% in 2009, peaking at 24.18% in 2014.

On the other hand, factors which determine international liquidity include: (i) macroeconomic factors (real costs of financing, expectations for return, and economic risks); (ii) public sector policies (for example, central bank liquidity policies necessary when facing nonliquid global capital markets and high financial stress, and policies of financial regulation which, among other objectives, seek to achieve more profitable use of funds); (iii) financial factors which determine the behavior of participants and brokers in the financial market (these are affected by financial innovation which promotes the transformation of nonliquid assets into liquid assets through processes of securitization, and use of lendable funds and derivatives); and (iv) risk propensity, which is greatest when there are three characteristics: (1) positive balances, (2) growing leverage, and (3) short-term wholesale financing, particularly in the banking sector (Bruno and Shin, 2015; Landau, 2013; Caruana, 2013).

Mechanisms for transmission of international liquidity include, on the one hand, interest rates which reflect the performance of the growth of private credit and the general terms of domestic financing, as well as risk-free rates (or YTM of short-term bonds) which show risks due to liquidity. On the other hand is risk propensity, which has a two-way relationship with liquidity because it is influenced by the conditions of liquidity, whereas liquidity depends on the investors' capacity and willingness to assume risk (Landau, 2013). Another mechanism of transmission of international liquidity is the exchange rate, where its volatility is a source of systemic risk or market risk, which influences a large number of macroeconomic variables.

In this sense, the study of international liquidity has been framed in international financial stability. As a result, on the one hand, the credit aggregates approach, in which private banks occupy a central position because they have a monopoly on both creation of debt and leverage, is significantly important in estimating international liquidity. In today's financial system, the banking sector creates liquidity by means of credit which, once converted to debt, boosts liquidity through a process of securitization which makes use of the non-banking sector. On the other hand, monetary aggregates added to international reserves are also a measure of liquidity. Consequently, the two approaches: credit aggregates and monetary aggregates, will prioritize financial stability as a desirable scenario and even as the ultimate end to guarantee the financial income which drives economic growth.

Moreover, expanding international liquidity depends on the availability of markets, instruments, and infrastructure for cross-border financing and how financial brokers organize their international activities. For example, bank and non-bank financial brokers play a decisive role in the operation of international liquidity, particularly in credit boom periods. The elements which influence accelerated credit growth are: (i) increasing liquidity, (ii) compressed risk premiums, and (iii) rising asset prices, three elements which, at the same time, affect financial stability.

In order to overcome potential problems of financial instability which arise from significant changes in international liquidity, central banks and the governments of some developed countries have bolstered three processes: (i) determining the level of liquidity which guarantees financial stability, (ii) estimating the amount of credit in the private sector which limits the increase of asset prices, and (iii) establishing the proper size of liquidity to achieve favorable conditions for financing. Thus, interventionist policies are needed to control liquidity, and by extension the cost of capital.

Having defined domestic liquidity, the capital market, and international liquidity, it is time to explain the orthodox and unconventional views of liquidity in corporate financing. The former perspective postulates that international liquidity, through its different instruments, produces global-scale financial stability through capital and debt markets which function efficiently and the Capital Asset Pricing Model reinforces the claim that there is a common pattern in the average yield of developed markets (Fama and French, 2011). Considering this perspective, in case of a financial crisis in the developed region the solution is to "lower interest rates to boost economic activity and prevent speculation on relevant assets" (Muñoz, 2011: 14), a phenomenon which, as we will see below, resulted from the application of QE in the 2008 crisis.

On the other hand, from an unconventional perspective, in principle, the financial markets do not operate efficiently. The most formal critique is that formulated by Behavioral Finance Theory, whose leading proponent is Robert Shiller. Its central positions include questioning the random variation of prices (Shiller, 2000: 171–175). In Shiller's view, prices do not depend only on past information from markets guided by the actions of rational agents; instead, uncertainty[4] can trigger irrational behavior in the market, causing it not to achieve the efficiency needed to correctly assess the price of an asset (Akerlof and Shiller, 2009).

Also, continuing with a critical approach, the growth of capital markets has produced an international or global financial cycle closely tied to the global liquidity cycle, which is subject to disruptions like the global financial crisis of 2008. Anaya et al. (2017) define a "global financial cycle" as a global movement of prices and terms of credit which had a strong presence between 2008 and 2015. Here it is important to ask, first, what are the factors which determine a cyclical behavior or may amplify global liquidity cycles? The answers may be: (i) sudden changes in risk propensity, (ii) a preference for liquidity, and (iii) changes in leverage. The second question is, on what does how an economy performs in the international financial cycle depend? On these factors: (i) structural characteristics, (ii) the state of financial development, and (iii) the degree of integration in the global financial system (Landau, 2013). The first of these refers to endogenous macro- and micro-economic conditions of a given economy; the second to the corporate functioning which estimates the efficiency of techniques used to assess financial assets; and the last refers to the impact of financial integration on international flows of capital, on the dynamic of credit, and on the prices of financial assets.

Having described the specificities of global liquidity cycles, it is time to explain how they can be "amplified" and what measures can be taken to avoid profound economic instability. Technically, in terms of monetary policy, to *amplify* means to intensify both increases and scarcity of liquidity. Due to the effects of these processes, according to Landau (2013), there is a political response which should consider the following factors: (a) stabilizing global liquidity cycles, (b) reducing the pro-cyclicality of the financial system, (c) stabilizing global flows of liquidity through the Basel Committee,[5] and (d) considering a macroprudential perspective in economic policy.

Furthermore, there is a heterogeneous relationship between the robust liquidity cycle, yields, and financial asset prices. Darius and Radde (2010) and Baks and Kamer (1999)[6] find a positive link between the (excessive) global growth of money and stock yields. In relation to bonds, Asada et al. (2011), following Sargent's model from 1987, propose a model portfolio with three assets, which we will develop in the next section: money M (issued by the central bank), bonds B (issued by the government), and stocks E (issued by companies), which takes stocks and bonds as imperfect substitutes, and consequently establishes that the effects of a robust liquidity cycle are not direct for all the variables involved in the portfolio.

Finally, from an unconventional perspective, excess liquidity is a contributing factor in creating financial instability. This macroeconomic perspective embraces a hypothesis of financial instability. "The idea is that stability is destabilizing in a capitalist system since processes are driven by internal financial developments" (Muñoz, 2011: 17). In this sense, the dynamic of cash flows is as unstable as changing expectations for financial asset prices. This, it bears mentioning, places uncertainty and expectations at the center of changes in corporate balance sheets. Thus, intervention by central banks is important to stabilize interest rates and asset prices, so "central banks should make monetary policy and regulate, and reform, the financial system" (Muñoz, 2011: 20).

Precisely, as we shall show in section 9.3, the monetary policy adopted by the United States Federal Reserve, QE, affected the U.S. economy through changes in its economic structure.

contrast, Mexican corporate financing was not affected by the externalities of that policy. First, because it was not the purpose of QE policy. Also, from an orthodox perspective, because QE did not represent a supply shock for Mexico which could have increased alternative domestic sources of financing, for example, through an expansion of bonds in response to the expectation of falling domestic interest rates. And, from an unconventional perspective, because levels of investment and actual demand would not have experienced a significant change in Mexico as a result of the implementation of QE.

9.2   THE INTEREST RATE AS THE KEY PRICE IN THE INVESTMENT PORTFOLIO AFFECTED BY INTERNATIONAL LIQUIDITY

In this section, we develop the three asset model, with the aim of synthesizing the effect of changes in the interest rate, as a key price, on assets in the investment portfolio, which depend on international liquidity and are altered by policies which affect it, like QE. Traditionally, interaction between the assets market and the financial sector is analyzed based on Tobin's "q," on the assumption that the wage level is exogenous and workers will not have a disposition to save (Asada et al., 2011: 14–43). Thus, the model establishes that households "should allocate all their wealth, but no more, between bonds, variable income [...] or stocks, and money" (p. 18). This can be confirmed in equation 9.4, where demand for money, demand for bonds, and demand for stocks depend on the interest rate (r) and the rate of return on assets/ stock (r_e^e), which is the sum of the rate of dividends on yields $\dfrac{r}{q}$ and capital gains expected on stocks/assets π_e^e, equation (9.6).

Considering Tobin's portfolio structure:

$$\bar{M} = M^d = f_m\left(r, r_e^e\right) W_c^n \tag{9.1}$$

$$\bar{B} = B^d = f_b\left(r, r_e^e\right) W_c^n \tag{9.2}$$

$$P_e\bar{E} = P_e E^d = f_e\left(r, r_e^e\right) W_c^n \tag{9.3}$$

$$W_c^n = \bar{M} + \bar{B} + P_e\bar{E} \tag{9.4}$$

$$f_m\left(r, r_e^e\right) + f_b\left(r, r_e^e\right) + f_e\left(r, r_e^e\right) \equiv 1 \tag{9.5}$$

$$r_e^e = \frac{r}{q} + \overline{\pi_e^e} \tag{9.6}$$

Equations (9.1) to (9.3) establish that demand for a financial asset depends positively on its own rate of return, and negatively on the rate of return of other assets, whereas demand for money depends negatively on both the interest rate and the rate of return on stocks (Asada et al. 2011). These relationships can also be established in the Keynes–Metzler–Goodwin (KMG) model, developed by Asada et al. (2011: 40–74). According to this model, which has the same foundations as Tobin's structure, demand for monetary balances is determined by a function fm(r, re^e) which depends on the interest rate on short-term bonds, r, and on the expected rate of return on stocks r_e^e. The product of this function and the nominal wealth Wc^n determine the nominal demand for money, Md. This relationship is repeated for the nominal demand for bonds and for the nominal demand for stocks. The conditions the model must satisfy are as follows: fm(r, r_e^e), fb(r, r_e^e), and fe(r, r_e^e):

$$Md = f_m (r, r_e^e) \; Wc^n \tag{9.7}$$

$$Bd = fb(r, r_e^e) \; Wc^n \tag{9.8}$$

$$P_e E^d = fe (r, r_e^e) \; Wc^n \tag{9.9}$$

$$Wc^n = Md + Bd + P_e E^d \tag{9.10}$$

Having assured that the number of independent equations is equal to the number of endogenous variables (r, r^e), we can establish the two fundamental inequalities of the model:

$$f_m(r, r_e^e) + fb(r, r_e^e) + fe(r, r_e^e) = 1 \tag{9.11}$$

$$\frac{\partial f_m \left(r, r_e^e\right)}{\partial i} + \frac{\partial f_b \left(r, r_e^e\right)}{\partial i} + \frac{\partial f_e \left(r, r_e^e\right)}{\partial i} = 0$$

These conditions guarantee that:

$$\frac{\partial f_b \left(r, r_e^e\right)}{\partial i} > 0; \frac{\partial f_m \left(r, r_e^e\right)}{\partial i} < 0; \frac{\partial f_e \left(r, r_e^e\right)}{\partial i} < 0$$

$$\frac{\partial f_b \left(r, r_e^e\right)}{\partial r_e^e} > 0 \; \frac{\partial f_m \left(r, r_e^e\right)}{\partial r_e^e} < 0 \; ; \; \frac{\partial f_b \left(r, r_e^e\right)}{\partial r_e^e} < 0$$

In such a way that the demand for bonds is positively related to the interest rate, while the demand for money and for financial assets are negatively related to the interest rate, the same as the expected interest rate.

Theoretically, the growth of the capital market this model assumes is tied to a set of factors, to wit: (1) the advance of institutional investors (pension funds, insurance companies, private capital funds, and investment funds); (2) the function of investment banks which distribute increasingly attractive securities or instruments; (3) the activity of rating agencies which determine the cost of capital as it impacts the costs of issuing corporate bonds; and (4) the functioning of corporate governance, an especially influential factor because it intervenes in issuance costs, best practices, accountability, and the reduction of asymmetries in information.

Finally, the cost of capital in instruments depends on a combination of factors, the most important of which include macroeconomic structure, the characteristics of issuers, and issues. Also, this cost depends on financing regimes (relationship between commitment to pay debts and expected revenue streams), which may be stable and unstable.

To link the theoretical framework described thus far with one of the most prominent economic policies of the 21st century with regard to its impact on financial asset prices, we describe the QE monetary policy and its potential impact on the structure of corporate debt in Mexico below.

9.3 THEORETICAL AND EMPIRICAL ASPECTS OF THE MONETARY POLICY OF QUANTITATIVE EASING

In fall 2008, the United States, together with other developed countries: the United Kingdom, Japan, and the Euro Zone, implemented an unconventional monetary policy by means of an emergency liquidity program to address the process of endogenous destruction of liquidity resulting from the financial crisis in the real estate market (Fawley and Neely, 2013). The primary goal of the QE policy was to reactivate the economy by increasing the monetary base by means of a Large-Scale Asset Purchase program (LSAP) implemented by the Federal Open Market Committee of the Federal Reserve.

In the United States, the main goal of purchasing long-term assets was to reactivate the economy by reducing long-term yields including real interest rates and the cost of capital. In 2007, the real interest rate in the United States was 5.22, following a downward tendency which reached its low point of 1.14% in 2011. Meanwhile, in Mexico the real interest rate fell even further, reaching -0.88% in 2011.[7]

Formally, the Federal Reserve implemented this monetary mechanism of injecting liquidity in three stages: QE1, November 2008, purchases of $600 million in instruments; QE2, March 2009, purchase of $1.75 billion in assets; QE3, September 2011, purchase of $400 billion in bonds (Fawley and Neely 2013: 58, 59). This process is reflected in the composition of the LSAP in which, in addition to representing a growing percentage of the GDP, as we remarked in the first section, the share of mortgage assets continued to grow, based on data published by the Federal Reserve, at a maximum rate of 54.28% in the second quarter of 2010.

Bauer and Neely (2014) showed that, during its implementation in the United States, the effect of QE was reflected in: (a) GDP growth, (b) a drop in bond yields (particularly ten-year bonds), and (c) an increase in prices of financial assets or stocks. It bears mentioning that rising asset prices are a characteristic of expansive credit cycles. Therefore, by boosting consumer confidence, QE helped bring an end to the negative cycle of endogenous destruction of liquidity by means of a mechanism in which the Central Bank flexibilizes monetary conditions by purchasing instruments by issuing money, where the demand for assets resulting from this process boosts their prices and increases capital gains, helping in turn to flexibilize monetary conditions, both domestic and international.

QE policy had effects on developing countries. Calvo (2016: 20) refers to a "liquidity wall" created by the flow of capital toward emerging markets, where this disposition for liquidity, more than responding to the expectations for growth of emerging economies, was the product of low interest rates on highly liquid instruments in the developed economies, such as United States treasury notes and bonds.[8] Moreover, QE has a "spillover effect" on emerging economies. Bhattarai and Chatterjee (2015), using a Bayesian VAR model, estimated the effects of QE policy on a group of emerging economies; specifically the group known as the "fragile five" (Brazil, India, Indonesia, Turkey, and South Africa) experienced the most intense effect. In a strict sense, these authors found that in emerging markets the expansive shock of QE policy caused an appreciation of exchange rates, an impulse for flows of capital, a drop in yields on long-term bonds, and a positive impulse on the stock market or asset prices, with no effect on the GDP of emerging economies.

On the other hand, Anaya et al. (2017) identified that QE policy had "spillover effects" on emerging economies due to the changes it produced in international capital flows. As a result, as Calvo (1993) had suggested, portfolio outflows in the United States have been associated with inflows of that kind of capital to emerging markets. In the latter economies it produced, the authors cited maintain, growth of real production, an increase in yield on capital, appreciation of exchanges, and a drop in real lending rates.

Bowman et al. (2014) showed that the effect of QE policy on the three key variables of emerging markets: yields, exchange rate, and stock prices, was not uniform and depended on the particularities of each country. The authors even found that the effect on yields of sovereign bonds would have been similar to the changes which other domestic policies had produced in interest rates (descending).

Bauer and Neely (2014) confirmed that the primary effect of QE policy was in the financial variables of emerging markets, in particular, in the exchange rate due to its impact on portfolio flows. By accelerating the flow of capital toward emerging economies, QE strengthened local currencies against the dollar, an effect which, in terms of corporate financing, could have affected emerging countries by deflating the value of debt contracted in dollars.

The findings described above are confirmed by the performance of the following indicators (Figure 9.1). Between 2007 and 2014, a few years beyond the formal QE program, U.S. liquidity increased, especially due to the monetary base, which grew more than reserves; even between 2007 and 2008, the first indicator doubled, and in contrast reserves grew only 8.25%; in 2013, the monetary base grew 38.92%, as reserves fell sharply from 2008, bottoming at a growth rate of -11.88%. Meanwhile, in Mexico Gross Fixed Capital Formation (GFCF) and portfolio investment, which could have responded positively to the effects of QE due to falling interest rates in the case of the first variable and the interest differential favorable to Mexico for portfolio investment did not present substantial changes. GFCF was approximately 22% of the GDP after QE, which was not a significant variation from the years before that policy. Portfolio investment remained unstable without surpassing 1%, while the current account deficit rose significantly. In 2007, the current account deficit accounted for -0.364% of the GDP, while in 2008 it tripled to represent 1.514%. Although, as the U.S. has begun to abandon QE policy Mexico's current account deficit has risen constantly since 2015.

9.4   CORPORATE FINANCING IN MEXICO IN A CONTEXT OF INTERNATIONAL LIQUIDITY AND FLEXIBLE U.S. MONETARY POLICY

From the outset, we need to establish certain facts about corporate financing in Mexico: (i) the deregulation and globalization of financing have boosted liquidity, with a reduction in total financing to the non-financial private sector, (ii) securitization techniques have expanded financing for the capital market, (iii) the impact of new non-bank financial instruments on financing of a sector is low, (iv) present and past gains are what determine the level of investment, and (v) sources of liquidity may include credit or debt contracts (Levy and Bustamante, 2019).

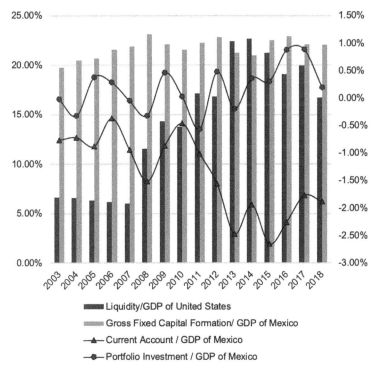

Source: Own based on the Federal Reserve and World Bank database.

Figure 9.1   *Liquidity in the United States and investment in Mexico (proportion of domestic GDP)*

Starting in the year 2000, a change in capital flows toward emerging markets triggered the development of a series of financing instruments in the capital and debt markets, specifically variable income instruments and fixed income instruments. In particular, the growth of markets for debt instruments in Latin America in recent years helped extend channels for corporate financing in the region. It bears recalling that the sustainability of financing through stocks depends on the rate of profitability exceeding the price of the assets and in the case of bonds there is a capital gain as long as the present value is greater than the nominal or face value of the bond. Also, the Latin American Integrated Market created in 2009, of which Mexico has been part since 2011, permits the expansion of financing instruments in Latin America through issuance of stocks on the stock exchange.

The expansion of liquidity through QE has no direct link to this process given that, based on data published by the Bank for International Settlements,[9] corporate debt globally and in Latin America and the Caribbean has maintained constant growth since the 1980s. In 1997, Latin America's share in global corporate debt reached a high point at 7.98%, after which the share fell to a low point of 1.58% in 2008. Then, growth of debt in LA and the Caribbean was reactivated, reaching 3.50% of global corporate debt in 2019. In the 1990s, Mexico's share in

Latin American corporate debt fell, reaching 19.15% in 2003. Since then, corporate debt in Mexico has recovered, totaling 33.30% in 2019.

The bond market in Latin America has been used to pay existing credit lines, refinance indebtedness, and acquire assets, for which reason it is important to make a distinction between corporate financing by means of private bonds in local currency and in foreign currency, and the market for bonds issued by the central banks of countries in the region (Nuñez et al., 2018). The Report on Capital Flows toward Latin America (Velloso, 2019) indicates that issuance of sovereign debt in the region reached 35.7% of total debt, and fifteen countries – Brazil, Chile, Colombia, Costa Rica, the Dominican Republic, Ecuador, El Salvador, Guatemala, Jamaica, Mexico, Panama, Paraguay, Peru, Surinam, and Uruguay – distinguished themselves by maintaining the largest share, with Mexico, Peru, and Brazil accounting for 47% of the total sovereign debt. Meanwhile, in 2019, the corporate sector (including corporations, banks, and quasi-sovereign and supranational issuers) represented 64.3% of total debt issues in Latin America, surpassing the 59.5% share reported in 2018 (Velloso, 2019: 23).

Usually, corporate issues are divided by investment grade and high yield. In 2019, Latin American companies with investment grade totaled 56%, with high-yield companies making up 44%. Also, Brazilian (32.3%), Mexican (31.0%), and Chilean (13.4%) corporations accounted for 77% of total corporate issues. By sector, the top performers were, first: commercial banking and financial services (20%); second: energy – oil, gas and power (18%); third: agriculture, agroindustry, and food (17%); fourth, minerals and metals (11%); fifth: telecommunications; sixth: utilities (energy, 8%); seventh: chemical industry (6%); retail, consumer goods, real estate, resorts, and hotels (3%); eighth: transportation (3%); ninth: construction (1.9%); and tenth: infrastructure (1%) (Velloso, 2019: 27).

In Mexico, in the second decade of the 21st century, considering the statistics reported by SIF ICAP of the National Baking and Stock Commission, Mexico (CNBV), the total amount of corporate financing through bonds showed significant growth in Mexico. For example, between 2014 and 2015, the corporative bonds in terms of the average amount 28 days per operation grew at 40%. However, the stock market remains an important mechanism for financing.

Why is the stock market still attractive to large corporations? It is due to the yield the capital market offers and its relatively fast recovery. With America Movil, for example, in 2008 the total yield on stocks, which includes yield from capital gains and yield from dividends, fell drastically by 30.65%, when in 2004 it had reported almost 100% growth. But in 2009, yields started to rise again with 50.57%.[10] To date, the performance of yields has followed a random trajectory, without fulfilling the maxim of Fama's first studies (1970). See Figure 9.2.

The same firms which distinguish themselves in Mexico due to higher volume of sales also stand out in corporate financing through issuance of bonds (Forbes, 2017). In 2006, America Movil made its first corporate issue worth 8 billion pesos at 30 years with a 8.46% coupon, which represented a differential of 80 base points on the yield of United States Treasury Notes at 30 years, in other words a premium for preferring corporate bonds. Meanwhile, in the same year America Movil issued ten billion pesos in unsecured bonds.[11] Recently, as shown in Table 9.1, America Movil has continued to do well in the bond market with a coupon rate above the Federal Reserve (Table 9.1), which confirms the demand for financing in the U.S. market due to the drop in interest rates which makes the America Movil bond issue attractive, but in the U.S. market.

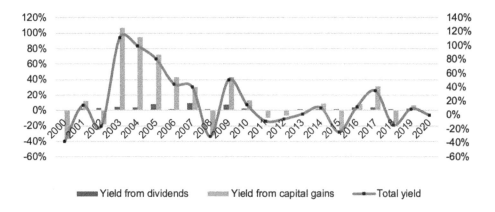

Source: Own based on *Yahoo Finance.*

Figure 9.2   America Movil stock performance

Based on America Movil's annual reports, the corporation's sources of financing come from "cash flows generated by its operations [...] international capital markets, Mexican capital markets, domestic and foreign banks, equipment suppliers and financing para entities for exports" (America Movil 2019: 43). In Table 9.2 we can see America Movil's financing dynamic and the significant drop in bank debt before QE with a temporary increase of such debt after QE. Therefore, in the last decade, credit has not been a primary financing mechanism for the firm. Also, corporate bonds have maintained a weak participation in recent years, and the noteworthy instrument is the Senior Note. These and bonds offer a coupon rate which represents a fixed income every period of time based on the established agreement. However, there are significant differences between a Senior Note and bonds. In first place, the term of financing for bonds is greater, in America Movil's case, as we see in Table 9.1, up to 25 years, for which reason the price (present value) of the bond fluctuates more than the notes, whose term to maturity is between one and ten years; second, in case of liquidation of a company's debt, in the order of precedence Notes occupy a preferential place. This confirms that long-term bonds with a fixed rate like those America Movil has issued are a limited instrument in corporate financing.

This performance held steady both in periods when America Movil's total long-term and short-term debt grew significantly, that is, the 24% annual growth of debt between 2003 and 2004, and when it fell by double digits, that is, -19.19% annual, between 2005 and 2010 (see Table 9.2).

9.5   CONCLUSIONS

The conclusions of this chapter are centered on three main ideas. First, changes in international liquidity occurred in inefficient markets which seek to synchronize economic changes of

Table 9.1   *America Movil bond issue*

2019	America Movil made its first bond issue on the New York Stock Exchange for 1 billion dollars with maturity in 10 years, a yield to maturity (YTM) or yield of 3.706%, and a 3.625% annual coupon rate. America Movil made a second bond issue on the New York Stock Exchange for 1.25 billion dollars with maturity in 30 years, YTM of 4.409%, and a 4.375% coupon rate.	The yield on the Bond with maturity in 2029 is 115 base points above the yield on Treasury Notes. The yield on the second Bond with maturity in 2049 is 145 base points above the yield on Treasury Notes.
September 10, 2015	Mexico City, September 10, 2015. America Movil, S.A.B. de C.V. ("AMX") [BMV: AMX] [NYSE: AMX] [NASDAQ: AMOV] [LATIBEX: XAMXL] announces that its Dutch subsidiary America Movil B.V. (the "Issuer") completed the bond placement for a principal amount of EUR 750 million (the "Bonds"), which will be guaranteed and exchangeable for ordinary shares of Koninklijke KPN N.V. (the "Exchangeable Bond Offer").	The Bonds will mature in 3 years and are expected to pay an annual coupon between 5.25% and 5.75%, which will be payable quarterly in arrears, and additional interest equal to 85% of the gross amount of cash dividends received by the Issuer in relation to the underlying common shares of Koninklijke KPN N.V. ("KPN").
Thursday, September 1, 2011	2.75 billion dollars 2 billion dollars (5 years) 750 million dollars with maturity in 2040	2.549% or 158 base points over comparable U.S. Treasury bonds. 5.502% or 190 base points over Treasury papers.
	America Movil made its first corporate issue for 8 billion pesos at a term of 30 years	The bond had a 8.46% coupon, which represented a differential of 80 base points over the yield of the 30-year federal government bond.

Note: Between 2004 and 2005, the obligations were mostly placed among institutional investors in the United States.
Source: Own based on Annual Reports of America Movil, 2002–2019.

Table 9.2   *Composition of America Movil's financing*

	2002	2005	2010	2015	2019
Senior Notes		55.63%	57.13%	74.44%	87.33%
Denominated in Dollars		86.89%	66.01%	42.87%	31.02%
Denominated in Mexican pesos		13.11%	10.03%	11.97%	10.66%
Denominated in Euros			16.71%	30.92%	40.75%
Denominated in Pound sterling			7.24%	10.96%	10.08%
Denominated in Swiss francs				2.77%	
Denominated in Japanese Yen				0.51%	0.41%
Denominated in Chilean pesos					0.65%
Denominated in Brazilian real					6.41%
Hybrid Bonds				13.72%	4.06%
Denominated in Euros				85.14%	45.82%
Denominated in Pound sterling				14.86%	54.18%
Bonds	10.04%	3.08%			
Denominated in Dollars	80.81%				
Denominated in Colombian pesos		100%			
Denominated in Brazilian real	19.19				
Bank and Other Loans	58.69%	16.04%	22.68%	8.49%	8.60%
Denominated in Dollars	96.42%	36.21%	48.17%	68.10%	
Denominated in Mexican pesos	2.95%	54.58%	0.07%	4.54%	
Denominated in Chilean pesos					

	2002	2005	2010	2015	2019
Denominated in Brazilian real			4.31%	4.75%	
Denominated in Euros			0.27%	12.62%	
Denominated in Colombian pesos		2.43%	5.82%	4.24%	
Denominated in other currencies	0.63%	6.77%	41.37%	5.76%	
Stock Certificates		18.31%	20.19%	3.35%	
Mexican pesos		100.00%	100.0%	100.0%	
Others[1]	31.27%	6.94%			

Note: [1]Others: BNDES, Suppliers, Commercial paper, Leases.
Source: Own based on Annual Reports of America Movil, 2002–2019.

two nations, because the lead price of international liquidity, in this case the cost of capital, does not provide the full information on the changes that occur in developed countries, and therefore uncertainty regarding the economic and structural conditions of developing countries increases. In this sense, one would expect an underreaction by capital and debt markets in developing countries like Mexico to the economic policies of developed countries like the United States. However, the effect of capital flows on the exchange rate and the cost of debt in foreign currency does not reflect such an underreaction, a thesis backed by studies which identified the trade deficit as indicative of an overreaction to QE in terms of the commodities market. Thus, the factors of attraction and expulsion were present during QE as established by the specialized literature and international organizations.

Second, there are endogenous limitations on the Mexican economy which, despite the greater investment QE produced, did not transform the structure of Mexican corporate financing, which continued to depend on the capital market with little effect, for example, on the banking system in support of productive investment, because the effects of QE unfolded in an unstable financial cycle, which increases the volatility of the stock market.

Third, with the implementation of QE, the cost of capital fell in the United States and the interest rate differential favored Mexico by increasing opportunities to find financing in the U.S. market, as shown by the premium companies like America Movil granted on the coupon rate for its bonds, taking as base the Federal Reserve rate. In other words, U.S. monetary policy had a tangential effect on America Movil's cost of capital which is reflected in the extra percentage over the Federal Reserve rate when, without QE monetary policy, the coupon rate could be higher.

Nevertheless, the most propitious scenario for growth of debt in corporate bonds in a context of excessive international liquidity is a process which has not been consolidated in Mexico, since corporate bonds represent a minimum share, and in the particular case of America Movil, another kind of financial instrument has gained relevance, specifically financial notes. In that sense, a theoretical structure like that which explains the composition of an investment portfolio is limited to recognize the real effect of an unconventional monetary policy based on increasing the magnitude of international liquidity. Finally, America Movil's experience is an example worth revisiting for subsequent analyses, above all in a climate of instability like that presented by the present global economic scenario.

NOTES

1. Unconventional monetary policies like QE have been applied in other countries, solely for ease of reading in this text the acronym QE will be used to refer to the case of the United States.
2. Based on data published by Grupo Expansion (annual publication *Las empresas más importantes de México*), PAPIIT IA302318 project database.
3. "The STLFSI2 measures the degree of financial stress in the markets and is constructed from 18 weekly data series, all of which are weekly averages of daily data series: seven interest rates, six yield spreads, and five other indicators. Each of these variables captures some aspect of financial stress. Accordingly, as the level of financial stress in the economy changes, the data series are likely to move together.
    How to interpret the Index:
       The average value of the index, which begins in late 1993, is designed to be zero. Thus, zero is viewed as representing normal financial market conditions. Values below zero suggest below-average financial market stress, while values above zero suggest above-average financial market stress." Federal Reserve Bank of St. Louis, St. Louis Fed Financial Stress Index

[STLFSI2] (n.d.), retrieved from FRED, Federal Reserve Bank of St. Louis; https://fred.stlouisfed
.org/series/STLFSI2, July 10, 2020.

4. According to Akerlof and Shiller (2009), "Uncertainty is something which cannot be measured
    because there are no standard objectives to express probabilities," location on Kindle 3309–3310.
5. The Basel Committee on Banking Supervision was created in 1974. The resolutions taken by the
    meeting of central bank governors on the Committee are focused on establishing levels of capital,
    risk management, and competitiveness, ultimately more centered on risk management.
6. Cited by Landau (2011).
7. Source indexmundi, based on the International Monetary Fund and the World Bank. https://www
    .indexmundi.com/es/datos/estados-unidos/tasa-de-inter%C3%A9s-real.
8. It bears mentioning that there is a substantial difference between Quantitative Easing and Credit
    Easing. According to Fawley and Neely (2013), the latter is a policy which "seeks to lower interest
    rates and restore market functions, whereas QE describes any policy which unusually increases the
    magnitude of central bank liabilities – currencies and bank reserves – especially in zero bonds"
    (p. 55).
9. BIS Quarterly Review: September 2015. International debt securities – all issuers.
10. Own estimates based on data from Yahoo Finance.
11. Source: Grupo Financiero Inbursa (2006) *América Movil, S.A. De C.V. Programa De Certificados
    Bursátiles*. Aut: 2723-4. 15-2006-005 date April 11, 2006.

BIBLIOGRAPHY

Akerlof, G., and Shiller, R. (2009). *Animal Spirits: How Human Psychology Drives the Economy and
    Why It Matters for Global Capitalism*. Princeton, NJ: Princeton University Press.
America Movil. (2019). Construyendo redes para un futuro mejor, Annual Report, Mexico.
Anaya, P., Hachula, M., and Offermanns, C.J. (2017). Spillovers of US unconventional monetary policy
    to emerging markets: The role of capital flows. *Journal of International Money and Finance*, *73*,
    275–295.
Asada, T., Flaschel, P., Mouakil, T., and Christian, P. (2011). *Asset Markets, Portfolio Choice and
    Macroeconomic Activity: A Keynesian Perspective*. London: Palgrave.
Bauer, M.D., and Neely, C.J. (2014). International channels of the feds unconventional monetary policy.
    Journal of International Money and Finance, *44*, 24–46.
Bhattarai, S., and Chatterjee, A. (2015). Effects of US quantitative easing on emerging market econo-
    mies. *Working Paper* No. 255, Federal Reserve Bank of Dallas, 1–68.
Borio, C.E. (2010). Ten propositions about liquidity crises, Bank for International Settlements, *BIS
    Working Papers* No. 293, 1–21.
Borio, C.E. (2013). Commentary: global liquidity: private and public. Global dimensions of unconven-
    tional monetary policy. *Proceedings of the Jackson Hole Symposium*. Federal Reserve Bank of Kansas
    City, 261–273.
Bowman, D., Londono, J.M., and Sapriza, H. (2014). U.S. unconventional monetary policy and trans-
    mission to emerging market economies. *International Finance Discussion Papers, 1109*. Board of
    Governors of the Federal Reserve System. United States, 1–44.
Bruno, V., and Shin H.S. (2015). Cross-border banking and global liquidity. *Review of Economic Studies*,
    82(2), 535–564.
Calvo, G.A. (1993). Capital inflow and real exchange rate appreciation in Latin America: the role of
    external factors. *Staff Papers (International Monetary Fund)*, *40*(1), 108–151.
Calvo, G.A. (2016). *Macroeconomics in Times of Liquidity Crises*. Cambridge, MA: The MIT Press.
Caruana, J. (2013). Global liquidity: where do we stand? Assessing global liquidity in a global frame-
    work. *Bank of Korea Annual Conference*, Seoul, 1–15.
Cerutti, E., Claessens, S., and Puy, D. (2015). Push factors and capital flows to emerging markets: why
    knowing your lender matters more than fundamentals, *Working Paper*, WP/15/127, International
    Monetary Fund, 1–42.
Cerutti, E., Claessens, S., and Ratnovski, L. (2014). Global liquidity and drivers of cross-border bank
    flows. *IMF Working Paper*, WP/14/69, 1–27.

Cerutti, E., Claessens, S., and Ratnovski, L. (2016). Global liquidity and cross-border bank flows. Economic Policy. *63rd Economic Policy Panel meeting in Amsterdam*, 1–36.

Fama, E. (1970). Efficient capital markets: a review of theory and empirical work. *The Journal of Finance*, 25(2), 383–417.

Fama, E. (1998). Market efficiency, long-term returns, and behavioral finance. *Journal of Financial Economics*, 49(3), 283–306.

Fama, E., and French, K. (2011). Size, value, and momentum in international stock returns. *Fama-Miller Working Paper*.

Fawley, B., and Neely, C. (2013). Four stories of quantitative easing. *Federal Reserve Bank of St. Louis Review*, 95(1), 51–88.

Gelos, G., Gornicka, L., Koepke, R., Sahay, R., and Sgherrill, S. (2019). Capital flows at risk: taming the ebbs and flows. *Working Paper* No. 19/279, International Monetary Fund, 7–8.

Landau, J.P. (2011). Global liquidity – concept, measurement and policy implications. *CGFS Papers*, 45, Report submitted by an Ad-hoc Group established by the Committee on the Global Financial System, Bank of France, Bank for International Settlements, 1–33.

Landau, J.P. (2013). Global liquidity: public and private, *Proceedings – Economic Policy Symposium – Jackson Hole*, Federal Reserve Bank of Kansas City, 223–259.

Lavigne, R., Sarker, S., and Vasishtha, G. (2014). Spillover effects of quantitative easing on emerging market economies. *Bank of Canada Review Autumn*, 23–33.

Levy, N., and Bustamante, J. (2019). Crédito, inversión y ganancia: un análisis empírico para la economía mexicana (2000–2014). *Análisis Económico*, 34(87), 125–148.

Muñoz, J. (2011). Orthodox versus heterodox (Minskyan) perspectives of financial crises: explosion in the 1990s versus implosion in the 2000s, *Working Paper* No. 695, Levy Economics Institute of Bard College.

Nuñez, G., Perrotini, I., and López-Herrera, I. (2018). Gobierno corporativo y deuda internacional de empresas latinoamericanas. *Revista de la CEPAL*, 126, 31–45.

Osina N. (2019). Global liquidity, market sentiment, and financial stability indices. *Journal of Multinational Financial Management*, 52, 1–60.

Shiller, R. (2000). *Irrational Exuberance*. Princeton, NJ: Princeton University Press.

Velloso, H. (2019). *Capital Flows to Latin America and the Caribbean*. Washington, D.C.: ECLAC.

Vermeulen, R., Hoeberichts, M., Vašíček, B., Žigraiová, D., Šmídková, K., and De Haan, J. (2015). Financial stress indices and financial crises, *Open Economies Review*, 26, 383–406.

Newspapers

Federal Reserve Bank of St. Louis, St. Louis Fed Financial Stress Index [STLFSI2] (n.d.), retrieved from FRED, Federal Reserve Bank of St. Louis, https://fred.stlouisfed.org/series/STLFSI2, July 10, 2020.

Forbes (2017, May). América Móvil se dispara 140 lugares en raking de las compañías más grandes del mundo, https://www.forbes.com.mx/.

Grupo Expansion, Annual publication *Las empresas más importantes de México*, https://expansion.mx/empresas/.

La Jornada (2006, December 14). *Crece América Móvil*, Mexico City.

Lizbeth, P. (2014, November 10). 13 grandes emisiones de bonos en América Latina, Forbes Staff.

Santiago, J. (2019, April 16). América Móvil obtuvo 2,250 mdd en bonos. Mexico City: *El Economista*.

10. Foreign direct investment in Latin America: effects on growth and development, 1996–2017

Marcelo Varela-Enríquez and Gustavo Adrián Salazar

10.1 INTRODUCTION

The literature on the relationship between foreign direct investment (FDI) and economic growth has marked positive relationships and, in some cases, negative relationships and positive effects on economic development. This literature, for the most part, has been linked to the increase in capital mobility and the expansion of the globalizing process that has allowed, some authors say, the spread of technology. All this, depending on the success of the economic policies issued in a country. In this regard, the Inter-American Development Bank (IDB, 2020, p. 16) points out that:

> Effective free competition offers a competitive environment for companies and numerous advantages for consumers (lower prices, better quality, greater choice, etc.). In this sense, competition is one of the keys to more efficiently integrate Latin America and the Caribbean (LAC) with global markets, improving the flow of FDI, and promoting economic growth and development.

In other words, for the IDB, state stimulus for free markets and the attraction of foreign direct investment (FDI) are effective mechanisms for growth and development.

Is what the IDB proposes effective and accurate? If this were the case, Latin America should have been, many decades ago, a region that had converged to development, not a region that is still considered developing or underdeveloped. But reality shows Latin America not only as the most unequal region in the world, but the region where economic growth is tied to the extraction of natural resources and exports of primary goods, and its economy moves in line with commodity prices and world economy, given the high dependence on the external market.

Therefore, to understand these factors that have not been studied or defined in most studies, this research measures the relationship between foreign direct investment and economic growth, as well as its relationship with human development in Latin America, considering variables such as the Human Development Index and GDP per capita based on purchasing power parity (PPP). Two econometric models developed under the same technical criteria are used for the measurement. For this purpose, a study group made up of 21 Latin American countries in the period 1996–2017 will be used, and two models have been proposed that reflect the effect of foreign direct investment for both human development and economic growth. This study aims to show not only that growth is not equal to development, but also to estimate how FDI affects economic growth and development in Latin America differently.

In the first model, to measure the relationship between FDI and development, the Human Development Index is used as the dependent variable. The independent variables used are the outward per capita net income based on purchasing power parity (PPP) as a proxy of FDI, the share of natural resource income in GDP, GDP per capita based on purchasing power parity (PPP), government final consumption expenditure, life expectancy at birth, and average years of schooling.

While in the second model, to measure the relationship between FDI and economic growth, GDP per capita based on purchasing power parity (PPP) is used as a proxy for economic growth, and as independent variables, FDI per capita based on purchasing power parity (PPP), real household and government consumption based on purchasing power parity (PPP), per capita merchandise exports and imports based on purchasing power parity (PPP) of GDP at constant prices, percentage of people employed, and government effectiveness.

The idea of defining two different models that differentiate the effects that FDI has on economic growth and development is to establish parameters different from conventional economics and move towards a heterodox measurement of the existing relationships given in traditional or conventional literature.

The structure of the chapter includes five sections. The first section addresses the introductory part of the chapter. The second section deals with foreign investment in Latin America, which allows observing the evolutionary process of foreign investment from 1996 to 2017, the direction towards the extraction of natural resources, and the income from foreign investment. The third section focuses on a literature review to understand the role of direct foreign investment in economic growth and development. The fourth section presents the methodology used and the results obtained, where the methodological process applied is explained in detail, and the two models used to explain the effects of foreign investment on both growth and development. The fifth section consists of the conclusions, where, based on the results, the fundamental conclusion is set out: Foreign direct investment contributes positively to economic growth as measured by variations in GDP, while money flows sent abroad captured from the balance of net income sent abroad in the balance of payments negatively affects human development. This indicates that the results found differ because growth is not the same as development. Given that the variations in GDP contribute to a lesser extent to the HDI compared to variables such as life expectancy and average years of schooling, the empirical evidence in Latin America for the last two decades shows that foreign direct investment does not generate positive results in the welfare of the population. Finally, the bibliography used as a basis for the theoretical and applicative understanding of the methodology is defined.

10.2   FOREIGN DIRECT INVESTMENT IN LATIN AMERICA

It has always been stated that foreign direct investment is beneficial for the economy, especially for developing or underdeveloped countries like those in Latin America. Similarly, the idea has spread that foreign direct investment must be stimulated because it brings foreign currency into the country and stimulates the economy. However, Figure 10.1 shows that while FDI has an average participation of 3% of GDP, the income from FDI abroad has the participation of 4% of GDP, that is, more foreign currency leaves than enters. As Morales

(2010, p. 151) indicates, "International capital flows in our countries, do not register a positive account detail, since the outflow via investment income (profits, dividends, interest, and portfolio) is higher than the foreign direct investment."

Furthermore, it should be considered that the return of neoliberal governments in Latin America from 2012 onwards has generated the deregulatory conditions that have benefited foreign and national capital, as well as the acceptance of international arbitration, which has undermined national sovereignties, affecting growth and development in the region. In the same manner, it should be pointed out that the FDI not only takes out more foreign currency than it brings to Latin America, but that this foreign direct investment is speculative and directed towards the extractive sectors of our countries; which in the majority of cases are sustained by the export of primary goods, especially oil and minerals, where foreign income from FDI is tied to income from natural resources, as GDP participation. And when we analyze FDI income growth and compare it to GDP per capita based on purchasing power parity (PPP), it turns out that FDI income grows faster than GDP per PPP.

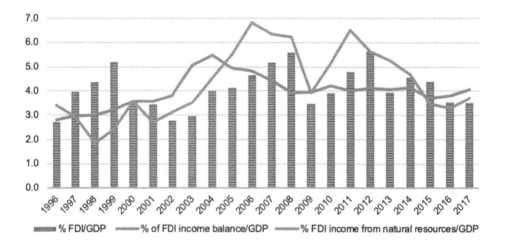

Source: CEPAL (2019a, 2019b), World Bank. Elaboration: authors.

Figure 10.1   Percentage of FDI income balance, and FDI income from natural resources over the gross domestic product, average Latin America (1996–2017)

Finally, when we compare GDP pc PPP with the human development index (Figure 10.2), we can see that GDP pc PPP grows in a volatile manner and in some periods contracts negatively. This affects purchasing power because it is in line with the economic cycle of the economy, and the volatility of commodity prices, in contrast to human development, which grows steadily during the period of analysis, and depends largely on public investment policies.

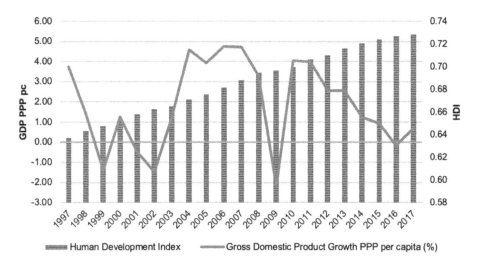

Source: United Nations Development Program, World Bank. Elaboration: authors.

Figure 10.2   Human development index and gross domestic product growth PPP per capita, Latin America (1997–2017)

10.3   LITERATURE REVIEW

In explaining the relationship between foreign direct investment and economic growth, different roles have been defined for foreign direct investment, based on the impact on economic growth as a result of assuming markets of perfect competition, decreasing marginal productivity, and constant returns to scale, as neoclassical models indicate. Based on these assumptions, exogenous increases in foreign direct investment can only positively affect capital per person temporarily, given the decreasing returns. In this way, the only way to affect economic growth in the long term is by modifying two exogenous factors: technology and work. In contrast, endogenous growth models indicate, in general, that foreign direct investment has a positive effect on economic growth indirectly through both capital formation and the development of human resources.

The explanation linked to the levels of capital mobility that affect the growth of countries has also been conditioned. It has been indicated that the phenomenon of globalization has promoted such mobility. It has even been stated that foreign direct investment is less volatile than other types of investment, and in addition to generating greater economic growth, have been accompanied by greater development, as indicated by the IDB (2020); Álvarez Herranz et al. (2009), among others.

Literature also indicates that foreign direct investment per capita promotes growth. As pointed out by Borensztein et al. (1995); Hermes and Lensink (2000); Alfaro et al. (2004), and Ozturk (2007), who have found a positive relationship between foreign direct investment per capita and economic growth, conditioned by the behavior of other explanatory variables such as the level of human capital, the levels of public and private capital per capita, the previous levels of per capita income, the interaction between human capital and foreign direct investment, and institutional quality. In comparison, Barro and Sala-i-Martin (1990) and Blomström et al. (1994) assume that countries converge to higher economic growth in terms of their per capita income, and the impact of foreign direct investment on the accumulation of private capital per capita, as defined by Borensztein et al. (1995).

Alfaro et al. (2004) indicate that, given the development of financial markets in a country, the effects of foreign direct investment become a key factor for economic growth. Meanwhile, Hermes and Lensink (2000) point out that in addition to the development of financial markets, the level of the human capital of a country generates a positive impact on economic growth. Other authors, such as Balasubramanyam et al. (1996), incorporate the degree of economic openness, and Blomström et al. (1994) define the level of income as the generator of more significant benefits in conditions where FDI is transferred to underdeveloped countries with higher levels of income.

In contrast, Boyd and Smith (1992) state that FDI causes adverse effects on economic growth under commercial and financial distortions. Also, there are studies such as that of De Mello (1999), Lipsey (2000), Carkovic and Levine (2005), which show the absence of any significant positive relationship between FDI and economic growth.

Barro and Sala-i-Martin (1990) point out that FDI tends to move towards underdeveloped countries with a higher financial return; therefore, FDI generates conditional convergence of economic growth. Meanwhile, Galindo and Escot (2004) estimate that, based on the similarity of the liquidity and risk levels of the countries, underdeveloped countries grow faster than developed countries from which the FDI comes due to higher rates of return. Blomström et al. (1994) show that FDI, the fixed investment rate, changes in the labor force participation rate, and a price structure generate convergence towards economic growth conditional on education levels.

On the other hand, authors such as Bertola (1993), Alesina and Rodrik (1994), Persson and Tabellini (1994) show that more significant state intervention based on active public policies negatively affects economic growth because it tends to displace private investment, generating the crowding-out effect. While Bénabou (1996a, 1996b) and Bourguignon and Verdier (2000) affirm the opposite, there is a positive impact on economic growth when there are redistributive policies via public investment, and public investment policies exert a positive effect on growth. On the other hand, Galor and Zeira (1993), Perotti (1993), Banerjee and Newman (1993), Piketty (1997), Aghion and Bolton (1992), point out that redistributive policies via public investment tend to impact economic growth, when these public policies tend to reduce imperfections in the credit markets or liquidity restrictions that negatively affect investment in both physical and human capitals.

Furthermore, the literature indicates that the externalities produced by foreign direct investment are reflected in technology transfer and the generation of spillovers. In this sense, Romer (1993) indicates that given the existence of spillovers, the FDI that comes from more developed countries to underdeveloped ones provides the know-how and technology transfer, increasing the productivity of companies and countries. Similarly, Borensztein et al. (1995) indicate that FDI contributes more than a national investment to economic growth; therefore, it is a fundamental element in the transfer of technology under conditions of determining factors in the country receiving the FDI, such as the minimum level of capital human and the conditions of attraction to FDI.

For the case of studies in Latin America, Mamingi and Kareem (2018) analyze the relationship between foreign direct investment (FDI) and economic growth in the countries of the Organisation of Eastern Caribbean States (OECS). These authors show that, although direct foreign investment has a positive effect on economic growth, if foreign direct investment is considered in isolation in each country, it would have a minimal impact on economic growth; that is, there is an indirect effect of foreign direct investment on economic growth. These authors also analyze the policy implications and point out that if the foreign direct investment were to generate healthy infrastructure development in the countries, it would impact on the increase in economic growth. However, if this happened, the foreign direct investment would end up displacing domestic investment.

Álvarez Herranz et al. (2009) also carry out an analysis of the relationship between foreign direct investment and economic growth in Latin America, where they analyze the relationship between the increase in gross domestic product per capita (as an approximation to economic growth) and the accumulation of private capital per capita during the period between 1996 and 2003. These authors find a positive relationship, in which "Foreign Direct Investment drives both the accumulation of Private Capital per capita and the increase in Per Capita Income" (p. 115), but indicate that the protection of private property, the freedom of individuals, and the quality of institutions, are fundamental variables that affect economic growth. Also, they consider that public investment stimulates economic growth; therefore, countries in Latin America are converging towards more significant economic growth, as the literature on this topic mentions.

The Inter-American Development Bank (IDB, 2020), in its study "The benefits of foreign direct investment: Promoting economic development in Latin America and the Caribbean," points out that "Foreign Direct Investment (FDI) is a fundamental pillar of economic development policy as it has a direct and indirect impact on various areas of the local economy and productivity and tax revenues. FDI is one of the main sources of external financing for developing economies."

In this IDB study (2020), it is pointed out that the host economy can generate $187 in production for every one dollar of foreign direct investment arriving in a country, but when comparing total FDI and gross domestic product (Figure 10.1), this is not shown as the IDB (2020) indicates. Additionally, foreign direct investment generates the same amount of domestic investment and doubles exports. For every dollar of foreign investment, there is an additional dollar in domestic investment, and a dollar of foreign direct investment is associated with 2 dollars of additional exports.

These findings by the IDB surely do not consider that in Latin America, foreign direct investment generates a greater outflow of income abroad, as shown in Figure 10.2; nor does it consider that foreign direct investment is directed to a greater extent towards the extraction of natural resources, generating a higher income from natural resources. Worse still, it considers that foreign direct investment does not generate any impact on the Human Development Index (HDI), as shown in this study. The latter may be because the IDB considers economic growth to be the same as economic development, undoubtedly based on the theory of economic progress tied to the theory of modernization, supporting the vision of economic development of neoclassicism or neoliberalism.

Regarding the relationship between FDI and development, Morales (2010, pp. 149–150) indicates:

> When examining the relationship between FDI and development in Latin America in the last twenty-five years, the first thing that stands out is the little or no correlation between FDI growth and the region's economy, let alone development. The lost decade saw a large outflow of capital from the region due to interest payments that were not offset by the growing flow of foreign investment (table or data). Already in the 1990s, the growth rates of FDI and non-traditional exports did not match those of Economic Growth either; poverty indicators increased significantly, and behind them, the unequal inequality of income distribution has deepened and further polarization of the economic and social structure.

This approach, given by Morales, clearly defines the inexistence of any positive relationship between FDI and development, which is also demonstrated in this research.

As Morales (2010, p. 152) points out, "the evaluation of FDI in national development is more complex, since it requires not ignoring the harmful presence of foreign capital in its various forms. That is, as credit and financial investment capital." Furthermore, privatized pension funds under the weight of new national and transnational financial subjects, as well as the change in "fiscal policies to favor the arrival of foreign capital, depress the income of public resources. Likewise, its predatory impact on the environment must be borne in mind" (p. 152).

Finally, international capital flows in our countries do not register a positive balance on our balance, since the outflow via investment income (profits, dividends, interests, and portfolio) is higher than the FDI, since, between 1991 and 2017, the first accumulated 3.3 billion dollars and the second was 20% lower (CEPAL, 2019a, 2019b). "The cyclical behavior of our economies is accentuated in this speculative phase, to the extent that there is greater integration dependent on international capital markets and the US economy. This was shown by the recurring financial crises since 1995, in Mexico, Argentina, or Brazil" (Morales, 2010, p. 153).

10.4 METHODOLOGY AND RESULTS

Long N and T Panel Data Methodology

To measure the relationship between the movement of capital and economic growth, as well as its relationship with human development in Latin America, two econometric models developed under the same technical criteria, are presented. Based on the classical assumptions in econometric modeling, the results of various methods for calculating the estimators are presented following the analysis proposed by Ron P. Smith and Ana-María Fuertes (2016) for static models with large N and T. The commands and recommendations described by Cameron and Trivedi (2009) were used, beginning with the Stata program. Collaterally, the theoretical foundation, with emphasis on the asymptotic properties of the estimators, is based on the following authors: Baltagi (2005), Hoechle (2007), Kennedy (2008), and Pesaran (2015).

The study group is made up of 21 Latin American countries in the period 1996–2017. The countries analyzed are Argentina, Belize, Bolivia, Brazil, Chile, Colombia, Costa Rica, Ecuador, El Salvador, Guatemala, Haiti, Honduras, Jamaica, Mexico, Nicaragua, Panama, Paraguay, Peru, Dominican Republic, Uruguay, and Venezuela. Since work is carried out using variables in first differences, we have a total of 441 observations. Under the criterion of including the largest number of Latin American countries, a simple data imputation technique was applied in countries with minimal missing values. Two models have been proposed that capture the effect of foreign direct investment both for human development (10.1) and for economic growth (10.2):

Human Development Model

$$\Delta LnHDI_{ij} = \alpha + \beta_1 \Delta LnNREper_{ij} + \beta_2 \Delta LnNRR_{ij} + \beta_3 \Delta LnGDPper_{ij} +$$
$$\beta_4 \Delta LnGGCper_{ij} + \beta_5 \Delta LnLEB_{ij} + \beta_6 \Delta LnMYS_{ij} + \mu_{ij} \qquad (10.1)$$

Where:

This preposition *Ln* implies that the variable is expressed as its natural logarithm. Δ is the annual variation of the variables. So, *j* (time) is the difference between two consecutive years.

$i = 1 \ldots, 21$ (countries)

$j = 1996–1997 \ldots, 2016–2017$

LnHDI = Human Development Index. This variable was obtained from the United Nations Development Programme. It summarizes the achievement of countries in three dimensions for human development: a long and healthy life, access to knowledge and a decent standard of living. In this sense, the HDI is the geometric mean of the normalized indices of each dimension.

LnNREper = Net ret foreign per capita based on purchasing power parity (PPP) in constant 2011 international dollar. This is the variable of interest in order to calculate the relationship with the human development. It was obtained from CEPALSTAT, and it is calculated from the balance of payments, as the difference between the credit income (enters the country) and the debit income (leaves the country), was transformed into PPP from GDP. For the study period, all the countries present a negative net income, that is, more money leaves than enters through this type of item, except in some specific years being exceptions.

LnNRR = Total natural resources rents (% GDP). Includes the total natural resources rents of oil, natural gas, coal (hard and soft), mineral, and forest. The World Bank calculated the rents as the difference between the price of a commodity and the average cost of producing it. This variable shows the level of extractivism that exists in an economy.

LnGDPper = Gross Domestic Product per capita based on purchasing power parity (PPP) in constant 2011 international dollar. GDP is the value of all end-use goods and services generated by the economic agents of a territory in a period. Being transformed into international dollars, each dollar has the same purchasing power over GDP as that of the US dollar in that country.

LnGGCper = General government final consumption expenditure in constant 2010 US$. This variable was obtained from the World Bank, it includes all government expenditures on goods and services, including salaries. It includes the majority of national expenditures on defense and security. It does not include government military spending for capital formation.

LnLEB = Life expectancy at birth in years. This variable was obtained from the United Nations Development Programme. It is related to the improvement of living conditions and medical advances.

LnMYS = Mean years of schooling. This variable was obtained from the United Nations Development Programme. It is related to the formal education of the society measured in years.

μ_ij = Model error.

Economic Growth Model

$$\Delta LnGDPper_{ij} = \alpha + \beta_1 \Delta LnFDIper_{ij} + \beta_2 \Delta LnCHGper_{ij} + \beta_3 \Delta LnXIper_{ij} +$$
$$\beta_4 \Delta LnPPE_{ij} + \beta_5 \Delta LnGEE_{ij} + \mu_{ij} \qquad\qquad (10.2)$$

Where:

This preposition *Ln* implies that the variable is expressed as its natural logarithm. Δ is the annual variation of the variables. So, *j* (time) is the difference between two consecutive years.

$i = 1$ ......, 21 (countries)

$j = 1996$–1997 ......, 2016–2017

LnGDPper = Gross Domestic Product per capita based on purchasing power parity (PPP) in constant 2011 international dollar. GDP is the value of all end-use goods and services generated by the economic agents of a territory in a period. Being transformed into international dollars, each dollar has the same purchasing power over GDP as that of the US dollar in that country.

LnFDIper = Foreign direct investment per capita on purchasing power parity (PPP) in constant 2011 international dollar. This variable was obtained from the World Bank, and transformed into PPP from GDP, and it is the sum of equity capital, reinvestment of earnings, and other capital in the reporting economy.

LnCHGper = Real consumption of households and government, at current PPPs per capita 2011 US$. Data series was obtained from Penn World Table 9.1, from which the variation and impact of living standards via consumption on GDP can be quantified.

LnXIper = Merchandise exports and imports per capita based on purchasing power parity (PPP) of the GDP in constant 2011 international dollar. Data were obtained from the World Bank, which shows the variations in international trade adjusted to the population.

LnPPE = Percentage of persons engaged. Data series was obtained from Penn World Table 9.1, from which the impact of the percentage of employed people on GDP can be quantified.

LnGEE = Government Effectiveness Estimate. Data were obtained from the World Bank, they correspond to the perception of the quality of public services and degree of independence from political pressures, as well as the quality of formulation, implementation and government commitment to policies, the indicator was built in a normal distribution and varies between -2.5 and 2.5.

μ_ij = *Model error.*

By way of general characteristics, the panels analyzed are balanced; this implies that for each unit observed (countries), complete data are available throughout the study period (1996–2017). In Static Models, Smith and Fuertes propose the following: "When T is small, the data have to be interpreted as a set of cross-sections and when N is small, as a set of time series. But when both N and T are large there is a choice" (Smith and Fuertes, 2016, p. 8). In that sense, the data can be treated as a cross-section or time series, and the parameters will differ in time or units being an essential choice in determining the purpose of the model.

The regressors of the models can have variation within that occurs for the same unit observed in several periods of time and between when it occurs between the units observed in a time when combining both variations, the overall variation is obtained. In this sense, the variations are specified as follows (10.3), (10.4) and (10.5). Where S^2 represents the variance, N the number of observations, T the number of periods, X the regressors (independent variables), subscript i for the observed units, and subscript t for the observed times,

$$S_w^2 = \frac{1}{NT-1}\sum_i\sum_t\left(x_{it} - \bar{x}_i + \bar{x}\right)^2 \tag{10.3}$$

$$S_B^2 = \frac{1}{N-1}\sum_i\left(\bar{x}_i - \bar{x}\right)^2 \tag{10.4}$$

$$S_O^2 = \frac{1}{NT-1}\sum_i\sum_t\left(x_{it} - \bar{x}\right)^2 \tag{10.5}$$

Given the general specification of a pooled model equation (10.6), it is established that the error of the u model is the sum of a time-invariant component α plus an idiosyncratic error component ε. Depending on the characteristics of the time-invariant component, the fixed effects and random effects models are defined. The fixed-effects model (10.7) assumes that the component that is invariant in time, but that varies between the observed units, exists and is not random. As it is part of the error, it is accepted that it is correlated with the regressors, even though endogeneity is generated in the calculation of the estimators, this problem is corrected as long as the regressors do not correlate with the idiosyncratic term. The random-effects model (10.8), on the other hand, assumes that the time-invariant component is purely random and therefore does not correlate with the regressors.

$$y_{it} = \beta X_{it} + u_{it} \text{ where } u_{it} = \alpha_i + \varepsilon_{it} \tag{10.6}$$

$$(y_{it} - \bar{y}_i + y) = \alpha + \left(X_{it} - \bar{X}_i + X\right)'\beta_k + \left(\varepsilon_{it} - \bar{\varepsilon}_{it} + \varepsilon\right) \tag{10.7}$$

$$(y_{it} - \hat{\theta}_i\bar{y}_i) = \left(1 - \hat{\theta}_i\right)\alpha + \left(X_{it} - \hat{\theta}_i\bar{X}_i\right)'\beta_k + \left\{\left(1 - \hat{\theta}_i\right)\alpha_i + \left(\varepsilon_{it} - \hat{\theta}_i\bar{\varepsilon}_{it}\right)\right\} \tag{10.8}$$

Where

$$\theta_i = 1 - \sqrt{\frac{\sigma_\varepsilon^2}{\left(T_i\sigma_\alpha^2 + \sigma_\varepsilon^2\right)}}$$

To obtain the Best Unbiased Linear Estimators, the model must ensure that its errors are independent and have a normal distribution. When the errors of different units are correlated with each other in the same period, it is a new or spatial correlation (10.9). Whereas, if the errors within each unit are temporally correlated, it is a serial correlation or autocorrelation (10.10), specified in a first degree autoregressive process. Collaterally, it is necessary to correct heteroscedasticity problems, for which the observations of Daniel Hoechle (2007) are followed, among which a regression with Driscoll-Kraay standard errors and regressions based on linear models by using feasible generalized least squares.

Let ε idiosyncratic error, Cor (ε_it, ε_is) = σ_ts   (10.9)

Let μ model error, ⟦μ⟧ _it = ρ_1 μ_ (it-1) + ε_it   (10.10)

In the study of the effects of estimators on panel data, it is stated that: "Between estimator (based on the cross-sectional component of the data) tends to give long-run estimates, while the Within estimator (which based on the time-series component of the data) tends to give short-run estimates" (Baltagi, 2005, p. 200). As Kennedy (2008, p. 287) mentions, if only cross-section observations are available, the regression in OLS produces long-term estimators, while if only one unit is observed in several periods, the regression will estimate short-term effects. Since the fixed-effects regression is based on the time component, the estimators are short-term, while the random-effects regression generates estimators that result in a mixture of short and long term.

Effects of Foreign Direct Investment in Latin America, Empirical Evidence 1996–2017

Next, the results of the human development model are presented in the different specifications: Clustered Model (OLS), Clustered Model without Constant Trend Term (MCON), Random Effects Model (RE), Fixed Effects Model (FE), Model Clustered with Driscoll-Kraay (DK) standard errors, Linear model using feasible generalized least squares corrected for heteroscedasticity (FGLSH), and Linear model using feasible generalized least squares, corrected heteroscedasticity and new correlation (FGLSC). Cluster errors by country were used in the pooled, random effects, and fixed effects regressions to correct inference problems due to heteroscedasticity.

Table 10.1 shows that there is a negative effect of the variations in Net rent foreign per capita and Total natural resource rents (% GDP), that is, both the increase in the variation of money that leaves Latin American countries to other locations due to foreign direct investment, as well as the greater weight given to extractive activities generate negative variations in the HDI. On the other hand, the foreign net income variable, as its variation increased by 1%, generates a negative impact of 0.0003% in the variations of the HDI, while extractivism generates approximately 0.0007%. Therefore, in the face of substantial variations in these variables, development conceived from a broader perspective is restricted. The rest of the regressors

Table 10.1   HDI econometric model results in first differences (1996–2017)

Variable	MCO	MCON	RE	FE	DK	FGLSH	FGLSC
LnNREper	-0.00028**	-0.00023*	-0.00028**	-0.00026*	-0.00028*	-0.00047*	-0.00025***
LnNRR	-0.00070*	-0.00080*	-0.00070*	-0.00066	-0.00070**	-0.00079**	-0.00082***
LnGDPper	0.06915***	0.07210***	0.06915***	0.07030***	0.06915***	0.07121***	0.06787***
LnGGCper	0.00895*	0.01231**	0.00895*	0.00950*	0.00895*	0.001494	0.00835***
LnLEB	0.58060***	0.86978***	0.58060***	0.72171***	0.58060***	0.53492***	0.58042***
LnMYS	0.12144***	0.12971***	0.12144***	0.12121***	0.12144***	0.12216***	0.11926***
_cons	0.00164***		0.00164***	0.00114*	0.00164**	0.00194***	0.00177***
r2	0.49093	0.75612			0.49093		
r2_b			0.72821	0.72591			
r2_w			0.47776	0.47863			

Notes: *, ** and *** significant 15%, 5% and 1% respectively.
Source: Authors' elaboration.

generate a positive impact on the HDI variations, the most decisive being life expectancy and mean years of schooling. Economic growth, as such, measured by the variation in GDP per capita, positively affects the HDI, but not to the same extent as the previous variables, as well as, and to a lesser extent, variations in government consumption.

The model has a better fit in r^2 when the trend constant is eliminated; see MCON. Also, for both fixed and random effects, the variation between (r2_b) is greater than the variation within (r2_w), which indicates that the model explains the changes between Latin American countries more strongly than the changes in a specific country over time. In summary, from the results obtained, for a static model, the OLS with cluster errors is the most indicated. Likewise, also given the new correlation, the significance of cluster errors with Driscoll-Kraay errors does not vary representatively. Also, the results of the tests applied to the different specifications of the HDI model are presented. Initially, the null hypothesis that the model does not present omitted variables verified with the Ramsey test is accepted. Heteroscedasticity problems are evident from the Wald test, so cluster-type errors are used in the grouped models. Upon carrying out the Wooldridge test, the model does not present first-order autocorrelation, so an autoregressive process is not established in the specifications. The model presents contemporary correlation problems given the Pesaran test, problems with Driscoll-Kraay errors, and feasible generalized least squares. With the Breusch and Pagan Test, the OLS estimators prevail before RE or FE. It should be mentioned that the regressors are not related to each other, since the inflation of the variance is less than two in all cases, and also given the transformation of the variables into first differences, all are stationary and do not have a unit root, therefore that there are no spurious regression problems.

The results of the economic growth model (Table 10.2) in its different specifications are presented next: Pooled Model (OLS) with cluster errors, Pooled Model with an order 1 autoregressive process (AR1) with robust errors, Random Effects Model (RE) with cluster errors, Fixed Effects Model (FE) with cluster errors, Pooled Model with Driscoll-Kraay (DK) standard errors and in fixed effects, Linear Model using feasible generalized least squares, corrected

Table 10.2   *GDP econometric model results in first differences (1996–2017)*

Variable	MCO	AR1	RE	FE	DK	FGLSHA	FGLSCHA
LnFDIper	0.00067**	0.00054**	0.00064**	0.00061**	0.00061	0.00057*	0.00054***
LnCHGper	0.47387***	0.47375***	0.46813***	0.46190***	0.46190***	0.49100***	0.48099***
LnXIper	0.05033***	0.04406***	0.04687***	0.04319***	0.04319***	0.05654***	0.04394***
LnPPE	0.00149*	0.00137*	0.00147**	0.00144***	0.00144***	0.00073	0.00129***
LnGEE	0.19443**	0.17639**	0.19328**	0.19197**	0.19197***	0.10388***	0.17258***
_cons	0.00118	0.00162	0.001433	0.00169	0.00169	0,00234*	0.00155***
r2	0.59752						
r2_b			0.72257	0.71655			
r2_w			0.59731	0.59743			

Notes: *, ** and *** significant 15%, 5% and 1% respectively.
Source: Authors' elaboration.

heteroscedasticity, order 1 autocorrelation (FGLSH), and Linear Model using feasible generalized least squares corrected heteroscedasticity, new correlation, and autocorrelation (FGLSC).

It is also evidenced that there is a positive effect on the variations of the regressors selected for the economic growth model, the most representative being household and government consumption. This is followed by governance, whose impact on GDP growth is 0.2% on average for every 1% increase in improved good governance perceptions. On the other hand, variations in foreign direct investment per capita influence the GDP in the following manner: upon an increase of 1% in the variations of this variable, it is expected that on average, GDP will increase by 0.006%. It is also observed that there is a greater impact on economic growth due to the growth of foreign trade rather than from foreign direct investment.

Like the previous model, this one has a more significant adjustment in r^2 for between (r2_b) variations than those within (r2_w), indicating that the model explains more strongly the changes between Latin American countries than the changes of a specific country over time. In summary, from the results obtained in Table 10.2, the most suitable estimators for a static model are those calculated by feasible generalized least squares.

Furthermore, the tests' results applied to the different specifications of the GDP model show that the null hypothesis that the model does not present omitted variables is rejected. Heteroscedasticity problems are evident, so clusters or robust errors are used. The model presents both serial and contemporary correlations, indicating that it is feasible to apply generalized least squares. With the Breusch and Pagan Test prevailing FE or RE estimators before OLS. As in the development model, the regressors are not related to each other since the inflation of the variance is less than two in all cases; thus, all the series are stationary and do not present unit roots; consequently, there are no spurious regression problems.

As the results found indicate, direct foreign investment contributes positively to economic growth as measured by GDP variations. Simultaneously, money flows sent abroad captured from the balance of net income sent abroad in the balance of payments negatively affect human development. This indicates that the results found differ because growth is not the same as development. Given that variations in GDP contribute less to the HDI than variables such as life expectancy and average years of schooling, empirical evidence in Latin America for the last two decades shows that foreign direct investment does not generate positive results in the well-being of the population.

10.5   CONCLUSIONS

Literature on the relationship between foreign direct investment (FDI) and economic growth has marked positive and, in some cases, negative relationships, as well as positive effects on economic development. This literature, for the most part, has been tied to the increase in capital mobility and the expansion of the globalizing process that has allowed, some authors say, the spread of technology.

In explaining the relationship between foreign direct investment and economic growth, different roles have been defined for foreign direct investment, based on the impact on economic growth as a result of assuming markets of perfect competition, decreasing marginal productivity, and constant returns to scale, as neoclassical models indicate. In contrast, endogenous growth models indicate, in general, that foreign direct investment has a positive effect on economic growth indirectly through both capital formation and the development of human resources.

The relationship between foreign direct investment and economic growth, as well as its relationship with human development in Latin America, considering variables such as the Human Development Index and per capita GDP based on purchasing power parity (PPP), were measured in this investigation. Two econometric panel data models, elaborated under technical criteria, have been suggested and were used for this purpose and a study group of 21 Latin American countries participated in this study that compiles the effect of direct foreign investment on both human development and economic growth from 1996–2017.

This study aimed to show not only that growth is not the same as development but also to estimate how FDI affects economic growth and development in Latin America differently. The idea of defining two different models that allow differentiating the effects that FDI has on economic growth and development was to establish parameters different from those of conventional economics and to move towards a heterodox measurement of the existing relationships given in traditional or conventional literature.

In Latin America, the FDI has an average participation rate of 3% over the GDP, while foreign FDI income has a 4% share of the GDP; this means that more currency leaves than enters the region. Furthermore, this foreign direct investment is speculative and directed towards the extractive sectors of our countries. Also considered should be that the return of neoliberal governments in Latin America since 2012 has generated deregulatory conditions that have benefited foreign and national capital and the fact that the acceptance of international arbitration has undermined national sovereignties, affecting growth and development in the region.

The GDP pc PPP grows in a volatile manner and in some periods contracts negatively, which affects purchasing power because it goes in accord with the economic cycle of the economy, and the volatility of commodity prices, unlike human development, grows steadily during the period of analysis, and very much depends on public investment policies.

Under the premise that growth is not the same as development, foreign direct investment contributes positively to economic growth measured by variations in GDP, while money flows sent abroad, and calculated from the balance of net income sent abroad, negatively affect human development. Given that economic growth affects to a lesser extent than life expectancy or average years of schooling, variables that can be improved through government action, it is concluded that the negative effect on development is greater than the positive effect on growth. Therefore, the empirical evidence in Latin America for the last two decades shows that foreign direct investment does not generate positive results in the well-being of the population.

BIBLIOGRAPHY

Aghion, P. and P. Bolton (1992). Distribution and growth in models of imperfect capital markets. *European Economic Review*, 36, 603–611.

Alesina, A. and D. Rodrik (1994). Distributive politics and economic growth. *Quarterly Journal of Economics*, 436, 465–490.

Alfaro, L., A. Chanda, S. Kalemli-Ozcan and S. Sayek (2004). FDI and economic growth: the role of local financial markets. *Journal of International Economics*, *64*(1), 89–112.

Álvarez Herranz, Agustín, J. Santiago E. Barraza and Ana M. Legato (2009). Inversión Extranjera Directa y Crecimiento Económico en Latinoamérica. *Información Tecnológica*, *20*(6), 115–124. doi: 10.1612/inf.tecnol.4116it.08.

Balasubramanyam, V., M. Salisu and D. Sapsford (1996). Foreign direct investment and growth in EP and IS countries. *The Economic Journal*, *106*(434), 92–105.

Baltagi, B. (2005). *Econometric Analysis of Panel Data* (third ed.). West Sussex: John Wiley & Sons.

Banco Mundial (2019). *Datos del Banco Mundial*. Retrieved from https://databank.bancomundial.org/home.aspx.

Banerjee, A. and A. Newman (1993). Occupational choice and the process of development. *Journal of Political Economy*, 101, 274–298.

Barro, R. and X. Sala-i-Martin (1990). Economic growth and convergence across the United States. *NBER*, Working Paper No. W3419.

Bénabou, R. (1996a). Unequal societies. *NBER*, Working Paper No. 5583.

Bénabou, R. (1996b). Inequality and growth, *MIT Press*, 11–74.

Bertola, G. (1993). Market structure and income distribution in endogenous growth models. *American Economic Review*, 83, 1184–1199.

Blomström, M., R. Lipsey and M. Zejan (1994). What explains developing country growth? In Baumol, W., R. Nelson, and E. Wolff (eds.), *Convergence and Productivity: Gross-National Studies and Historical Evidence* (243–259). Oxford: Oxford University Press.

Borensztein E., J. de Gregorio and J.-W. Lee (1995). How does foreign direct investment affect economic growth? *NBER*, Working Paper No. W5057.

Bourguignon, F. and T. Verdier (2000). Oligarchy, democracy, inequality, and growth. *Journal of Development Economics*, 62, 285–313

Boyd, J. and B. Smith (1992). Intermediation and the equilibrium allocation of investment capital: implications for economic development. *Journal of Monetary Economics*, 30, 409–432.

Cameron, C., and P. Trivedi (2009). *Microeconometrics Using Stata*. College Station, TX: Stata Press Publications.

Carkovic, M. V. and R. Levine (2005). *Does Foreign Direct Investment Accelerate Economic Growth?* In Moren, T. H., E. M. Grahma and M. Blomström (eds.), *Does Foreign Direct Investment Promote Development?* (195–220). Washington, D.C.: Institute for International Economics.

CEPAL (2019a). *La Inversión Extranjera Directa en América Latina y el Caribe*. www.cepal.org/es/publicatios.

CEPAL (2019b). *Bases de datos y publicaciones estadísticas*. https://estadisticas.cepal.org/cepalstat/WEB_CEPALSTAT/estadisticasIndicadores.asp?idioma=e.

De Mello, L.R. (1999). Foreign direct investment-led growth: evidence from time series and panel data. *Oxford Economic Papers*, 51.

Galindo, M. A. and L. Escot (2004). International capital flows, convergence and growth. *The Journal of Economic Asymmetries*, *1*(1), 49–69.

Galor, O. and J. Zeira (1993). Income distribution and macroeconomics. *Review of Economic Studies*, *60*(1), 35–52.

Hermes, N. and R. Lensink (2000). Foreign direct investment, financial development and economic growth. *SOM Theme E*, Workings Papers 27.

Hoechle, D. (2007). Robust standard errors for panel regressions with cross-sectional dependence. *Stata Journal*, *7*(3), 281–312.

IDB (2020). *Los beneficios de la inversión extranjera directa: Promoviendo el desarrollo económico en América Latina y el Caribe*. Edición fue escrita por Juan Pablo Etchegaray y Ana Arias Urones en colaboración con Jaime Granados, Christian Volpe y Fabrizio Opertti.

Kennedy, P. (2008). *A Guide to Econometrics* (sixth ed.). Malden, MA: Blackwell.

Lipsey, R. E. (2000). The role of foreign direct investment in international capital flows, *NBER*, Working Paper No. 7094.

Mamingi, N. and M. Kareem (2018). La inversión extranjera directa y el crecimiento en los países en desarrollo: el caso de los países de la Organización de Estados del Caribe Oriental. *Revista de la CEPAL*, 124, April.

Morales, J. (2010). Inversión extranjera directa y desarrollo en América Latina. *Revista Problemas del Desarrollo*, *163*(41), October–December.

Ozturk, I. (2007). Foreign direct investment – growth nexus: a review of the recent literature. *International Journal of Applied Econometrics and Quantitative Studies*, *4*(2), 79–98.

Perotti, R. (1993). Political equilibrium, income distribution and growth. *Review of Economic Studies*, 60, 755–776.

Persson, T. and G. Tabellini (1994). Is inequality harmful for growth? *American Economic Review*, 84, 600–621.

Pesaran, M. (2015). *Time Series and Panel Data Econometrics*. Oxford: Oxford University Press.

Piketty, T. (1997). The dynamics of wealth distribution and the interest rate with credit rationing. *Review of Economic Studies*, *64*(2), 173–189.

Programa de Naciones Unidas para el Desarrollo (2019). *Estadísticas*. https://estadisticas.pr/index.php/en.

Romer, P. (1993). Idea gaps and object gaps in economic development. *Journal of Monetary Economics*, *32*(3), 543–573.

Smith, R. and A. Fuertes (2016). *Panel Time-Series*. London: Birkbeck University of London.

PART III

Capital movement and economic patterns

11. Latin American international integration and global value chains: what changed after the 2008 global financial crisis

Juan Pablo Painceira[1] and Alexis Saludjian

The Covid-19 pandemic has led to a crisis of global dimensions. An unprecedented health shock caused an enormous disruption in the production and circulation of goods and services, having serious consequences still to be seen for the global development. The objective of this chapter is to discuss the development strategies based on the international integration for the Latin American economies after the 2008 Global Financial Crisis (GFC).

In the last two decades, the mainstream development strategies have been based on the importance of the economies' integration into the Global Value Chains (GVCs). These chains have emerged and flourished in the context of free trade and expansion of the international trade. This chapter shows that those development strategies, which had already shown their limits in the environment of economic liberalization, can be even more problematic for Latin American (LA) economies in the context of major changes in the development strategies of advanced countries and of financialized capitalism. Major advanced countries changed their development strategies towards protectionist policies since the GFC, while LA economies, outstandingly Brazil, have followed uncritically the same international integration regarding to GVCs, consequently keeping the mainstream view on international trade.

This chapter has three sections. Section 11.1 discusses the integration of major developed and LA economies into the global economy. We argue that since the GFC, the development strategies of the key developed economies have changed to higher protectionism and less favourable free trade policies. These changes put at odds their theoretical and ideological perspectives on development in which they have supported and imposed for international integration strategies in most of developing economies.

Section 11.2 analyses the economic and financial development put at the service of the most comprehensive strategy for international integration in the context of the global capital dynamic after GFC. Since the late 1990s, theoretical and policy debates on development have supported the integration into GVC. We show that policies towards higher competitiveness are at the centre of the international integration. This question to boost economies' competitiveness has manifested through a number of industrial, monetary and labour market policies. These policies are implemented in a specific context, but they carry the same imperative of seeking certain comparative advantages in the globalized competition. We analyse the case of the Brazilian economy through various policies (production, trade and finance) seeking to improve competitiveness. This development strategy is implemented in the context of predominance of finance in global contemporary capitalism, denominated as financialization.

Similarly, to international economic integration, financialization has a subordinated character in emerging economies due to the subordinated position of these countries in the international monetary system. In the LA economies, specifically Brazil, it is shown through the foreign direct investment (FDI) dynamic how these characteristics of the contemporary capitalism have shaped their strategies of development. Finally, section 11.3 contains the conclusions of this chapter.

11.1   POST-GFC DEVELOPMENT STRATEGIES: IS FREE TRADE AN ENGINE FOR ECONOMIC GROWTH AND DEVELOPMENT?

In this section, we present how the GFC has profoundly changed the development strategies of the major countries in global capitalism. This characteristic has been of great importance to LA economies and has shaped their international integration into a globalized and financialized capitalism.

Before and after the GFC

The GFC was profound and comparably the worst crisis in 21st century in relation to the 1929 crisis. Reasons for a comparison include similarities in the scale of the crisis; that both crises occurred after a period of financial liberalization; and they had their original causes in the financial sphere. They also spread rapidly throughout the world and had economic, political and social consequences. Nonetheless, there are crucial differences between the 2008 and 1929 global crises in the global capitalist dynamics, expressing different phases of international development.

These differences have an important role to define the development strategy based on the international integration and to differentiating developed countries from developing countries. For example, trade globalization is different nowadays from that of the early 20th century. In the contemporary capitalism, it is about the fragmentation of the production or value chain (Salama, 2016). In our opinion, the period of expansion of the GVCs has four fundamental elements: first, international trade and multilateral institutions (GATT/WTO) as development engines; second, multinational companies that have become the main actors of capitalist dynamics; third, the role of finance (since the late 1970s and in the GFC); and lastly, the role of China in the reorganization of the industrial sector in a global scale. The first two elements have been at the centre of discussion since the beginning of the capitalist development. In the contemporary capitalism, the new fact is the process of deglobalization since the GFC. The volume of goods exports has suffered the highest contraction (-12%) in 2009. In the period 1952–2016, the lowest annual growth rate in the volume of exports ever (2.9% on average) happened between 2012 and 2016. Since 2016, despite the modest rebound in 2017, the downward trend in the international trade in 2018 and 2019 has supported the claims on deglobalization (ECLAC, 2019 p. 23, OECD, 2020, p. 21; Salama, 2016). In addition to the lack of dynamism in trade, the 2020 WTO's report clearly indicates the increase in commercial notifications, such as the use of dispute resolution measures, particularly in agriculture with a record level, since 2005, of over 400 notifications in 2018 and 2019. In the anti-dumping measures, the largest share was from the US initiative: 21 new anti-dumping notifications in the first semester of 2019 and the technical Barriers to Trade (record level since 2015 and the higher increase since 2008).

In this scenario of lack of dynamism in the world economy, it is important to analyse how different countries have reformulated their development strategies. The economic growth trend in LA was also negatively affected by the GFC, being close to zero in 2019 (ECLAC, 2019, p. 58). The OECD countries were already facing a complex situation with very low growth rates compared to previous periods.[2]

Since the 2000s, the development of the global capitalism cannot be discussed without China's fundamental role. Between 2000 and 2015, China's share of global exports increased from 4% to 14% and developing Asian countries accounted from 20% to 26% (see ECLAC, 2016, pp. 61, 94). Meanwhile Africa and Latin America did not change their share, 2% and 6% respectively. On the other hand, developed countries lost percentage share in global exports: the USA from 16% to 12% and the European Union (EU) from 38% to 33%.

It is in this context of deceleration of the international trade that GVCs have expanded. The Transnational/Multinational Companies (TCs/MNCs) and technological developments had consequences for the dynamics of capitalism, particularly in the industrial sector.

In the third element (finance) it is important to address the relevance (and complexity) of the GVCs in the context of the globalized and financialized economy, further discussed in the next section. The fourth element is China. Since 1990 and its entry into WTO in late 2001, the Chinese economy has changed the capitalist dynamics. It was precisely the period of expansion of the GVCs. The incorporation of hundreds of millions of rural workers into China's major industrial centres had a significant impact on both industrialization, global trade and poverty reduction (Nogueira and Hao, 2019).

The global capitalism accumulation requires comparative perspective since some economies are undergoing a deindustrialization process (declining importance of industrial sector) and other countries are industrializing. There has been a profound change in the configuration of the global economy (Salama, 2016). Thus, the understanding of a specific region's development strategies must take in consideration the strategies of other groups of countries. This relationship is far from symmetrical. In the context of dependence, the developing countries' strategies are shaped by the developed countries' strategies.

Before and After the GFC for Developed Countries

After World War II, named as the Bretton Woods era, a rise in imperialism took place, being international trade at the centre of the development strategy, reaching a consensus to lower tariffs (General Agreement on Tariffs and Trade – GATT) that culminated five decades later with the creation of the World Trade Organization (WTO) in 1995. In the theoretical field, discussions around the GVCs gained strength as the central tool to justify the advantages of free trade and for the international economic insertion. The central players (MNCs) have actively engaged in this transformation and in the path of deindustrialization in developed economies. This movement is related to the debate of relocation and outsourcing by the multilateral institutions and by the GVCs.

The US economy, due to GFC, suffered a strong economic and social impact. The Federal Reserve responded by implanting a huge strategy of monetary easing (around 15% of the US GDP) which had positive effects on economic growth. However, despite the economic growth, the post-GFC period can be characterized by the increase in wealth and income inequality and by stagnant wages.

The election of the US's President Trump in 2016 had significant impacts on the world economy. The key themes during the campaign "*Make America Great Again*" have been quickly implemented, such as trade protectionism (against China), migration protectionism (anti-Islamic measures and the border wall between the US and Mexico) and the tax reduction for US companies. In addition, the Trans-Pacific Partnership (TPP), discussed since 2005, was eliminated in 2017 from the US agenda.

The EU has also undergone major changes in this scenario of deglobalization. In the light of not being able to generate sustainable and equitable economic growth for decades; unemployment rates reached record levels after the GFC, and the strong heterogeneity of the region, rising tensions took place in policy orientations among the countries' members. In addition, some severe economic, political and social crises took place in some member countries (Greece, Spain, Portugal and Italy) and recently, due to the outcome of the UK referendum (Brexit) which imposed further problems to the EU's development strategy. The Brexit vote was supported mainly by the precarious employment situation, xenophobic debates against immigration and claims on the strategy of free trade agreements. Economic liberalism has always been at the heart of the EU's integration in the world economy, but the pro-trade liberalization policy has important counterpoints, such as the Common Agricultural Policy (supported by France). There has also been a shift in the defence of liberalism by placing restrictions and denouncing irregularities primarily by China.[3] The effects of the crisis as well as the power of China in the global market imposed a big challenge for the EU liberalization policy.

In relation to LA economies, the Mercosur trade agreement was signed in 2019. This agreement started to be discussed in 1995 (as well as the TPP) and was part of the pro-liberalization era; and when finally signed the EU was facing a different context and new dynamic in the world economy, increasing the position of protectionist policies. Finally, since the GFC, the EU has motivated the strengthening of restrictive measures within the framework of the Common External Policy (CEP) as well as in the national level. In Germany, Chinese investment projects have been opposed.

The political tensions linked to austerity policies and the end of the commodities boom in 2014 also had significant impacts on the world economy so as in the international trade. Since 2015, the growing number of people discontent with the economic situation has elected political leaders that challenged the multilateralism principles. The Brexit process and Trump's triumph are major examples.

Thereby, the main developed countries suspended their pro-liberalization approach, reversing their international integration strategies, in relation to the Bretton Woods era. The next section discusses how developing countries have implemented their integration strategies after the GFC.

Developing Countries before and after the GFC in Terms of Development Strategy

In the last decades, the world trade gravity centre changed for Asian countries, mainly with China's demands of raw material (major cause of the commodity boom), its manufactured goods and the investment flows. In the same period, LA recovered from the emerging market crises of the late 1990s and early 2000s, and several countries in the region benefited from the commodities boom between 2003 and 2014.

It is important to highlight that neither China in the "New Normal" era (low global growth) nor LA economies changed their international integration strategies after the GFC, despite the substantial impacts of the crisis in economic and social terms.

The Chinese Communist Party (CCP), in its 12th five-year plan (2011–2015), reoriented its policies to design strategies radically favourable to trade liberalization. In LA, several countries implemented some reorientation in their economic policies, but the pro-free trade framework persisted across the region.

This section merely points out the key aspects on the development strategy after China's entry into the WTO in 2001. For decades China planned to project itself into the 21st century as the centre of the world economy.

China was affected by the GFC like all economies, but unlike advanced countries, its strategy did not change. It remained pro-trade liberalization proposing the Silk Road Economic Belt initiative (2013), which goes beyond the trade framework and it has been enshrined in China's constitution since 2017. In Davos, in 2017, the Chinese president's speech clearly indicated the Chinese strategy:

> This is a path of pursuing common development through opening-up. China is committed to a fundamental policy of opening-up and pursues a win–win opening-up strategy. (…) China stands for concluding open, transparent and win–win regional free trade arrangements and opposes forming exclusive groups that are fragmented in nature. (https://www.weforum.org/agenda/2017/01/full-text -of-xi-jinping-keynote-at-the-world-economic-forum)

In the same conference, the US president addressed one of first speeches on the US strategy of development and international insertion, which was contrary to the "*globalism*" of the WTO and based on protectionist measures. Since then, trade tensions have escalated further, leading to an open trade war, exacerbating US protectionist strategy but without changing the Chinese one.

LA Countries Development and Integration Strategies Before and After the GFC

This section offers a synthesis on the development strategies of the LA economies based on the periodization proposed by Salama (2016), grouped in four periods, between 1930 and 2010,[4] and we add a fifth period, starting after the GFC.

The first period (1930s to 1970s) was marked by a modest and incomplete process of industrialization via Import Substitution (ISI), characterized by high growth economic rates, along with external vulnerability, and significant inequalities. National states conducted the process of regional integration to achieve productive cooperation by promoting industrialization and development.

The second period (1980s) was characterized by the external debt crisis. The supporters of liberalism attributed these consequences to the wanderings of the *developmentist* state strategy of the Bretton Woods era. For them, the crisis was due to international integration strategy based on the ECLAC's structuralist vision. International financial institutions, along with powerful levers in the academy and politics did everything to ensure the revival of the economies in the region, either through terms of favourable conditions to repay external debt or through a business-friendly atmosphere. This new atmosphere was led by the orthodox mac-roeconomic framework, in particular austerity policies and the reduction of the state's role in the economy. The macroeconomic orthodoxy legacy has taken various forms in LA countries that have shaped their development strategies. LA integration followed the liberalization trend with the creation of ALADI in 1980 and by the Economic Integration Program (PICE) which foreshadowed the Constitution of Mercosur between Argentina and Brazil.

The third period (1990s) was characterized by the end of hyperinflationary processes, market liberalization, and the establishment of the Washington Consensus building blocks of the end of the Cold War. This period coincided with the emergence of the discussions on GVCs.

The fourth period (early 2000s and 2010) experienced higher growth rates up to 2008, a new type of external vulnerability, a slight drop in inequality and in poverty. In terms of integration and development strategies, GVC consolidated; and the "commodities boom" was an important characteristic of this decade; but the major event of the period was the GFC. Other important events were the constitutions of the BRICS (2006) and the creation of CELAC (Caribbean and Latin America Community) in 2010. In this period there were important politi-cal discussions, and economic objectives continued to be guided by liberal strategies, focusing on open regionalism and commercial liberalism.[5]

The rise of finance is a major characteristic of the global capitalism during these periods, initiated in the late 1970s and reinforced during the 2000s (before the GFC). This period can be broadly defined as financialization, with important impacts on the development strategies mentioned above. We adopt Lapavitsas' (2014) general perspective on financialization, which argues that the major economic agents (banks, non-financial companies and households) have fundamentally changed their behaviour due to structural changes in the global capitalism. In the next section, the discussion on finance and its influence on the development strategies is further developed.

The fifth period (which we add) starts after the GFC and ends in 2019. LA economies have been badly hit by the end of the commodities cycle (2014), with raw materials falling, and global demand decelerating, especially in China; which has led to a lasting economic slow-down with significant economic, political, and social consequences. The LA industrial sector share of the regional economies declined, reinforcing neo-extractivism, early and/or incom-plete industrialization, in the context of structural and social heterogeneity and dependence (Salama, 2016).

Some countries led state anti-cyclical policies (including consumer and investment support programs in Argentina and Brazil) were notable; without major impact on integration strat-egies and were far from reversing the early deindustrialization trend (Salama, 2016, Chapter 3). Since 2015, neoliberal reforms in the labour market and in the pensions system were implemented on the assumptions that were fundamental to achieve a better international inte-gration. However, these strategies of insertion and development unfolded in a world economy without dynamism and rising trade tensions. International trade growth, in 2019, was negative (0.1%, WTO, 2020). In this year, the deterioration was substantial, since the growth forecast in April, was positive (2.6%) and fell to 1.2% in October. Moreover, the WTO forecasts report for 2020 indicated that the world economy dynamics would be slower than anticipated by the end of 2019 (2.7% of world trade growth instead of 3% previously forecast). Even before the

Covid-19 pandemic, economies were already close to recession. In 2020, the global trade is expected to have a huge fall between 13% and 32% due to the pandemic (WTO, 2020).

Moreover, the economic structure of Brazil and Argentina (and to a large extent LA) cannot be considered competitive due to their late and dependent insertion into the world economy, reinforcing the unequal and combined character of their development in contemporary capitalism, which has China/Asia at the centre of the global industrial scenario. Since 2015, in the context of orthodox macroeconomic policies, the reversion of the so-called progressive governments cycle had profound consequences on LA strategies for international and regional integration, with falling trade among LA countries, since the GFC (see ECLAC, 2016, p. 120). For example, UNASUR was deactivated, and the Pacific Alliance, discussed since 2012, came into force in 2015. The Chilean President proposed PROSUL (March 2019) as a counterpoint to UNASUR, joined by seven countries, including Brazil, Argentina and Colombia.

From the above it can be seen an opposition between developed and developing countries strategies in terms of international integration. The 2020 UNCTAD report illustrates this trend, stating that there is an increase in restrictive/regulatory investment policies at a global level since 2015, even though liberalization measures account for three quarters of the total. When distinguishing these restrictive or liberalizing policies by type of country of origin, in developed countries of the total investment measures promoted, 10 are restrictive, one neutral and four liberalizing. On the other hand, LA (and Caribbean) countries are promoting 10 liberalizing measures, two neutral and two restrictive measures out of the total of 14 in 2019. This is the opposite of the Bretton Woods context, in which advanced countries supported liberalization and trade opening, while some developing countries, such as LA countries, including Brazil, promoted an international integration strategy via the IIS. In the next section we analyse how these development strategies from developing countries can be related to the contemporary form of global industrial dynamic implemented by MNCs through GVCs in which those countries can be considered in a dependent or subordinated position.

11.2   THE CONTEMPORARY GLOBAL CAPITALIST DEVELOPMENT CONFIGURATION: GVC TURNING INTO GLOBAL INEQUALITY CHAIN

This section analyses critically the development strategies in LA economies regarding productivity and competitiveness, and the expansion of the GVCs after the GFC.

The mainstream economic theory that supports the discussion of GVCs presents a segmented and fragmented view of the major issues in this area (Selwyn, 2019). The international economy, the production function, and the labour economics, disconnected from economic dynamics. In the perspective of Political Economy, it is worth analysing the relations between economic development strategies and international integration, and how these factors may interact in the contemporary capitalism through GVCs. Since the mid-1990s, the GVCs have become a central part in economic development. The key argument on the merits of a higher integration into the world economy through GVCs is that this type of integration benefits workers from all over the world, mainly from developing countries by guaranteeing them better wages. This will allow them to catch up in these chains if their governments undertake the correct (or prescribed) policies, creating a "win–win" situation for workers (better wages) and for capitalists/entrepreneurs, creating a beneficial distribution.

Selwyn (2019) developed a critical analysis of GVCs, highlighting that the integration of developing countries energizes global capitalism. New forms of poverty are linked to the integration into GVCs, characterized by super-exploitation of the labour force in developing countries, even though the level of productivity had periodically been higher than in developed countries. Case studies are presented and allow us to reconsider some of the premises of GVCs and their results in promoting greater integration into the global economy. The author defines the relation between GVCs and developing countries as Global Poverty Chains (GPC), developing an alternative theory of value and new strategies of socio-economic development, which is more inclusive and egalitarian. The orthodox theory argument on GVC justifies workers' lower wages in developing countries because of their low productivity, following the marginal utility theory that determines the level of wage according to marginal productivity.

Selwyn shows that the GVCs are based on the neoclassical theory of value by focusing on value-added to account for the global economy (Selwyn, 2019). This author resorts to Marx's theory of labour value to overcome the concept of added-value and to grasp the dynamics of globalized capitalism; since it provides an alternative approach to analyse the relation among firms and the dimensions of worker exploitation across global capitalism. The return to Marx's value theory is mainly related to the characteristics of the intensification of the exploitation. In the case of the developing countries, Marini in the early 1970s, was the pioneer of the concept of super-exploitation of the labour force, in the context of the Marxist dependency theory. He argued that:

> the sub-continent's productive structure is based in greater exploitation of the workers' [than in the economic core] and technical progress made possible capitalist intensification of the rhythm of the worker's labour, increasing his productivity and, simultaneously, sustaining the tendency to remunerate him at a lower rate than his real value. (Marini, 1973, pp. 71–72)

Selwyn points to the importance of TNCs in the dynamics of the GVC, which are the big winners for Medeiros and Trebat (2018). On the one hand, he distinguishes the leading firms that engage in research and development, marketing, management, and design of goods, benefiting developed countries workers with better working conditions and wages. However, small companies or subcontractors/suppliers, fully involved in production, even with low wages, have worse working conditions and are forced to accumulate overtime to survive. The case of the Apple brand iPhone is presented to reflect this dynamic between different firms and workers within the current globalized and financialized economy. Important case studies (e.g., clothing industries in Cambodia and electronics in China) show that the wage/productivity relationship mobilized towards GVC to justify low wages has not been found. In the traditional view, low wages are due to low productivity, but these recent studies show instead that in developing countries, productivity in specific sectors (not on average) have been higher than in developed countries. In the case of the Brazilian automobile industry, there is a higher average productivity than for workers in the US or Germany (Selwyn, 2019, p. 83). The explanation lies rather in the differential of workers' wages and in the relative strength of the unions to negotiate advantageous wage agreements in developed countries. In relation to the place and strength of trade unions, labour market reforms are essential elements and have had an important influence on the level of wages and productivity.

In LA economies, the wage level in the commodities boom increased;[6] with competitiveness becoming a central issue in the debate, especially since the 2000s, which is marked by

China's entry into the WTO that was initiated with a radical transformation of GVCs through 700 million new workers. Wage increases can only impact the country's competitiveness if MNCs do not find lower wages in other countries, taking place in a "race to the bottom". The economy "offering" the best conditions for extracting value and capital gains would win it all.

Workers in developing countries, included in GVCs, receive wages that barely exceed the minimum level of the World Bank's poverty line, which does not mean that their working conditions are dignified, and they are often forced to have multiple jobs or work overtime. Selwyn (2019) points out that the authors, supporting the GVCs, have used precisely this argument to justify that a full insertion into GVCs would increase their salaries through "upgrading" and the acceptance of policies aimed at increasing the competitiveness of the company or sector in question. By indicating the way forward along the Smile Curve, the GVCs seem to solve the problem of low wages in developing countries. In this process, in order to reach the point of the curve where high wages are located, it is necessary to improve competitiveness and innovation, by placing entry barriers to these sectors or segments and benefit from rent due to this technological monopoly. In relation to this neoclassical Smile curve, Selwyn (2019) opposes a Marxist curve in the form of a grimace. In this curve, the highest level of value and surplus value production from the exploitation of the labour force takes place in developing countries where, for example, the production of iPhones and the vast majority of consumer goods in the world are produced, and strong competition over labour costs exists. The productivity in developing countries can be higher than in the developed countries, putting in doubt the "upgrading" solution of GVC theory. In this same curve, other sectors of value production in developed countries (marketing, design, research and development) employ relatively less workers but capture the value from countries with lower labour costs.

For Selwyn (2019), the discussion of Global Poverty Chains (GPCs) criticizes this argument with a theoretical discussion about key Marxist concepts (value, distribution and coordination of the chain) and, on the other hand, at empirical level analyses specific cases that contradict the GVCs' central argument.

These elements allow to address GPCs rather than GVCs, since the former promotes the continuity of capitalist dynamics by arguing that developing countries can improve by upgrading their competitiveness. This policy of international integration comes at the cost of greater exploitation of the labour force.

The potential of this discussion for LA economies on super-exploitation, neo-extractivism, or modern slave labour issues is just highlighted, but not analysed in this chapter.

GVCs: the Case of Brazil since the GFC

In this subsection some Brazilian economic and industrial policies to gain competitiveness are discussed. In addition, we analyse synthetically the major premises of these policies. The reduction of the cost of labour has occupied the main place along with the reduction of state participation. These institutional elements echo Selwyn's discussion on the importance of these factors in competitiveness and GVC.

Economic policy plans involve the interconnection of key issues such as international insertion, fiscal sustainability, labour and financial markets, infrastructure, and development financing, in short, socio-economic development policies. These issues have often presented as a question of "competitiveness" for the economies to integrate in a "positive" way. This question has become the central issue. As Selwyn notes, theories around the GVC evoke the possibility of upgrading. Firms with the lowest productivity can modernize and catch up with the most modern firms and increase their productivity. In LA, the most modern firms are often connected to foreign companies. The main plans for development and international insertion after the GFC have been policies geared towards expanding physical infrastructure to improve competitiveness. These infrastructure projects are expected to affect productivity and attractiveness of the country to foreign and large domestic investors. The role of the Brazilian Development Bank (BNDES) has also been important in setting up and supporting some public–private partnerships (PPPs). In 2007, a Growth Acceleration Program (GAP)[7] was launched. It is also before the first extraction of the huge oil field (pre-salt oil, discovered in 2006) in 2008. This PPPs broad program in the area of infrastructure and logistics has also included social and urban infrastructure to reduce housing inequality.[8] It projected investment of R$657 billion (25% of the GDP in 2007) in eight years. This program assumed a 5% economic growth, per year, between 2007 and 2012; which was not reached due to the deleterious effects of the GFC. Measures to contain the growth of government expenditures were imposed, such as a ceiling for the public sector payroll growth and a minimum wage policy, which affected the pension system, with definition of adjustment rules every four years. Concerns about the cost of social security were already present as well as on the Treasury's revenues stemming from tax exemptions for economic sectors.

In 2010, GAP 2[9] was developed, with investments spending around R$955 billion (around 25% of the GDP) until 2014. In this context, there was government concern to support the economy with anti-cyclical measures, without affecting the fiscal accounts. Regarding industrial development, there were several industrial and exports policies, focusing on innovation and competitiveness, to be implemented between 2011 and 2014, that followed other initiatives such as PITCE (Industrial, Technological and Foreign Trade Policy) that took place between 2003 and 2007 and the Productive Development Policy[10] (2008–2010), which intended to gain competitiveness in strategic sectors.

In addition, the Bigger Brazil Program – PBM – was developed[11] that aimed to expand markets through export diversification and Brazilian companies' internationalization (GVC *upgrading*); training and professional qualifications and competitiveness of small businesses. The PBM also included tax exemptions aimed to finance investments, focused mainly in the agro-industry (more than 25%), which is one of the most competitive sectors at the international level and promoted and supported large companies' groups that were already the major Trans-Latam (Petrobras, JBS, Sadia, Odebrecht and Gerdau).

In 2014, the crisis deepened, and the new PT government (initiated in 2015) was marked by austerity measures, reducing public spending and wages growth in order to boost the companies' profitability and their competitiveness, as well as trying to stabilize the trend of public sector indebtedness.[12] After President Dilma's impeachment (or rather a Parliamentary coup) in 2016, the arrival of the vice-president accelerated liberalization and the austerity agenda, imposing the PMDB Program, called "Bridge to the Future";[13] which was in line with the interests of the large national capitalist groups. These groups opposed the minimum wage gains during the period 2005–2014 and favoured the approval of the Labour Market Reform in 2017 that led a strong market flexibilization, reducing workers' rights and, in general, increasing job insecurity. This reform changed profoundly labour stabled by the Labour Acts (CLT) of the Vargas era (1940s). On the other hand, it was in line with the creation of the

Individual Micro-Entrepreneur (2008), a formalized service provider without the same rights as CLT contracts.

However, the measures to improve competitiveness, whether in infrastructure, innovation and especially in the reduction of labour rights, did not permit Brazil or most LA economies to better integrate into the GVCs or achieve the "upgrading" predicted. This can be explained by the disconnection between development policy and the orthodox macroeconomic policies implemented in the last decades.[14] As indicated by Medeiros and Trebat (2018), developed countries have had a clear advantage in the expansion of GVCs, and in developing countries, only China and some Asia countries have benefited. According to these authors, LA remains poorly integrated in the GVC and these strategies have not produced the desired effect. In these authors' words:

> In general, the LA countries have integrated into global value chains through the adoption of 'easy' strategies based on weak regulatory systems and low wages. (Medeiros and Trebat, 2018, p. 197)

In line with the discussion of the weak integration of LA countries (exception may be Mexico due to its agreements with the US and Canada), recent studies show that net transfers from developing to developed countries have increased during the period 1995–2007, reinforcing the discussion of dependence and unequal exchange specifically in LA and Brazil.[15] After the discussion on GVCs with the changes in global capitalism led by China and analyses of the changes in the development strategies of developed countries after the GFC, it is necessary to integrate the major aspects of financialization to understand its impact on development strategies, particularly for developing countries.

GVCs in the Financialization Era

This subsection discusses how development strategies have been engaged in issues of finance or financialization, considering the peculiarities of developing countries, particularly LA and Brazil.

After the discussion of the major characteristics of financialization in the contemporary capitalism, especially in developed countries, based on Lapavitsas (2014), it is necessary to address the developing countries or the periphery of the global capitalism. Our approach on financialization in developing countries, particularly in LA economies, follows Kaltenbrunner and Painceira (2018) that shows that financialization in those countries has a subordinated characteristic, since it is not only determined by the subordinated position of developing countries in the international financial system but this process also cements and exacerbates an uneven development. This process of subordinated international integration has worked in the context of the real economy, through processes of trade and foreign direct investment, as well as in the new reality of financialized international markets. In this sense, uneven development works both through the "real" implications that financialization has and by the self-reinforcing processes within financial markets.

This approach on financialization in developing economies emphasizes the differentiated nature of financialization in relation to advanced countries, because it includes a subordination within a monetary hierarchical system. This differentiates from the orthodox theory that has treated separately the monetary phenomena of real phenomena. The dominant GVCs approach has not been an exception to the rule with very little debate on financialization, although some studies have been advanced lately.[16]

According to Kaltenbrunner and Painceira (2018), financialization shaped recent changes in the financial practices and relations of economic agents in LA economies through two major channels. The first channel is through the reserve accumulation of developing countries and the way it has altered the banks and household behaviour. The second is LA's continued vulnerability to large and sudden capital and exchange rate movements (largely independent of domestic economic fundamentals) with significant repercussions on the interaction of LA companies with financial markets.

Both processes are related to the global capital accumulation and thereby to GVCs. The rise in reserve accumulation allowed developing countries to sustain a rising participation in global investments and in international trade flows and, consequently, engaged in the global chains of production,[17] reinforcing the dependence on the US dollar financial networks, and has delivered much less than promised in terms of economic policy autonomy.[18] On the other hand, the continuation of LA's external vulnerability has been manifested in higher exchange rate volatility as one of the consequences. Non-financial companies have been more involved in financial operations in order to fund and hedge their productive operations. This dependence has also meant the rise in speculative operations in relation to the productive investments in the last decades.[19] In addition, financialization in Brazil has also been characterized by the privatization of public goods and social services (Lavinas et al., 2019).

In general terms, it can be said that finance in many LA countries, including Brazil, has had deleterious characteristics (which refers to the classical Marxist debate of the beginning of the 20th century with Lenin, Hilferding and others). The interests of finance have influenced economic policy decisions (and development strategies), preventing any transformation of the economies to a more inclusive and stable accumulation system. In this regard, finance has not been domesticated and channelled towards Brazil's full socio-economic development, but it has been an additional instrument for strengthening social inequality and concentration of wealth. It is important to mention that in LA economies, in general, the economic programs[20] were compatible with the Washington Consensus.

GVC and GWC, a Critical Perspective: GIC

The GVCs (or Global Poverty Chains) are necessary to understand the role of finance and of the TCs/MNEs. This chain is combined in a two-dimensional critical analysis through Global Inequality Chains (GICs) by Quentin and Campling (2017) that are also mobilizing the discussion on Global Wealth Chains (GWCs) by adding a dimension to the analysis developed by Selwyn (2019). They expand the GVC framework through its integration with the GWC approach.

For this reason, we argue that it is fundamental to promote an argument related to the objective rather than the subjective theory of value to discuss GVC (added-value). In general, this analytical framework has become the reference for multilateral institutions (OECD, WTO and World Bank). For GVC proponents, cash flows and value flows are equivalent and allow value-added to be treated as they were an increase in value creation. It is therefore fundamental to propose an alternative theory that would permit to demystify key differences. The Marxist value theory is the best approach to express these differences, particularly for the GVC phenomena because instead of focusing on the determination of prices, it sustains an objective value conception that is not limited to prices. According to Quentin and Campling (2017), it is possible to track the creation of value in the GVC regardless of where the amount of money determined by prices is found.

Once this critical analytical framework has surpassed the theory of neoclassical value (subjective and the confusion with its monetary form) the discussion moves to creation of surplus value within the production of goods and how it is appropriated by the owners of the means of production (capitalists) following Marx's approach. On the GIC, the authors point out that it is necessary to consider not only the formal productive work paid by wages, but also, other forms of labour. Indeed, it has often been the case of developing countries, in which the labour force is poorly paid and largely informal. The key question is on the distribution of the added-value among the various capitalists as Marx presents at the very beginning of *Das Kapital*, Volume III, whether they are industrial capitalists, bankers, landowners for rent or traders. Quentin and Campling (2017) mobilize another two categories of labour in the analysis of the political economy of the taxation of corporate profits: (i) work in the public sector and (ii) unpaid reproductive work and domestic work.

In contemporary capitalism, these two categories of work are essential to account for the weight of the state, being the unpaid work fundamental for the production of value and surplus value. It also allows us to address the case of developing countries or the issues of gender inequalities (as proposed by them). This discussion on value theory is not incidental and allows a critical view on the GVCs by integrating the spatial dimension and, thus the global nature of the development, and of the contemporary capitalist dynamics.

Following Quentin and Campling (2017) there are two dimensions. The first one relates the GVCs based on the Marxist value theory, focusing on the GVC's structure, particularly by differentiating the leading companies from the smaller companies and the companies located in developed countries and developing countries. The supporters of the GVCs present the case of leading companies that have market power as a goal to be achieved by small companies, being in developed countries or not. This process of "upgrading"/improvement of small companies would be done by the insertion into the GVCs, thanks to the market forces often represented by a smile curve. Leading companies that integrate into GVCs by participating in activities such as research and development, design, marketing or advertising, create a higher amount of added-value than the small companies that are restricted to production and distribution. The insertion into the GVCs would be a way for small firms to "climb" the value-added ladders, in the expectation of being a leader. This perspective for insertion into the GVC serves only to promote a narrative on the capture of value creation in the hands of certain places of the GVC and to maintain a hierarchy and domination within the GVC. The second dimension it critically tackles is the Global Wealth Chains (GWCs). These chains are the routes through which surplus is expanded in favour to owners of capital by minimizing the taxes payments.

Transnational companies are expanding their activities globally and are always looking to maximize their profits and minimize taxes and payments for other players (such as tax-based states). This taxation issue has a clear influence on the states that try to attract leading companies by proposing exemptions from taxes, often engaging in deleterious tax wars. In order to attract foreign capital, competition among states takes place through tax reductions for leading companies, which has caused problems for public financing, generating macroeconomic imbalances.

As the authors note, the mainstream framework of the GVC, although it can be considered contemporary to the changes in global production, is nevertheless a limited framework ("poor lens"). Since this framework does not account for the distribution between profits and wages due to obsession of the analysis in terms of added-value, it is concerned with proposals of political liberalization practices in the agendas of international institutions that do not consider the distribution effects of the tax systems in the countries in which GVC operate and increase the value added. Quentin and Campling and their research group attempt to go beyond these limits by combining critically GVC and GWC in order to propose an analytical framework, named Global Inequality Chains (GICs).

The GIC framework articulates two dimensions: horizontal, named GVC and vertical, referred to as GWC. The horizontal dimension deals with the creation of value throughout the production chain of its appropriation by the various players involved (transnational companies carving the lion's share, leaving the remains to small companies and workers) in the context of a financialized global system. The vertical dimension searches for better financial closure to reduce payment taxes as much as possible, juggling legal practices (tax optimization) along with illegal practices (tax evasion, tax havens).

In this context, the GICs are based by unequal appropriation of surplus value created by labour, taken over by capital, and unequal distribution of capital gains created at the expense of the state. This critical perspective profoundly alters the understanding of GVCs and the neoliberal proposals that promote uneven and combined capitalist development. However, it is important to highlight that it is not all multilateral institutions that support blindly the upgrade by GVCs as a critical concern on GWC is present in a recent UNCTAD (2020) report.

Latin America and Brazil in the GICs

From the beginning of the 2000s, the huge rises in international capital flows have been connected with the expansion of GVCs through the rise of foreign direct investment (FDI), undertaken essentially by transnational companies.[21] In this regard, it is important to analyse the dynamics of the FDI in LA, based on Brazil, in order to grasp the importance of this type of capital flow in shaping the GICs since the GFC.

After the GFC, emerging market economies, LA economies included, received a huge amount of short-term capital flows as a consequence of the large monetary easing policies promoted by major central banks of developed countries. Brazil, in particular started to get a substantial capital inflow as soon the crisis eased in the middle of 2009 (see Figure 11.1). In order to curb the domestic currency (BRL) appreciation, which was damaging the exports competitiveness, the Brazilian authorities started to implement capital controls, such as the imposition of taxes or quarantine on short-term capital flows (equities, bonds and loans instruments) by the end of 2009. In the middle of 2010, there was an acceleration of FDI flows which could not be explained by investment or productive reasons. This sudden and substantial rise in the FDI inflows is due to speculative motives to overcome restrictions in short-term capital flows movement. The speculative movement started to ease only when restrictions were imposed in the FX derivatives market.[22] There was a drop in the FDI inflows when capital controls ended by the middle of 2013.

In FDI stocks, there has been a rising importance of inter-company loans related to equity and investment fund shares in the last decade from around 15% in 2010 to over 30% at the end

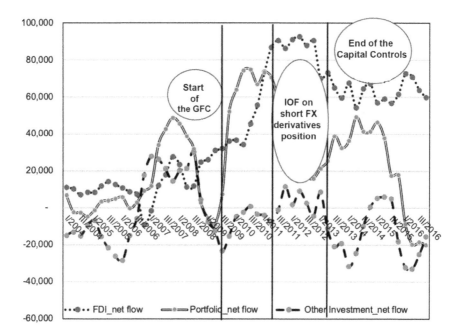

Source: Authors' calculations based on BCB (2020).

Figure 11.1   Capital controls and international capital flows (US$ millions, cumulated 12 months)

of 2019.[23] This increase can be attributed to an issue of valuation (depreciation of the BRL) and mainly to the subordination character of affiliated companies through lending operations in which the major driver has been the financial management of the multinational companies. These companies are at the top of the GVCs.

The subordinated position in international finance is also depicted in FDI coming from foreign investors based on offshore financial paradises. In Brazil, there has been a large share of these investors. In 2018, it was around 35% from the total FDI inflow. The wealth management is crucial for the FDI decisions, and consequently for the GVCs ones.

Finally, the taxation system has regressive characteristics[24] in the Brazilian economy, unchanged since the 2000s, favourable to companies, particularly to TCs/MNEs which benefit from broad tax exemptions for settlements which are often subject of a taxation war on the part of provincial governments. In the same direction, in the midst of the debate on the Brazilian pension reform in 2019, the issue of unpaid taxes and overdue debt to the public pension scheme (INSS) on the part of large groups (TCs/MNEs or large domestics groups) was put in place. Beyond the astronomical amount of the overdue debt (hundreds of billions BRL) of these groups, for example Itaú and Original Banks, JBF Investimentos, JBS, Eldorado Celulose and Havan, the proponents of the reform approved a series of provisions reducing the amount of pensions for the majority of Brazilians and increasing their period of contribution. On the other hand, they reduced the social contributions of companies (DIEESE, 2017). This kind of taxation framework is one of the components raised by Quentin and Campling in the GICs' approach.

11.3   CONCLUSIONS

This chapter has discussed the key elements related to the development strategies of the international insertion of developing countries, focusing in LA, particularly, in Brazil. We have shown that the changes related to development strategies since the GFC concentrate in developed countries with significant impacts in the world economy. From a long-term perspective, after the GFC, the international strategies moved towards protectionism in developed countries (US and EU), while developing economies still favour trade liberalism, outstandingly China, but also LA economies. Therefore, we are witnessing a reversal of strategies for international integration between countries of the centre and the periphery at a time of profound upheavals in the capitalist dynamics, such as multinational companies' strategies, China's role and finance.

These challenges in the new international trade configuration have emerged in the context of the predominance of multinational companies' strategies based on the expansion (and consolidation) of GVCs. These chains have shaped development strategies in developed economies and, fundamentally, in developing countries, which have a subordinated position in international trade markets. Also was revised the debate on GVCs from a critical perspective that presents how they can deteriorate the working and living conditions of workers, especially of developing countries. This is far from the mainstream approach, particularly when it is considered the global reorganization of trade and production in combination with the China's power.

In opposition to the mainstream view which split issues of trade and finance, we developed a critical approach between these two spheres based on the Marxist theory of value in the context of GVCs and financialized capitalism (or financialization). By having a subordinated position in international monetary markets, developing countries have a subordinated financialization. Our critical discussion, based on the approach of Global Poverty Chains, of the dominant view of the multilateral institutions (GVCs) points out the challenge of competitiveness without this being at the expense of wages and working conditions of the labour force. The Global Inequality Chains approach highlights the inequalities linked to tax systems, to the appropriation of value and to the capacity of multinational companies to carry out wealth and tax optimization at the expense of public taxes, which could finance the development. Finally, taking the Brazilian experience, it has raised some challenges for international integration. It is highlighted by the recent FDI dynamic how the combination of multinational strategies, consequently GVCs, and finance can be useful to analyse the unfolding of development strategies in LA economies.

NOTES

1.   The opinions of this chapter do not express the BCB's opinion.
2.   See OECD (2020, p. 15). Global GDP growth rate of 3.4% and 2.7% for 2018 and 2019 respectively compared to the average 3.3% for the period 2012–2019. For OECD countries, 2.3% and 1.7% compared to the average of 2.1% for the same period. For Brazil, 1.3% and 1.1% for 0% to the period 2012–2019. Finally, China and India also slowed down in terms of growth rates.

3.   https://www.touteleurope.eu/actualite/la-politique-commerciale-commune.htm.
4.   In addition to works by ECLAC and its authors, there is substantial literature on the LA develop-
     ment. A good synthesis is found in Bielschowsky (2000). For a critical perspective, see Carcanholo
     (2017).
5.   On this issue, see Saludjian (2005).
6.   In Brazil, for example, the wages increase is related to the minimum wage policy from 2005 to 2015
     and must be considered within the framework of global capitalism and being compared with the
     wage levels of other countries.
7.   http://www.fazenda.gov.br/noticias/2007/r220107-PAC-integra.pdf/view.
8.   http://www.pac.gov.br/infraestrutura-social-e-urbana/minha-casa-minha-vida8.
9.   http://www.planejamento.gov.br/servicos/faq/pac-programa-de-aceleracao-do-crescimento/visao
     -geral/qual-a-diferenca-entre-pac1-e-pac28.
10. See https://iedi.org.br/admin_ori/pdf/20080529_pdp.pdf and https://www.dieese.org.br/notatecnica/
     2008/notaTec67PoliticaDesenvolvimento.pdf.
11. http://www.brasil-economia-governo.org.br/2013/10/23/o-que-e-o-plano-brasil-maior/.
12. On this issue and the level of profitability (ROE) of large economic groups during this period, see
     Pinto et al. (2019).
13. https://www.fundacaoulysses.org.br/wp-content/uploads/2016/11/UMA-PONTE-PARA-O
     -FUTURO.pdf8.
14. On financialization, GVC and technological change in LA, see Abeles et al. (2018).
15. On this dependence, see Ricci (2019). For example, in LA the net transfer (as % of value-added) to
     developed countries increased from 4.98% in 2000 to 6.4% in 2007. In Brazil, net transfers almost
     doubled from US$39 billion in 2000 to US$63 billion in 2007.
16. A good discussion of the virtuous or vicious circle of financialization can be found in Salama
     (2016).
17. Since the beginning of the 2000s, the process of reserve accumulation has happened with the rise in
     foreign direct investment towards emerging and developing countries. The relation between finan-
     cial and productive aspects has been connected in the expansion of capital flows and productive
     investments to those countries. On this discussion, see Painceira (2009).
18. For more details, see Painceira (2021).
19. Important Brazilian and Mexican companies went to bankruptcies as they were involved in spec-
     ulative operations in derivatives markets during the GFC. The LA economies have been the target
     for carry trade operations among investors, including domestic non-financial companies, since the
     beginning of the 2000s.
20. For example, the Law of Convertibility (1991) in Argentina and the Real Plan (1994) in Brazil.
21. On this relation, see Andrenelli, A. et al. (2019), "Micro-Evidence on Corporate Relationships in
     Global Value Chains: The Role of Trade, FDI and Strategic Partnerships", OECD Trade Policy
     Papers, No. 227, OECD Publishing, Paris.
22. This is the market where the FX rate is determined in Brazilian markets and there was a fundamental
     international dimension in the FX rate dynamic. For more details see Kaltenbrunner and Painceira
     (2015).
23. BCB (2020).
24. On this regressive character, see https://brasildebate.com.br/wp-content/uploads/Austeridade-e
     -Retrocesso.pdf.

REFERENCES

Abeles, M., Pérez Caldentey, E. and Valdecantos, S. (2018). *Estudios sobre financierización en América
     Latina*. Libros de la CEPAL, N° 152 (LC/PUB.2018/3-P), Santiago, Comisión Económica para
     América Latina y el Caribe (CEPAL).
BCB (2020). Time series. Retrieved from https://www.bcb.gov.br/.
Bielschowsky, R. (2000). *Cincuenta años de pensamiento en la CEPAL: textos seleccionados*. Santiago:
     CEPAL.

Carcanholo, M. (2017). *Dependencia, superexplotación del trabajo y crisis. Una interpretación desde Marx*. Madrid: Maia Ediciones.

DIEESE (2017). Reformar para excluir. *Departamento Intersindical de Estatística e Estudos Socieconomicos*. Retrieved from https://www.dieese.org.br/evento/.

ECLAC (2016). *Panorama de la Inserción Internacional de América Latina y el Caribe*. Santiago: CEPAL.

ECLAC (2019). *Preliminary Overview of the Economies of Latin America and the Caribbean*. Santiago: CEPAL.

Kaltenbrunner, A. and Painceira, J. P. (2015). Developing countries' changing nature of financial integration and new forms of external vulnerability: the Brazilian experience. *The Cambridge Journal of Economics*, *39*(5), 1281–1306.

Kaltenbrunner, A. and Painceira, J. P. (2018). Subordinated financial integration and financialisation in emerging capitalist economies: the Brazilian experience. *New Political Economy*, *23*(3), 290–313.

Lapavitsas, C. (2014). *Profiting Without Producing: How Finance Exploits Us All*. London: Verso Books.

Lavinas, L., Araújo, E. and Bruno, M. (2019). Brazil: from eliticized to mass-based financialization. *Revue de la régulation*, *25*, Spring 2019. Retrieved from http://journals.openedition.org/regulation/14491; doi: 10.4000/regulation.14491.

Marini, R. M. (1973). *Dialética da Dependência*, Petrópolis: Editora Vozes; Buenos Aires: CLACSO; Rio de Janeiro, RJ: Laboratório de Políticas Públicas, 2000.

Medeiros, C. A. and Trebat, N. (2018). Las finanzas, el comercio y la distribución del ingreso en las cadenas globales de valor: implicancias para las economías en desarrollo y América Latina. In *Estudios sobre financierización en América Latina*, 171–203. Libros de la CEPAL, Santiago: CEPAL.

Nogueira, I. and Hao, Q. (2019). The state and domestic capitalists in China's economic transition: from great compromise to strained alliance. *Critical Asian Studies*, *51*(4), 558–578.

OECD (2020). *Perspectives économiques de l'OCDE, 2020(1)*. Paris: Éditions OECD.

Painceira, J.P. (2009). Developing countries in the era of financialisation: from deficit accumulation to reserve accumulation. *RMF Discussion Papers*, 4.

Painceira, J.P. (2021). *Financialisation in Emerging Economies: Changes in Central Banking*. London: Routledge (forthcoming).

Pinto, E., Guedes Pinto, J. P., Saludjian, A., Nogueira, I., Balanco, P., Schonerwald, C., and Baruco G. (2019). A Guerra de todos contra Todos e a Lava Jato: a Crise Brasileira e a Vitória do Capitão Jair Bolsonaro, *Revista da SEP*, *54*, 107–147.

Quentin, D. and Campling, L. (2017). Global inequality chains: integrating mechanisms of value distribution into analyses of global production. *Global Networks*, *18*(1), 33–56.

Ricci, A. (2019). Unequal exchange in the age of globalization. *Review of Radical Political Economics*, *51*(2), 225–245.

Salama, P. (2016). *La tormenta en América latina. Hacia dónde van las economías de la región?* Guadalajara: Universidad de Guadalajara and Colegio de la Frontera Norte.

Saludjian, A. (2005). Critique of open regionalism from the geographic economy applied to Mercosur. *Journal of Latin American Geography*, 4(2), 77–96.

Selwyn, B. (2019). Poverty chains and global capitalism. *Competition and Change*, *23*(1), 71–97.

UNCTAD (2020). World investment report 2020, *United Nations Conference on Trade and Development*. Retrieved from https://unctad.org/.

WTO (2020). Annual report. World Trade Organization. Retrieved from https://www.wto.org/.

12. From "downpour of investments" to debt crisis: the case of Argentina 2015–2019

Cecilia Allami, Pablo Bortz and Alan Cibils

On 15 December 2015, Mauricio Macri took office as President of Argentina after 12 consecutive years of *kirchnerismo*.[1] During those years, Argentina's economy experienced a remarkable recovery from the 2001–2002 crisis, with high growth rates and a significant improvement in employment, income distribution and social indicators. Furthermore, a successful debt restructuring negotiation and high international prices of commodities – Argentina's main exports – resulted in a process of significant international reserve accumulation and a progressive reduction of the debt-to-GDP ratio.

However, a series of macroeconomic imbalances began to emerge in the second half of 2011. First, a moderate but persistent inflation rate caused tensions between the monetary and exchange rate policies. Second, and more importantly, Argentina's historic foreign exchange constraint reappeared, resulting in the implementation of a series of policies aimed at external accounts management, such as import and foreign exchange controls.

This was the context in which the 2015 presidential campaign took place, where mainstream media actively campaigned against the continuity of *kirchnerismo* and in favour of Macri's opposition coalition *Cambiemos*, using exchange controls and inflation as battering rams against *kirchnerismo*. During the campaign, Macri made a great number of promises and predictions about what he would do if elected, including "zero poverty" (a virtual elimination of poverty), a "downpour of investments" that would arrive from abroad once exchange controls were lifted and capital markets deregulated, and an efficient and transparent government which allegedly would be guaranteed by appointing CEOs from large corporations to key posts in government.

However, once in office it became clear that economic policy would have two key drivers, namely trade liberalization and the deregulation of the capital market and financial sector. As we show below, Macri's policy framework did not contribute to achieve the promised outcomes. Indeed, the Macri administration radically changed the orientation of monetary and financial policies compared to his predecessors, dismantling prudential and exchange controls, deregulating the capital account and interest rates. Monetary policy also changed radically, abandoning the managed float exchange rate policy and quantitative targets monetary policy in favour of an inflation targeting monetary policy and a freely floating exchange rate. This new policy framework, purportedly more transparent and market-friendly, was supposed to attract foreign investment which in turn would result in higher growth rates.

However, the Macri administration's liberalization and deregulation policies only deepened Argentina's macroeconomic imbalances, resulting in a massive accumulation of external debt as the only compensating alternative in the chosen policy framework. Indeed, Argentina's insertion into the global system of finance and trade as a dependent periphery nation, whose main source of foreign exchange is primary exports or debt, imposes serious restrictions on its policy space. This is especially the case in the event of a sudden reversal of capital flows in the face of which the only alternatives are to default or turn to the IMF – which is what Macri did in mid-2018 when capital markets stopped bankrolling his scheme. Not taking foreign exchange restrictions seriously and implementing the standard orthodox policy package results in crisis and economic paralysis as Macri's four years in office patently show.

This chapter is structured in four sections. In the following section we take the insights from the currency hierarchy bibliography to analyse the theoretical restrictions of Argentina's periphery status. In section 12.2 we present an overview of the main policy changes implemented by the Macri administration, followed by an analysis of the empirical results of these policy changes in section 12.3. The chapter concludes with a summary of findings.

12.1   CURRENCY HIERARCHIES, DEPENDENCY AND LIQUIDITY

There are three concepts to be kept in mind to understand Argentine financial dynamics since December 2015 and the crisis that erupted in May 2018, prompting a hasty return to an IMF stand-by agreement. The first relates to the role of the Argentine peso (ARS, from now on) in the international currency hierarchy (ICH from now on, see Dow 1999; Andrade and Prates 2013; De Paula et al. 2017; De Conti and Prates 2018, among many others). The second major concept, linked to the ICH, is the ensuing financial dependency of developing economies on the global financial centres. A third major concept to consider is the permanent regulatory arbitrage, financial innovation and changes in liquidity and indebtedness norms and conventions that characterizes "money-manager capitalism" (Minsky 1986). Changes in leverage, a willingness to take on more debt followed by a sudden reversal of external financial conditions is one of the major corollaries of Minsky's Financial Instability Hypothesis. The liberalization of the financial account in the balance-of-payments is one example of the "relaxation" regarding increasing indebtedness, both by borrowers and lenders. This liberalization is one of the requirements for the implementation of the Inflation Targeting (IT) monetary policy regime announced by the Macri administration in September 2016 and implemented in January 2017. This section will present and explain these different (though interrelated) concepts, the theoretical framework that guides this chapter.

In its role as the reference currency in the international monetary system, the US dollar takes part in 85% of transactions around the world (Auboin 2012; Gopinath 2016). It is the safest asset in the world, even more so after the global financial crisis in 2008 because of the international liquidity network unfolded by the Federal Reserve (Tooze 2018). Its influence is not only related to the US financial system: in 2014, US banks accounted for a quarter of all cross-border dollar bank claims (McCauley et al. 2015: 5; Avdjiev et al. 2016: 427), but rather to the dominant geopolitical role that the US plays in the world system. The dollar is therefore the go-to currency in times of stress, and the reference currency in times of great uncertainty, high inflation and weak domestic financial systems (what is called "currency substitution", see Giovannini and Turtelboom 1992; Eichengreen et al. 2003).

The dollar sits at the top of the ICH. Underdeveloped countries' currencies, in turn play the role of speculative, short-term investment vehicles, to be discarded as soon as risk perceptions tighten, margin haircuts are increased, refinancing and roll over are restricted, and liquidity is the supreme ordinal principle. This role as a speculative investment vehicle forces under-developed countries to pay a liquidity premium over the dollar (Kaltenbrunner 2015; Bonizzi 2017). Their financial systems, their liquidity, their interest rates and public debt management are inextricably linked to the US dollar. This is not to say that the link is invariant to economic policy, to economic history and the characteristics of each country. But the ICH influences, limits and restricts the policy space of underdeveloped economies, even more so in the case of financial openness and external deregulation.

This financial dependency on the dollar partly manifests itself in the liquidity premium that underdeveloped countries have to pay on the dollar. It also manifests itself in the need to accumulate foreign reserves, to countervail domestic capital flight, and in its exposure to the fluctuations of external financial conditions outside the scope of domestic authorities. The IT monetary regime is a perfect conduit for these fluctuations. IT presupposes external finan-cial deregulation in underdeveloped economies for a smooth transmission of the monetary policy. In these economies, the interest rate influences prices mainly through its effect on the exchange rate. And financial deregulation is required for a sufficient "elasticity" of external and domestic finance to the domestic interest rate. Additionally, some authors recommend reserve accumulation as a complementary tool to exchange rate management, to counteract the exposure of domestic financial conditions to changes in external risk perceptions in a deregu-lated financial system (Ostry et al. 2012).

Pressures for financial deregulation move in a sort of "cycle" linked to the ebb and flow of external liquidity. Although Minsky wrote mostly about the US economy, his theory (1986) gives us elements to understand the evolution of this regulatory cycle and the feedback of investors and their reactions. Kregel (1998), Wolfson (2002) and Schroeder (2002) provide a blueprint to extend Minsky's analysis to the international sphere. Based on their work, we would like to stress two points. The first point relates to the role of financial innovations. Fear of external disruption usually leads to different types of capital and exchange controls, both to inflows and outflows. Investors develop innovative channels to jump these restrictions (Alami 2019). A proper dynamic approach is required when implementing capital control measures.

The second point refers to conventional standards regarding the accepted leverage levels by lenders. Minsky affirmed that a major driving factor of instability was that "the acceptable and desired liability structures of business firms and the organizations acting as middlemen in finance change in response to the success of the economy" (Minsky 1986: 193). Low leverage levels call for more indebtedness. In underdeveloped economies this manifests itself not only in firms but also in governments, mainly with regard to international indebtedness. This is important to keep in mind when analysing the Macri administration, that faced a very low level of external indebtedness when it took office in December 2015.

The Argentine experience with financial deregulation has also moved to the fore different aspects of international financializaton (Bonizzi 2017; Bortz and Kaltenbrunner 2018; Cibils and Allami 2018; Cibils and Arana 2019). International financializaton is characterized by new actors entering into financial markets and adopting guiding principles related to finan-cial management more than productive and public management. Other features include the development of new financial instruments, the involvement of external investors in domestic financial markets, and the growing influence of global asset managers in underdeveloped economies, both as owners of liabilities and as managers of financial surpluses by elites.

With these concepts in mind, we turn to describe the Argentine experience with deregulation and unsustainable debt accumulation during the Macri administration.

12.2 FINANCIAL DEREGULATION DURING THE MACRI ADMINISTRATION IN ARGENTINA (2015–2019)

As stated earlier, the Macri administration's policy framework had two main drivers: trade liberalization and capital market and financial sector deregulation. As a result, Macri's economics team radically changed the orientation of monetary and financial policies inherited from the preceding Kirchner administrations, dismantling prudential and exchange controls, and deregulating the capital account and interest rates. Monetary and exchange rate policies also changed radically, abandoning the managed float exchange rate policy and quantitative targets monetary policy in favour of an inflation targeting monetary policy and a freely floating exchange rate. Dismantling the policy framework inherited from the Kirchner administrations resulted in a deepening of existing macroeconomic disequilibria, generating a profound crisis. Three years after taking office, the Macri administration had to turn to the IMF as the only remaining source of financing, signing a stand-by agreement for a loan of an unprecedented – for the IMF and for the country – amount.

In the remainder of this section we present a brief overview of the regulatory changes in trade, finance and monetary and exchange rate policies. In the following section we examine the impact of these changes on the external imbalances, using official data.

External Accounts: Let a Thousand Speculators Bloom

One of the first policies implemented by the Macri administration soon after taking office was the deregulation of the foreign exchange market, lifting exchange controls, which had several important effects. First, individuals and businesses could freely purchase foreign exchange with an initial limit of two million dollars per month. In May 2016, the limit was increased to five million dollars and later that year (September) the limit was eliminated altogether. Second, requirements to transfer funds abroad were relaxed. Third, foreign exchange operations were increasingly freed from reporting requirements to the Argentine Central Bank (BCRA for its Spanish acronym) and it was no longer required to inform the country of origin, destination or the purpose of transactions. Fourth, the only regulations kept in place were related to international agreements on money laundering.

Finally, restrictions on capital flows, especially short-term flows were substantially reduced initially, and then fully eliminated. The BCRA first reduced the minimum period of inflows from 365 to 120 days, eliminating this requirement in January 2017. The 30% reserve requirement on short-term flows was also eliminated, resulting in a surge of short-term, speculative capital inflows in search of higher rates of return.

Trade was another major target of deregulation and liberalization. One of the first acts of Macri's government in this area was to eliminate import affidavits or sworn statements (*declaración jurada anticipada de importación*, DJAI), implemented during Cristina Fernández de Kirchner's second term in office. Import affidavits were designed as an instrument to restrict imports in a context of a growing foreign exchange shortage. In other words, DJAI were an attempt to exert control over the foreign exchange used for imports by restricting imports to strictly necessary uses, eliminating superfluous or luxury items. Additionally, it was hoped that these controls would act as an incentive to produce locally what would have otherwise been imported.

In this way, the country lost control over its foreign trade, opening up the economy in a global context that was moving to increased protectionism spearheaded by US president Donald Trump. Furthermore, early in his mandate Macri significantly reduced, and in some cases outright eliminated, export taxes on primary commodities, Argentina's main exports. Export taxes had become an important source of fiscal revenue during the Kirchner administrations, revenue which was now mostly lost and would result in a growing fiscal deficit. Export taxes are also an important policy instrument to decouple the price of key mass consumption items (beef, wheat, corn, etc.) which are also Argentina's main exports with prices set in international markets. Therefore, in addition to the fiscal impact, the elimination of export taxes resulted in an important increase in the price of mass consumption goods, which would then further increase with each successive devaluation.

The 2018 crisis, sparked by the sudden stop of foreign lending and resulting in a turn to the IMF to avoid an explicit default, resulted in the reintroduction of some of the regulations eliminated early in Macri's mandate. One of these regulations was the export tax on all exports, primary commodities and manufactures, but it was introduced as a fixed sum, in pesos, with no update clause for exchange rate movements and no differentiation by sector of the economy, region of the country, and so on.

One of the most controversial liberalization measures is related to the foreign exchange proceeds of exports. During the Kirchner administrations, exporters had 30 days to repatriate the foreign exchange earned from sales abroad. Soon after taking office in December 2015, the Macri administration changed the foreign exchange repatriation period from 30 days to five years, and later to ten years. Finally, in November 2017 the requirement to repatriate foreign exchange earning was eliminated altogether. Needless to say, this only deepened Argentina's foreign exchange shortage and dependence on capital inflows.

Monetary and Exchange Rate Policies

Once the foreign exchange market and the capital account had been liberalized, the Argentine Central Bank, with Federico Sturzenegger as its president, implemented an inflation targeting monetary policy with a freely floating exchange rate regime. The stated objectives were to drastically reduce inflation and to let the market freely determine the exchange rate.[2] Despite paying lip-service to the freely floating exchange rate regime, the BCRA still intervened in the foreign exchange market, often erratically.

Two years into the implementation of this policy package, including substantially higher real interest rates, inflation not only did not fall but increased significantly,[3] and external disequilibria became more acute. Furthermore, the Central Bank bonds (monetary policy sterilization instruments, LEBAC according to their Spanish acronym) became key vehicles for carry trade and financial speculation, which flourished in the newly deregulated environment. The ever-growing stock of LEBACs generated increasing pressure on the exchange rate, forcing the Central Bank to keep increasing interest rates to prevent foreign short-term investments (in LEBACs) from massively converting back to foreign exchange and flee the country. When the LEBAC bubble became dangerously destabilizing, the Central Bank changed its sterilization bonds (the new ones were named LELIQ), which could only be held by local institutional investors (mainly banks) in the hope that it would prove less destabilizing on the exchange rate. While this partially worked, it still required very high interest rates to prevent bondholders from dollarizing their holdings. High interest rates in turn attracted any surplus of local businesses and households, thus paralyzing consumption and economic activity more broadly. Following the crisis in early 2018 and the agreements with the IMF (July and October), the inflation targeting monetary policy was abandoned for a quantitative zero expansion monetary target policy.

The inflation targeting monetary policy, promoted by the IMF and mainstream economics, requires that the Exchange rate float freely, letting the foreign exchange market set the exchange rate. For most periphery countries, Argentina is no exception, the exchange rate is a key macroeconomic variable affecting not only the country's international trade, but also domestic prices, debt-to-GDP ratios, and so on. Free floats, in countries like Argentina where economic agents rapidly dollarize portfolios in the face of uncertainty, lead to a highly unstable exchange rate, often with rapid succession of devaluations and runs on the currency.

In this context, one of the first measures implemented by the Macri administration after taking office in December 2015, was the removal of all exchange controls, thus allowing free access by businesses and households to foreign exchange. Additionally, Macri paid off the vulture funds the full amount of their demands, with no prior negotiation.[4] The expectation was that such a gesture would normalize relations with Northern financial markets, allowing Argentina to, once again, be able to issue public debt in those markets. This indeed happened, initiating an accelerate process of debt accumulation which served to fulfil local foreign exchange demand, to cover an incipient but growing trade and tourism deficits, and debt service payments.

As long as international capital markets were willing to bankroll Argentina's foreign exchange demand, the Macri administration's rickety policy framework endured. However, when in March 2018 foreign markets closed their doors to Argentina, the country's monetary and exchange rate regimes collapsed. A series of runs on the peso, with their usual inflationary consequences, turned the whole Macri administration's macroeconomic policy regime unsustainable, resulting in a hasty bailout agreement with the IMF.

12.3 BALANCE OF PAYMENTS IMPLICATIONS OF FINANCIAL LIBERALIZATION AND DEBT ACCUMULATION

Data from the financial account of Argentina's balance of payments provides a clear panorama of the effects of the Macri administration's liberalization policies on Argentina's external imbalances. Foreign direct investment (FDI) remained practically constant during the entire period, an indication that the "downpour of investments" never really materialized. Indeed, total FDI for the period 2016–2019 was $33 billion, compared to $42 billion during Cristina Fernández de Kirchner's second term in office (2011–2015). Even during Macri's first years in office, when the international financial establishment massively approved the change in political and economic orientation of the Argentine government, FDI flows never surpassed the Kirchner administrations' high points. According to BCRA data, FDI flows represented only 4.3% of total capital inflows for this period.

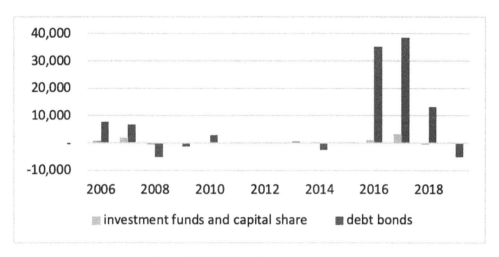

Source: Authors' calculations based on official (INDEC) balance of payments data.

Figure 12.1   *Annual portfolio investment: equities (capital shares and investment funds)*
and debt (net liabilities) (millions of dollars)

Financial liberalization had a much more significant effect on portfolio flows. Figure 12.1
shows net liabilities for the two main components of portfolio investment flows: equities
(capital shares and investment funds) and debt bonds (private and public). The figure shows
a dramatic growth of debt holdings by non-residents during the Macri administration, especially during 2016–2017.

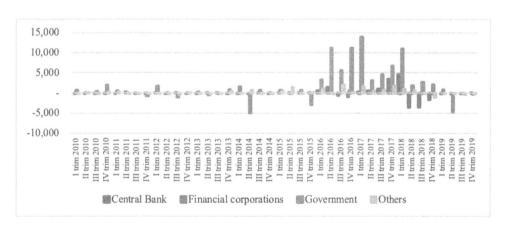

Source: Authors' calculations based on official (INDEC) balance of payments data.

Figure 12.2   *Portfolio investments: debt by holder (net liabilities) (millions of dollars)*

Figure 12.2 shows quarterly debt by issuer, expressed as net liabilities, as recorded in the portfolio investment section of the balance of payments. There are two salient phenomena one can observe in the figure. First, foreign holdings of government debt, and the debt itself, grew exponentially as of the second quarter of 2016, reaching an all-time high in the first quarter of 2017. Second, Central Bank dollar-denominated instruments (mainly LEBACs) grew at a very high rate until the first quarter of 2018. After that, due to the substantial speculative bubble those instruments had generated, the Central Bank started cancelling those bonds, issuing new ones that could only be acquired by resident financial institutions. It is important to point out that these values do not include the IMF loan (even the segments of it destined to reinforce international reserves), as it is recorded in a different section of the balance of payments.

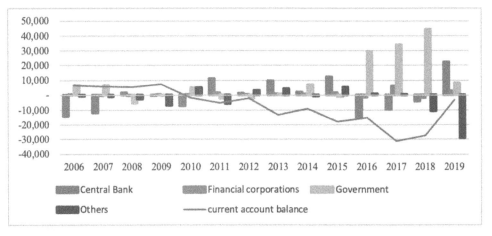

Figure 12.3   Balance of payments by sector (net liabilities) and current-account balance (millions of dollars)

In Figure 12.3 we show the sectoral balance of the financial account of the balance of payments. This allows for a different view of the central government's and Central Bank's contribution to the external balance. For further information, we have also added the current account balance. The figure clearly shows how the central government financed the current account deficit, mainly through new debt issues until 2018 and after that with the IMF loans.

At this point, it is important to highlight that during the entire Macri administration, resident foreign asset purchases tripled in value, totalling more that $86 billion according to a Central Bank report.[5] Even during Macri's first two and a half years in office when there were substantial capital outflows, with foreign asset purchases by residents totalling $41 billion. After Northern financial markets stopped bankrolling the Macri government in March 2018, foreign asset purchases accelerated till Macri left power in December of 2018. The same Central Bank report presents evidence that foreign asset purchases were concentrated in a reduced number of economic agents – 100 businesses and/or individuals made net purchases worth $24.7

billion and the top ten foreign asset purchasers account for almost 10% of total purchases for the entire period.

12.4 CONCLUSION

In this chapter we have discussed the changes that took place in Argentina after the neoliberal government of Macri took office in December 2015. Macri made many promises during his campaign which did not follow the typical neoliberal script, managing to convince sufficient voters to get elected. However, once elected, the policies implemented came directly from the neoliberal textbook.

Trade and finance liberalization policies were rolled out early on and in rapid succession, dismantling prudential and other regulations implemented during the twelve preceding years of Kirchner administrations. In this way, most export taxes and import controls were eliminated, capital controls were done away with and restrictions on capital inflows and outflows were also eliminated. Monetary and exchange rate policies also changed. The monetary targets monetary policy and a managed float exchange rate policies of the Kirchner years were replaced for an inflation targeting monetary policy and a freely floating exchange rate (albeit with erratic Central Bank interventions in the foreign exchange market).

This textbook neoliberal policy package is highly problematic for a periphery country like Argentina, whose currency is low in the international currency hierarchy, and is also cyclically subject to foreign exchange shortages and speculative currency attacks and sudden reversal of capital flows. In this context, the initial Macri administration policy package subsisted until early 2018, when foreign capital flows suddenly reversed. At that point, the only options as a financially dependent periphery country were to default or to seek IMF financing with the well known "austerity" conditionalities. Macri chose the latter.

The effects of Macri's neoliberal policies are clearly reflected in official balance of payments and Central Bank data. First, the "downpour of investments" never materialized, as FDI remained practically constant throughout the period and its highest point never surpassed the Kirchner era high points. Second, portfolio investment flows increased significantly, particularly debt-related flows. Third, debt portfolio flows were primarily related to official debt instruments. These instruments were primarily issued by the Treasury and the Central Bank (until 2018), promoting a huge inflow of speculative capital and deepening Argentina's dependence on such flows.

Clearly, once again, Argentina's experience with neoliberal policies ended in economic crisis and a virtual default, only masked by a huge inflow of IMF financing. This is not Argentina's first experience of the kind. Will it be the last?

NOTES

1. The term refers to the 12 years in which Néstor Kirchner (2003–2007) and Cristina Fernández de Kirchner (2007–2011 and 2011–2015) were president.
2. Under the Kirchner administrations, monetary policy was driven by monetary targets and the exchange rate regime was a managed float, with the dual objective of keeping Argentina's exports competitive and providing some level of protection for local production through import substitution. These policies had been implemented by Minister Roberto Lavagna under the transition government of Eduardo Duhalde, in April 2002, facing strong opposition from the IMF at the time.

3. Price formation in Argentina is closely linked to fluctuations in the exchange rate and when it increases, so do prices. Furthermore, the government linked key prices to the dollar, including electricity, gas, fuel and transport. The elimination of export taxes on primary products, a mechanism used to decouple domestic prices from world prices, also meant basic foodstuffs (wheat, maize, beef, dairy products) were now linked directly to world prices, leading to increases in lockstep with the exchange rate.
4. For further detail on Argentina's conflict with the vulture funds, see Cibils (2015).
5. "Mercado de cambios, deuda y formación de activos externos, 2015–2019". At: http://www .bcra.gob.ar/Pdfs/PublicacionesEstadisticas/Informe-Mercado-cambios-deuda-%20formacion-de -activos%20externo-%202015-2019.pdf.

REFERENCES

Alami, I. (2019). Taming foreign exchange derivatives markets? Speculative finance and class relations in Brazil. *Development and Change, 50*(5), 1310–1341.

Andrade, R. and D. Prates (2013). Exchange rate dynamics in a peripheral monetary economy. *Journal of Post Keynesian Economics, 35*(3), 399–416.

Auboin, M. (2012). Use of currencies in international trade: any change in the picture? *Working Paper ERSD-2012-10*. Geneva: World Trade Organization.

Avdjiev, S., R. McCauley and H.-S. Shin (2016). Breaking free of the triple coincidence in international finance. *Economic Policy, 31*(4), 409–451.

Bonizzi, B. (2017). International financialisation, developing countries and the contradictions of privatised Keynesianism. *Economic and Political Studies, 5*(1), 21–40.

Bortz, P. and A. Kaltenbrunner (2018). The international dimension of financialisation in developing and emerging economies. *Development and Change, 49*(2), 375–393.

Cibils, A. (2015). Towards justice-centred debt solutions: lessons from Argentina. Report written for Debt and Development Coalition Ireland, at: http://www.debtireland.org/download/pdf/towards _justice_centred_debt_solutions_2015.pdf.

Cibils, A. and C. Allami (2018). Financialization of commodities, reserve accumulation and debt: the case of Argentina. In Levy, N. and J. Bustamante (eds.), *Financialisation in Latin America: Challenges of the Export-Led Growth Model*, 102–138. New York: Routledge.

Cibils, A. and M. Arana (2019). Financierización y restricción externa en Argentina desde 2015. In Levy, N. and J. Bustamante (eds.), *América Latina: Movimiento de capitales y su efecto sobre modelo liderado por las exportaciones*, 123–148. México: UNAM.

De Conti, B. and D. Prates (2018). The international monetary system hierarchy: current configuration and determinants, *Texto Para Discussao 335, IE – UNICAMP.*

De Paula, L., B. Fritz and D. Prates (2017). Keynes at the periphery: currency hierarchy and challenges for economic policy in emerging economies. *Journal of Post Keynesian Economics, 40*(2), 183–202.

Dow, S. (1999). International liquidity preference and endogenous credit. In Deprez, J. and J. Harvey (eds.), *Foundations of International Economics: Post Keynesian Perspectives*, 153–170. New York: Routledge.

Eichengreen, B., R. Hausmann and U. Panizza (2003). Currency mismatches, debt intolerance and original sin: why they are not the same and why it matters. *NBER Working Paper No. 10036*, Cambridge, MA.

Giovannini, A. and B. Turtelboom (1992). Currency substitution. *NBER Working Paper No. 4232*, Cambridge MA.

Gopinath, G. (2016). The international price system. *Jackson Hole Symposium Proceedings.*

Kaltenbrunner, A. (2015). A post Keynesian framework of exchange rate determination: a Minskyan approach. *Journal of Post Keynesian Economics, 38*(3), 426–448.

Kregel, J.A. (1998). East Asia is not Mexico: the difference between balance of payments crises and debt deflation. In Jomo, K.S. (ed.), *Tigers in Trouble: Financial Governance, Liberalisation and Crises in East Asia*, 44–62. London: Zed Press.

McCauley, R., P. McGuire and V. Sushko (2015). Global dollar credit: links to US monetary policy and leverage. *BIS Working Papers No. 483*. Bank for International Settlements, Basel.

Minsky, H. (1986). *Stabilizing an Unstable Economy*. New Haven: Yale University Press.

Ostry, J., A. Ghosh and M. Chamon (2012). Two targets, two instruments: monetary and exchange rate policies in emerging market economies. *IMF Staff Discussion Note 12/10*, Washington: International Monetary Fund.

Schroeder, S. (2002). A Minskyan analysis of financial crisis in developing countries. *CEPA Working Paper 2002-09*.

Tooze, A. (2018). *Crashed: How a Decade of Financial Crises Changed the World*. London: Allen Lane.

Wolfson, M. (2002). Minsky's theory of financial crises in a global context. *Journal of Economic Issues*, *36*(2), 393–400.

13. The hegemony of big corporations and the internationalization of capital: a stagnation model with restricted democracy[1]

Gonzalo Cómbita-Mora and Álvaro Martín Moreno-Rivas

Capital flows move at relative velocities while goods and individuals are subject to Newtonian velocities. The financial markets are transnational while the goods and labour markets are subject to the norms of the national state. The sovereignty of Leviathan is diluted in privatization – deregulation – globalization, amplifying the exertion of hegemony by the great corporations which curve the space–time of the exertion of power, while restricting the reach of the exercise of democracy by the citizens. The consequences of these asymmetries are not easily incorporated in the economic models of the *mainstream*.

In fact, the conventional interpretations of the balance of payments establish an ontological equivalence between the current account and the capital account. The current account balance is the difference between savings and investment, whose counterparts are the capital account flows. Foreign direct investment, portfolio investment, foreign indebtedness, and transfers with the rest of the world expresses the so-called foreign savings.[2]

The world described by the intertemporal approach of the balance of payments, the countries with a current account deficit can compensate them with domestic and foreign savings, with no long-run negative consequences. The larger returns of their investments or the higher marginal productivity of capital allows the country with a deficit to pay its obligations with the rest of the world with its future foreign surpluses. Any evidence contradicting these conclusions is interpreted as a paradox (i.e., Lukas Lucas's paradox and the Feldstein–Horioka puzzle).

Households solve their intertemporal consumption-saving optimization problem and firms maximize the present value of their future profit flows, highlighting that all agents are sovereign and independent. Thus, "(the) free markets promote democracy because they lead to economic development, which produces wealthholders independent of the government, who will demand a mechanism through which they can counter the arbitrary actions of the politicians: democracy" (Chang, 2007, p. 200). Clearly, for the *mainstream* there are no power relations in the economic space, only exchange equivalents. In Palermo's (2019) words: "In the mystified approach of mainstream economics, power is the negation of competition" (p. 10).

The above considerations exerted significant weight when establishing restrictions in developing economies growth rate. The analysis starts arguing that the main obstacle for the economic take-off of Latin American countries is their inability to generate enough internal savings and thereby cannot accelerate their accumulation rate and increase per capita income in the long run. From where follows that foreign investment becomes a supplement of internal savings, productive investment, and economic growth. Domestic saving is a scarce resource and accordingly a price must be paid for it. In context, free market policies advocates promote financial market deregulation, capital account liberalization and the opening of national economies to international competition.

However, the history of capital flows in the 20th century does not sustain *mainstream* arguments. Poor countries' current account deficits and capital–labour ratios should have moved capital flows and foreign investment from developed to developing countries and this has not been the case (Davidson, 2003). Actually, a net flight of both financial capital and human capital has taken place from the periphery countries to the centre. Likewise, the major flows of capital and foreign investment did not supplement the internal saving, nor reflect in larger investment rates. On the contrary, foreign saving has displaced domestic saving, thereby diminishing, or keeping investment at its initial level (Bresser-Pereira and Gala, 2008; Bresser-Pereira, 2010).

Capital flows volatility has unleashed cycles that have led to financial and balance of payments crises. The current account deficits might fulfil the long-run stability conditions, that is, the rate of capital flows to the economy is equal to the interest and return rates paid on the obligations with the rest of the world. However, this scheme corresponds to a Ponzi position, which of its instability is too well known. A small change of conditions suffices to unleash a system crisis (Kregel, 2004). It has been recently shown that an increase in foreign indebtedness results in external shock, followed by economic growth declines and the deterioration of functional and personal distribution of income (Bortz et al., 2020).

In developing countries, in which the capital account predominates, they are more likely to experience financial fragility (Amico et al., 2012).

> The current account is simply stating whether a country is, on net, releasing resources to the rest of the world (if in surplus) or drawing on it for those resources (if in deficit). But the corresponding expenditures could be financed entirely at home or abroad, regardless of the current account position. (Borio and Disyatat, 2015, p. 2)

The above problems are addressed in this chapter by first characterizing large (international and domestic) corporation decision-making processes. Following Hymer's (1979) argument that this form of transnational organization dominates contemporary capitalism structure, and that their objective is to maximize their hegemony, we built up an historical block (Gramsci, 1980) between foreign and national capital based on strategical alliances. From where it is argued that companies underspin their power through *corruption*, investment policies and coercion, as a means to appropriate the returns, limiting market competition and coercing national democracies.

The corporation microeconomic analysis is complemented with the essential features of modern financialized capitalism of concrete national economies. Here, the impact of multinational companies on the policy sovereignty on productive development, economic growth and employment, and the strength of democracy for the case of a small and open economy are considered. Particularly, we focus the discussion on the Colombian economy dynamics and the consolidation/reinforcement of a productive structure, which strengthens big corporation interests. The mining sector and more recently the tourism industry, as well as the agroindustry biodiesel and palm oil have been structured through foreign investment.

This chapter's hypothesis is that these activities entrain the displacement of Afro-descendant and indigenous peoples, peasants and *colonos* in the Colombian territory through the revival of internal armed conflict along with the drug war, favouring the international projects.

The chapter is divided into three sections. The first section presents a conceptual model that uses the analytical structure of the post-Keynesian firm to show the effects of financialization and corruption on the rate of capital accumulation and economic growth. The second section uses data of the Colombian economy to show the main regularities and consequences of both the foreign – saving – led model of economic growth and the neoliberal policies on the growth pattern, followed by a discussion of the required conditions to change the model and the policies needed to attain an equitable growth with long-lasting stable peace. Finally, the conclusions of this chapter are presented.

13.1   CAPITAL FLOWS, CORRUPTION AND ECONOMIC STAGNATION

Financial deregulation and the opening of the capital account are usually presented as a prerequisite for attracting foreign savings and attracting foreign direct investment to developing countries. Is assumed that the discipline and transparency imposed by the international financial markets ensure that capital flows and the foreign investment would invigorate capital accumulation in the most profitable sectors of the developing economies.

We argue that that set of ideas lacks conceptual and analytical foundations. The current account and capital accounts are not ontologically identical despite both being part of an accounting identity (Borio and Disyatat, 2015). The capital account records foreign flows, both for the short and the long run, with no reference on how these resources are allocated nor how they contribute to increase productive investment. Actually, the capital flows can be directed towards speculative activities, corruption, financial assets purchases, mergers and acquisitions of firms, with no important effect on the rate of capital accumulation.

Clearly, the allocation and use of capital inflow and outflows don't follow market signals nor national state regulations. In today's world, the international corporations have a hierarchical organization with pyramidal and centralized structures, which allow them to centralize strategical planning at a global level. Therefore, in a decentralized manner, they can make the operative decisions of their subsidiary and satellite companies in different territories; first, determining their resource allocation.

Hymer (1979) shows that the investment assessment criteria instead of following local market conditions are moved by rent-seeking financial objectives that can be linked either to market entrance barriers, the sale of patents and licenses, exports costs versus domestic production; and concludes that "under an oligopoly situation, certain part of foreigners' earnings may constitute a fee for the service to restrict competition and reduce efficiency in the allocation of resources" (Hymer, 1979, p. 261).

The centralization and concentration of capital at national and global levels allow multinational corporations to act like demiurges of the future of these economies, deciding which investment projects to implement.

> Whatever the force of technology, it is clear that the growth of multinational corporations, by itself tends to weaken nation-states. Multinational corporations render ineffective many traditional policy instruments, the capacity to tax, to restrict credit, to plan investment, etc., because of their inter-

national flexibility. In addition, multinational corporations act as a vehicle for the intrusion of the policies of one country into another with the ultimate effect of lessening the power of both. (Hymer, 1979, pp. 307–308)

Indeed, Bhaduri (2011) shows that in the attraction of foreign direct investment, developing countries need to engage in a race that deteriorates their industrial policies and labour standards. This ultimately leads to a direr precariousness of employment and growth, and current account disequilibria since not all countries can simultaneously gain from trade.

The mechanisms through which the big corporations exert their hegemony are not always explicit. Reveiz (2016) put forward the concept of "meso-contracts", which are non-written ad hoc agreements, outside the public institutions and constitutional norms, through which different actors – large economic groups, multinational corporations, politicians and high-ranking officials – establish the non-market rules of exchange to obtain privileges, tax benefits, deals and franchises, and concessions for the exploitation of natural resources.

> The meso-contract ruptures the legitimacy of impartially since it clandestinely bestows privileges to particular political, economic and social groups through several mechanisms and lobbies. It tears the legitimacy of *réflexivité*, since it generally uses the Co (corruption), Ca (capture) and Coop (co-optation) of the E (state) in order to set up capture networks and maps that substitute the formal institutions and outwits the legitimacy of proximity, thereby allocating public resources outside the social contract, e.g. by diverting royalties in Colombia. (Reveiz 2016, p. 69)

Following the above discussion, the consequences of foreign resources access are discussed, specifically debt and investment, and its consequence on firms' capital accumulation rates and returns. To this effect, are considered some aspects related to exertion used by hegemonic corporations (i.e., corruption). In this way is extended firms' post-Keynesian theory, discussed by Lavoie (2014) in terms of small and open economy, with free capital flows.

This model incorporates recent theoretical developments on financialization, the dominance of the corporate model of *maximization of the owner's(owner's) share value*, as well as corporate corruption (Stockhammer, 2004, 2005; Dallery, 2009). This last element plays an essential role in promoting privatization and market deregulation during the neoliberal period. Chang (2007, p. 198) comments that "The corruption often exists because there are too many market forces, not too few".

The models mentioned above are based on the separation of *property* and *management* within the firm, from where the principal–agent problem emerges – the conflict between the shareholders who seek to maximize their rate of profits and the top managers who seek to maximize the *power* of the enterprise, following Gramsci's central concept (Gramsci, 1980, p. 124). In the case of the multinational companies, this conflict becomes larger because of asymmetric information between the operative units *in situ* and parent company (head offices).

Also, as mentioned by Lavoie (1992), in the process of capital accumulation, firms are driven by survival and growth mechanisms. In this context, multinational companies exert their hegemony (in terms of Gramsci, 1980) on the different agents that interact and compete in the market, using the three "c" instruments: consensus, coercion and corruption.

The first element, consensus, is linked to the legal contractual processes that the firm establishes with its providers, consumers, banks and shareholders, to set a non-zero sum game. The second one, coercion, refers to price wars, technology control, overcapacity, labour control, and the use of powerful financial sources in order to unfold mergers and the acquisition and

liquidate their competitors. And, corruption, which by definition is illegal, conveys the allocation of resources for bribery, presents, lobbying and other activities aimed at obtaining rents,
contracts, concessions, and permits from public institutions and market regulators.

Following Dallery's (2009) analysis, is discussed the way in which the different aspects
mentioned above affect the firm's process of capital accumulation in the context of financialization. This would allow integration to the main model the principal market features for the
power hegemony-seeking multinational corporation, discussed in case 3.

The construction of the model begins with the discussion of the firm's financial frontier, following Dallery's model 2009. Then, two elements are added: the open economy condition as
it is the case for the multinational company; and the corruption expenditures that the company
requires to attain market hegemony. These two features are incorporated to the accounting
identity (firms' sources and uses):

$$\pi - iD - (i^* + \rho)D^* e + x_A I + x_c I + x_{c^*} I = I + x_f I + (1 - s_f)$$
$$(\pi - iD - (i^* + \rho)D^* e) + kI \tag{13.1}$$

Where: π – gross profits, i – domestic rate of interest, D – debt in local currency, i^* – international rate of interest, ρ – risk-premium, D^* – debt in foreign currency, x_A – share issue, x_c –
indebtedness in local currency, x_{c^*} – indebtedness in foreign currency, I – investment, x_f
– investment in financial assets, s_f – profits withholding rate, and k – in-balance corruption
resources. For simplicity, static expectations on the exchange rate are assumed, that is, and
$P = P^* = 1$.

Reordering the terms in equation (13.1) and normalizing by the value of the capital stock
(K), equation (13.2) is then obtained:

$$r = \frac{g\left[1 + x_f - x_A - x_c - x_{c^*} + k\right]}{s_f} + id + (i^* + \rho)d^* \tag{13.2}$$

Where: r – rate of profits (π/K), g – rate of growth or rate of accumulation of productive capital
(I/K), d – domestic debt as a proportion of stock of capital (D/K), and d^* – foreign debt as
a proportion of stock of capital ($D^* e/K$).

Equation (13.2) is the financial frontier of the firm. This restriction determines the minimum
rate of profits required for the firm to sustain a given rate of investment. Actually, what this
equation says is that in order to finance their projects the firms need to own resources obtained
from their profits, thus smoothing the risk premium that entails their financing with the credits
from the financial sector.

The second restriction firms are confronted with is the expansion frontier, which relates to
the rate of profits that the firm can attain under given technological conditions and costs structures. The financial frontier is a linear curve and the expansion frontier is an inverted U-curve
in the r,g-space, allowing to explain the so-called "Penrose effect", that is, the non-lineal
relation between the rate of profits and the rate of growth of the firm linked to management
diseconomies that come up when changes in the rate of growth or investment take place
(Lavoie, 1994, 2014).

Figure 13.1 shows the solution for three cases. The first case occurs when firms' managers
have the absolute power and shareholders play a passive role in the market. This solution of

this case – point *a* – corresponds to the traditional model of firm decision-making processes in the post-Keynesian theory.

In the second case, managers must incorporate the shareholder power as a restriction, present during the financialization processes and the transition towards a maximization value model, in which the shares are held by the owners; which also corresponds to the traditional model. The incorporation of this restriction triggers an upward shift of the financial frontier, which occurs mainly due to the additional costs that firm incur, when distributing dividends, which can contradict with investment and the managers' innovation decisions. Additionally, financialization causes new expenses in non-productive investments that are leveraged with both internal and external new debt. This latter element – a key modification – pushes further upwards the financial frontier, affecting negatively the rate of capital accumulation. Accordingly, point *b* in Figure 13.1 shows a lower rate of capital accumulation and a larger rate of profits that suits the interests of the share owners.

The third case incorporates corruption as an instrument of corporate hegemony that allows the company to obtain privileged treatment in the host country – for example tax benefits, flexibilization of labour rights, removal of environmental constraints, contractual privileges. This new cost reduces further the rate of capital accumulation and, at the same time, it increases the corporate profits.

A trade-off improvement between profitability and capital accumulation, moving from point *b*, can be attained through further actions that displace upwards the expansion frontier, allowing for a solution at point *d*. This solution can be reached through legal or illegal actions that reduce both the bargaining power of the trade unions and firms' labour costs. Consequently, the rate of capital accumulation and the rate of profits increases.

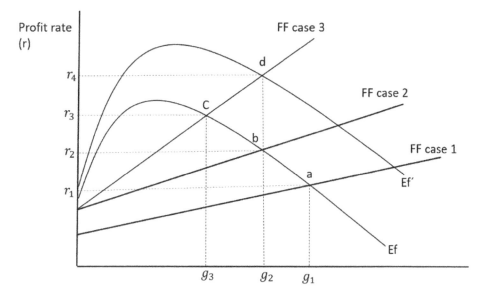

Source: Own elaboration based on Dallery (2009).

Figure 13.1   *The multinational corporation from a post-Keynesian perspective*

Table 13.1   Accumulation and profit rate of Colombia's firms

Year	gk		ROA	
	Multinational	**Others**	**Multinational**	**Others**
2009	0.47	0.58	2.25	2.66
2010	0.47	0.55	2.65	2.75
2011	0.43	0.47	2.52	1.87
2012	0.48	0.47	1.98	1.14
2013	0.47	0.47	-0.26	-0.79
2014	0.53	0.51	-0.22	-0.20
2015	0.52	0.53	-1.54	-4.55
Average	0.48	0.51	1.05	0.41

Source: Authors' own elaboration on United Nations database.

The solutions for cases 1, 2 and 3 shed new light on the Colombian economy. Clearly, the institutional and ideological changes unleashed by the conservative counterrevolution together with the implementation of the neoliberal model and the rentier's revenge in the mid-1980s lead to lower rates of economic growth and investment, though the shareholder profits rate were higher. This was attained by larger dividend flows that were capitalized through in the stock market.

Table 13.1 verifies this result. This was constructed on the results of 19 multinational corporations and nearly 150 Colombian companies operating in different sectors. The table shows that the rate of capital accumulation – that is, the ratio of gk between tangible assets and total assets – and the rate of profits – that is, the index ROA – differ for the two firms group in almost all years and in the period average. Particularly, the rate of capital accumulation (gk) is lower for the multinational corporations when compared with the other group. By contrast, the rate of profits of the former is larger than in the case of the latter.

From the data presented it can be observed that the new scenario facilitated higher corporations' profits rates that, however, was attained through lower rates of capital accumulation. It should be pointed out that the latter "cost" was transferred upon the workers by both the lobby of the co-opted society and the illegal society through the pressures of the Congress and the use of violence.

In effect, the labour reforms and the deterioration of the working standards together with restrictive monetary policy of higher real interest rates in relation of labour productivity (Moreno, 2014) shifted upwards the expansion frontier, reducing the initial effect on the rate of capital accumulation, and expanding the rate of profits even higher. In this way, both foreign investment and capital flows respond to the so-called investor confidence policy, that is, a model based upon corruption, along with the State alignments with big capital interests (Reveiz, 2016).

Alternatively, the negative effect of the multinational corporation decisions on the rate of capital accumulation can be discussed through the Colombian share prices real index. Between 2002 and 2007, it increased by around 9.4 times, which coincides with the boom commodities period that mainly benefited the multinational corporations (Botta et al., 2014; Ocampo, 2013); which created an economic bubble in the Colombian economy (that increased around 1.2 to 1.3 times in real terms, well above the GDP growth rate and the real estate prices (second-hand homes) (Combita, 2020)).

A similar behaviour occurred between the end of 2008 (subprime crises bursting) and 2012, when the largest Colombian stock agent went bankrupt, dragging down the firms boom gains and the stock markets increments of the preceding decade. The Bolsa de Valores de Colombia (Colombian Stock Market) stock prices are highly correlated with the commodities prices, particularly with the energy commodities prices (Combita, 2020).

Also, during these periods the stock market was manipulated by Interbolsa (the stock agent that went bankrupt in 2012) (González, 2013) and Grupo Nule (speculative investments whose directors were highly corrupted – its principle directors were indicted for diverting Bogota public funds). Even repo operations were used for speculative purposes, facilitating both the rate of exchange and stock price inflation (Mayorga, 2013).

A key player of the commodity stock bubble was Pacific Rubiales, a well-known multinational corporation that, later, was proven to have carried out illegal speculative practices in the stock market, on the basis of short-lived investments in the oil sector (see Justicia Tributaria 2019).

This fact shows that the gradual economic specialization towards the primary energy sector was the result of an agreement of policy makers, reinforced by both national and international interests that beforehand decided the economic future of the region (Leon, 2002; Misas, 2016; Nova, 2014). Different aspects such as the hydrocarbons policy in 1974 (Ocampo, 2007) and other tax breaks and facilities policies, streamlining of mining concessions, and the repatriation of earnings in the case of multinational corporations, show the effects of foreign direct investment on both the financial system and the productive structure, thereby determining the growth model and the creation of employment (Banco Mundial, 1997; Leon, 2012; Nova, 2014).

An additional negative effect of foreign investment in Colombia has been the increasing of the dispossession and displacement of vulnerable groups – peasants, *colonos*, indigenous and Afro-descendant communities – excluded from the growth model, in order to favour the extraction of natural resources by the mining and agro-industrial companies, including the extraction of landscape rents by the tourism industry (Hylton, 2017). In this respect, Sintraminercol (2004, p. 103) shows a strong correlation between the location of the exploitation of mining resources by multinational corporations and the intensification of violence-related events linked to the presence of paramilitary groups, the displacement of vulnerable groups and massacres of civilians.

The presence of the multinational companies in Colombia has deep economic, political, and social effects. First, the action of these companies reduced the rate of capital accumulation and increased their profits, at the cost of labour rights and biodiversity deterioration, as well as ethnic diversity. This process was reinforced by financial deregulation policies and capital and trade liberalization, during the 1990s, the privatization of public companies, and public utilities provisions, which created investment opportunities for large corporations.

Also, the permits and concessions for the construction of infrastructure mega-projects were obtained by means of large bribery operations. This has been the case of the ongoing corruption scandals around the multinational company Odebrecht, which also involved top Colombian politicians and executives, and a hegemonic financial group.

13.2   STRUCTURAL CHANGE, DISTRIBUTIVE CONFLICT AND MACROECONOMICS IN COLOMBIA

Here we discuss the macroeconomic context and the impact of how multinational corporations act in the Colombian economy. We focus on the impact of large corporations on the economic growth rate, the rate of capital accumulation, and the distribution of income. It is shown that the investment decisions and resource allocation deepened the regressive process of economic structural change,[3] whose origins can be traced back to the Keynesian crisis and the Bretton Woods collapse in the 1970s.

During the 1960s and 1970s, Latin American countries followed import-substitution industrialization policies, restricting multinational companies' foreign direct investment (Bértola and Ocampo, 2013), abandoning this industrialization policy by the late 1980s. The Cartagena Agreement (1987) handed over the regulation of multinational corporations' foreign direct investment to "free" market forces (Estrada, 2010). These so-called structural reforms were expanded in the 1990s.

This new Colombian economics, which emerged in the 1990s, is analysed through Robinson's theory of growth (Robinson, 1962); which captures the critical changes of the Colombian economy through key variables – the rate of capital accumulation, labour productivity, structural changes, and the profits share in the GDP, which explain the distribution conflicts, "solved" through different forms of violence.

First Condition: The Return of the Golden Age of Growth

The taxonomic classification of growth, proposed by Joan Robinson (1962) and recently applied to describe the history of Latin American countries (Fuentes Knight, 2015; Vernengo, 2015) are classified by the golden age, leading age, galloping platinum, and creeping platinum.

The golden age is characterized for the adjustment of the desired capital growth to the potential rate of growth under full employment conditions. In this case wages growth, productivity and the rate of profit are constant. In the leading age, the investment rate falls under the potential growth rate, productivity growth is zero or decreasing, unemployment increases, and income distribution worsens. The platinum age is a transitional period. Galloping platinum features an accumulation rate greater than the potential, requiring sectoral changes for satisfying the needs of the capital goods sector, while the employment rate grows above the rate of growth of labour supply, without an inflationary barrier, that is, with no distributive tensions between workers and capitalists. Creeping platinum also features an investment rate higher than the potential growth, but the excess of accumulation of capital goods deaccelerates the accumulation rhythm and reduces the size of the capital goods sector.

In underdeveloped countries, unlimited labour supplies or informal low-productivity sectors relax the distributive tensions, while demand for capital goods can be met through imports, which can turn into an active external constraint (Vernengo, 2015). In this context, Latin American economies' golden age took place between the 1950s and 1960s. From the late 1960s to the early 1970s appeared the galloping platinum age, followed by the leading age of the 1980s lost decade. From the early 1990s to 2015 there was a creeping platinum period characterized by accelerated de-industrialization and de-agriculturization, and large capital inflows and currency appreciation. This reversed the productive specialization towards commodities exports, mining, natural-resource-intensive goods, and *maquilas* with low-value-added content (Fuentes Knight, 2015; Vernengo, 2015).

In this period, foreign direct investment was closely linked to this process. According to Botta et al. (2014, 2015), Flóres (2001), Garcia (2002), Goda and Torres (2013), Misas (2016) and Sarmiento (2014) argue that after the 1990s structural reforms, the Colombian economy became highly dependent on the balance-of-payments capital flows, especially on foreign direct investment. Hence the capital account liberalization led to the overvaluation of both the nominal and the real exchange rate in two periods.

Table 13.2 shows the evolution labour productivity (YL), measured by an average value, as an indicator of Colombia structural change between 1970 and 2014. The pattern of behaviour of this variable coincides with Joan Robinson's ages of growth. In the galloping platinum age (1970s), labour productivity shows high growth rates; in the leading age (1980s) it stagnated, with negative growth rates; finally, in the creeping platinum age labour productivity recovers. It also contains the standard deviation of investment. It shows that the economy went from creating stable macroeconomic conditions that favoured productive investment to unstable macroeconomic scenarios that fostered the accumulation of capital in rent-producing sectors – that is, the building sector, financial system, mining and energy sector – and speculative activities as well (Ffrench-Davids, 2010; Lorente, 2002).

The new productive specialization based on mining and finance reduced manufacture and agriculture activities (Table 13.2). Value-added fall in these two sectors shrank significantly after the 1990s due to capitals inflows (foreign portfolio and direct investment). The exchange rate overvaluation deteriorated even more the productive structure. Thus, during the so-called creeping platinum period, those sectors that were supposed to create jobs and foster the economic growth were moving persistently backwards. This affected negatively the rates of capital accumulation in a macroeconomic environment that was getting increasingly unstable, with no domestic aggregate demand pulling up the economy. Another critical aspect has been the intensification of distributive conflicts, shown by the increasing profit share. The multinational corporations played a key role in fostering the deterioration of the labour conditions to increase their rate of profits in order to compensate the loss capital accumulation.

Multinational corporations also increased property ownership concentration and production reallocation, followed by a higher conflict between labour and capital power (Gonzaga, 2015), which led to a sustained reduction of the wage share in the GDP. In developed countries this process took place, reducing working places, while in developing countries of labour rights were diminished; and this certainly attracted large companies' foreign direct investment (Lavoie and Stockhammer, 2013a; Bhaduri, 2011; Bhaduri and Marglin, 1990).

Robinson's arguments of the different periods is considered in Table 13.2 through the gap between the real wage (Rw) and the productivity of labour (YL). In the golden age both the real wage and the mean of labour productivity grow at the same rate, leaving unchanged the functional distribution of income. In the platinum age there are no inflationary tensions because investment capacity is expanded, adjusting the utilization capacity. In the leading age there is an important reduction in the employment rate, affecting negatively the distribution of functional income, which adjusted to the Colombian growth patterns.

In the leading age all indicators deteriorated, the real wage shrank, the productivity of labour stagnated, and the distribution of functional income and wealth distribution worsened. Finally, the creeping platinum age showed inflationary tensions in the early 1990s that later were "cor-

Table 13.2   *Robinson's ages of growth in Colombia macroeconomic variables (1960–2014)*

Period	Age	YL	ΔYL	Investment Std. Deviation	Agriculture GDP %	Δ Agriculture GDP %	Industry GDP %	Δ Industry GDP %	Rw - YL	strikes	Forced displacement
1960–1969	Golden age									75.71	
1970–1980	Galloping platinum age	1.14	0.03	0.01	0.24	0.00	0.23	0.00	-0.09	92.73	
1981–1989	Leading age	1.21	0.00	0.01	0.22	0.00	0.21	0.00	0.16	139.11	69200
1990–1992	Inflation barrier	1.44	0.00	0.01	0.22	0.00	0.21	0.00	-0.16	138.00	83666.66667
1993–2014	Creeping platinum age	1.68	0.03	0.04	0.10	-0.01	0.14	0.00	-0.20	89.00	254197.2

Sources: DANE, CODHES, CIDER. Own calculations.

rected" during the 1999 crisis. This downturn was followed by a lasting pattern of larger ine-quality, higher interest rates and double-digits unemployment, thus widening the gap between the stagnant real wage and the productivity of labour which barely increased in this period.

In Table 13.2 is recorded the number of strikes as a measure of distributive conflict in Colombia (excluding critical historical conflicts such as the peasant struggle for land). During the golden age, distributive conflicts are fewer; in the galloping platinum age, the labour strikes increased ostensibly, and the workers achieve their targets since the real wage grew faster than labour productivity. The leading age reveals high conflictive index followed by unfavourable workers' conditions.

Lastly, the creeping platinum age shows a drastic reduction of strikes, which is explained by the *pax uribista*: increased violence against social movements along with regressive mac-roeconomic policies that coincided with the process of de-industrialization and the rise of the mining and agribusiness sectors; with macroeconomic and regional policies which weakened the popular urban movements' strength. The increased organized violence in the countryside eliminated all peasant resistance against the so-called "extractive locomotives". Table 13.2 last column shows the dramatic rise of social tensions within the Colombian society, which led to a huge number of victims, forced to move from their living places during the galloping platinum age.

The return of the golden age requires a change in the accumulation patterns and the dis-tribution of income. First, full-employment macroeconomic policies are required (interest rates equal to the growth of labour productivity (the average) accompanied by active fiscal policies); second, strategic industrial and commercial policies directed towards reducing the participation of mining and finance in economic activity and increase the industrial and agri-cultural sectors in GDP. Colombia requires a New Deal to promote and expand the domestic market via higher incomes and social security in the case of urban workers, and provide higher life-standards and sustainable productive units in the peasant and indigenous, Afro-descendant groups in rural areas.

Second Condition: Structural Change and Power De-concentration

The creeping platinum age in Colombia (1992–2014) main characteristic has been, on the one hand, huge levels of investment in extractive and financial sectors and, on the other hand, the processes of de-industrialization and de-agriculturization are widening the lag of real wage with respect to labour productivity, particularly since the late 1990s crisis, accompanied by an escalation of violence in the countryside accompanied by a reduction in open distributive conflict in urban areas.

The reduction of poverty and inequality attained in the period of the commodity boom came along with a deterioration of functional distribution of income, which has led to an unsustain-ability rent-seeking model, based on the extraction of limited natural resources determined by international commodity prices (Cimoli et al., 2016; CEPAL, 2012).

A political-economical regime based on rent-seeking, along with public goods reduction and private property in the rural area, and the institutional dominance by illegal agents, config-ured a scenario of natural resource-curse, characterized by highly concentrated resources and a rent-seeking administration of public affairs. In this context, "transferring the property rights of these enterprises, either to domestic or foreign private sector, may not change the fundamental fact related more with the attitude towards wealth accumulation than with a particular form of property" (Fajnzylber, cited by Cimoli and Rovira, 2008, p. 337).

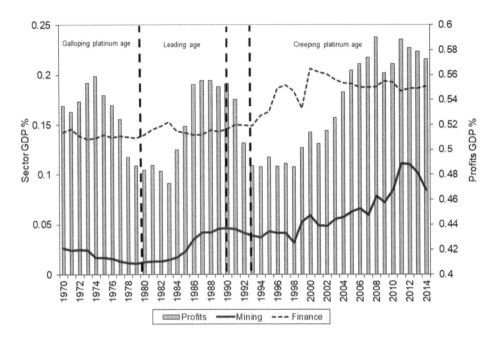

Source: DANE. Own calculations.

Figure 13.2   Profit and sector shares of Colombia's GDP (1970–2014)

The consequences of this model of accumulation and structural change are reflected in the share of mining and financial sectors in GDP compared with the functional income distribution. In Figure 13.2 the larger importance of these sectors is linked to the worsening of the functional distribution of income, that is, a higher share of profits (through non-earned rents such as interests and land-rent). This model also impacts deeply in the tax structure since it demands, on the one hand, a higher indirect taxation, thereby worsening the equality of income distribution and, on the other, the reduction of tax rates on profits and as a means to attract domestic and foreign investors to risk capital in natural resources and non-tradeable high-profit sectors (construction and tourism, for example).

As can be seen, during the golden and galloping platinum ages, both mining and financial sectors lost or kept their importance in GDP, whereas the industry and the agricultural sectors increased their share, with positive results: the real wages increased their share of value added, which partly helped to solve distributive conflicts. The increase in formal labour demand and the gains in labour productivity allowed for higher real wages without extreme inflationary pressures nor marked deterioration in balance of payments. On the other side, the creeping platinum age shows a pattern of growing inequality of functional income distribution and a regressive structural change that, instead of compensating the higher import demands, have contributed to a deterioration of the current account.

Given this scenario, the regressive structural change, and the concentration of economic and political power it involved must be reversed. The increasing importance of the mining and financial sectors is prejudicial in the long-run for the economy: the former implies high ecological costs, rent-seeking behaviours, corruption and Dutch disease; the latter is a cost for the economy, and it is necessary to minimize and regulate it in order to better fulfil its function of offering the credit resources for financing productive investment (Nell and Semmler, 2010).

Third Condition: From Neoliberal Policy to the Consolidation of a Wage-Led Regime

During the creeping platinum age, the philosophy of "investor confidence" and "communitarian state" pretended to solve the distributive conflicts through authoritarian and rent-seeking means. All efforts were focused on ignoring social conflict and confrontation of interests of different social classes, setting-up the Manichean logic of "friend-and-enemy" (Cardona Zuleta, 2016), which supposes to reflect apparent disagreements among elites, hides an "invariant" that guarantees extraordinary rent appropriation through subsidies to the wealthy and via a scheme of contingent warranties for assuring zero investment risk in mining, finance, construction and agri-business.

These mechanisms have combined to attract foreign direct investment through huge privileges: labour market flexibilization to reduce both money and real wages; monetary policies oriented towards inflation control, thus keeping the real interest rate above productivity growth as a means to reduce the wage-share; tax and social security reforms that gave more degrees of freedom to the financial sector for it to profit from the pension savings and health system of Colombian citizens; the introduction of balanced-budget fiscal rule and the subsequent abandonment of full-employment policies; and the privatization of public assets and enterprises.

However, this model is not sustainable because it is based in keeping low living standards to guarantee high levels of rent income, while the reduction of poverty and inequality is conditioned by extraordinary good conditions in the international markets (boom in the commodity prices, terms of trade improvement, easy access to credit) or a deeper exploitation of natural resources. A different sustainable scenario is a wage-led economy: the expansion of the domestic market through higher incomes, while the re-industrialization of the economy can increase both productivity and exports (Lavoie and Stockhammer, 2013b; Cassetti, 2010). This can only be attained through a reconfiguration of political power. Such a scheme would also allow reducing the degree of open violence that is usually exerted by powerful elites both at the national or local level as a means to keep their privileges and command in low-productivity and rent-seeking economies.

As Hirschman (1977) claimed, one of the conditions for the transit of societies based on princes' nepotism and arbitrariness towards modernity was the displacement of "passions" in the public agora towards the so-called "interests". The peace deal was a first condition in this direction of recognizing a society of conflictive interests, and political and economic adversaries. The recognition of the distributive conflict and the provision of the means to solve it through economic rules and institutions are necessary in order to reduce the violence and the power concentration that has characterized the apparently successful but now obsolete model of growth during the creeping platinum age of the Colombian economy.

13.3   CONCLUSIONS

In this chapter is offered a multidimensional analysis on the effects of big corporations in the process of capital accumulation in the Colombian economy. First, two theoretical frameworks, which complement each other, are presented adapting post-Keynesian firm theory to the behaviour of the multinational corporation; for which is considered firms finance in foreign currency and the corruption expenses as factors that facilitate the operation of these corporations in host countries. The results indicate that multinational companies seek to increase their profits rate at the expense of capital accumulation. Also, it is shown that multinational corporations lead to the deterioration of the labour conditions as a mechanism to expand even more their profits.

Second, a growth macroeconomic theory is incorporated to study the historic patterns of capital accumulation and distribution in Colombia in the context of the recent phase of trade and financial globalization. The model is adapted to study how the incursion of the multinational corporations is no more than a worldwide phenomenon in which the developing countries have led their economies towards a systematic deterioration of the labour conditions as a means to attract foreign direct investment, and their increasing specialization towards the export of prime commodities. This process is the reflex of a productive structural change that slowed down the dynamic of capital accumulation in employment-and-growth leading sectors, thus reinforcing the model of economic exclusion while slowing the accumulation of capital. This result is consistent with the microeconomic model of capital accumulations adapted in this chapter.

An additional contribution in this chapter is the reassessment by the data of the hypotheses advanced on the consequences of the actions of the multinational corporations both at firm level and in the aggregate. Some of the most interesting evidence refers to the verification of the decrease of the rate of accumulation due to the presence of this type of firm, which goes hand-in-hand with a significant increase of the rate of profits when compared with other types of firms. It can also be seen that the geographical location of the multinational corporations that extract natural resources is correlated with the higher intensity of war conflicts and violence. Also, at the macroeconomic level since the 1970s there has been a breaking moment in the process of capital accumulation in Colombia which became both increasingly excluding and regressive in terms of its productive structure. This is also consistent with the direction of the microeconomic results that followed from the presence of the multinational corporations.

At the same time, both at macroeconomic and microeconomic levels it is apparent that the role played by the multinational corporations has been that of a catalyser of social and political violence in Colombia, as they contribute to the reinforcement of the excluding model through the consolidation of rent-seeking and speculative sectors highly dependent on the external booms which also favour wage repression. Even worse, these corporations have directly taken part by financing illegal armed groups for their own benefit.

Finally, in Colombia the solutions to distributive tensions demanding structural and institutional *reforms*, are aborted or delayed by means of two mechanisms. In the case of the first mechanism a dissident faction of the "historical block" (Gramsci, 1980) emerges with the intention, either to catch the citizen impatience for progressive changes, or to lead, from right-wing positions, the reactionary yearnings of those terrified by the ascent of social and popular sectors through institutional means. The second mechanism has been historically the use of violence as an "adjustment variable" to close the distributive gap needed by the accumulation pattern, leaving aside less violent macroeconomic mechanisms such as inflation (Hirschman, 1984; Revéiz, 1989). What are the necessary conditions to lead a process of sustained growth and structural change that will reduce inequalities in the long term and respond effectively to the demands of the popular sectors and victims of the armed conflict? This work aims to make a modest effort in this regard, in order to open discussions within the Colombian society.

NOTES

1. The authors want to thank Hernando Matallana and David Cano for their comments and help during translation process.
2. Borio and Disyatat (2015) show that this definition is false. Though the balance of payments is an accounting identity, the current account reflects the resources restriction of the economy and the capital account is the financing restriction. "Saving, a national accounts concept is simple income (output) not consumed: financing, a cash concept, is access to purchasing power in the form of an accepted settlement medium (money), including through borrowing. Investment, and expenditures more generally, require financing, not saving" (pp. 1–2). They also observe that "The current account is simply telling us whether a country is, on net, releasing resources to the rest of the world (if in surplus) or drawing on it for those resources (if in deficit). But the corresponding expenditures could be financed entirely at home or abroad, regardless of the current account position" (p. 2).
3. Cimoli and Porcile (2011) argue that the structural change has a regressive type, following periphery countries which suffered external supply and demand shocks, inducing patterns of specialization.

REFERENCES

Amico, F., Fiorito, A. and Zelada, A. (2012). Expansión Económica y Sector Externo en la Argentina de los años 2000: Balance y desafíos hacia el futuro. *CEFIDAR*, Documento de Trabajo, 45.

Banco Mundial. (1997). *Estrategia minera para América Latina y el Caribe*. Banco Mundial.

Bértola, L. and Ocampo, J. (2013). *El desarrollo económico de América Latina desde la independencia*. México: Fondo de Cultura Económica.

Bhaduri, A. (2011). *Repensar la economía política*. Buenos Aires: Manantial.

Bhaduri, A. and Marglin, S. (1990). Unemployment and the real wage: the economic basis for contesting political ideologies. *Cambridge Journal of Economics*, 4 (14), 375–393.

Borio, C. and Disyatat, P. (2015). Capital flows and the current account: taking financing (more) seriously. *BIS*, Working Paper, No. 525.

Bortz, P., Michelena, G. and Toledo, F. (2020). Shocks exógenos y endeudamiento externo. Impacto sobre el crecimiento y la distribución en economías emergentes y en desarrollo. *El Trimestre Económico*, LXXXVII (2), 346, 403–436.

Botta, A., Godin, A. and Missaglia, M. (2014). Finance, foreign (direct) investment and Dutch Disease: the case of Colombia. *DEM*, Working Papers Series No. 90.

Botta, A., Godin, A. and Missaglia, M. (2015). Finance, foreign direct investment, and Dutch Disease: the case of Colombia. *Levy Economics Institute of Bard College*, Working Paper No. 853.

Bresser-Pereira, L. C. (2010). *Globalization and Competition. Why some Emergent Countries Succeed while Others Fall Behind*. New York: Cambridge University Press.

Bresser-Pereira, L. C. and Gala, P. (2008). ¿Por qué el ahorro externo no promueve el crecimiento? *Investigación Económica*, LXVII (263), 107–130.

Cardona Zuleta, L. M. (2016). *La culebra sigue viva: miedo y política. El ascenso de Álvaro Uribe al poder presidencial en Colombia (2002–2010)*. Universidad Nacional de Colombia, Sede Medellín-Colombia: Folios.

Cassetti, M. (2010). *Macroeconomic outcomes of changing bargaining relationships in open economies. The feasibility of a wage-led economy reconsidered*. Mimeo.

CEPAL. (2012). *Cambio estructural para la Igualdad*. Naciones Unidas-CEPAL.

Chang, H.-Joon. (2007). *¿Qué fue del buen samaritano? Naciones ricas, políticas pobres*. Spain: Intermón Oxfam Editorial.

Cimoli, M. and Porcile, G. (2011). Tecnologia, heterogeneidad y crecimiento: una caja de herramientas estructuralista (Munich Personal Repec Archive No. 33801). *Munich*. Retrieved from https://mpra.ub .uni-muenchen.de/33801/.

Cimoli, M. and Rovira, S. (2008). Elites and structural inertia in Latin America: an introductory note on the political economy of development. *Journal of Economic Issues, XLII*, 327–347.

Cimoli, M., Neto, M., Porcile, G. and Sosdorf, F. (2016). Productivity, social expenditure and income distribution in Latin America. *CEPAL Series Production and Development*, 201.

Combita, G. (2020). *Canales de transmisión entre el cambio estructural y la fragilidad financiera en Colombia*. Universidad Nacional de Colombia.

Dallery, T. (2009). Post-Keynesian theories of the firm under financialization. *Review of Radical Political Economy, 41* (4), 492–515.

Davidson, P. (2003). Are fixed exchange rates the problem and flexible exchange rates the cure? *Eastern Economic Journal, 27* (3), 393–408.

Estrada, J. (2010). *Derechos del capital. Dispositivos de protección e incentivos a la acumulación en Colombia*. Bogotá: Universidad Nacional de Colombia.

Ffrench-Davids, R. (2010). Macroeconomía para el desarrollo, desde el financiarismo hasta el productivismo. *Revista de La Cepal, 102*, 7–27.

Flóres, L. (2001). Colombia tras diez años de reformas políticas y económicas. *Cuadernos de Economía, XX* (34), 31–55.

Fuentes Knight, J. A. (2015). Hacia una interpretación robinsoniana de la acumulación del capital en América Latina. In A. Barcena and A. Prado (eds.), *Neoestructuralismo y corrientes heterodoxas en América Latina y el Caribe a inicios del siglo XXI* (pp. 185–221). Santiago de Chile: CEPAL and IDRC.

Garcia, J. G. (2002). Liberalización, cambio estructural y crecimiento económico en Colombia. *Cuadernos de Economía, XXI* (36), 190–243.

Goda, T. and Torres, A. (2013). Overvaluation of the real exchange rate no. 13-28 and the Dutch Disease: the Colombian 2013 case. *Ensayos de Política Económica, 13*, 197–206.

Gonzaga, L. (2015). La reciente internacionalizacón del capital. In A. Bárcena and A. Prado (eds.), *Neoestructuralismo y corrientes heterodoxas en América Latina y el Caribe a inicios del siglo XXI* (pp. 101–116). Santiago de Chile: CEPAL and IDRC.

González, J. (2013). *¿Quién se llevó el dinero de interbolsa?* Bogotá: Planeta.

Gramsci, A. (1980). *Notas sobre Maquiavelo, sobre política y estado moderno*. Buenos Aires: Editorial Nueva Visión.

Hirschman, A. (1977). *Las pasiones y los intereses*. México: Fondo de Cultura Económica.

Hirschman, A. (1984). *La matriz social y política de la inflación: elaboración sobre la experiencia Latinoamericana*. Mexico: Fondo de Cultura Económica.

Hylton, F. (2017). *La horrible noche*. Medellín: Universidad Nacional de Colombia.

Hymer, S. H. (1979). *La Compañía Multinacional. Un enfoque radical*. Madrid: H. Blume Ediciones.

Justicia Tributaria. (2019, 19 April). Quiebra de Pacific Rubiales se advirtió durante años. *Noticias*. Retrieved from https://justiciatributaria.co/quiebra-de-pacific-rubiales-se-advirtio-durante-anos/.

Kregel, J. (2004). External financing for development and international financial instability. *United Nations*, Discussion Paper No. 32, October.

Lavoie, M. (1992). *Foundations of Post Keynesian Analysis*. Aldershot, UK and Brookfield, VT, USA: Edward Elgar Publishing.

Lavoie, M. (1994). A post Keynesian approach to consumer choice. *Journal of Post Keynesian Economics, 16* (4), 539–562.

Lavoie, M. (2014). *Post-Keynesian Economics: New Foundations*. Cheltenham, UK and Northampton, MA, USA: Edward Elgar Publishing.

Lavoie, M. and Stockhammer, E. (2013a). *Wage-Led Growth: An Equitable Strategy for Economic Recovery*. New York: Palgrave Macmillan.

Lavoie, M. and Stockhammer, E. (2013b). Wage led growth: concept, theories and policies. In E. S. Marc Lavoie (ed.), *Wage Led Growth* (pp. 13–39). New York: Palgrave Macmillan.

Leon, N. (2012). Crisis, reprimarización y territorio en economías emergentes: caso Colombia. *Crisis económica e impactos territoriales – V Jornadas de Geografía Económica AGE. Univ. de Girona.* Genova.

Leon, P. C. (2002). La industrializacion colombiana: una vision heterodoxa. *Revista Innovar*, *20*, 83–100.

Lorente, L. (2002). *Entorno macroeconómico y crecimiento en Colombia*. Bogotá: Ensayos sobre Colombia y América Latina.

Mayorga, D. (2013, 8 November). Interbolsa, la historia de un desplome, in: *El Espectador*. Retrieved from https://www.elespectador.com/noticias /economia/interbolsa-la-historia-de-un-desplome/.

Misas, G. (2016). El lapso 1990–2010: una coalición en el campo de poder. In *Macroeconomía y bienestar* (pp. 13–44). Bogotá: Universidad Nacional de Colombia, Facultad de Economía.

Moreno, A. (2014). La política monetaria y la distribución funcional del ingreso: lo que usted quiso saber y no se atrevió a preguntar. *Documentos FCE-CID*, No. 50. Bogotá.

Nell, E. and Semmler, W. (2010). After hubris, smoke and mirrors, the downward spiral: financial and real markets pull each other down; how can policy reverse this? *New School*, Working Paper, May.

Nova, M. (2014). Derechos del capital. Dispositivos de protección e incentivos a la acumulación en Colombia. *Revista Finanzas y Política Económica*, 6 (2), 367–385.

Ocampo, J. A. (2007). *La búsqueda, larga e inconclusa, de un nuevo modelo (1981–2006)*. Bogotá: Planeta.

Ocampo, J. A. (2013). *Diez años de revaluación*. Bogotá: Universidad Javeriana.

Palermo, G. (2019). Power: a Marxist view. *Cambridge Journal of Economics*, doi:10.1093/cje/bey055, pp. 1–23.

Revéiz, E. (1989). *Democratizar para sobrevivir*. Bogotá: Poligrupo.

Reveiz, E. (2016). *La Transgresión moral de la Élites y el Sometimiento de los Estados*. Academia Colombiana de Ciencias Económicas, Bogotá-Colombia.

Robinson, J. (1962). *Ensayos sobre la teoría del crecimiento económico*. México: Fondo de Cultura Económica, 1973.

Sarmiento, E. (2014). *Crecimiento con distribución es posible*. Bogotá: Escuela Colombiana de Ingenieros Julio Garavito.

Sintraminercol. (2004). *La gran mineria en Colombia: las ganancias del exterminio*. Bogotá: Sintraminercol.

Stockhammer, E. (2004). Financialisation and the slowdown of accumulation. *Cambridge Journal of Economics*, *28*, 719–741.

Stockhammer, E. (2005). Shareholder value orientation and the investment-profit puzzle. *Journal of Post Keynesian Economics*, *28* (2), 193–215.

Vernengo, M. (2015). From restrained golden age to creeping platinum age: a periodization of Latin American development in the Robinsonian tradition. *Brazilian Journal of Political Economy*, *35* (4), 683–707.

14. Extractive capitalism: transnational miners and Andean peasants in Peru

Alejandro Garay-Huamán

The inflow of foreign direct investment (FDI) increased dramatically after the economic liberalization of the Peruvian economy during the early 1990s. The extractive sector, mainly mining, has been a mayor recipient of this massive inflow of FDI. The neoliberal impetus for promoting the extractive industry has profoundly impacted the socio-economic structure of the non-capitalist, peasant societies of rural Peru. This chapter not only aims at illuminating the impact of extractive transnational capital on indigenous peasant communities of the northern highlands of Peru, but also provides an alternative conceptual framework for its analysis. I start by critically engaging with the contemporary Marxist literature on imperialism. The objective of this critique is to develop an alternative Marxian class-analytic and non-essentialist framework to understand the interaction of capitalist and non-capitalist social formations. This alternative framework is presented in the next section of this chapter.

Analysing capitalism development in Peru requires a foremost acknowledgement of its complexities and contradictions. The Peruvian highlands constitute an intricate configuration of social relationships, where indigenous communities, petty commodity producers, wage labourers, transnational corporations, and so on, contradictory coexist. This socio-economic mosaic has been shaped over centuries and it is the putative outcome of the pre-colonial, colonial, and post-colonial systems. In the third section, I explore some of these complexities and contradictions using the alternative conceptual framework previously developed. In particular, I discuss the transnational mining corporation (TNMC)/indigenous peasant interaction in two regions of the northern highlands of Peru, focusing on mining-related dispossessions and displacements of indigenous peasants. Finally, some concluding remarks are presented in the last section.

14.1 CHALLENGING CONTEMPORARY THEORIES OF IMPERIALISM: RE-CONCEPTUALIZING THE CAPITALIST/NON-CAPITALIST ARTICULATION

The social economic transformation of the periphery has been usually discussed within the theoretical confines of development and underdevelopment. Marxist literature has emphasized the notions of dependency, modes of production, and imperialism to explain the complex articulation of capitalist and non-capitalist social formations (Bartra 1978; Frank 2009; Kay 1989; Kvangraven 2020; Laclau 1971; Montoya 1980). Marxist notions of imperialism and primitive accumulation have played a central role in these discussions. Marxist orthodoxy assumes that, once capital penetrates into the non-capitalist world, direct producers (e.g., peasants) are forcibly separated from their means of production (i.e., primitive accumulation), and then both labour and the means of production are incorporated into the circuits of capital. As capital transforms the non-capital in its own image, it becomes universal and self-sufficient. Concomitantly, the non-capital ceases to exist, its articulation to capital vanishes, and thus the *transition* is completed.

Despite the burgeoning literature about imperialism and primitive accumulation in the recent years, the current theoretical discourse seems to be attached to the old dualistic thinking, so recurrent in the traditional Marxist's theorizing of imperialism and primitive accumulation.[1] Under capitalism, it is argued, the economic logic becomes dominant, subduing the non-economic coercion that characterizes pre-capitalist modes of production (Brenner 2006; Harvey 2003, 2006; Wood 2003, 2006).

Wood's (1981) long-standing argument about the formal separation of the political and economic puts forward a characterization of capitalist imperialism. She argues that capitalism's uniqueness lies in its "capacity to detach economic from extra-economic power" (Wood 2003: 5), imposing its hegemony without openly relying on political coercion, violence, or other non-economic forms of power. The subordinated condition of the extra-economic to the economic logic implies that the political logic is completely determined by the economic logic, so as the need for accumulation increases the nation-states respond mechanically to these requirements (Arrighi 2010; Amin 2015; Panitch and Gindin 2012). For Harvey (2003), capitalist imperialism operates through two logics of power: "the logic of capital", which involves the process of capital accumulation, and the "territorial logic" of political, diplomatic, and military management of the state. As the capitalist system experiences crisis of overaccumulation due to the lack of profitable investment outlets, "spatial-temporal fixes" are required to restore the process of capital accumulation.[2] These solutions include forcing non-capitalist spaces to open up for capital investments, as well as using them as sources of cheap labour and raw materials (Harvey 2003). The contradictory relation between the expanded reproduction of capital (i.e., economic logic) and the "often violent processes of dispossessions" (i.e., territorial logic) is both what defines contemporary capitalist imperialism and shapes its geography (Harvey 2003: 142).

In these discourses, the political and economic belong to two different realms, if not completely separated, each with its own logics and dynamics, generating an artificial disconnectedness and false ontological hierarchy within and between these two realms. The delimitation of two spaces, the space of capital and non-capital, poses another tension. The space of capital is the constitutive centre of the process of capital accumulation, its *internality*. The space of non-capital is characterized by the ubiquity of pre-capitalist social relations, the *externality* of capital, its negation. Non-capital is the negation of capital for it is in the process of becoming, it is not yet being capital. *Creating* capital – that is, restoring capital accumulation – implies the violent and coercive transformation of pre-capitalist social relations, that is, a process of primitive accumulation. As the space of capital experiences internal problems of accumulation, there is an external need for the imperial subjugation of the spaces of non-capital. Primitive accumulation *qua* accumulation by dispossession is no more than an external phenomenon, giving ontological primacy to the space of capital.

All these theoretical constructions are essentialist, which depending on the type of essentialism that the commentator favoured it would be capital-centric (economic logic), power-centric (territorial logic), or both. For capital-centric theories, capital is the ultimate *essence* of social reality. Thus, capitalist imperialism is reduced to the economic logic of capital, that is, the accumulation of capital through a variety of mechanisms: labour arbitrage, monopoly rent and unequal exchange, super exploitation, and income deflation (Cope 2019; Patnaik and Patnaik 2017; Smith 2016; Suwandi 2019). Given the subordinated condition of the extra-economic logic, nation-states are reduced to entities whose main role is to act in behalf of capital, and its need for accumulation (Arrighi 2010; Amin 2015; Panitch and Gindin 2012). For power-centric conceptions, the ultimate essence of imperialism is the power of the hegemonic state(s). Imperialism is reduced to the strategic needs of the dominant states, these needs can be economic, political, military, or a combination of them (Boron 2005; Gordon and Webber 2016; Kiely 2010).

Imperialism, as a theoretical category, has also made its re-entry to the study of Latin America natural resource dependence. It is argued that the imperialism of the 21st century is the "extractive imperialism". This new imperialism emerged as a response to the systemic crisis of contemporary capitalism, a crisis nurtured by the neoliberal policies, which accelerated the transition towards a strategy of natural resources extraction in order to both boosting capital accumulation and bringing a solution to the capitalist crisis (Girvan 2014; Petras and Veltmeyer 2014). Extractive imperialism represents an interesting departure from the traditional literature on natural-resources, which has mainly focused around economic concepts of cost–benefit analysis. Even though their conceptualization of class remains essentialist, proponents of the extractive imperialism thesis have to be acknowledged for bringing class analysis back into the core of the natural-resources research agenda.

Given the shortcomings of conventional theories, I offer an alternative conceptual framework for studying the capital/non-capital interaction. The building blocks of this alternative framework are a particular Marxian epistemological position (overdetermination) and the concept of class as a theoretical entry-point. An overdetermined epistemology implies that all *processes*[3] comprising a social totality are mutually constitutive, that is, each one process influences all other processes, and each process' existence is the effect of all other processes. Overdetermination rejects reductionist causality of essentialist/determinist approaches that identify one process, or a subset, as the essence, that is, the ultimate cause of the phenomenon under study. Moreover, given the overdetermined nature of each societal process, change and contradiction are ubiquitous features of them (Resnick and Wolff 1987).

A complete analysis of this complex, overdetermined social totality would demand a herculean effort, which no theory is equipped to accomplish. Partiality is the common denominator of all social theories, but their partial analyses differ as a consequence of using different theoretical entry-points (Wolff and Resnick 2012). Marxian theory approaches social totality with class as its entry-point. In other words, the particular concept of class is used as the starting point for theorizing society. Class is not defined in the traditional Marxist sense, that is, power or property-based notions of class (Resnick and Wolff 2003). Instead, class is defined as the process of production, distribution, and appropriation of surplus labour (Hindess and Hirst 1975; Marx 1973; Resnick and Wolff 1987). Theorizing society requires, first, to specify the different class processes existing within that particular social formation; then to examine how these class processes are overdetermined by all the non-class processes, and finally how the former participate in over determining the latter (Resnick and Wolff 1987).

My proposed conceptual framework relies upon and extends the seminal contributions of Resnick and Wolff (1979, 1987, 2001), Chakrabarti and Cullenberg (2003), Ruccio (2003),

Table 14.1   Capitalist and non-capitalist class structures

Capitalist class structure	Non-capitalist class structure
$\sum CSV_i^j + \sum CSCR_i^j + \sum CNCR_i^j =$ $\sum CSCP_j^k + \sum X_j^k + \sum Y_j^k$	$\sum NCSL + \sum NCSCR + \sum NCNCR_{a,b} =$ $\sum NCSCP + \sum X + \sum Y_{a,b}$
Where:	Where:
$i =$ indexes the various global locations from where the surplus-value is produced, subsumed class revenues are received, and non-class revenues are collected.	$a =$ indexes the various non-capitalist locations from where subsumed class revenues are received and non-class revenues are collected.
$j =$ indexes the various global locations from where the surplus-value, subsumed class revenues, and non-class revenues are appropriated.	$b =$ indexes the various capitalist locations from where subsumed class revenues are received and non-class revenues are collected.
$k =$ indexes the various global locations of recipients of subsumed class and non-class payments that the capitalist enterprise (TNC – transnational corporations) and the capitalist state must make to secure their class and non-class revenues.	$NCSL =$ non-capitalist surplus labour. $NCSCR =$ non-capitalist subsumed class revenue. $NCNCR_{a,b} =$ non-capitalist non-class revenues drew from non-capitalist *ath* location and capitalist *bth* location. $NCSCP =$ non-capitalist subsumed class payments.
$CSV_i^j =$ capitalist surplus-value produced at the *ith* location and appropriated at the *jth* location.	$X =$ expenditures needed to secure subsumed class revenues. $Y_{a,b} =$ expenditures needed to secure non-class revenues.
$CSCR_i^j =$ capitalist subsumed class revenue drawn from *ith* location and appropriated at the *jth* location.	
$CNCR_i^j =$ capitalist non-class revenue drawn from *ith* location and appropriated at the *jth* location.	
$CSCP_j^k =$ capitalist subsumed class payments to recipients at *kth* locations.	
$X_j^k =$ expenditures needed to secure the subsumed class revenues at *kth* locations.	
$Y_j^k =$ expenditures needed to secure the non-class revenues at *kth* locations.	

Bhattacharya (2010), and Callari (2008, 2010). In this alternative framework, imperialism and its capitalist/non-capitalist interaction are no longer confined to the narrow and problematic dualistic theorizing of contemporary Marxist theories. The economic and non-economic logics, as well as the spaces of capital and non-capital, are integrated as non-reducible aspects of an overdetermined social totality. Now, this particular Marxian conceptualization can be represented in terms of class structural equations (CSEs).[4]

Some conceptual clarifications are required in order to make sense of the CSEs presented above (Table 14.1). First, non-class processes are all those aspects of society that are not directly related with the production of surplus labour. The class process is subdivided into the fundamental class process and the subsumed class process. The former makes reference to the production and appropriation of surplus labour, and the latter "refers to the distribution of already appropriated surplus labour and its products" (Resnick and Wolff 1987: 118).[5]

Although related to each other, class process and classes are conceptually different. Classes refer to the grouping of people around their particular position in the class process. The fundamental class process entails two class positions: performers of surplus labour, and extractors of surplus labour. Likewise, there are two class positions associated with the subsumed class process: distributors and recipients of surplus labour. It is worth noting that individuals occupy more than one class position, for instance, TNMC's executive officers are not only distributors of appropriated surplus value but also recipients as they collect their salaries.

CSE 01 and 02 (Table 14.1) can be interpreted as revenue-expenditure equations, representing all flows of surplus value (labour), subsumed revenues, and non-class revenues produced, appropriated, and distributed at different spatial locations. The left-hand side of both equations represents all class (fundamental and subsumed) and non-class revenues produced; the right-hand side represents all the class and non-class expenditure flows used as payments to secure the reproduction of all revenues.

In a globalized system of production, characterized by the pervasiveness of decentred networks and value chains (Cope 2019; Smith 2016; Suwandi 2019), surpluses are produced at ith locations and are appropriated at jth location, the same applies for other sources of subsumed and non-class revenues (Resnick and Wolff 2001). In other words, there is hardly a spatial correspondence between the production, appropriation, and distribution of surpluses. This non-fixed spatiality of contemporary capitalist production is represented by the indexes i, j and k (CSE 01, Table 14.1).

CSE 01 and 02 (Table 14.1) intend to represent the *aggregate* class structure of the capitalist and non-capitalist social formations. Nevertheless, both class structures can be *disaggregated*, and an individual CSE can be specified for each entity existing in these social formations. For instance, the CSE of a capitalist firm would represent the total surplus value produced by wage workers and appropriated by the capitalists in the left-hand of the equation, and all the subsumed class payments to its management, shareholders, financiers, landlords, merchants, and the state in the right-hand. Likewise, all the subsumed (e.g., interest, dividends, ground rents, etc.) and non-class revenues captured by the capitalist firm, and its corresponding payments are included in the left and right-side of the equation respectively. Another *site*[6] of class structuration for the capitalist social formation is the state, whose CSE can also be specified as a revenue-expenditure equation. For the non-capitalist social formation (CSE 02, Table 14.1), for example peasant societies, it is possible to identify, at least, three *sites* of class structuration: peasant households, non-capitalist productive units, and the communal organization (e.g., *comunidad campesina*). Thus, disaggregated CSE can be formulated for each of these entities. In general, larger class sets, and its variations, could be identified for any specific non-capitalist social formation, or capitalist social formation.[7]

Finally, studying contemporary capitalism requires to move beyond the confines of the nation-state as the basic unit of analysis (Robinson 2014). The global commodity chain/global value chain (GCC/GVC) analysis constitutes an alternative to the nation-centric approach (Bridge 2008; Gereffi, Korzeniewicz and Korzeniewicz 1994). Nevertheless, conventional literature on GCC/GVC narrowly focuses on the economic concepts of transaction costs and value added (Newman 2012). For instance, it argues that rent-captures (i.e., appropriation of surpluses) within extractive global chains are a "function of the relative power of [its] different actors, and (…) changes in price" (Bridge 2008: 402). A superficial analysis that provides only a "typological description of the immediate outer manifestations of the determinations at stake" (Starosta 2010a: 435). In short, conventional GCC/GVC's empiricist focus and its lack of theoretical attention to the general dynamics of capitalist accumulation are highly problematic (Starosta 2010b).

Few Marxist scholars have devoted substantial attention to studying GCC/GVC (Cope 2019; Hudson 2008; Smith 2016; Starosta 2010a, 2010b; Suwandi 2019; Taylor 2007). Marxism's indifference towards GCC/GVC analysis would not be an issue if the intellectual roots of the GCC/GVC approach were not to be found in the Marxist World-System theory (Hopkins and Wallerstein 1977). For World-System theorists, the GCC/GVC can be conceived as "a network of labour and production *processes* whose end result is a finished commodity" (Hopkins and Wallerstein 1986: 159, emphasis added). The emphasis on processes is, according to Hopkins and Wallerstein (1994: 50), "the greatest virtue of a commodity chain". Likewise, for Resnick and Wolff (1987: 19), whose contributions inform the theoretical perspective advanced in this chapter, "the basic unit of analysis in Marxian theory is 'process'". These commonalities facilitate the bridging of these two theoretical frameworks, resulting in a GCC/GVC grounded in the Marxian epistemology of overdetermination and class analysis. This framework provides an analytical and conceptual apparatus to study the complex interaction of capitalist and non-capitalist social formations in contemporary capitalism.

14.2 TRANSNATIONAL MINING CAPITAL AND PEASANT COMMUNITIES: SOME VIGNETTES FROM A NON-ESSENTIALIST GCC/GVC ANALYSIS

The conceptual framework sketched out above allows us to explore the complexities of TNMC/indigenous peasant interaction in two regions of the northern highlands of Peru: *Ancash* and *Cajamarca*. In what follows, I organize the discussion in two parts. First, I briefly contextualize the importance of FDI for the Peruvian neoliberal experiment, highlighting its industry and macro-level effects. Second, using the proposed conceptual framework, I focus on the micro-level impacts of extractive FDI upon indigenous peasant communities. Some preliminary findings of an ongoing research project are presented in this section. Not all stages of the mining chain are discussed herein due to space constraints. I only focus on the mining-related dispossessions and displacements of indigenous peasants during the exploration and exploitation phase of the commodity chain.

Transnational Mining Capital and the Neoliberal Development Strategy

The inflow of FDI increased dramatically after the economic liberalization of the Peruvian economy by Alberto Fujimori's regime during the early 1990s. From experienced net foreign disinvestment (1991–1992) and an accumulated FDI value of US$1.3 billion (1990), the stock of FDI reached US$104.4 billion in 2018, a 7500 percent increase. For the 1990s the annual average of FDI inflows was US$1.6 billion, increasing to US$3.2 billion for the 2000s, and reaching US$7.9 billion for 2010–2019 (UNCTAD 2020). The main investors by country of origin have been Spain, USA, UK, and Chile, representing more than 60 percent of overall FDI (ProInversion 2020). Over this period, Peru has become an important destination for FDI in Latin America, only surpassed by Mexico, Brazil, Colombia, Chile, and Argentina, although in some years outranking Chile and Argentina (ECLAC 2019a). Fujimori's government implemented one of the most radical privatization programs in Latin America, which partly explains the massive inflow of FDI, accounting 35 percent of registered FDI for the 1990s (UNCTAD 2000).

Like most countries in the region, global capital's main targets were the primary sectors of the Peruvian economy (e.g., mining), favouring a primary export-oriented production. A new phase of domination and dependency emerged from this process of re-primarization (Higginbottom 2013). A process that was decidedly driven by all neoliberal regimes ruling the country since 1990. Economic liberalization, privatizations, changing in the tax regimes, and enforcing rigid property and mining rights were key elements favouring the inflow of foreign capital into the mining sector (Sánchez Albavera, Ortiz and Moussa 2001). The most important state-owned companies were privatized during the period 1991–1997, providing more than U$S1 billion in revenues for the state, and investment commitments for U$S1.1 billion (Sánchez Albavera, Ortiz and Moussa 2001). By 1997, Latin America concentrated 29 percent (US$1.17 billion) of the worldwide exploration budgets. Peru's share reached 15 percent of this total expenditure, making it the sixth largest recipient of exploration investment in the world (Sánchez Albavera, Ortiz and Moussa 2001). Over the last three decades, FDI in mining has represented around one fifth of the overall FDI. It declined after the Asian financial crisis of 1997, reaching its lowest point in 2002 (12 percent of total FDI), recovering its pre-crisis level in 2006, since then it has steadily increased to represent 23 percent of total FDI in 2019 (ProInversion 2020).

Legal amendments, including a new constitution in 1993, were introduced to safeguard the neoliberal reforms. The mining legislation was changed to favour foreign private investment and to limit state participation through public enterprises. Not only are these legal and constitutional changes still in place but also new draconian laws were passed to criminalize social movements and activists opposing mining and other extractive projects (Lust 2014).

Under the 1993 constitution, contract-laws (also known as legal stability contracts) were introduced to attract foreign investment through a legal framework that gave foreign investors constitutionally protected contracts. For the government, it was based in the simple notion that "nations with favourable geology and lower tax impositions have an advantage over higher taxing nations" (Otto 2002: 2), a race to the bottom strategy. Legal stability agreements are notorious for granting excessive long-term benefits to foreign investors, ranging from tax stability contracts, especial exchange rate and tariff regimes, profit repatriations, and more. Neither Congress nor any other legislative body could modify those contracts. Since 1993, many transnational mining investors have signed those contracts. TNMCs have benefited from reimbursement of sales taxes levied on inputs, services and capital goods. The Peruvian government did not impose any regulation to the repatriation of dividends and capital by foreign mining corporations, its remittances were tax free (Sánchez Albavera, Ortiz and Moussa 2001). Royalty payments were not introduced until 2004, and much of the corporate income taxes were not collected until 2005 due to the tax stability agreements (Lasa Aresti 2016).

At the industry level, prior to the neoliberal reforms, the mining industry was characterized by the presence of both large state-owned operations and numerous, small, privately owned firms. After the 1990s, the industry became highly concentrated, with few large TNMCs controlling most of the mining sites. Since the mid-1990s copper production is dominated by few TNMCs: Southern Copper Corporation (owned by Grupo Mexico), BHP, Glencore (previously Xstrata), and Freeport-McMoRan, controlling more than 80 percent of the overall production, equivalent to 6 percent of the worldwide production (MINEM 2011). Similarly, few TNMCs have controlled more than 50 percent of the production of silver and gold: Newmont, Barrick, Glencore, and BHP. *Compañia de Minas Buenaventura* has been the only

Peruvian corporation with a considerable market share participation. In most cases, mining operations have been operated through joint ventures among these TNMCs, and in some cases in partnerships with domestic corporations but, usually, as minority shareholders.

The gold mines in Cajamarca and Ancash account for almost 30 percent of the entire gold production of Peru. *Minera Yanacocha S.R.L.* is the largest gold mining company in Peru, operating in the highlands of Cajamarca. It is a joint venture between the US based Newmont Mining (51.35 percent) – the largest transnational gold mining producer in the world – Peruvian *Minas Buenaventura* (43.65 percent) and Sumitomo Corporation (5 percent). *Yanacocha* mine is its largest mine and is considered the largest gold mine in South America. In 2019, its production reached 524,000 of fine ounces representing almost 13 percent of the overall production; however, its production has declined by 60 percent over the last decade (MINEM 2020).

Ancash is also one of the largest producers of copper. In 2019, 19 percent (466,106 FMT – fine metric tons) of the nationwide copper concentrates were produced in Ancash (MINEM 2020). *Antamina* mine is Peru's second largest copper and zinc mine and one of the biggest mines in the world. It is owned by a larger transnational conglomerate of leading global resources companies: the Anglo-Australian based BHP Billiton (33.75 percent), the Anglo-Swiss Glencore (33.75 percent), the Canadian Teck (22.50 percent), and the Japanese Mitsubishi (10 percent) (Antamina 2016). Antamina's operations are located in the highlands of Ancash, nearby the *Huascaran* National Park, declared a Natural World Heritage Site and Biosphere Reserve by UNESCO.

Since the 1990s, every president in office has highlighted the importance of attracting FDI, especially extractive capital, for the Peruvian economy, making FDI the cornerstone of their so-called *development* strategies. A modernization creed that put foreign capital "as the positive subject bringing progress" to the country (Higginbottom 2013: 186). This consensus has been built based on the good economic performance during part of the 1990s and most of the 2000s. For the 2000s, the average growth rate of Peruvian GDP was 6 percent, a figure twice that of Latin America and the Caribbean as a whole; similarly, inflation was one of the lowest in the region, and unemployment decreased rapidly. Poverty, measured as a percentage of the population living on less than US$3.2 a day, also dropped 18 percentage points between 1997 and 2010 (World Bank 2020). In the external front, after a period of marked deterioration in the terms of trade (1980–2000), it showed an improvement for the period 2000–2018. The net barter terms of trade index reached its peak in 2011 (195.2, 2000=100), to slowly fall to 178.6 points in 2018, reflecting the impact of the latest commodity boom (World Bank 2020). The extractive sector played a major role in improving Peru's balance of trade, although making its performance extremely dependent on the wild swings of the global markets. The mining sector accounts for 60 percent of the total value of the country's export, increasing from 52 percent in 2003 to 61 percent in 2017 (Ávila Palomino 2019). The increasing price index of traditional exports has positively impacted government tax revenues, especially those collected from the mining sector. Mining accounted, on average, for 13 percent (around US$2.2 billion per year) of the total fiscal revenue for 2005–2018, in addition to yearly royalty payments for US$2.1 billion, in average, for the same period (Ávila Palomino 2019). Those fiscal revenues have increased public spending, and compensatory social programs have become the central strategy of Peruvian neoliberalism.

The neoliberal establishment took all the credit for this unprecedented economic performance, and neoliberal policies were presented as the panacea for economic development. The "Peruvian miracle" soon became the exemplary of independent, technocratic management of the economy, a successful case of market reforms. In actuality, most of this growth was fuelled by the favourable international context of historically lowest interest rates and the massive inflow of capitals, and the growing global demand for natural resources, especially mining commodities by China. Among the neoliberal establishment, even though some of them recognize the importance of the favourable international context, the *correct* short-term macroeconomic policies are highlighted as a pivotal element for explaining the "Peruvian miracle" (Mendoza Bellido 2013). An argument supported by the International Monetary Fund (2012), whose findings show that 60 percent of the economic expansion of emerging market economies and developing countries, including Peru, during 1990–2007, is explained by good policies. Obviously, what constitutes correct, or good, macroeconomic policies are the standard neoliberal policies oriented to keep low inflation rates, fiscal surpluses, and strong external positions. Yet the "Peruvian miracle" started to show its limits, the rate of growth of GDP plummeted from 8.3 percent (2010) to 2.1 percent (2019), even though the inflow of FDI was higher than in the previous decades (World Bank 2020).

Despite the official figures showing a drastic reduction on the country's poverty levels, the impressive economic growth did not modify the long-standing, structural inequities of the country.[8] Even the World Bank (2006) recognizes that the Peruvian economic growth fuelled by commodity exports was insufficient for changing the structural patterns associated with high levels of poverty. Relying on an econometric estimation, the study concludes that patterns of economic growth based on labour intensive sectors reduced poverty more rapidly (World Bank 2006). Alternatively, heterodox economists have showed the positive effect of wage-led growth strategies on the wage shares, thus improving functional income distribution. Increasing wage shares also have effects on the supply side, as increases in real wages would increase labour productivity (Lavoie and Stockhammer 2013). In other words, the Peruvian neoliberal pattern of economic growth led by a capital intensive extractivist sector was unable to generate new employments and to increase the wage income share, that is, it was not a pro-poor growth. The total number of direct employments generated by the mining industry was less than 90,000 for 2010–2019 (MINEM 2020).

Instead of changing the structural problems of the country, the neoliberal consensus has actively promoted extensive compensatory social programs as long-term strategies to face poverty and inequality. But even this strategy falls short as public spending on social programs, and overall public expenditure, is in the lower bound among Latin American countries (ECLAC, 2012, 2019b). Peru's total social expenditure has increased from 4 percent of the GDP in 1994 to stay around 8 percent for most of the 2000s, reaching 11 percent of the GDP in 2014 and it was kept at the level since then (INEI 2020). For this decade, public expenditure on education and health has been 5.2 percent of the GDP. Compensatory social programs accounted for 2 percent of the GDP, almost the same amount allocated to the entire health system of the country (INEI 2020).

Peasants, *Comunidad Campesina*,[9] and Transnational Mining Capital

The exploration process is the initial stage of the mining chain. The mining claims and concessions are granted by the state at this stage. The extractive industry is characterized by an intense intra-firm competition for "reserve replacements and reserve growth" (Bridge 2008: 403). The latter generates differential rents, which are captured by those firms that are able to access and control the richest ores, but also with the lowest costs of production (Bridge 2008). Competitive pressures to access and control these reserves necessarily imply large processes of land and water appropriation, and labour displacements. The number of mining claims and concessions have skyrocketed from 2.2 million hectares in 1992 to 17.7 million hectares in 2020, reaching a peak of 26.8 million hectares in 2013 (Cooperacción 2020). It is estimated that 14.2 percent of Peru's territory is currently under mining claims and concessions (Cooperacción 2020). In a country where 50 percent of overall territory is under some type of indigenous communal landholding, and two fifths of total agricultural lands belongs to rural communities (De Echave 2005; IBD 2016), it is hardly surprising that a large percentage of allocated lands for mining concessions is overlapping with lands traditionally occupied by peasant communities.

Over the last two decades, Cajamarca and Ancash have seen a dramatic increase in the number of mining concessions. Ancash has currently more than 41 percent of its territory under mining concessions, 18 percent lower than it was in 2014, when 9 out of 20 provinces had over 60 percent of its territories under mining concessions, and 3 of them have more than 90 percent (Cooperacción 2014, 2020). Likewise, in 2014, Cajamarca had more than 47 percent of its territory under mining concessions, and for some of its provinces were 80 percent (De Echave and Diez 2013). As a consequence of large social protests, mining concessions in Cajamarca have plummeted, covering 23 percent of its territory in 2019 (Cooperacción 2020).

This geographic expansion of mining operations and its penetration into communal lands have become a main source of social conflicts. Communal lands, as well as natural water supplies, have been seized by TNMCs with the support of the state (Borras, Franco, Gómez, Kay and Spoor 2012; Burneo de la Rocha and Chaparro Ortiz de Zeballos 2010; Sosa and Zwarteveen 2012). The number of conflicts surrounding mining operations has increased from 74 in 2006 to 211 in 2015, and declined to 176 in 2019, almost 20 percent of these social conflicts happened in Cajamarca and Ancash (Cooperacción 2015, 2020). Yanacocha's gold-mining operation has a long story of social and environmental conflicts in Cajamarca. Since the exploration stage, in 1992, Minera Yanacocha has had a conflictual relationship with the surrounding peasant communities. These early conflicts emerged due to the low prices paid by Yanacocha for the acquisition of peasants' lands.[10] Later, during the exploitation, there were several confirmed reports of chemical spills and other accidents associated with hazardous substances, affecting hundreds of people (Tanaka and Meléndez 2009). Yanacocha's nefarious background sprung massive demonstrations against the *Conga* mining project, an expansion of Yanacocha's operation, forcing Newmont to stop the expansion in 2011, and walking away from a multibillion project in 2016.

The main productive activities of a *campesino* household of the northern highlands of Peru are farming and grazing. Members of the household usually spend most of their time grazing their flock of sheep, and in petty agricultural production. Both activities are based on family labour, which sustains the social reproduction of the household. This is the fundamental class process characterized by its collective appropriation of surpluses, employing unpaid family labour. At the most basic level, this would be represented by $NCSL = \sum NCSCP$. In general, most of the output is consumed by the household, and a small part goes to the market for monetary and/or for in-kind exchanges with other households inside and outside the community. It is also possible to find a variation of this fundamental class. Individual appropriations by the head of the household of surpluses produced employing both unpaid family labour and *hired* labour paid in kind. The head of the household decides whether the surpluses are allocated to the subsumed class and non-class recipients. Output, likewise, is consumed, sold in commodity form, and/or exchanged for other goods. Additionally, peasant households could farm under a sharecropping agreement with a member of the community or *rent* the land from a landowner. Depending on the type of agreement, peasant households make in-kind or monetary subsumed payments (e.g., ground rent) to the landowner. The head of the family is usually a member of the *comunidad campesina*, the communal organization that regulates the social, political, and economic relations within the community and with outside entities. The *comunidad campesina* has the legal right to establish communal enterprises. In these non-capitalist economic units, the surplus is collectively appropriated. Production is carried on employing a combination of wage labourers and non-wage labourers, and output is typically sent to the markets for sale.

Neoliberal dispossessions and displacements cannot be seen as isolated processes. There is a large historical development that facilitated it, a continuity in the Peruvian land politics (Mayer 2009). The radical agrarian reform of the 1960s broke down the exploitative hacienda system and granted land rights to indigenous peasants and communities. Since the 1990s, this land tenure system has indirectly favoured TNMCs in their negotiations with indigenous peasants over lands in mining concessions, facilitating legal dispossessions. In general, rural property rights are not clearly established. Thus, TNMCs in alliance with the national government have actively fostered land titling. But if neither of these alternatives be favourable for the TNMC, they could easily restore, as Antamina did, a strategy in which their "community relations staff were required to convince landowners [i.e., peasants] to sell using a pre-set package of inducements and threats" (Szablowski 2002: 260). The role of the national government has been to enforce the rule of law, which means to facilitate the land acquisition under proper market conditions, even though no real market for these lands exist at all. In reality, the state has willingly used its monopoly on violence to enforce the law in favour of TNMCs. For the state, this is a necessary condition to keep the proper investment climate that would attract more extractive FDI. In exchange, the government receives increasing royalties and tax-revenues.

The internal socio-political and economic structure of peasant communities also play a role in facilitating land appropriations by TNMCs. In San Marcos (Ancash), before Antamina's operation started, indigenous peasants had a complex system of vertical structuration, across different ecological zones, of different households and their extended families; each of them played a particular role in a complex system of kinship and reciprocity among all neighbouring territories (Salas Carreño 2008). Families living in the valley, whose main activity was farming rather than grazing, owned the pastures in the highlands. Families of the highlands, mainly shepherds, have access to the pasture lands through their networks of kinship and reciprocity with the peasant families of the valley.

Antamina needed those lands for its mining operations, so they established negotiations with both the *comunidad campesina* and individual peasants. The power asymmetries during the negotiations and the promise of monetary compensations, although miniscule compared to the multimillion returns for the TNMC, made impossible for the peasant families to reject Antamina's offer. Families located in the valley decided to sell their lands without consultation or approval from the families of the highlands who not only used the pastures for grazing but also have lived there for decades. Legally, in order to sell an indigenous communal land, two thirds of the community members should reach an agreement. In this case, two thirds of the community were located in the valley and without further consultation the decision was made (Salas Carreño 2008). Historians have pointed out factionalism as a common characteristic of Peruvian highlands politics (Taylor 1998; Mallon 1983). Antamina took advantage of this and pursued a divide and conquer strategy aimed at gaining support for its operations from the community. Factional politics, inflamed by the mining corporation, were central in shaping alignments for and against the mining operations, and subordinating the local political structure to Antamina's interest.

After the negotiations, the *comunidad campesina* received almost US$1 million, which was used to build public infrastructure in the community (Salas Carreño 2008). As Antamina was not yet in operation, the TNMC used appropriations of surplus value made in different locations around the world to make these subsumed payments. For the TNMC, these were necessary allocations to secure its future appropriation process. More importantly, what we have here is an instance of capitalist/non-capitalist *articulation*, which can be represented by $\sum CSV_i^j \rightarrow \sum NCSCP$. There are many other instances of articulation that could be traced back by using the CSEs. For instance, rural development programs sponsored by the capitalist state, which use taxes and royalties collected from the capitalist sector to reproduce the conditions of existence of both the state's receipts and the TNMC's production and appropriation of surplus value; TNMC's corporate social responsibility (CSR) programs whose goal is to secure its own reproduction. It is worth noting that the transfer of surplus value in the form of development programs and CSR programs to the peasant communities are as important to secure the existence of the capitalist fundamental class process as are other political, cultural, natural and economic processes.

For decades, neither the national nor the local government provided the basic public infrastructure to these rural communities. It is understandable that once a huge flow of money entered to the community, they embarked on hectic spending to catch *development* and *modernize* their community. They built a high school and a small hospital, electrified the village, set up a satellite dish, and bought two trucks. The high school and the hospital were never implemented with teachers and doctors, nor with educational and medical equipment (Salas Carreño 2008). Sadly, corruption and internal conflicts were the main results of the modernization process.

Once the indigenous peasants were dispossessed from their lands, the TNMC started an accelerated resettlement program. A process that inflected a material and symbolic violence on the community, destroying their historical way of life. The peasant system involved not only monetary transactions but also transactions based on kinship and reciprocity, which were essential for their social reproduction. Peasants were separated from their means of subsistence and production in exchange for money, yet not attention, or compensations, were possible for the loss of their non-monetary assets. Few families were capable of rearticulating their socio-economic activities to the larger socio-economic structure of the basin system (Salas Carreño 2008). For most of them, as all neighbouring territories were occupied by other peasant communities sharing a complex socio-economic structure, their integration into these surrounding communities was hardly possible.

Both the Peruvian state and TNMCs' response were compensatory policies. The national government, as a recipient of subsumed payments through rent-captures, has emerged as the "compensatory state", ruling through the combination of neoliberal macroeconomic policies and *pro-poor* social programs (Gudynas 2016). These measures have been incapable of changing the long-lasting structural problems of the country. TNMCs presented, from the outset, as the champions of socially and environmentally responsible mining. CSR became the buzzword of the mining industry. The transnational and domestic neoliberal establishment played a major role promoting the CSR ideology. The World Bank and the International Monetary Fund have been central to the process of promoting self-regulation, and voluntary codes of conduct for the mining industry (Kirsch 2014). The resettlement program used by Antamina was originally developed by the World Bank (Szablowski 2002). In general, CSR programs have been used to depoliticize the local community–TNMC contested interaction (Szablowski 2002). Finally, the limited presence of the national state vis-à-vis the presence of the TNMC has created new sites of governmentality (Kirsch 2014; Sanyal 2014). These are sites where new forms of governance have been created. TNMCs assuming the state's traditional roles and responsibilities, a process that is radically modifying the citizen–state relationship.

14.3   CONCLUSIONS

This chapter provides an alternative conceptual framework to analyse the complex interaction of the capitalist and non-capitalist social formations. The Marxian epistemological position of overdetermination and the concept of class as process are the key elements of this alternative framework. Unlike Marxist contemporary theories of imperialism, this novel framework sees the non-capitalist and capitalist social formations as constitutive, non-reducible, elements of an overdetermined social totality. This framework is proposed in terms of class structural equations (CSEs). The analysis presented above suggests that CSEs are useful for studying the complex and contradictory interaction between extractive transnational capital and non-capitalist, peasant communities. Mining-related dispossessions and displacements of indigenous peasants are the main outcomes of this interaction in the northern highlands of Peru.

Foreign direct investment (FDI) has played a central role in the economic strategy of Peru since the 1990s. Peruvian neoliberal *development* strategy has mainly relied on attracting foreign direct investment to feed a large extractive sector capable of funding government compensatory programs. A primarily export-led growth boosted GDP, but it barely changed the structural inequities of the country. In a favourable international context, with rising demand and prices for mining commodities, leading TNMCs have eagerly invested in the country increasing their market share and profits but also creating the widespread dispossession of peasant lands. Reconversion of agricultural lands into lands for mining use have dramatically impacted the peasantry. As a result, peasant communities, and their complex socio-economic structure, are increasingly destroyed. Mining-related dispossessions have intensified and become a major source of social conflicts during the neoliberal period.

NOTES

1. This dualism is somehow similar to G.A. Cohen's (2000) distinction of the material from the social. It also resembles the mechanical metaphor of the base/superstructure so prevalent among orthodox Marxists.
2. For Harvey, the spatio-temporal fixes "is a metaphor for solutions to capitalist crises through temporal deferment and geographical expansion" (Harvey 2003: 66).
3. Process is a basic unit of analysis in this Marxian framework. All societal relationships are composed of a set of processes. These processes are grouped, for simplicity, into natural, economic, political and cultural. All of them complexly intervene to overdetermine any relationship in society (Resnick and Wolff 1987).
4. The structural class equations are based on the contributions of Resnick and Wolff (1987), Resnick and Wolff (2001), and Bhattacharya (2010).
5. Marx (1973) identifies several historical fundamental class processes: primitive communist, slave, feudal, ancient, capitalist, and other variations.
6. "A site in Marxian theory specifies the context of analysis". It can be defined as the "conceptually defined space where groups of relationships occur and whose effects constitute the site" (Chakrabarti and Cullenberg 2003: 163–164).
7. For instance, Chakrabarti and Cullenberg (2003) identify 12 class sets to show the complex class configuration of the Indian society.
8. The official statistics of poverty and inequality have been criticized on methodological grounds (see Chacaltana 2006; Alarco, Castillo and Leiva 2019).
9. *Comunidad campesina* (peasant community) is an indigenous communal organization legally recognized by the Peruvian state. It is composed of peasant families who occupy and control a territory. It is characterized for having both individual (family) and collective control over its lands, as well as the labour process. Communal life is usually regulated by reciprocity and kinship relationships.
10. Tanaka and Meléndez (2009) argue that Minera Yanacocha paid around US$40–60 per hectare.

REFERENCES

Alarco, G., Castillo, C., & Leiva, F. (2019). *Riqueza y desigualdad en el Perú: Visión panorámica*. Lima: Oxfam.
Amin, S. (2015, July–August). Contemporary Imperialism. *Monthly Review, 67*(3), 23–36.
Antamina. (2016). *Sustainability Report 2016*. Antamina S.A. Mining Company. Lima: Antamina.
Arrighi, G. (2010). *The Long Twentieth Century: Money, Power, and the Origins of Our Times*. New York: Verso.
Ávila Palomino, G. (2019). *Reporte Nacional No 23 de Vigilancia de las Industrias Extractivas*. Lima: Grupo Propuesta Ciudadana.
Bartra, R. (1978). *Modos de Producción en America Latina*. Ciudad de México: Ediciones de Cultura Popular.
Bhattacharya, R. (2010). *Capitalism in Post-Colonial India: Primitive Accumulation under Dirigiste and Laissez Faire Regimes* (Doctoral dissertation). University of Massachusetts Amherst, Amherst. Retrieved from http://scholarworks.umass.edu/cgi/viewcontent.cgi?article=1204&context=open_access_dissertations.
Boron, A. A. (2005). *Empire and Imperialism: A Critical Reading of Michael Hardt and Antonio Negri*. New York: Zed Books.
Borras, S. M., Franco, J. C., Gómez, S., Kay, C., & Spoor, M. (2012). Land Grabbing in Latin America and the Caribbean. *The Journal of Peasant Studies, 39*(3–4), 845–872.
Brenner, R. (2006). What Is, and What Is Not, Imperialism? *Historical Materialism, 14*(4), 79–105.
Bridge, G. (2008). Global Production Networks and the Extractive Sector: Governing Resource-Based Development. *Journal of Economic Geography, 8*(3), 389–419.

Burneo de la Rocha, M. L., & Chaparro Ortiz de Zeballos, A. (2010). Poder, Comunidades Campesinas e Industria minera: El Gobierno Comunal y el Acceso a los Recursos en el Caso de Michiquillay. *Anthropologica, 18*(28), 85–110.

Callari, A. (2008). Imperialism and the Rhetoric of Democracy in the Age of Wall Street. *Rethinking Marxism, 20*(4), 700–709.

Callari, A. (2010). 2008: A New Chapter for U.S. Imperialism. *Rethinking Marxism, 22*(2), 210–218.

Chacaltana, J. (2006). *¿Se puede Prevenir la Pobreza?* Lima: Consorcio de Investigación Económicas y Sociales.

Chakrabarti, A., & Cullenberg, S. (2003). *Transition and Development in India*. New York: Routledge.

Cohen, G. A. (2000). *Karl Marx's Theory of History*. Princeton: Princeton University Press.

Cooperacción. (2014). *Informe de Seguimiento de las Concesiones Mineras en el Peru*. Lima: Cooperacción.

Cooperacción. (2015). *16° Observatorio de Conflictos Mineros en el Perú – Reporte Primer Semestre 2015*. Observatorio de Conflictos Mineros en el Perú – OCM. Lima: Cooperacción.

Cooperacción. (2020). *26° Observatorio de Conflictos Mineros en el Perú: Reporte Primer Semestre 2020*. Observatorio de Conflictos Mineros en el Perú – OCM. Lima: Cooperacción.

Cope, Z. (2019). *The Wealth of (Some) Nations*. London: Pluto Press.

De Echave, J. (2005). Peruvian Peasants Confront the Mining Industry. *Socialism and Democracy, 19*(3), 117–127.

De Echave, J., & Diez, A. (2013). *Más allá de Conga*. Lima: Cooperacción.

ECLAC. (2012). *Social Panorama of Latin America 2012*. Santiago: ECLAC.

ECLAC. (2019a). *Foreign Direct Investment in Latin America and the Caribbean*. Santiago: ECLAC.

ECLAC. (2019b). *Social Panorama of Latin America 2019*. Santiago: ECLAC.

Frank, A. G. (2009). *Latin America: Underdevelopment or Revolution. Essays on the Development of Underdevelopment and the Immediate Enemy*. New York: Monthly Review Press.

Gereffi, G., Korzeniewicz, M., & Korzeniewicz, R. P. (1994). Introduction: Global Commodity Chains. In G. Gereffi, & M. Korzeniewicz (eds.), *Commodity Chains and Global Capitalism* (pp. 1–14). Westport: Greenwood Press.

Girvan, N. (2014). Extractive Imperialism in Historical Perspective. In J. Petras, & H. Veltmeyer (eds.), *Extractive Imperialism in the Americas: Capitalism's New Frontier* (pp. 49–61). Boston: Brill.

Gordon, T., & Webber, J. R. (2016). *Blood of Extraction: Canadian Imperialism in Latin America*. Winnipeg: Fernwood Publishing.

Gudynas, E. (2016). Beyond Varieties of Development: Disputes and Alternatives. *Third World Quarterly, 37*(4), 721–732.

Harvey, D. (2003). *The New Imperialism*. New York: Oxford University Press.

Harvey, D. (2006). *The Limits to Capital*. New York: Verso.

Higginbottom, A. (2013). The Political Economy of Foreign Investment in Latin America: Dependency Revisited. *Latin American Perspectives, 40*(3), 184–206.

Hindess, B., & Hirst, P. Q. (1975). *Pre-Capitalist Modes of Production*. London: Routledge & Kegan Paul.

Hopkins, T. K., & Wallerstein, I. (1977). Patterns of Development of the Modern World-System. *Review (Fernand Braudel Center), 1*(2), 111–145.

Hopkins, T. K., & Wallerstein, I. (1986). Commodity Chains in the World-Economy Prior to 1800. *Review (Fernand Braudel Center), 10*(1), 157–170.

Hopkins, T. K., & Wallerstein, I. (1994). Conclusions About Commodity Chains. In G. Gereffi, & M. Korzeniewicz (eds.), *Commodity Chains and Global Capitalism* (pp. 48–50). Westport: Greenwood.

Hudson, R. (2008). Cultural Political Economy Meets Global Production Networks: A Productive Meeting? *Journal of Economic Geography, 8*(3), 421–440.

IBD. (2016). *Tierras Comunales: Más que Preservar el Pasado es Asegurar el Futuro*. Lima: Instituto del Bien Común.

INEI. (2020). *Instituto Nacional de Estadística e Informática*. 15 April. Retrieved from Estadisticas: https://www.inei.gob.pe.

International Monetary Fund. (2012). *World Economic Outlook: Coping with High Debt and Sluggish Growth*. Washington, DC: IMF.

Kay, C. (1989). *Latin American Theories of Development and Underdevelopment*. New York: Routledge.

Kiely, R. (2010). *Rethinking Imperialism*. New York: Palgrave Macmillan.

Kirsch, S. (2014). *Mining Capitalism: The Relationship Between Corporations and Their Critics*. Oakland: University of California Press.

Kvangraven, I. H. (2020). Beyond the Stereotype: Restating the Relevance of the Dependency Research Program. *Development and Change*, advanced online publication. https://doi.org/10.1111/dech.12593.

Laclau, E. (1971). Feudalism and Capitalism in Latin America. *New Left Review*, *67*, 19–38.

Lasa Aresti, M. (2016). *Mineral Revenue Sharing in Peru*. New York: Natural Resources Governance Institute.

Lavoie, M., & Stockhammer, E. (2013). *Wage-led Growth: An Equitable Strategy for Economic Recovery*. New York: Palgrave Macmillan and ILO.

Lust, J. (2014). Peru: Mining Capital and Social Resistance. In H. Veltmeyer, & J. Petras (eds.), *The New Extractivism: A Post-neoliberal Development Model or Imperialism of the Twenty-first Century?* (pp. 192–221). London: Zed Books.

Mallon, F. E. (1983). *The Defense of Community in Peru's Central Highlands: Peasant Struggle and Capitalist Transition, 1860–1940*. Princeton: Princeton University Press.

Marx, K. (1973). *Grundrisse: Foundations of the Critique of Political Economy* (M. Nicolaus, Trans.). New York: Penguin Books.

Mayer, E. (2009). *Ugly Stories of the Peruvian Agrarian Reform*. Durham: Duke University Press.

Mendoza Bellido, W. (2013). Milagro Peruano: ¿Buena Suerte o Buenas Políticas? *Economía*, *45*(72), 35–90.

MINEM. (2011). *Mining Yearbook 2010*. Lima: Minister of Energy and Mining of Peru.

MINEM. (2020). *Mining Yearbook 2019*. Lima: Minister of Energy and Mining of Peru.

Montoya, R. (1980). *Capitalismo y No-capitalismo en el Perú: Un Estudio Histórico de su Articulación en un Eje Regional*. Lima: Mosca Azul.

Newman, S. (2012). Global Commodity Chains and Global Value Chains. In F. Ben, & A. Saad-Filho (eds.), *The Elgar Companion to Marxist Economics* (pp. 155–161). Cheltenham, UK and Northampton, MA, USA: Edward Elgar Publishing.

Otto, J. M. (2002). *Position of the Peruvian Taxation System as Compared to Mining Taxation Systems in Other Nations*. Ministerio de Economía y Finanzas del Perú. Lima: MEF.

Panitch, L., & Gindin, S. (2012). *The Making of Global Capitalism*. New York: Verso.

Patnaik, U., & Patnaik, P. (2017). *A Theory of Imperialism*. New York: Columbia University Press.

Petras, J., & Veltmeyer, H. (2014). *Extractive Imperialism in the Americas: Capitalism's New Frontier*. Leiden: Brill.

ProInversion. (2020). *Agencia de Promoción de la Inversión Privada*. 2 March. Retrieved from Estadisticas Generales: https://www.proinversion.gob.pe/modulos/JER/PlantillaStandard.aspx?ARE=0&PFL=1&JER=5701.

Resnick, S. A., & Wolff, R. D. (1979). The Theory of Transitional Conjunctures and the Transition from Feudalism to Capitalism in Western Europe. *Review of Radical Political Economics*, *11*(3), 3–22.

Resnick, S. A., & Wolff, R. D. (1987). *Knowledge and Class: A Marxian Critique of Political Economy*. Chicago: University of Chicago Press.

Resnick, S. A., & Wolff, R. D. (2001). Empire and Class Analysis. *Rethinking Marxism*, *13*(3/4), 61–69.

Resnick, S. A., & Wolff, R. D. (2003). The Diversity of Class Analyses: A Critique of Erik Olin Wright and Beyond. *Critical Sociology*, *29*(1), 7–27.

Robinson, W. I. (2014). *Global Capitalism and the Crisis of Humanity*. New York: Cambridge University Press.

Ruccio, D. F. (2003). Globalization and Imperialism. *Rethinking Marxism*, *15*(1), 75–94.

Salas Carreño, G. (2008). *Dinámica Social y Minería: Familias Pastoras de Puna y la Presencia del Proyecto Antamina (1997–2002)*. Lima: IEP.

Sánchez Albavera, F., Ortiz, G. & Moussa, N. (2001). *Mining in Latin America in the Late 1990s*. Santiago: ECLAC.

Sanyal, K. (2014). *Rethinking Capitalist Development: Primitive Accumulation, Governmentality and Post-colonial Capitalism*. New Delhi: Routledge.

Smith, J. (2016). *Imperialism in the Twenty-First Century*. New York: Monthly Review Press.

Sosa, M., & Zwarteveen, M. (2012). Exploring the Politics of Water Grabbing: The Case of Large Mining Operations in the Peruvian Andes. *Water Alternatives, 5*(2), 360–375.

Starosta, G. (2010a). Global Commodity Chains and the Marxian Law of Value. *Antipode, 42*(2), 433–465.

Starosta, G. (2010b). The Outsourcing of Manufacturing and the Rise of Giant Global Contractors: A Marxian Approach to Some Recent Transformations of Global Value Chain. *New Political Economy, 15*(4), 543–563.

Suwandi, I. (2019). *Value Chains: The New Economic Imperialism*. New York: Monthly Review Press.

Szablowski, D. (2002). Mining, Displacement and the World Bank: A Case Analysis of Compania Minera Antamina's Operations in Peru. *Journal of Business Ethics, 39*, 247–273.

Tanaka, M., & Meléndez, C. (2009). Yanacocha y los Reiterados Desencuentros: Gran Afectación, Débiles Capacidades de Acción Colectiva. In J. De Echave, A. Diez, L. Huber, B. Revesz, R. Lanata, & M. Tanaka (eds.), *Minería y Conflicto Social* (pp. 73–98). Lima: Instituto de Estudios Peruanos.

Taylor, L. (1998). Indigenous Peasant Rebellions in Peru during the 1880s. In K. Gosner, & A. Ouwenee (eds.), *Indigenous Revolts in Chiapas and Andean Highlands* (pp. 183–205). Amsterdam: Centro de Estudios y Documentación Latinoamericano.

Taylor, M. (2007). Rethinking the Global Production of Uneven Development. *Globalizations, 4*(4), 529–542.

UNCTAD. (2000). *World Investment Report 2000: Cross-border Mergers and Acquisitions and Development*. New York: United Nations.

UNCTAD. (2020). *United Nations Conference on Trade and Development*. 17 February. Retrieved from Data Center: https://unctadstat.unctad.org/EN/.

Wolff, R. D., & Resnick, S. A. (2012). *Contending Economic Theories: Neoclassical, Keynesian, and Marxian*. Cambridge: The MIT Press.

Wood, E. M. (1981). The Separation of the Economic and the Political in Capitalism. *New Left Review, 1*(127), 66–95.

Wood, E. M. (2003). *Empire of Capital*. London: Verso.

Wood, E. M. (2006). Logics of Power: A Conversation with David Harvey. *Historical Materialism, 14*(4), 9–34.

World Bank. (2006). *A New Social Contract for Peru: An Agenda for Improving Education, Health Care, and the Social Safety Net* (D. Cotlear, ed.). Washington, DC: World Bank.

World Bank. (2020). *The World Bank*. 29 March. Retrieved from The World Bank Open Data: https://data.worldbank.org/.

Index